Introduction

The three gigantic mobilizations in Cuba in April and May 1980, responding to military threats from U.S. imperialism, are powerful testimony to the dynamism of the Cuban revolution. The largest of these mobilized *half* the island's population.

Twenty-one years after the revolution, the Cuban people and their leadership maintain their revolutionary perspective, in spite of all the attempts by imperialism to beat them down.

The revolutions in Grenada and Nicaragua have greatly strengthened the Cuban revolution and, as Fidel has observed, reinforced the confidence of the most revolutionary-minded and internationalist forces in Cuba. At the same time, the extension of the socialist revolution in this hemisphere has dealt a blow to the careerists, routinists, and bureaucratic-minded elements in Cuban society.

The Nicaraguan revolution is also inspiring the oppressed masses throughout the Caribbean and Central America, including thousands of revolutionary fighters who want to make the socialist revolution in their countries. Most notable now is the struggle taking place in El Salvador.

The revolutionary developments in the Caribbean and the grave threats by Washington to counter them are occurring in the context of a weakening U.S. imperialism worldwide. Ever since the 1975 victory in Vietnam, the relationship of forces has continued to shift against the imperialist rulers and to the benefit of the toiling masses. Furthermore, the deepening economic crisis in the imperialist countries is placing increasing pressures on the working class, leading to a growing radicalization and militancy.

Sizing up this situation, the revolutionary socialist leadership in Cuba has taken bold initiatives in the fight against imperialism. It has become a bigger and bigger factor in world politics. But more than that, its own political consciousness is being expanded as it learns from these new developments in the class struggle, especially from the growing centrality of the urban working class in struggles within both the imperialist and semicolonial countries. The Cuban leadership is taking further steps in deepening its Marxist understanding of world politics.

The changes in the world political situation, their relationship to Cuban society and the Castro leadership, and Cuba's role in world politics have opened up an important political discussion among revolutionists outside Cuba. The documents and articles included in this selection represent the initial stage of discussions in the Socialist Workers Party on these important developments.

In the report adopted by the SWP's 1979 national convention, included in this selection, SWP leader Larry Seigle notes that for a period of several years during the early 1970s, the party stopped following the developments in Cuba as closely as it did in the 1960s. We did not read carefully the main speeches and reports of the central Cuban leaders or their press nor did we send reporters to observe first hand what was happening in Cuba. Very little was written in the party's press to inspire members and sympathizers and other readers with the achievements of the revolution or to explain the latest developments.

Following the blows dealt to imperialism in Africa, in which the use of Cuban troops played a key role, the party took a fresh look at the Cuban revolution and began to catch up on what had been happening there. As the discussion in the party unfolded, different evaluations were expressed.

In the party's internal discussion bulletin prior to the 1977 national convention, an exchange took place between David Keil and Joseph Hansen. Keil presented the view that the Castro leadership had become Stalinist in the early 1960s and should be replaced by a political revolution in Cuba. Hansen, a long-time leader of the SWP and the author of many of the party's resolutions and major articles on Cuba, defended the party's established positions on Cuba and the method used to reach them. His article, "Two Interpretations of the Cuban Revolution," is included here as background to understanding developments in Cuba today.

Since so many SWP members and sympathizers of the party were unfamiliar with the SWP's early discussions and positions, Pathfinder Press published in 1978 the principal articles and resolutions on Cuba written by Hansen. They are available in *Dynamics of the Cuban Revolution: A Marxist Appreciation*, Pathfinder Press.

In August 1978 the party's Political Committee held an expanded meeting to discuss Cuba. National Committee members, party organizers, and international guests were invited to participate in the discussion which was initiated by Larry Seigle. Cuba was also on the agenda of the December, 1978, national committee plenum and three reports were presented. Seigle reported on behalf of the Political Committee majority in defense of the Cuban revolution and the revolutionary character of its leadership. Bruce Levine reported from the standpoint that Cuba is a state capitalist society, and Tim Wohlforth argued that Cuba is a bureaucratized workers state requiring a political revolution.

The general line contained in Seigle's reports to the expanded PC meeting and the plenum was adopted by the National Committee. The vote was 29 regular members for, 2 against; 29 alternate members for, 1 against. There were no abstentions. The document incorporating the essential political points from Seigle's two reports, "In Defense of the Cuban Revolution," was submitted to the party membership for discussion. It is included in this selection.

The Cuban question was then discussed by the entire party membership in the internal discussion bulletin and at branch meetings during the three months prior to the August, 1979, national convention. At the convention Seigle reported for the National Committee majority. His report "Cuba and the Castro Leadership" is included in this selection. The general line of this report and the document "In Defense of the Cuban Revolution" was adopted by the delegates. The vote was 121 for, 1 against. The consultative vote was 75 for, 1 against, and 4 abstentions.

Wohlforth's minority report received no votes from the elected delegates and only one consultative vote. There were two abstentions.

Levine reported that he and the two other national committee supporters of the view that Cuba is state capitalist had changed their minds since the national committee plenum and now considered Cuba a workers state. They abstained on Seigle's report. One delegate, however, did vote for the general line of the document "The Cuban Revolution: A State Capitalist Analysis." There were no abstentions.

While the convention was taking place, José Pérez, editor of *Perspectiva Mundial*, was in Cuba as part of the second tour of the Antonio Maceo Brigade. When he returned he wrote an account of his observations that was published in *Intercontinental Press/Inprecor* (Dec. 3, 1979). It is also included in this selection.

As part of the discussion in the party, differences were also expressed over the character of the 1977 Ethiopia-Somalia war and Cuba's role in that conflict. Two articles are reprinted here from the 1979 SWP discussion bulletin which were part of that exchange: "Ethiopia, Somalia, and the African Revolution" by Eric Flint and Bruce Levine, and "The Ethiopia-Somalia War, Eritrea, and Cuba—What the Facts Show: A Reply to Flint, Levine, Kramer, Wohlforth and Keil" by Ernest Harsch and Larry Seigle.

One issue raised in the SWP debate was whether to designate the Castro leadership as revolutionary or centrist. The different views expressed on this question are also reflected in the Fourth International. We are reprinting here a public exchange on this question between Alan Jones, a central leader of the International Marxist Group, British section of the Fourth International, on the one side, and Larry Seigle and David Frankel on the other. The articles appeared in the July 2 and August 6 issues of the *Intercontinental Press/Inprecor* respectively.

Doug Jenness
JUNE 7, 1980

CUBA AND THE CASTRO LEADERSHIP
by Larry Seigle

The general line of the following report was adopted by the 30th National Convention of the Socialist Workers Party, August 6, 1979. The vote was 121 for, 1 against. The consultative vote was 75 for, 1 against, and 4 abstentions.

At this convention we are completing a thorough and rich discussion on Cuba. We began the discussion at an expanded two-day Political Committee meeting one year ago. Discussion was continued in the National Committee at its December 1978 plenum. The majority and two minority positions from the plenum have been before the membership of the party, for discussion in written form, for more than four months. (See SWP Discussion Bulletin Vol. 36, Nos. 1–3.) Oral discussion has also taken place in the branches on the documents before us.

What we have been considering is how to deepen our understanding of the Cuban revolution, and our participation in its defense; how to help extend the revolution, and how to learn more from and get more of a hearing from its revolutionary leadership. The delegates at this convention have a big decision to make. We have to decide whether to reaffirm the line we have had on Cuba for almost two decades. We will make that decision here. We will act on it throughout the country and, as much as we are able to do so, throughout the world. We will also make our views known throughout the Fourth International, which will open a discussion on Cuba sometime after its World Congress later this year. This will be one of the most important discussions since the reunification of the Fourth International in 1963. We are convinced it will have a decisive bearing on the capacity of the world Trotskyist movement to act to advance the growing opportunities to bring together a mass revolutionary international.

While we have been debating how to deepen our involvement in defending and extending the Cuban revolution, the Cuban leadership has been discussing how to deepen the impact of the example of Cuba on politics in the United States. They have begun to develop a new relationship with the Cuban community in the United States, a relationship known as the Dialogue. They are seeking ways to cooperate with those in this country who favor launching a campaign to demand an end to right-wing anti-Cuban terrorist attacks, an end to the U.S. economic blockade, and normalization of relations between the United States and Cuba—all of whose demands are in the interests of the workers and farmers of both Cuba and the United States. They have greeted the formation of the Antonio Maceo Brigade, made up of young Cubans in this and other countries who are prosocialist and favorable to the Cuban revolution. We have been participating in the Brigade. The editor of *Perspectiva Mundial*, José Pérez, now in Cuba, is part of the month-long tour sponsored by the Brigade.

Both we and the Cuban leadership are moving toward a better understanding of the deepening interaction and interpenetration of the fortunes of our two revolutions, the Cuban socialist revolution and the coming socialist revolution in this country. This interaction is occurring in the context of the increasing class polarization in this country, the escalating offensive of the U.S. ruling class against working people, and the growing desire and willingness of working people to fight back in defense of our rights and standard of living.

As we deepen our turn we are more and more in a position to be part of and influence the growing resistance in this country. Internationally, the Cubans are more and more directly involved in anti-imperialist and anticapitalist struggles on many fronts. As the world relationship of forces shifts against the imperialists, the Cubans are pushing forward wherever they spot an opening or a possibility of countering imperialist intervention. They are probing, moving, advancing. They are using their doctors, teachers, and engineers, in Africa, Indochina, South Yemen, and the Caribbean. They have repeatedly offered to send troops to Vietnam. They are using their army against imperialism in Africa.

Solidarity with Nicaragua

And right now—today—the Cubans are, in words and deeds, leading the international campaign of solidarity with Nicaragua. Twenty years after the overthrow of Batista by the July 26 Movement, Somoza and his gang of butchers have been overthrown by a massive popular uprising led by the FSLN. This is a great event for the Latin American revolution, for the world revolution. It is the opening of the socialist revolution in Nicaragua, the extension of the Cuban revolution to the Americas. And the Cubans have responded to that momentous step as we have:

First, by hailing, embracing, celebrating, and identifying 100 percent with that revolution as *their* revolution, and declaring that they intend to learn from it.

Second, by organizing an international campaign to send supplies, food, and whatever else the Nicaraguans need.

Third, by telling the truth about what is happening in Nicaragua, what the masses are fighting for, and how the imperialists are trying to block the revolution from moving forward.

Fourth, by pledging everything to defeat any effort by Washington to use economic pressure to strangle the revolution, to blockade Nicaragua, to invade, or to intervene in any other way in that country. The Cubans are urging competition among all the countries of the world to aid the Nicaraguans rebuild their shattered economy and reconstruct their devastated homeland.

And they are warning, as we are, any imperialist power or reactionary regime that wants to attempt to turn back history: *Hands off Nicaragua!*

Fidel's July 26 speech

At the July 26th celebration in Cuba a week and a half ago Fidel discussed the revolution in Nicaragua. He explained he had prepared a speech discussing some of the domestic problems facing the Cuban revolution, but he had to throw that out. How could anyone give a speech on this July 26, Fidel asked, and talk about anything other than the Nicaraguan revolution?

> What should we talk about, what else could we talk about, what more extraordinary event of our times, what act of greater historical importance, of greater significance and implications has taken place in recent times than the victory of the Sandinistas in Nicaragua?" he said. "What has touched us more deeply, what has captured our attention more during these weeks, what could have excited or inspired us more than this popular and heroic victory?

Twenty-six Sandinista rebel commanders participated in the July 26 anniversary rally in Cuba. This was a tremendous show of solidarity. Fidel said, "I say solidarity, because we too need solidarity; I say stimulating, because we also need that stimulation."

He explained why the victory over Somoza is such an important victory for the Cuban revolution: "Solidarity, stimulation, because for a long time it was almost a crime to visit Cuba; for a long time imperialism tried to cut the ties with our sister peoples of Latin America and the Caribbean, and for a long time blockaded us, prohibited and thwarted the coming together and development of the natural, historical and logical ties between the Nicaraguan and the Cuban peoples."

Then he proposed an international campaign to mobilize aid to the Nicaraguan people and to block any imperialist intervention. This is according to the text in *Granma*:

> There's much hunger in Nicaragua. I believe that Nicaragua needs help from everybody. In the past few weeks, a large number of leaders have expressed their readiness to help Nicaragua.
> I think that's very good.

Governments of different hues, of different ideologies, of different political systems have expressed their readiness to assist the people of Nicaragua on a large scale. And Nicaragua certainly needs this help.

Even the United States has stated that it's ready to send food and organize other kinds of help. We're glad to hear it. They said they were going to start an airlift and send 300 tons of food a day. We think that's a very good idea.

. . . because it's much better in every sense, more productive, and makes for better relations among the peoples and for a climate of peace all over the world, to send food instead of sending bombs and Marines, like they did in Vietnam and so many other places.

Naturally—since I mentioned Vietnam—if the United States had intervened in Nicaragua it would have been an act of suicide for United States' policy in this hemisphere, because we haven't the slightest doubt that the Sandinistas would have continued fighting in spite of U.S. intervention. There's no question about that.

What U.S. intervention would mean
We're extremely happy that it didn't happen—who knows how many lives have been spared for that very reason—but we are also convinced that had there been an intervention it would have met with tremendous resistance on the part of Sandino's people. And not only that, but also that a gigantic Vietnam might have developed throughout Central America and in the rest of Latin America, a gigantic Vietnam. . . .

We are glad to know the United States is sending food to Nicaragua. We are glad to know that everybody is sending food and giving aid of all kinds to the people of Nicaragua.

We are not rich; we cannot compete with the United States in numbers of planes and tons of food. But we will send something; because even though we are poor we can always spare some of what we have. (Applause)

And something very important: we may not have great financial or material resources, but we do have human resources. (Applause)

Engineer Robelo said here that they need doctors, that they need campaigns to wipe out illiteracy. And we know our doctors and teachers. (Applause) They'll go wherever they're needed. If they have to go to the mountains, they go to the mountains; if to the countryside, the countryside. In Cuba and in Ethiopia, in Vietnam, in Yemen, in Angola, anywhere.

Nicaragua is much nearer, right nearby. There's practically the same distance between Cape San Antonio [Cuba's westernmost point] and Managua as between Cape San Antonio and Maisí Point [Cuba's eastern tip]. So it's really close.

Therefore, I believe that we are expressing the feelings of our Party and of our people when we say to our Nicaraguan brothers and sisters that, if they plan to put into effect a broad health and medical care program and there aren't enough Nicaraguan doctors, we are ready to send all the doctors they need to support this health program. (Applause)

Of course, we do have more than 1,000 doctors working abroad, but we still have some to spare. We have our commitments and we can meet them. . . .

If our doctors collaborate—and of course I'm sure they will—if our hospitals, the heads of hospitals, the health sectors, everybody collaborates, we can find all the doctors we need to tell the people of Nicaragua that we will send them all they need if they haven't enough themselves.

This means that if they need 100, we'll send them 100. If they need 200, we'll send them 200. And if they need as many as 500, we'll send them 500. No trouble at all. (Applause)

The need for a large-scale education campaign has also been mentioned here. And it looks as if there are some teachers here who are quite enthusiastic at the idea. A great educational campaign. (Applause)

Only a revolutionary government can carry out a great health and education campaign. . . .

I know how much people appreciate a health campaign; I know how much people appreciate an educational campaign.

Even in the midst of destruction and ruins,

a revolutionary government can wage a great campaign in these fields, and since our country has plenty of experience in these things we can offer some advice in both the health and the education campaigns. And, I repeat, if they don't have enough teachers in Nicaragua to put this education campaign into effect, we are ready to send them as many as they need. (Applause). . . .

We also know that our teachers go wherever they are sent—to the most remote places, to the farthest mountains, to the most forgotten little town. (Applause). . . .

It's not a case of our going to engage in politics in Nicaragua—and there will certainly be some who will say that we are.

Who's going to engage in politics, who's going to influence the Sandinistas? On the contrary, our teachers and our doctors will be influenced by the Sandinista spirit, and we are very pleased and happy about this. (Applause) The revolutionary spirit of the Sandinistas will have a great effect on them. Everyone knows our technicians' dedication to their work.

I repeat that we're glad that the United States and other countries are to help Nicaragua. What's more, we're ready to enter an emulation campaign with the United States, an emulation campaign (Applause) to see who can do the most for Nicaragua. We invite the United States, we invite all the countries of Latin America, we invite all the countries of Europe, the countries of the Third World, our sister socialist nations, everybody, to take part in an emulation campaign to help Nicaragua. (Applause)

This is a revolutionary leadership in action. A leadership responding to a revolution in process by turning toward it, determined to learn from it, and doing everything they can to move it forward—and being ready and willing to take the consequences for that active solidarity.

The Nicaraguan revolution is a clear and decisive test for every current in the world claiming to be revolutionary. The positive response of the Castroists to this challenge is confirmation of their continued revolutionary capacities and course of action. A similarly positive response to this challenge by Trotskyists will get us, the Castroists, and the Sandinistas working on a common campaign internationally. We will have new opportunities to collaborate with, learn from, and get a hearing from these revolutionary forces. A sectarian stance toward the Nicaraguan revolution and its leadership, or a routinist, lethargic response to the need and opportunity for an international solidarity campaign (which amounts politically to the same thing), would cut us off from this opportunity. This would be a default of historic magnitude for our world movement. We are confident that that mistake will be avoided.

Our internal discussion

Before turning to the major questions to be taken up, I want to say something on the discussion we have had with Comrade Wohlforth, who thinks revolutionaries should call on the workers and peasants of Cuba to arise and overthrow the Castro leadership in a political revolution. And I want to take up the discussion we've had with the comrades who hold the state capitalist view.

We have had an educational debate with comrades who came to the SWP from the Revolutionary Marxist Committee. These comrades had a state capitalist background, and they had not rejected the position of state capitalism when they joined the SWP two years ago. In the course of the Cuba discussion—with a little help from Nicaragua and a deeper study of Cuba—a number of these comrades have changed their minds, which is a step forward for the entire party. Among those who have changed their minds on the character of the Cuban revolution and who now recognize that a workers state exists in Cuba, are the three ex-RMCers who are members of the outgoing National Committee: Eric [Flint], Shelley [Kramer], and Bruce [Levine]. They had earlier signed the document "The Cuban Revolution: A State Capitalist Analysis," which is one of the three resolutions on Cuba we are going to vote on. These comrades themselves will explain the change in their thinking to you. Everybody will be interested in what each has to say. I'm sure comrades who still hold a state capitalist position and have not yet changed their minds on the class character of Cuba will give this the most serious consideration.

The comrades of the ex-RMC were attracted to the SWP because they are revolutionists. They found themselves more and more drawn toward the Cuban revolution for the same reason. And when they found the facts about Cuba and their own attitude toward the Cuban revolution in contradiction with their theory that Cuba remains capitalist, they junked the theory of state capitalism.

We have also been debating with Comrade Wohlforth. I won't take much time on this. There are not many people in this party who agree with him. The total number of votes his document received in all the branches was less than one-half of 1 percent of the membership.

By pointing out this fact I am not at all belittling the question at issue. If there were a substantial segment of this party that favored calling for a political revolution in Cuba, for the overthrow of the Castro leadership, that would be by far the weightiest question before this convention. Everything else, including our turn to industry would be third-rate by comparison. Because this party would be finished as a revolutionary workers party if we called for the overthrow of the only revolutionary socialist leadership in power anywhere in the world.

Before we began our discussion in the SWP on Cuba a number of comrades, without thinking both the question and all its implications through seriously, were drifting into adopting this position. Now, fortunately, the number of comrades in our party who hold this position is negligible, and in the Fourth International as a whole the number is shrinking. Our discussion in the SWP has convinced many comrades to pull back and think the question through to the end.

The discussion on these questions in the Fourth International is only just beginning. No section of the Fourth International has had any organized discussion on Cuba in recent years. The international discussion will, as I indicated, begin sometime after the World Congress. And when that discussion gets underway we will have an important role to play in sharing what we have learned and relearned about the Cuban revolution and about the strategic questions of party building on a world scale that are so bound up with the Cuban—and now the Nicaraguan—revolution and their leaderships.

Inside the camp of the revolution

What is at the heart of this discussion? What do we need to affirm so that we can *act* with a campaign spirit and in a united way to take advantage of the new openings before us?

What we are discussing is whether our twenty-year policy toward the Cuban revolution has been correct and remains correct today.

What has our line been?

We hailed the Cuban revolution and greeted its leaders, the team around Fidel Castro, as fellow revolutionaries *who had successfully led the toilers to make a revolution*. The Fidelistas were not a grouping thrust into power despite an anti working-class program or practice, but a leadership who *led* the working masses to conquer power through a socialist revolution. No small accomplishment. The first since the Bolsheviks.

From the first we have been part of the Cuban revolution. As part of the international working class it is our revolution. And from Cuba's proximity and its influence on us it is *our* revolution. We view its problems and contradictions from the standpoint of being participants in the revolution.

Within that framework we have put forward our programmatic ideas, our suggestions and criticisms, our proposals on how to move the revolution forward. A few comrades have said they don't think we are being critical enough of the Cuban revolution. This indicates a lack of understanding of our entire policy—our starting point. Joe Hansen's book, *The Dynamics of the Cuban Revolution*, is an extremely critical look at Cuba. I believe it is the most profoundly critical book written about the Cuban revolution. But some people miss that aspect because the framework of Joe's book is from within the camp of the Cuban revolution and its revolutionary leadership, and against all their enemies and opponents, including the Stalinists. That is our approach.

James P. Cannon summed this up in 1961 in solidarizing himself with the course of the SWP Political Committee against the Healyite minority. Cannon said, "The only *revolutionary* policy for [us in regard to] Cuba is to *recognize* the revolution there, as it is and as it is developing as a *socialist* revolution—and to *identify* ourselves with it, and to act as a part of it, not as scholastic wiseacres standing outside the living movement." (SWP Discussion Bulletin, Vol. 22, No. 17, p 3.) The heart of the discussion on Cuba is whether we are going to continue that approach.

A party-building stance

But what underlies that approach? What are we really trying to accomplish? How did we arrive at it and how does it relate to our strategic approach to building a mass revolutionary international? A world party of socialist revolution?

Beginning in 1959, the SWP and the YSA plunged into the tasks of defending the Cuban revolution, fully and completely. We didn't worry about getting in too deep, becoming too closely connected to Castroism, or putting too many eggs in the Cuban basket.

As we were carrying out our elementary responsibility to defend the Cuban revolution against imperialism we began to learn more and more from and, even though we were very small in numbers, get a hearing from Cuban revolutionaries. We also began to win to the YSA and SWP young people in this country who were attracted to the revolution and its leadership. The Castroist leadership represented a new generation of revolutionary fighters. This was a development of historic importance for the world revolution. Of decisive importance was the fact that they had succeeded in bypassing the Stalinists in Cuba. This breakthrough advanced to a new stage the struggle to bring into existence a revolutionary leadership on a world scale, to push aside the Stalinist roadblock.

The best way to understand what we have been doing in regard to Cuba is to view our approach as part of our broader party-building strategy. We have been engaged in party-building activity in regard to the Cuban revolution since 1959. Both national and international party building.

On one level, this was an almost instinctive reaction. More than anything we are trained to respond positively to revolution and to a revolutionary leadership, to turn toward forces moving in a revolutionary direction, and to seek ways to advance the process of organizing them into Leninist parties in each country, and into a world party.

It is parallel to the way we respond, as a party, to opportunities and challenges for our class in places like Newport News, Virginia—we do everything possible to advance the struggle and strengthen the organization, consciousness, and combativity of our class, we collaborate with leftward-moving forces, and we move decisively into action to build the party.

Our approach toward Cuba was the response of a party educated and trained to *act*, to participate, to *affect* the course of events as we learn from them. We are a party of cadres trained as revolutionary politicians. We are trained to judge those who claim to be revolutionaries by their actions. We understand that is how we will be judged—and how we *should* be judged. And we know it is only by orienting toward those who act as to advance the interests of the working class that we can assemble the forces for the revolutionary party—internationally and here in the United States.

To the SWP and the YSA, this is the ABC of revolutionary working-class politics.

Bolshevik approach

In approaching the Cuban revolution in this way we relied on what we had learned from the Bolshevik leadership—what we had learned from Lenin, and what had been transmitted directly to us by Trotsky.

This was the approach, for example, followed by Lenin when the Communist International was being organized. The Bolsheviks held power in the Soviet Union and had immense authority among revolutionary-minded workers and other toilers throughout the world because they had led the October revolution. But despite this commanding political authority, not all revolutionary forces were in the parties of the Communist International. Not all revolutionary forces were yet Leninists. So the leaders of the Communist International had to carry out a policy of trying to reach out to these forces, within their overall strategy of party building. One expression of this approach was their decision to invite revolutionary organizations that were not Leninist to come to Moscow to attend the early congresses of the Communist International. Among those organizations that did send delegations were the Industrial Workers of the World in the United States, the Shop Stewards Movement in Britain, and others.

When the Bolsheviks grappled with the problems of party building in the colonial and semi-colonial countries, they recognized they faced a special challenge. The proletariat itself was small, the workers movement weak, the influence of Marxism faint. But revolutionary currents, often based on the poorer peasantry, were appearing in a number of countries. Lenin explained, at the Second Congress in 1920, that the Comintern had to turn toward these forces and win them to the international party.

Lenin, who was precise on questions of terminology, even argued strongly for a change in language to help advance this orientation. In his report to the congress from the commission on the National and Colonial Question, Lenin explained that the commission "came to the unanimous decision to talk not about the 'bourgeois-democratic' movement but only about the national-revolutionary movement...."

> It would be utopian to think that proletarian parties, insofar as it is at all possible for them to arise in these countries, will be able to carry out Communist tactics and Communist policies in the backward countries without having a definite relationship with the peasant movement, without supporting it in deeds. But objections were raised that, if we say 'bourgeois-democratic,' we lose the distinction between the reformist and revolutionary movement which has become quite clear in the backward countries and the colonies recently....
>
> [W]e believed that the only correct thing would be to take this difference into consideration and to replace the words 'bourgeois-democratic' almost everywhere [in the 'Theses on the National and Colonial Question'] with the expression 'national-revolutionary.' The point about this is that as communists we will only support the bourgeois freedom movements in the colonial countries if these movements are really revolutionary ... (*The Second Congress of the Communist International*, New Park, pp. 110–111.)

Lenin understood that the revolution surges ahead faster than the party. He also knew that the party is decisive to the victory of the revolution. He combined these two facts in the Bolshevik's strategic approach to party building.

If this approach was correct for the Bolsheviks in 1920, isn't it correct—even more correct—for the Fourth International today, which is the continuator of the program and method of the Bolsheviks and the early Comintern? The Fourth International has nothing like the authority Lenin and Trotsky had after 1917. We are still a tiny nucleus of the future vanguard. We have yet to build a mass party and none of our nuclei are as yet composed in their large majority of industrial workers. And yet the objective conditions for revolution are far more favorable today than they were in 1920. Revolutionary forces will come forward outside the ranks of the Fourth International. They won't start as Leninists, and they will make lots of mistakes. How are we going to approach these forces to build a mass world party of socialist revolution?

Party building involves one-by-one recruitment, as we know only too well. But the SWP is not going to be built just by recruiting individuals until we gradually get to be a mass party. We will fuse with and link up with all kinds of forces moving in a revolutionary direction. And we may be in a minority on some questions for a while. The same is true for the Fourth International.

This is our attitude in regard to the Cuban revolutionaries. We have been trying to link up with them, to battle shoulder-to-shoulder with them against the imperialists, to explain and resist the misleadership and faintheartedness of the Stalinists, to learn from the Cubans, and to get a hearing from them through the example of our actions and the power of our ideas. This is the only way to proceed if we are going to build an international party of revolutionaries—not an international sect or cult, but a politically homogeneous party whose different components have come to revolutionary Marxism from different starting points and along different paths.

Jim Cannon explained this very well in 1961 in regard to the Cuban revolution. He recalled that in the 1930s Trotsky spent a good deal of time and energy trying to win left-centrists to the Fourth International. These were people, Jim recalled, who never led revolutions, they only talked about it—"and even that not very convincingly."

Jim asked, if it was correct for the Fourth International to orient to and try to win those forces, aren't we one hundred times more justified in considering the leaders of the Cuban revolution as candidates for membership in the revolutionary international? "If such people are not considered as rightful participants in a discussion, and possible collaborators in a new party and a new International—where will we find better candidates?" (ibid., p. 15) To Cannon, as to the entire experienced leadership of our party, the supreme test of those who claim to be revolutionary was leading forces in class combat, making a revolution. "The Cuban revolutionists have done more than talk, and they are not the only ones on trial from now on. We are also on trial," Jim stressed (ibid, p. 15). If we had failed to turn toward this opening when it presented itself, we would have joined the "scholastic wiseacres"—as Jim called the sectarians—on the sidelines.

Our approach to Malcolm X a few years later was the same. When Malcolm started moving toward revolutionary politics, we turned toward him and the forces around him. We understood the promise and potential of that development. We greeted Malcolm as a fellow revolutionist even though he was not a Marxist. In fact, he was still a Muslim.

What was at the heart of our orientation to Malcolm? We were not cheerleaders. We wanted to learn from, and try to link up with fresh revolutionary forces, to move toward the larger revolutionary party that must be built. We tried to design every word we wrote, everything we said and did to advance that goal. Our comments, analysis, and proposals were presented in that critical spirit.

If we had gone wrong on Cuba and the Castroist current, we would not have been able to orient toward Malcolm X correctly either. If we had not waged a war in our party on sectarian attitudes to the Castro team, we would not have been in a position to respond positively to Malcolm X when he began moving in a revolutionary direction. It's worth noting that the sectarian opponents of the SWP have always pointed to our analysis and approach to Malcolm and Fidel as the two supreme examples of the utter opportunist degeneration of the party. The two are totally linked—and correctly so. In their eyes negatively, in ours positively.

Politics first

The fight we had in the party almost twenty years ago in regard to Cuba was not over the theory of the Cuban revolution, although of course there were major theoretical questions involved. The fight was over political line. In essence, it was over our party-building strategy. We had a minority in the party then, led by Tim Wohlforth, James Robertson, and Shane Mage, who feared we were getting in too deep. They said we had to be more critical. We had to put more distance between ourselves and the Castroist current—lest we become infected. As the fight unfolded it became clear that we had a sectarian minority in the party.

This petty-bourgeois current labored under two misunderstandings. They suffered from others also, but I'll point out these two. One, they had the impression that the decisive test of Trotskyists was their ability to criticize! They thought that a really astute Trotskyist must be an expert critic. And if god didn't want Trotskyists to criticize all the time, he wouldn't have given them a tongue or a typewriter!

For the SWP, criticism from the sidelines is anathema. To the sectarians, shaking their fingers at forces in revolutionary motion is the be-all and end-all of politics. That's where we part company.

The second misunderstanding of the Wohlforth-Robertson-Mage minority was over the question of party-building strategy that I have been talking about. They accused the party of not being interested in building the Fourth International. They said we were adapting to Castroism and liquidating the party and the international. These comrades simply didn't understand what was going on. They didn't see that everything we were doing in relation to Cuba was part of a worldwide party-building perspective.

As Joe Hansen put it in his debate with Wohlforth at the 1961 National Committee plenum, "We have been party-building in Cuba right along, and I don't know if anybody noticed it. Apparently some comrades didn't notice it. What were we doing with those articles? Just writing for the fun of writing? The fun of observing the Cuban revolution? In a pig's eye. We were working there with a design, we were always writing with regard to its influence in Cuba, that is, party-building influence." (SWP DB, Vol. 22, No. 3.)

Joe explained that the minority thought the task of building a party internationally or in Cuba as primarily an organizational question, one of running down to Cuba and opening up a headquarters in order to expose, outflank, and denounce the Castroists. So they missed out on the fact that we've been party building in our relations with the Cuban revolution all along. They missed the fact that to build a party, a world party of socialist revolution, we've got to orient toward revolutionary-minded forces, toward the forces that are most like us. We've got to seek areas of agreement, seek ways to collaborate with them so we can learn from them, gain a hearing by the effectiveness of our example, and convince them by the correctness of our ideas. Our goal is to bring together forces capable of leading a revolution—not push them aside and proclaim ourselves to be the only genuine revolutionaries.

There is still another aspect to this question of party building. We have always stressed the fact that the Castroists need an international organization of revolutionaries, an international party, to extend the Cuban revolution. For example, Che Guevara paid with his life for relying on the treacherous Bolivian Stalinist party.

But the other way to look at this is from the standpoint of the Fourth International, which was organized in order to advance the rebuilding of a mass world party of socialist revolution. From this standpoint—the standpoint of *our* responsibilities and opportunities—the revolutionary international organization, in skeletal form, does exist. It is the Fourth International. And its program is revolutionary Marxism—the summation of the lessons of a century and a half of working-class struggle.

Our reason for being is to bring together on a world scale the revolutionary forces and to forge them into a powerful force, steeled to counter the bourgeois nationalists, Stalinists, and reformists of all stripes, and to provide resolute leadership to the toilers. That is what we are in business for. The Castroists should be part of this international organization that we are trying to bring into being. And they must be part of it if their goal of defending and extending the Cuban revolution is to be reached.

We have not yet been able to make that linkup. It is a challenge that remains before us. We have often discussed the contradictions in the development of the Castroists, which present barriers in the way of this process. But let's look for a few minutes at the problems on our side.

The Fourth International has been handicapped by two factors. The first is our small size and the fact that we don't command mass influence. This is determined by conditions beyond our control, but it is not a decisive handicap in our ability to move toward linking up with the Cuban revolutionaries.

The second factor is more important. It is also the one we can do the most to change. The Fourth International missed the two best opportunities presented to it to influence the Cubans and take steps toward this linkup.

The sectarianism of Juan Posadas

The first opportunity opened up right after the Cuban revolution. But the only organized group in Cuba that called itself Trotskyist at that time was a sectarian outfit led by Juan Posadas. It was affiliated to the International Secretariat, one of the two public factions of the Fourth International.

Posadas's line was that the biggest threat to the Cuban revolution lay in the Castro leadership and its alleged determination to strangle the mass movement. They considered it a petty-bourgeois leadership that had to be pushed aside if the revolution was to proceed. They attacked the Castroists for not being radical enough, not going far enough, fast enough, even at the height of the revolutionary process in 1960. They set out to take the leadership of the Cuban revolution out of the hands of the Fidelistas. Thus they cut themselves off from ever attracting any serious revolutionary forces in Cuba.

To give you an example of their criminal sectarianism, in October 1962, in the midst of the missile crisis, the Posadistas distributed in Havana—in the name of the Cuban section of the Fourth International—a mimeographed sheet asserting: "The concrete measure that must be adopted is the immediate expulsion of Yankee imperialism from Guantanamo." Guantanamo is the naval base maintained by force by U.S. imperialism in Cuba. A military move against it would have been disastrous, an adventure of the worst kind. To call for such a move under the circumstances was an extreme provocation.

Moreover, with imperialism pushing the world to the brink of nuclear war, the Posadistas urged the Soviet Union in one of the headlines on the leaflet to "strike the first blow." If their position on Guantanamo can justly be called an irresponsible provocation, their advocacy of a Soviet first strike against the United States can only be described as madness. Advocacy of a preemptive Soviet nuclear strike—accompanied by the "theory" that a world socialist order would arise out of the ashes of a nuclear holocaust, became one of the Posadas sect's special hobby horses.

Of course, the Stalinists seized on the politically irresponsible positions of the Posadistas to smear Trotskyism. At that time our world movement was split into two public factions, which made it more difficult to minimize the damage. The positions expressed by Posadas were not the line of either of the two wings of the world movement. Posadas and Pablo together were a minority at the 1960 World Congress held by the International Secretariat. By early 1962 the faction Posadas led had walked out of the International Secretariat wing altogether. He held his own rump world congress and proclaimed his sect the *real* Fourth International.

Well before Posadas split the majority of both wings of the Fourth International recognized the revolutionary character of the Castro leadership team. However, because the reunification was delayed, the international was hamstrung in exerting its influence on Trotskyists in Cuba who were led by followers of Posadas from other Latin American countries. The opportunity was lost. (Despite the obstacle of the Posadistas, the Fourth International did succeed in establishing collaboration with the Cuban leadership on the decisive issue of defense of the revolution against Yankee imperialism. In particular, the Trotskyists in Canada and the United States threw their forces into building the Fair Play for Cuba Committee.)

After Bolivia: rethinking the guerrilla-war strategy

A second great opening presented itself to the Fourth International in the late 1960s, when the Cubans began to rethink the guerrilla-warfare strategy in the wake of the death of Che and the debacle of the efforts at guerrilla war in country after country. Confronted with growing economic difficulties as well, the Cuban leadership pulled back. They were thinking about how to move forward in an effective way to extend the revolution. But instead of pointing the way forward at the critical turning point, the majority of the International adopted a guerrilla strategy itself. As Joe Hansen put it, the Fourth International majority passed the Cubans going the opposite direction. Needless to say, this didn't provide any help to the Cubans. And, until this error began to be corrected at the end of 1976, with the adoption by the majority leadership of their "Self-Criticism on Latin America," (See *The Leninist Strategy of Party Building: The Debate on Guerrilla Warfare in Latin America*, by Joseph Hansen; Pathfinder Press, Inc.; New York; 1979; Appendix II) this line was disastrous for the Fourth International. Some cadre were unnecessarily lost and thousands more were miseducated and trained with ultraleft sectarian ideas, not the Leninist strategy of party building and the method of the Transitional Program.

A new opportunity

Now we have a third opportunity. The former majority tendency has rejected the erroneous line adopted at the 1969 World Congress, of elevating guerrilla warfare to a strategy. This will be formalized at the upcoming World Congress.[1]

---

1. The document on Latin America adopted at the World Congress in November 1979, stated:

    The Fourth International promoted an incorrect political orientation in Latin America for several years. The clearest and most developed expression of this incorrect line is contained in the . . . reports and resolutions on Latin America adopted by a majority vote at the 1969 and 1974 World Congresses of the Fourth International. . . .

    As a result of this erroneous line, many of the cadres and parties of the Fourth International were politically disarmed in face of the widespread, but false idea that a small group of courageous and capable revolutionaries could set in motion a process leading to a socialist revolution. The process of rooting our parties in the working class and oppressed masses was hindered. The line that was followed not only cut across the possibility of winning cadres from the guerrillaist tendencies to a revolutionary Marxist program, but also led to adventurist actions and losses from our own ranks. The consequences for our small movement were most severe in Argentina and Bolivia.

    Accordingly, the Fourth International rescinds the erroneous line on Latin America adopted at the 1969 and 1974 World Congresses. The line of this resolution on Latin America now supersedes the previous line.

    One of the most important tasks for the education of the revolutionary Marxist forces in Latin America is the critical evaluation of this whole experience. With the debate now over, the documents can be studied in an educational way, as part of the history of our movement.

The changes in the relationship of forces on a world scale have enabled the Cubans to take some extremely important initiatives. This has included increased political attention and interest in the class struggle right here in the United States. That is the significance of the Dialogue with the Cuban community.

Most importantly, the revolutionary triumph in Nicaragua opens new prospects for extending the revolution, new tasks in the fight to stay the hands of the imperialists, and new opportunities for common activities, especially throughout Latin America and in the United States.

We must decisively reject any sectarian line toward the Cuban leadership that would be an excuse for not responding to this opening. We must wage this fight. Because if we turn our backs on this opportunity, if we choose to act as sideline critics, then the Fourth International will pay the heaviest price. And that is what this discussion is about.

The frame-ups against Cuba

If we are going to join hands with the Cuban revolutionaries to defend the revolution, we have got to know who we're defending it against.

In the past few years a growing number of what can only be called frame-up charges against Cuba have been circulated. We should take a look at these. We don't have to bother with the right-wing frame-ups—the slanders from Somoza's pal in Congress, Larry McDonald, or the CIA-planted stories about Cuban soldiers raping Angolan women, and the like. What we need to scrutinize are some of the more sophisticated frame-ups, those that attack Cuba ostensibly from the left. This is quite the fashion these days among petty-bourgeois radicals.

One example of this trend is an anthology cited by Comrade Wohlforth in his article in the preconvention discussion bulletin as a "good" source of information on Cuba. It is called *The New Cuba: Paradoxes and Potentials* (edited by Ronald Radosh, William Morrow and Company, Inc., New York, 1976). I had looked through it some time ago and put it aside because it seemed to be singularly lacking in factual material. But a few months ago I went back to it because of the person who edited and wrote key parts of it. His name is Ronald Radosh. He is the "radical" who recently coauthored the article in *New Republic* concluding that Julius Rosenberg was in fact guilty. This article was jubilantly hailed by right-wingers and reactionary forces. Even a "radical" agrees that Julius Rosenberg was proved guilty, they trumpeted. Of course, Radosh's article was a "balanced" reexamination of the Rosenberg case. Julius was guilty, he found, but Ethel Rosenberg was framed-up. What could be more objective?

Radosh takes the same "balanced" approach to Cuba—so watch out! His book, he explains, is an answer to the unbalanced "Cubaphiles." These are the people who love the Cuban revolution. That's us, among others.

Radosh states he writes from the standpoint of "western intellectuals," by which he really means petty-bourgeois radicals who live in the academic world, who fear and hate the working class, and who reject the dogmatic notion that workers should rule society.

Radosh's first indictment against the Cubans is that they haven't yet figured out how to produce things without factories and assembly lines. You see, he visited a factory in Cuba. He says workers in Cuba "are engaged in repetitive and boring jobs, as they would be on an American assembly line. One cannot help thinking that no matter what the social goals and programs of the Revolution, the working hours of the people at this factory are being spent at dull and meaningless jobs." This intellectual knows that there is no point making a revolution just so you can work in a factory—what kind of life is that?

Radosh eventually comes out with his opposition to the revolution itself: "As I spend more time in Cuba, I keep coming back to the conclusion that socialism simply cannot be built on one island, particularly one that is also subject to underdevelopment and an economy of scarcity."

True. That is why the Cubans dedicate their lives—unlike Radosh—to *extending* the socialist revolution as they struggle to improve their lives in Cuba. But the Cuban masses long ago rejected the counsel of those who urged them not to make a socialist revolution in Cuba because the country was too small and weak to accomplish anything on its own. They have proved those chicken-hearted advisers wrong. And how!

Another article in this anthology is by Martin Duberman, who is recommended to us by Comrade Wohlforth as a "radical gay activist," an authority worth listening to on Cuba. Duberman begins by suggesting a more "balanced" view of the Bay of Pigs invasion:

> As early as the Bay of Pigs invasion in 1961—discontented elements in Cuba included people not readily reduced to the classic Marxist category of a 'parasitic elite.' Dominated though the invading brigade unquestionably was by middle-and upper-class elements [not to mention the imperialists!], it included a number of men (the San Roman brothers, for example) who had earlier tried to overthrow Batista or had initially been strong supporters of Castro, as well as some 50 blacks and 100 workers.

Looking back on all the trouble and bother, Duberman thinks the revolution wasn't really worth the effort. The Cubans have solved the petty problems—hunger, unemployment, disease, illiteracy, and things like that. But so what? Nothing fundamental has really changed because the Cubans have not yet achieved "psycho-sexual transformation." That is, they are not as advanced in this area as Martin Duberman, who is the true yardstick of liberation. Duberman says true revolutionaries "seek the path to this transformation through intra- and interpersonal explorations which at least in part involve the denunciation or transcendence of material accumulation."

Showing how totally reactionary this "radical activist" really is, he then says that this "more encompassing vision, the redefinition of sex roles . . . cannot proceed without absolute freedom of inquiry and expression, and that it is in the presumed heartland of counterrevolution [the *"presumed"* heartland!], the United States of America, that we are beginning to glimpse its emerging contours."

What an inspiring message to the peoples of the world: Don't worry about—how does the Church put it?—"temporal" things. Concentrate on intrapersonal liberation. This guy makes the pope in Rome look progressive! This fellow that Comrade Wohlforth recommends to us as a "radical gay activist" has an out-and-out counterrevolutionary position on Cuba.

The 'pink grapefruit'

Sad to say, even worse material than this has appeared in the press of sections of the Fourth International. In January, 1979, *Rouge*, the newspaper of the Ligue Communiste Révolutionnaire, the French section of the Fourth International, ran a full-page article by "a reader" who had recently returned from a tourist trip to Cuba. This reader was dismayed and distressed by the experience:

> It is to be noted that Cuba, like the other countries of the socialist bloc, is rather reluctant to accept any sort of individual tourism. Individual imagination and initiative are considered 'not very revolutionary.' Mass tourism in groups, on the other hand, is encouraged, because it can be supervised, closely regulated, and most of all the tourists can be kept track of. Trips by buses specially for tourists follow fixed itineraries [how suffocating!] and, of course, offer only a relatively limited interest. . . .
>
> It is sad to note that in Cuba, the 'free territory of America,' tourists coming from capitalist countries have the painful feeling of being trapped and being kept in blinders. This is done under organizational pretexts that are far from convincing. These tourists have come as friends, and paradoxically they are considered as 'potential internal enemies.' So, anything goes. Lies and mistrust go hand in hand in a terrifying climate of hypocrisy. . . .
>
> This defensive and suspicious attitude, unfortunately is not taken just toward mere tourists coming from the Western world looking for a chance to breathe some 'free air.' It is in fact a sinister reflection of the sort of relationship the government maintains with the people. This is a people that has been robbed of what is held most dear, of its achievement of freedom and happiness. Frustrated by a government that exerts its power at every level of society, the people suffocate and fall into indifference. This is a system based on fear.

This reactionary diatribe did not appear in one of the CIA-financed counterrevolutionary sheets—where it would be appropriate—but in the newspaper of the French section of the Fourth International.

Our suffocating tourist goes on to complain about the architecture of the tens of thousands of new apartments built since the revolution. "The new section of Havana looks like a phantom city, a ghost town. Hastily painted for the youth festival last year, the modern buildings conjure up a depressing image of the suburbs that serve as dormitories for workers in France. The paint is coming off . . ." How horrid! New buildings, but not as stylish as the better neighborhoods of Paris! And paint peeling. What is the matter with those Cubans?

> The Cuban people daily face bureaucratic hassles, rationing, inevitable lines, military officers, police, speechifying—all the characteristic signs of a pathological regime that is suffocating itself. It is a regime that hides behind opportunist rhetoric and a lamentable parody of what is supposed to be consulting the people, and is, in fact, nothing but the expression of an institutional void, a void that goes to the frontiers of the absurd. This void is one created by a military dictatorship that justifies its power in the name of a 'revolutionary' ideology.

To back up the accusation that Cuba is ruled by a "military dictatorship," this French tourist submitted to *Rouge*, along with the article, a poem, entitled "The Grapefruit Are Pink," which the editors prominently featured with the article. The poem is introduced as being by Armando Valladares, who "has been imprisoned for nearly twenty years in Cuban jails. He is paralyzed as a result of being denied food for a long period. He is, if not the spokesman, at least one of the most representative voices from this gulag of the tropics."

And who is Armando Valladares? A dissident poet? Perhaps. Jailed for artistic deviations? Not quite. Valladares was convicted and sentenced for possession of bombs in 1960! While in prison, he began writing poetry. The poem reprinted in *Rouge* begins like this:

> *The sun was setting; we were ending twelve hours of forced labor covered with sweat and marks and bruises left by bayonets and kicks. The blue sky extended along the quiet mountains, over an inscription of green and gold an inscription telling of pine woods and pirates it was the Isle of Pines the Siberia of America. Our blood enriched the grapefruit groves, that is why some grapefruit are pink.*

It is hard to find appropriate words to describe this counterrevolutionary garbage, appearing in a Trotskyist newspaper! If in the early days of the Russian revolution, the editors of *l'Humanité* had published such poems by White Russians, the Comintern would have insisted on harsh action.

The editors of *Rouge* published this article and poem without comment. And to this day, nine months later, while other articles about Cuba have appeared, this one has never been explicitly repudiated, never disavowed in the pages of *Rouge!* What are the readers of *Rouge*—including those in Cuba—to think but that this vile reactionary stuff represents, at least, a current of opinion among Trotskyists?

The frame-up on Eritrea

Let us turn to another charge: the Cubans have been framed-up on Eritrea. There is no other word for it. This is an especially tricky frame-up, based on two counts. The first accusation is that the Cubans directly participated in the war in Eritrea. No matter how many times this charge is repeated, each time the evidence is examined it totally evaporates.

We have taken this "evidence" apart piece by piece, and I won't repeat that here. (See "The Revolutionary Character of the Castro Leadership," and "The Ethiopia-Somalia War, Eritrea, and Cuba—What the Facts Show" in this volume.)

We can say categorically that there is *no* evidence whatsoever, not a shred of proof, that the Cubans are lying when they say that they were not and are not involved in the military operations against the Eritrean liberation forces.

Unfortunately, it seems that some comrades are so convinced of the supposed counterrevolutionary character of the Cuban leadership that they want to believe this false accusation. And they *do* believe it, despite all the evidence against it. I hope we can finally be done with this charge because it's just a bum rap. It doesn't stand up.

But once you dispose of this slander there is the second count of the indictment against the Cubans on Eritrea, which is somewhat more complicated. This is the conspiracy count: Even if the Cubans aren't directly involved in the Dergue's war against the Eritreans, they are still responsible for it, militarily, politically, and morally.

We need to step back and look at this accusation to see where it takes us.

We disagree with the Cuban policy in Ethiopia in two important respects. First, they do not support self-determination for Eritrea: that is, they do not support the right of the Eritreans to decide if they want to be part of Ethiopia or have their own independent state. We have pointed out in our press that this mistaken policy weakens the Ethiopian revolution, and also serves to weaken the Cuban revolution. The Cubans should politically support self-determination for Eritrea.

But in making this criticism we have to know what the Cuban line actually is. Some Cubaphobes try to argue that the Cubans are for crushing the Eritrean struggle. This is false. The Cubans have repeatedly stated publicly that they oppose a military solution to the conflict. This is *not* the position of the Dergue or of Moscow. And the Cubans have resisted intense pressure, from the Dergue and Moscow, to fall in behind the Dergue's war against Eritrea.

In 1978, Cuban vice-president Carlos Rafael Rodriguez stated the Cuban position as follows: "We helped the Eritreans in their fight for self-determination from the time of Hailie Selassie onward. We feel there has to be some political solution to the Eritrean problem and there have to be talks between Eritreans and the central government." [*Intercontinental Press/Inprecor*, Vol. 17, No. 30, August 6, 1979, p. 800.]

In 1975, in Havana, Fidel Castro took up the question of Eritrea in a speech to ministers of the Coordinating Bureau of the Non-Aligned Countries. This speech has recently been reprinted in Spanish, English, French, Russian, and Arabic, and is being made widely available. Fidel said:

Unfortunately, a fratricidal struggle between the new government [in Ethiopia] that destroyed the old structures and a national liberation movement is now being waged within that very state. This situation in which two causes of progressive trends are confronting each other is indeed complex. Therefore what is the duty of the nonaligned? It is perhaps to stand idly by or to support one side to the detriment of the other? To urge the war on? Decidedly not.

The least that should be done is to make a serious effort and seek a peaceful and just solution that is acceptable to the parties in the conflict which is separating and pitting against each other the Ethiopian revolutionary process and the Liberation Movement of Eritrea. Only recently, the OPEC worked to seek peace between Iraq and Iran. Why don't the nonaligned countries do the same thing in Ethiopia? (*Granma*, March 30, 1975.)

So if we are going to talk about Cuba and Eritrea, we must start with what the Cuban position actually is.

The second mistake the Cubans make in Ethiopia is that they fail to distinguish between, on the one hand, the Cuban government's correct policy of maintaining friendly relations and extending material aid to Ethiopia and, on the other hand, the position that should be held by the Cuban Communist Party: that only by taking the road of socialist revolution can the workers and peasants of Ethiopia guarantee their victory over imperialism and move their revolution forward. As we know, this same mistake—the failure to distinguish clearly between maintaining friendly state-to-state relations and expressing political confidence in some bourgeois governments that are in sharp conflict with imperialism—marks Cuban policy toward other countries in the colonial and semicolonial world as well. It is the kind of mistake that would be more readily corrected if the Cuban revolutionaries were a component of a mass world party of socialist revolution.

We think the Cuban policy of expressing political confidence in the Dergue, or in the Neto government in Angola, is wrong, and have said so. But this is not the dispute in our party and in the International. Where we have a difference is on whether the Cubans should send military and other aid to these regimes at all. This is the difference we need to discuss, as has been made clear in several recent articles, including the article by Comrade Alan Jones (see "The Character of the Cuban Revolution," in this volume), several contributions to the SWP preconvention discussion bulletin, and in amendments that have been submitted to the Draft World Political Resolution by Comrade Gabriel of the French LCR (International Internal Discussion Bulletin Vol. XVI, No. 8.).

The basic line of argument advanced by these comrades is that no matter what the Cubans say or do on Eritrea, so long as they send aid to Ethiopia—military aid, administrative aid, or medical and educational aid—they bear political and moral responsibility for the policies and actions of the Dergue. In other words, what the Cubans consider to be internationalist aid in the struggle against imperialism just serves to strengthen these repressive, bourgeois regimes. If Cuba's military aid was decisive in defeating the imperialist-inspired Somali invasion of Ethiopia, then it simply freed the hands of the Dergue to send troops against the Eritreans. If Cuba sends administrators, doctors, teachers, or technicians to Angola to help get the economy moving, then that just strengthens the bourgeois regime there.

Stop Cuban aid?

The political logic of this position is to demand that Cuban troops get out of Ethiopia, no matter what ongoing imperialist-backed military threat there may be. And Cuban troops, by this logic, should get out of Angola regardless of the military threat from South Africa. Even if it would leave the door open for South Africans to march in and install a pro-South African regime in Angola—Cuban troops should get out. And, of course, by this logic, Cuba shouldn't send aid to Nicaragua, in which today capitalist property relations still exist.

This is the line proposed by Comrade Gabriel. He says that the Fourth International should demand that Cuba immediately stop all "military aid to the Dergue," and cut off "all support" to Ethiopia. [ibid.] If we followed this line, we would go to Cuba and start campaigning against the thing that the most politically conscious, the most revolutionary-minded Cubans, are most proud of, and consider one of the most important things the Cuban revolution is doing. That's its internationalist aid. And we would say, "The Fourth International stands for ending this counter-revolutionary garbage."

We would go to Ethiopia, and rally around our flag all workers and peasants in Ethiopia who want to see the Cuban troops and doctors and teachers out of there. We would be pretty lonely—wouldn't we? I would hope so!

Inside Cuba this line would put us on the side of the most conservative, fainthearted forces—those who think all this African business, this stuff in Central America, is too risky, too dangerous. Let's just stay home, they argue, and build socialism on our own island. This would put the Fourth International on the side of sectarian abstentionism at its worst. We would be blocking with the Stalinists, regardless of our broader program. Luckily, the Cubans wouldn't listen to us. They would dismiss us with the back of their hands.

But the differences in the Fourth International don't stop there. They get even worse. The argument was put forward by Comrade Jones in his article that so long as the Cubans don't *overthrow* the bourgeois regimes they bear responsibility for whatever they do. Comrade Jones complained: "Once the military victory [over South Africa] was achieved, however, the Cubans took no steps whatever—quite the reverse—to encourage the overthrow of capitalism in Angola. And this is no academic point when, with the prestige of their intervention and *their great military weight*, there is no doubt that a Cuban call for the overthrow of bourgeois rule in Angola would have had every chance of succeeding." (Emphasis added. See p. 95 of this volume.)

For the Cubans to use their "great military weight" to overthrow the Angolan regime would be a colossal adventure. Who would they replace the Neto leadership with? The Angolan workers and peasants are the only ones who can overthrow capitalism in Angola. Not the Cuban army.

For the Fourth International to call on the Cubans to substitute themselves for that forces would be wild adventurism. It would discredit Trotskyism in the eyes of serious revolutionaries in Angola as well as in Cuba.

The Cuban leadership's policy, I repeat, is wrong on a couple of counts. They do bear responsibility for the negative consequences that flow from their mistakes. But it is absurd to hold them morally and politically responsible for the Dergue's war against Eritrea—a war they do not endorse and have stayed out of—because they aid the Ethiopian government against imperialist-instigated assaults, or because they haven't used their army to overthrow the Dergue.

What is the point of making accusations—frameups—like that? If we seriously want to encourage the Cubans to *change* their policy, then we need a clear and cogent explanation of what is wrong with it—not false polemics, exaggerations, or Cubaphobic slander. That will only guarantee we have no impact.

Castroism: revolutionary or centrist?
One important question that has been raised is whether it is correct to call the Castro leadership revolutionary, or whether a more accurate term would be "centrist."

Some comrades might think that this belongs in the terminological hairsplitting department. After all, there is broad agreement on many important points between comrades who hold each position.

First, both those who think the Cuban leadership is centrist and those who are convinced it is revolutionary agree that there is no crystallized, privileged, bureaucratic caste in power in Cuba. Both reject any approach that equates Castroism with Stalinism. Second, both sides reject calling for political revolution in Cuba. Third, we agree that bureaucratism is a problem of substantial proportions in Cuba today, and that the revolution must find effective ways to combat it.

Even the gap in terminology narrows because comrades who have proposed using the term centrist recognize the term must be qualified in some way, such as "left centrist" or something similar.

But there is a very important question of political orientation behind this terminological discussion. It is not a hairsplitting controversy. Let's begin our discussion of this debate by recognizing that this question has two parts. First, were the Fidelistas centrists when they overthrew Batista, when they led the July 26 Movement to power? Second, is the Castroist current today, as the dominant and decisive force in the leadership of the Cuban workers state, centrist?

We have to separate these two periods in the evolution of the Castro leadership. Centrism in power in a workers state is quite a different phenomenon from a small centrist grouping with revolutionary pretenses. We have dealt with both of these questions extensively in the article by David Frankel and Larry Seigle in the August 6, 1979, issue of *Intercontinental Press/Inprecor*. (See pages 98–129 of this volume.) Let's summarize the key aspects of this question here.

We will begin with the first question. As we have already seen, we do not think the term revolutionary applies only to forces that are Leninists. Other revolutionary currents arise, and we have always been able to recognize this and call them by their right name.

But if there ever was a revolutionary current anywhere, tested in battle against imperialism, against their own bourgeoisie, against the compromisers and vacillators—it is the Castroist leadership of the July 26 Movement.

No one in the SWP made a serious challenge to this designation at the time, and I don't believe a serious challenge is possible. This was the view of the leadership of our party and of the majority of the International at the time the Fidelistas came to power and led the masses to establish the first workers state in our hemisphere. It was expressed in resolution after resolution, in article after article: the Castroists were a revolutionary current.

If anyone now proposes to go back and junk that, they will have to present a very powerful case because what is involved is junking the assessment and political orientation we have had for twenty years. Comrades who now want to label the Castroists as "centrists" can't slip over this point. No case has yet been made for any change here.

Bureaucratic centrism
Now what about the second question? Is Castroism in power today centrist? The only previous experience of centrism in power in a workers state is the Soviet Union between 1923 and 1933. In discussing the centrism of the Stalin faction, Trotsky explained that it was a particular form of centrism, which he called "bureaucratic centrism." Trotsky explained that this was a new form of centrism, which the workers movement hadn't seen before.

Previously, centrist groups always lacked an

independent social foundation. This explained why they wavered, they flip-flopped, they vacillated between two forces: between the reformist wing of the workers movement, which does have a solid social foundation in the labor bureaucracy which appeals to and draws support from the labor aristocracy and misleads millions of workers; and revolutionary Marxism, which also has a solid independent social foundation because it represents the material and historic interests of the proletariat.

Centrism as we saw it before 1923, Trotsky said, had no independent social foundation of its own. But bureaucratic centrism was different, because it had social roots in the emerging privileged bureaucracy in the Soviet Union. This bureaucracy had its own interests, which were distinct from and counterposed to the interests of the working class in the Soviet Union and internationally. This bureaucratic layer, not yet a hardened caste, was the social foundation on which bureaucratic centrism rested.

To say that the Castro leadership is bureaucratic centrist, therefore, we would have to show that this leadership bases itself on a developing and hardening privileged bureaucratic layer, rather than on the Cuban toilers. And we would have to show that this layer, while not yet crystallized into a counterrevolutionary caste, follows and defends policies in Cuba and internationally that promote and protect its own material interests, which are increasingly counterposed to the interests of the workers and peasants. This would dictate an increasingly repressive regime as well, in order to protect the bureaucracy's privileges.

In what ways, then, is the situation in Cuba today similar to, and in what ways is it different from, the Soviet Union from 1923 to 1933?

There are some significant parallels. In Cuba today there are severe scarcities. There are intense economic pressures stemming from the legacy of imperialist exploitation and from the ongoing imperialist blockade and aggression. These shortages and pressures are the medium for the growth of bureaucratism based on material privilege. There is in Cuba today, among the administrators, technicians, and professionals, a bureaucratic layer that is inclined toward political conservatism. Their first concern is protecting their own standard of living, their own material privileges. And in Cuba today, as in the Soviet Union in the stormy decade following 1923, there are differences between the revolutionary wing of the leadership, the left wing, and the conservative, right wing.

These are some of the parallels. But there are also important differences, qualitative differences. In Cuba, the revolutionary wing, the wing that made the revolution, the Castroist wing, remains in the saddle. It remains the dominant force in the leadership. It sets the line on the crucial questions. It is responsible for the major policy decisions.

In the Soviet Union after 1923, the center—that is, the Stalin grouping—defeated the revolutionary wing. It absorbed the bulk of the right wing, and it consolidated the bureaucracy's preeminence and power. The revolutionary left was defeated, driven from power, persecuted, hounded, exiled, jailed— and murdered.

In Cuba that's not true. There is a right wing in the Cuban leadership that reflects the interests and pressures of the more privileged layers. And its influence is felt throughout the country. But the Castroists, the revolutionary wing, the left wing, remain the dominant and decisive component. They remain the authoritative leaders with the Cuban masses solidly behind them. This gives them the power to drive through the fundamental policy decisions and hold the right wing in check.

The Communist Party of Cuba has both a right wing and a left wing, with some elements in the center. This is why Comrade Keil was dead wrong when he wrote in an article for the discussion bulletin that the key question before us is whether to label the Cuban *Communist Party* and its policies revolutionary. [SWP Discussion Bulletin, 1979, Vol. 36., No. 2.] The Cuban Communist Party is not identical to the Castroist current. The Castroists are a wing in that party, albeit the preeminent one.

I am not saying anything new; we have analyzed all of this before. The conflict between the Castroists and the right-wingers began well before 1959. The Fidelistas had the old Stalinist party, the Partido Socialista Popular, accurately pegged as a gang of collaborators and conciliators, an obstacle to the revolutionary struggle that had to be outflanked. Castro forced this conflict into the open in 1962, when he pulled the rug out from under Aníbal Escalante and his Stalinist cronies, who were building and trying to consolidate their faction in the new, united party, which fused the PSP into a single organization with the July 26 Movement.

Fidel, at that time, opened a campaign against bureaucratism and against privilege. And in that battle we were, and remain, totally on the side of the Castroist current against the Stalinists. We identify ourselves with, and we back, the revolutionary wing in Cuba against the Stalinists and against all the fainthearted, conciliationist, conservative forces that exist.

**Differences between Cuba
and the Soviet Union**

In the Soviet Union, in the decade of bureaucratic centrism, the ruling Stalin faction zigzagged back and forth, from extreme right to ultraleft. *But each step in the pattern was a step toward consolidating their privileged positions, a step toward weakening and isolating the revolutionary left, a step toward tightening their bureaucratic grip, terrorizing the party ranks, and strengthening the dictatorial rule of the Stalin faction.*

In the Soviet Union in this period, women, youth, and the oppressed nationalities were especially hard hit by the Thermidorean reaction that was setting in. In Cuba today, women, youth, and Afro-Cubans are reaping the greatest benefits and continue to register social advances.

In the Soviet Union, the peasants became victims of the monstrous policy of forced collectivization. In Cuba today, the alliance between the workers and peasantry is solid.

In the Soviet Union after 1923, the cultural freedom and creativity inaugurated by the October revolution was increasingly replaced by enforced conformity and party and state terror against artists. In Cuba today there is a broad expansion of cultural freedom. Havana today is increasingly being recognized as the cultural and literary capital of all of Latin America. Creative life is flourishing in the arts, encouraged by the Castroist leadership.

In the Soviet Union by the late 1920s, massive arrests of oppositionists had begun. The gulag was being constructed. In Cuba today the opposite is the case. The government has released thousands of political prisoners. And these were counterrevolutionaries—not revolutionaries. It was a wonderful kick in smiling Jimmy's "human rights" teeth. And what a powerful statement about the reality of social relations in Cuba today! It speaks volumes about the power and confidence of the Cuban revolution on its twentieth anniversary.

In the Soviet Union, the internationalism of the Bolsheviks under Lenin and Trotsky's leadership was jettisoned in favor of the line of building "socialism in one country." This meant protecting the privileges of the bureaucracy in one country and turning away from the perspective of world revolution. The prospect, hope, and goal of extending the revolution was replaced by a policy of making deals with imperialism in an attempt to protect the international status quo.

In Cuba the very opposite is the case today. Doesn't Havana's response to the revolution in Nicaragua, coming on the heels of its response to the openings in Africa, Grenada, South Yemen, and Indochina offer proof positive that the course of the Castroist leadership is the opposite of the course of the Stalin faction in the Soviet Union in the decade following 1923?

Every policy is confirmation of the revolutionary character, capacity, and direction of the Castroist current. It is the diametric opposite of the tightening grip of a hardening conservative bureaucratic caste such as Stalin defended and promoted.

**What is involved in the dispute
over terminology**

What is really involved in this dispute from the standpoint of our policy toward Cuba? In retaining the designation revolutionary we are reaffirming our orientation of twenty years standing. The Fidelista current is the *leadership* of the Cuban revolution. We seek to deepen our ties with this leadership, to strengthen it against all its enemies and opponents, including the Stalinists. In the struggle against privilege and bureaucratism inside Cuba, in the debate with the Communist parties of Latin America over the so-called peaceful road versus armed struggle, in the debate over the cultural policies—freedom for artists versus the Stalinist school of "socialist realism"—in all these struggles and others we are with the Castro current. We side with it. We operate within this framework.

If, on the other hand, we were now to reject the term revolutionary and label the Castro leadership "bureaucratic centrist," the axis of our participation in the Cuban revolution would shift qualitatively. We would be saying, in essence, that the approach followed by the Left Opposition in the decade after 1923 is the closest guide we have as to how we should orient toward the Castro leadership today.

While we might support the Castroists against the Stalinists on one or another question, we would start to emphasize the alleged betrayals of the revolution by the Castroists, by this ruling centrist faction. Even if we agreed on a specific policy or aspect of a policy, or with a specific action, we would insistently warn that the general line, the general course of development of the Castroist current is a deadly threat to the Cuban revolution and to the working-class movement internationally. We would begin to work toward advancing an alternative leadership, to replace those who supposedly can no longer lead the revolution forward.

This line, certified by this proposed change in terminology, would set us on a sectarian course that would prevent us from taking advantage of the new openings before us. We would block ourselves off from the third big chance we have to link up with revolutionary forces in Cuba to build a mass revolutionary international, and to maximize the chances of having a positive influence on the course of the revolution in Cuba and Central America. We reject this course as politically false—and fatal.

Rearming ourselves

In the course of this discussion we have reeducated and rearmed the party on Cuba. In doing so we have become conscious of the fact that we had slipped politically. We had lowered our guard a little, and stopped seeing ourselves as the most intransigent and energetic enemies of the Cubaphobes of all varieties.

For a number of years, comrades joining our movement got the impression that today there just wasn't much to get excited about in the Cuban revolution. We stopped having celebrations on July 26 and on New Year's. We stopped going to Cuba. We didn't write much about Cuba. We were negligent about gathering facts and analyzing them in our press. We didn't even say as much as we should have about the crimes being committed against Cuba by Yankee imperialism, with its blockade and other offensive weapons.

Most importantly, we stopped thinking about and acting to try to affect the course of the Cuban revolution and its extension. That is where we had slipped the most—on the party-building orientation. We did this without thinking about it, without discussing it.

It didn't take too much to get this all straightened out, once Cuba's role in Africa forced us to start reviewing the matter. That is a sign of how healthy this party is. And as we got straightened out we helped some of our comrades with the state capitalist line get straightened out.

Now we are going to participate in the discussion in the Fourth International, and we are going to try to convince the international as a whole that the position we are reaffirming here is the only possible course for a world party of Leninist politicians.

As we leave this convention, rearmed and prepared, we are setting ourselves six tasks.

One, we are going to join hands with the Cubans and with everyone else in Latin America, in this country, and throughout the world, to oppose in action any U.S. efforts to defeat the revolution in Nicaragua. We will combat any threats, any economic blackmail, any blockade, any move toward military intervention, any violence against supporters of the Nicaraguan revolution in this country. We are going to campaign in defense of the revolution in Nicaragua just as we have campaigned in defense of the Cuban revolution. We will work with others to mobilize support for the right of the Nicaraguans to determine their own future, without taking orders any longer from the United States. We are going to join with Fidel and others in demanding the U.S. government give the Nicaraguan people all the aid they need—without any conditions whatsoever—to rebuild their country.

We are going to tell the truth about Nicaragua. We have already sent reporters down there. Now we have to decide how fast we can get out a special issue of the *Militant* and of *Perspectiva Mundial*, to reprint Fidel's July 26 speech, to carry the dispatches from Fred Murphy, Pedro Camejo, Sergio Rodriguez, and the other comrades who have been down there. We can't wait till our normal summer break is over to do that, because we have to leave this convention and hit the mines, mills, and plants right away with the truth about this revolution. We have to sound the alarm about the danger of U.S. intervention and launch the solidarity campaign as fast as we can.

Two, we are going to step up our activity in support of the dialogue with the Cuban community in this country. Pulley and Zimmermann are going to campaign in a big way for an end to the blockade against Cuba, and against terrorist violence aimed at supporters of normalization of relations between the United States and Cuba.

Three, we are going to follow the lead of Fidel and pay more attention to what is going on inside the U.S. Cuban community. The Cuban community is not a monolithic bloc of gusanos. We're going to see it for what it is. In its large majority it is a component of the working class, a layer of the proletariat in this country, facing national oppression, along with the rest of the Latino population. In the Cuban community there are a growing number of supporters of the Cuban revolution. This means we will put a national priority on our work in Miami, where there is the largest concentration of Cubans in this country, where "Little Havana" is located. We're going to beef up that branch and orient a good part of its work towards building a revolutionary Cuban component of the SWP and the YSA. If we do that right, our Miami comrades will give a new and revolutionary meaning to the term Little Havana.

We're also going to pay increased attention to the Cuban communities in other areas, such as the New York City-Northern New Jersey area, where some 200,000 Cubans live.

Four, we are going to step up our work with the Antonio Maceo Brigade, to build its activities, to help it carry out its work, and to involve young revolutionary-minded Cubans in this country. And we are going to defend it and its members from the CIA-sponsored right-wing terrorists and other reactionary forces.

Fifth, we are going to try to get as many of our members, sympathizers, and co-workers as possible to take trips to Cuba. Take your vacation there. Take some *PMs*, *Militants*, election campaign materials, and other literature. Get names and addresses of people there who want to receive our publications in the mail. Ask them to send you theirs. We can do nothing better to further our party-building perspectives than to have a couple hundred socialist workers from this country take trips to Cuba to talk politics with a cross section of the few million socialist workers and peasants there.

We can and should take our co-workers with us, too. The Cuban revolution has helped us win quite a number of people to our movement over the past twenty years. Let's take advantage of that power. If you want a chance to do some really solid contact work, take your contact to Cuba for a week or two! You'll have a lot going for you there.

Sixth, and finally, a major theme of the Pulley and Zimmermann campaign will be to explain that the Cuban revolution shows what can be accomplished when working people kick out the capitalists and run the country for themselves. Through the discussion we have had on the Cuban revolution, we have increased our own consciousness about the Cuban revolution. Now we are in a stronger position to explain the meaning and importance of that revolution to American working people.

SUMMARY

The discussion on centrism has raised a number of historical points as well as a number of political points. We didn't get through them all today.

We will return to them in the international discussion that will be opened sometime after the World Congress.

If we were to change our designation of the Castroist leadership this would signify a change in political policy toward that leadership. It would, as several comrades pointed out in the discussion, mean a change in tone, in stance, in emphasis, and in balance. A response to this point was offered today, arguing that changing the terminology would not necessarily involve a change in our political approach to the Castroist leadership. We have explained why we think this is not so.

But if we were to grant this point, then we would have to ask the comrades who propose the terminological change, why do they insist so strongly on the point? Why is the issue being raised, if it is not connected to our political orientation? What would be the advantage to the party in abandoning the approach—including the terminology—we have had from the beginning toward the Castroists? Were we wrong twenty years ago? Or has a point of qualitative change been reached in Cuba? If so, when?

The comrades who advance the view that the Castroist leadership is centrist argue that the historic parallel that is most helpful to us in thinking out how to approach the Cuban leadership is the policy of the Left Opposition toward the Stalin faction in the Soviet Union between 1923 and 1933. We reject the parallel. Not only does it totally break down, but if we were to adopt it as a guide to action it would be a total disaster. It would be a disaster for the SWP and for the Fourth International.

From 1923 on, the authentic leaders of the Bolshevik revolution—beginning with Lenin himself and, after Lenin's last stroke, headed by Trotsky—fought to defeat the Stalin faction politically, and drive it out of control of the Soviet workers state and of the Communist International. The struggle between the Left Opposition and the Stalin faction wasn't a dispute over one or another policy or programmatic difference. It was a struggle between the representatives of the interests of the Soviet toilers, the Left Opposition, and the representatives of the privileged bureaucratic layer, the Stalin faction.

The role of the Castroist leadership is the opposite of the role of the Stalin faction. We don't fight to drive the Castroists from the leadership; we recognize them as the *leaders* of the Cuban revolution and the enemies of the bureaucratic layers. We don't call for a reversal of the line of march followed by the Castro team; we believe that the overall course of this leadership has been to deepen the revolution and to extend it. We don't believe the Castroists represent, or base themselves on, a privileged layer; the Castroists rely on the mobilized power of the Cuban workers and peasants.

Political disorientation

I want to make two points on what Comrade Wohlforth had to say—or didn't have to say. After listening to his report on Cuba at the National Committee plenum in December, several comrades pointed out a peculiar thing. Despite the fact that he devoted his report to the problems in Cuba, he didn't mention imperialism. He didn't once use the word "blockade." This omission revealed a rather glaring political disorientation, an utterly irresponsible approach to the problems facing the Cuban revolution.

You can't abstract Cuba from the world context in which it exists. You can't simply overlook the pressures bearing down from imperialism, as well as the pressures from Moscow. One important reason the imperialists maintain that blockade is to keep the Cubans dependent on Moscow, and therefore more vulnerable to pressure from the counterrevolutionary gang in the Kremlin.

This wrong approach was called to Comrade Wohlforth's attention by the National Committee. But he didn't seem to pay any attention. Because today he managed once again to omit from his report any mention of imperialist pressures and threats against Cuba. How can a revolutionist—right here in the United States, too!—even begin to approach the problems and perspectives of the Cuban revolution without taking as the starting point the continuing Yankee aggression against Cuba? How can you explain that? It is as though Comrade Wohlforth were on another planet. He is not here, within our framework, that's for sure.

There is another difference—on Nicaragua. And our difference with Comrade Wohlforth on Nicaragua sheds further light on what really separates us on Cuba. There are some differences that run so deep, that involve gut feelings we have as revolutionary internationalists, that if someone doesn't share our fundamental response, its hard to discuss it by taking up this or that particular question, this or that disputed point. The revolution in Nicaragua is one of those kinds of questions.

We get pretty excited when a revolution takes place. We get especially excited when a revolution throws out a bloody, U.S.-imposed regime of forty-five years standing. Events like that don't happen every day. So we felt pretty good about the victory over Somoza. We felt *part* of it. It was *our* victory. Everyone was rushing home to watch Walter Cronkite every night to see if Somoza was still there. The comrades in our print shop started a pool on when the old bastard would finally be sent packing. And when he went, we all celebrated. Didn't we all feel some special enthusiasm about selling the issue of the *Militant* with the banner headline on Somoza's downfall? This is what we *live* for, isn't it—revolution?

But Comrade Wohlforth doesn't share this reaction. He says, oh well, there are a lot of problems in Nicaragua. There are many dangers. The FSLN is making many mistakes. It doesn't look good. It looks bad. We have got to start criticizing, says Wohlforth. Be more critical. Don't get starry-eyed. Don't start adapting to the FSLN or to Castro, that counterrevolutionary Stalinist tyrant.

Well, comrades, what can you say to that? Wohlforth doesn't *feel* the revolution. He just doesn't feel it.

There are problems in Nicaragua. Of course. We don't know what will happen, whether the caliber of the leadership and the mobilization of the masses will be up to the tremendous challenge facing the revolution. We don't know how successful we can be in mobilizing international aid and support in time. We know there are dangers. But we think the revolution has gotten off to a pretty good start.

From listening to Comrade Wohlforth today, he is already pretty certain that only the worst can happen. At least he is consistent. In his pessimistic view the best that can happen in Nicaragua is . . . another Cuba! And that would be just another Stalinist dictatorship in Latin America, wouldn't it?

Cuba's revolutionary foreign policy

How do we size up Cuba's foreign policy? Our starting point should be inside Cuba itself. What does that policy mean from the point of view of Cuban workers and peasants? Here there is one compelling, overriding fact: Cuban workers and peasants are ready to give their lives for the revolution in Nicaragua. They are ready to give their lives for the revolution in Africa. They are ready to die in the fight against colonialism, against racism, against apartheid, against imperialism in Africa. That is revolutionary internationalism. And it is the consciousness, encouraged, taught, and advanced by the revolutionary leadership in Cuba.

This revolutionary foreign policy is an extension of the government's domestic policy. Not since the days of the Soviet Union under the leadership of Lenin and Trotsky has there been a government in power that pursued policies demanding and fostering that kind of proletarian internationalist consciousness.

What about some of the objections that have been raised to characterizing Cuba's international policy as revolutionary?

First, the charge is made that Cuba supports all kinds of neocolonial regimes. No. The regimes Cuba tries to aid are ones in more or less open conflict with the imperialists. When that happens, the Cubans start paying attention, looking for ways to reinforce the anti-imperialist actions and stands of these regimes. In carrying this out, they make mistakes, as we have seen. But it is *not* a mistake for the Cuban state to extend diplomatic aid and support, and material aid and support, to countries in the semicolonial world that are being squeezed by imperialism.

The class struggle in the colonial and semicolonial world cannot be reduced simply to the class conflict between the toilers and the weak semicolonial bourgeoisie. There is also the fight against imperialist domination, because it is only by getting imperialism off their backs that the masses can begin to solve the problems they face.

In these struggles the Cubans have consistently come down on the correct side. The same side we are on. This is what happened when the Vietnamese dumped Pol Pot; when China invaded Vietnam; when South Africa invaded Angola; when Somalia invaded Ethiopia. Each time the Cubans were on the correct side.

Second, the charge is leveled that Havana's foreign policy must be counterrevolutionary like Moscow's because Cuban international policy converges with that of the Soviet bureaucracy. Both Cuba and the Soviet Union lined up on the Ethiopian side against the Somalian invasion; both gave aid to Angola against the South African invasion; etc.

But what does this prove? Didn't we also "converge" with Moscow on the Ethiopian-Somalian war? Didn't we have a "convergence" in Vietnam? Don't we converge with the Kremlin bureaucracy on the question of defense of the Soviet Union itself against imperialism—although we propose different methods of carrying out that defense? So this "convergence" argument doesn't tell us anything about the nature of Cuban foreign policy.

Third, the critics of the Fidelistas charge that the Cubans never openly and explicitly criticize Moscow. They argue that this proves the Cubans have essentially the same line as the Kremlin bureaucracy.

How should we approach this question? We start by recognizing the fact that the Moscow Stalinists squeeze political consequences from the Cubans, using the tremendous leverage that Cuba's economic and military dependence gives them. That's where our fire is aimed: at the Kremlin.

Should the Cubans have refused as a matter of principle to make any concessions to the Kremlin? Had they taken that stand, they wouldn't be around today. They would have gone under, their revolution would have been crushed by imperialism.

Some sectarians find it hard to understand that in the real world of the class struggle you make concessions when the relationship of class forces requires it. You maneuver. You try not to get crushed. That doesn't mean you act in an unprincipled way. Nor does it mean we agree with every concession the Cubans have made. But we, like the Cubans, start with the existing world of class combat.

Example from U.S. labor movement

There is an analogy from the American labor movement that helps put this in perspective. It is an example of a revolutionary leadership, with a limited geographical and numerical base, that was forced to maneuver and obtain the tolerance of a rotten, class-collaborationist bureaucracy in order to be able to survive and try to extend its influence. For a long time this revolutionary leadership refrained from publicly and directly criticizing the bureaucracy. They had to operate within the limits they could force the bureaucracy to accept.

The example, of course, is the Minneapolis Teamsters, led by Farrell Dobbs, Ray Dunne, Carl Skoglund, and other comrades. They could not have survived as long as they did without the tolerance of Tobin, the head of the International Brotherhood of Teamsters. Farrell didn't go around denouncing Tobin as a right-wing, class collaborationist bureaucrat. The Minneapolis Teamsters tried to box Tobin in. They had to get his formal approval for their efforts to extend their operations—such as organizing the over-the-road drivers in the North Central states. And then they used that approval to advance their own program and policies—not Tobin's. And in doing so they used their methods, not Tobin's. And they divided Tobin's forces for a while in this effort.

Isn't that similar to what the Cubans are doing? They box in Brezhnev, then they move, they carry their line as far as they can. The Teamster analogy is not perfect. I am sure comrades can point to its many limitations. Most important of these is that the Trotskyists in the leadership of the Teamsters union had a Leninist party.

But the advantage of the analogy is that it helps us to think about the question of the Cuban revolution from the standpoint of the real world of the class struggle. The world is imperfect. Workers understand this because they live in this imperfect world, and they know that if you can make it better, that's worth fighting for, even given the limits imposed by the concrete relationship of forces. Petty-bourgeois sectarians live in a different world, one created by sitting at a typewriter writing the script for the perfect revolution—and always measuring the gap between the world as it exists and their ideal conception of it.

If we understand this, we have no trouble at all seeing the qualitative differences between Cuba's foreign policy and that of the Kremlin. Let me cite just a few examples.

One, detente. Detente is the all-consuming objective of Soviet foreign policy. All policy decisions take place within the framework of securing detente. The Cubans, however, as we have seen, subordinate everything to their goal of extending the revolution. They make no secret deals with Washington at the expense of the world revolution. Just the opposite. Do you think the Cubans—and the Soviets—aren't aware of the difference?

Two, political prisoners and Carter's "human rights" hypocrisy. The Stalinists hand the imperialists a powerful weapon with which to discredit socialism in the eyes of the world working class. Because they need a police state to protect their rule and secure their privileges, the Moscow bureaucrats often intensify their repressive measures as the imperialists press their anti-Soviet propaganda offensive. In contrast, Havana told Carter: We will release all the political prisoners—and you can have 'em! Do you think the Cubans weren't consciously following a different policy from Moscow? Do you think they are not aware of the difference between Cuba and all the other workers states on this?

Three, Cuba's internationalist aid. The Cubans take great pride in proclaiming that their aid to semicolonial countries is free and clear. No repayments required. No strings attached. No pressure. They say that anything else would be a grotesque violation of proletarian internationalism. This is a conscious and glaring contrast to the policy followed by the Soviet bureaucracy—a policy the Cubans, and many others, are only too familiar with from bitter experience. In this area, as in many others, the Cubans don't criticize Moscow's policies directly. They just do things the way they think they ought to be done, proclaiming and explaining their policy to the whole world, and letting people draw their own conclusions.

Four. Think for a minute about the way the Cubans have repeatedly and publicly offered to send troops to Vietnam. They made this offer during the U.S. war. They renewed it during the Chinese invasion. And they repeated it again just a few weeks ago. Now, who are those public statements aimed at? If it were just a question of an offer to the Vietnamese, why make them in public? Those statements are aimed squarely at Moscow—and at public opinion in the international workers movement—to challenge, to pressure, Moscow to do what it has always refused to do—send Vietnam the aid it needs in massive amounts to defeat the imperialist-inspired assault and economic squeeze.

Five, Nicaragua. When Fidel appeals publicly for a competition with "our sister socialist nations" to see who will send the most aid to Nicaragua, they are challenging Moscow. They know that if the revolution continues to advance in Nicaragua, the imperialists are going to start putting pressure on Moscow to put the screws to the Nicaraguans. Don't you think the Cubans are planning ahead, thinking how can we force Brezhnev not to stab the Nicaraguans—and us—in the back, but to help them? So the Cubans use the political power of their example, their aid—and even though it is modest by the standards of what the Soviets could and should provide, it carries great political weight.

The Cubans are acutely conscious of these factors. They are revolutionary politicians. They are like us. They are oriented toward affecting events outside Cuba; intervening in the real class struggle to change the course of history. That's what we have in common with them. That is the basis on which we seek to deepen our collaboration with them.

Finally, we have two international tasks. The first is our participation in the Fourth International's discussion on Cuba, which will be opened sometime after the World Congress.

The second international task is more immediate. Here at this convention we are launching a campaign to aid and defend the Nicaraguan revolution. We are going to return to our branches and start it right away. But what is objectively needed is an international campaign, a worldwide campaign into which the entire Fourth International throws itself. This is a campaign to stay the hands of imperialism in Nicaragua, a campaign to strengthen the Nicaraguan revolution, a campaign for aid to Nicaragua. It is an opportunity for a united action campaign by our entire world movement, an opportunity that can build the Fourth International. And such a campaign, of course, will be totally intertwined with our efforts to defend the Cuban revolution.

An international mobilization is called for. And we are confident that the entire Fourth International will respond to this challenge as we have at this convention.

IN DEFENSE OF THE CUBAN REVOLUTION
National Committee Majority Report
By Larry Seigle

The following document incorporates the essential political points from two reports. The first was given to an expanded meeting of the Political Committee of the Socialist Workers Party on August 14, 1978. The second was given to a National Committee plenum on December 18, 1978. The general line contained in both reports was adopted by the National Committee at the December meeting. The vote was 29 regular members for, 2 against; 29 alternate members for, 1 against. There were no abstentions.

Today, twenty years after the fall of the Batista dictatorship, the Cuban Revolution continues to inspire the oppressed and exploited throughout the world, including here in the United States.

Struggling to overcome the legacy of centuries of colonial bondage and two decades of imperialist assault and blockade, revolutionary Cuba stands as a living example of what happens when the workers become the ruling class and establish a government that acts in their interests, serving human needs instead of private profits. The standard of living and quality of life of the workers and peasants are markedly advanced over pre-revolutionary Cuba. Cuba today puts top priority on the needs of children, of youth, of humanity's future. It devotes the greatest part of its total national product to education and to health care, which are free to all. It is a country where a job is a basic human right; where unemployment—the scourge of capitalism everywhere—has been eliminated.

It is a country where the *latifundistas* have been sent packing, and the peasants have been given land; where the government is no longer the enemy of the poor peasants, but defends their interests; where the rural proletariat is guaranteed work year-round, as well as housing, schools, hospital care, other social services, and involvement in the cultural life of the country.

It is a country where rents have been slashed, where the ill or elderly are not cast onto the trash heap once they can no longer produce surplus value for some capitalist.

It is a country that has outlawed racial discrimination and taken gigantic, determined strides to eradicate all expressions of racism against Blacks, and to instill knowledge about and pride in the Afro-Cuban heritage.

It is a country that has built high-quality child care centers for tens of thousands of children, and is committed to expanding such facilities as rapidly as economically possible; a country where, by the mid-1970s, 26 percent of women were in the work force as compared to 12 percent, most of whom were maids, before the revolution; where abortion is legal and free; where doors to all education are open to women; where the government promotes the equality of women.

It is a country that has ended the human misery created by U.S. imperialism. The courage, pride, and confidence of an oppressed nation that has stood off the most brutal and powerful ruling class in history is today being expressed through the most deep-going revolutionary internationalist spirit of any people since the early years of the Russian Revolution. Cuba's unbending opposition to Yankee imperialism is expressed in the quote from Fidel Castro on the billboards one often sees on the highways of Cuba: Ser Internacionalista Es Saldar Nuestra Propria Deuda Con La Humanidad—To Be an Internationalist Is to Pay Our Own Debt to Humanity.

The Cuban leadership's stance and policy stands in stark contrast to the stance and policy of the

Stalinist bureaucrats in Moscow and Peking, who daily try to outdo each other in their efforts to betray revolutionary movements in order to curry favor in Washington.

While Peking was responding enthusiastically to Kissinger's ping-pong diplomacy and Moscow was stepping up the drive toward its own détente with Washington; while both were putting the squeeze on aid to Vietnam and clinking glasses with Nixon as the United States carried out its terror bombing of Hanoi and Haiphong—the Cuban leadership was declaring that Vietnam should be considered an inviolable part of socialist territory and pledging their blood in its defense. The Cuban leadership understood that Vietnam's fate was Cuba's fate. And they acted accordingly.

The clearest test and confirmation of the continued revolutionary character of the Cuban leadership is their policy in Africa today. Cuban armed forces have beaten back the South African imperialists in Angola. They have defeated in combat the imperialist-inspired attempt by the Somalian regime to roll back the Ethiopian revolution. They are throwing their resources behind the Black freedom fighters in the rising tide of revolutionary struggle in southern Africa.

Unlike Moscow and Peking, Havana hailed the revolutionary upsurge of the Iranian masses from the very start.

Cuba's refusal to put its revolution up for sale in the détente market, or trade its support to the world revolution "for a mess of pottage," as Raul Roa recently put it in a speech at the United Nations, has led to sharpened confrontations with Washington. The Carter administration has escalated its international propaganda campaign against Cuba. It has taken steps to shore up the economic blockade. And it continues to try to convince the American working class that it will be necessary at some point to take military action against Cuba.

A decisive test for the Fourth International

Given the role of Cuba in the world class struggle, our attitude toward the Castro leadership and its policies becomes a decisive question. It is a test for the revolutionary party in the United States and for the Fourth International.

In our world movement there are today two fundamentally counterposed political lines on Cuba, which lead to two incompatible courses of action.

One line is held by comrades who would alter the position the Trotskyist movement has maintained until now. They believe the Fourth International should today call for and, to the extent we are able, organize the workers and peasants of Cuba to overthrow the Castro leadership.

These comrades hold that the Castro leadership no longer has—if it ever did have—the political capacity to lead the Cuban revolution forward. This approach would orient us toward the Castro leadership in the same way that we approach the Stalinist castes in every other workers state: as class enemies, as representatives of a crystallized, petty-bourgeois, privileged, bureaucratic layer. These bureaucratic castes are opposed to advancing the international struggle against imperialism and capitalism because any advance of the world revolution will threaten their privileges. Every revolutionary development therefore only deepens their counterrevolutionary commitment to class-collaborationism.

Comrades who believe this to be a correct evaluation of the social character of the Cuban leadership would have us adopt the goal of exposing, discrediting, and trying to remove the Castro leadership from power.

Among those who believe the Castro leadership must be overthrown if the Cuban revolution is to advance are comrades who openly hold different positions on the origins, development, and nature of the Cuban revolution. Some believe that Cuba is a workers state deformed by Stalinism from the beginning. Others believe that the Cuban revolution has undergone a process of degeneration sometime in the last ten years, and a political revolution is now necessary. Others argue that Cuba is not a workers state at all, but a "state-capitalist" state.

Politically, each of these analyses leads to a common conclusion: the need for the workers and peasants of Cuba to overthrow the Castro regime.

The second, opposite, political line is the one held by the Socialist Workers Party and the Fourth International today. Despite our differences with the Castro leadership we view them as fellow revolutionaries who have demonstrated their capacities to lead the Cuban revolution. From the beginning we have supported the Castro wing of the Cuban leadership against the Stalinists. We try to win them to revolutionary Marxism, to our program and to the banner of the Fourth International rather than propose replacing them. We do not believe they respond to each new advance of the world working class, as the Stalinists do, by trying to join hands with imperialism in a common counterrevolutionary cause. We believe that further advances in the world revolution can have the effect of impelling the Castro leadership toward Leninist positions, coming more deeply into conflict with the Stalinist wing of the Cuban Communist Party in the process. We want to do everything in our power to facilitate that. In maintaining this stance, we will maximize the number of Cuban revolutionists we can win to Leninism, to the program of the Fourth International.

For the Socialist Workers Party and the Fourth International to call for a political revolution to overthrow Castro would be a colossal error. It would foreclose the chances of winning revolutionary forces to our ranks inside Cuba. It would place serious obstacles in the path of winning revolutionary-minded forces in the United States, in Latin America, in Africa, and throughout the world. It would profoundly disorient us politically concerning major developments on the world scene. It would lead us into errors on other questions as well, beginning to erode our revolutionary fiber and making us increasingly vulnerable to social-patriotic and other alien class pressures.

Imperialist pressure against revolutionary Cuba

There is a concerted imperialist propaganda barrage directed against the Cuban revolution. The pressure, which takes many and sometimes subtle forms, bears down on all those who are allies of the Cuban revolution. This pressure has increased since 1975, as the Cuban government, refusing to take the class-collaborationist road of détente, has stepped up its support for revolutionary struggles, especially in Africa.

The source of this anti-Cuba campaign is Wall Street and its government in Washington. Their goal is twofold. First, to convince supporters of the Cuban revolution that there is nothing much left worth defending in Cuba, and to discredit the Cuban revolution in the eyes of working people. Second, to convince American workers that Cuba is a dangerous aggressor against whom it will ultimately be necessary to use military force, and maybe not so far in the distant future.

This pressure dictates the hostile coverage Cuba gets in the capitalist press. It is reflected through the writings of the so-called Cuba experts at American universities, many of whom consider themselves some kind of radicals, who are turning out volume after scholarly volume explaining that the Cuban revolution has become "Stalinized."

This pressure affects the stance of petty-bourgeois radicals from the Social Democrats, to the Peking Stalinists, to currents that consider themselves Trotskyist, like the Spartacists.

Were we now to succumb to this pressure, after our twenty-year record of unbending defense of the Cuban revolution, it would be a disaster for the Socialist Workers Party and the Fourth International.

HOW THE SWP APPROACHED THE CUBAN REVOLUTION

We should begin by reiterating the method we have used in approaching the Cuban revolution from the beginning.

First, we started with the reality of the Cuban revolution. With the facts. We did not start with a model of proletarian revolution—either as set forth in Marxist theory or the experience of the Bolshevik-led revolution in Russia—and then match this with what was happening in Cuba in order to decide whether or not a socialist revolution was occurring. It *was* occurring in Cuba. And we recognized it and identified with it.

The Russian revolution provided some rich historical lessons from which we have learned how proletarian revolutions occur in our epoch. Included among the central features of the Russian revolution was the existence of workers, peasants, and soldiers councils, which the Russians called soviets. Most important, the Russian revolution provided a model as to how proletarian revolutions are led to victory. Key to this is the role of a revolutionary workers party, tested in struggle, with influence among the masses, leading the insurrectionary proletariat to power in alliance with the peasantry.

This is not the way things happened in Cuba.

But we did not say, "Well, the Cuban revolution

doesn't measure up to our norms; it didn't really happen." This may seem like an absurd way of putting it, but in the early 1960s we had a fight inside the party and the international over exactly this question. The Healyites said that the Cuban revolution did not live up to their preconceived notions, therefore it didn't qualify as a socialist revolution. That was their political response. They made the classical sectarian mistake of utilizing our programmatic heritage not as a tool for understanding reality and guiding our intervention in the living class struggle, but as a set of rigid schemas. When reality turned out to be more complicated they "solved" the contradiction by denying the reality and turning their backs on a revolution.

In 1961 Jim Cannon had a few words to say about this kind of sectarianism. As a Leninist politician with more than a half century of revolutionary experience, he recoiled from it in horror: "The only *revolutionary* policy for Cuba is to *recognize* the revolution there, as it is and as it is developing as a *socialist* revolution—and to *identify* ourselves with it, and to act as a part of it, not as scholastic wiseacres standing outside the living movement."

"What would our talk about revolution be worth," Jim asked, "if we couldn't recognize a revolution when we see it?" (SWP Discussion Bulletin, Vol. 22, No. 17, June 1961. Emphasis in original.)

The Cuban revolution was a gigantic test for the Fourth International on a world scale. The challenge was to recognize the revolution, to identify with it, in order to participate in it, defend it, and affect its course of development. The sectarians in the Fourth International failed that test, as did the petty-bourgeois minority inside the SWP who supported them.

Those who passed that political test—the ability to recognize and identify with a socialist revolution when it comes along—were then able to make the theoretical conquests required for understanding and explaining the Cuban revolution. Studying the developments in Cuba also enabled us to deepen our understanding of revolutionary processes in other countries as well, including China, Eastern Europe, Algeria, and Vietnam.

Partisans of the revolution

Second, we were unconditional partisans of it. We identified with it. We thought it was a great historic event, not just for Cuba but for the whole world. It was the opening of the socialist revolution in our hemisphere. We did everything we could to get American workers, farmers and students to identify the SWP and YSA with the Cuban revolution, with the conquests by the Cuban masses, with the audacity and capacities of its internationalist leadership.

Farrell Dobbs, our presidential candidate in 1960, went to Cuba along with Joseph Hansen. Dobbs then toured the United States explaining what was really happening in Cuba and why working people should defend the revolution there. The *Militant* answered the lies and slanders against the Cuban revolution and its leadership, and reported extensively on developments as they took place.

As revolutionists we found we had a great deal in common with the Cuban leaders. They led the Cuban masses to victory in a socialist revolution. That's what we are in business for, although our movement hasn't succeeded in doing this since October 1917. So we thought maybe we could learn something from the Cubans as well as share with them some of our ideas, our program, the historical experience of world revolution that they would have to absorb if they were to consistently move forward.

To influence, not abstain

Third, our stance was a totally conscious political response to revolutionary forces moving in our direction. From the beginning we sought points of agreement and ways to present our views that would maximize the chances that our ideas would be listened to and understood. How else can we win new forces to Trotskyism, to the Fourth International?

We saw the Cuban revolution as a decisive historical turning point. For the first time in forty-two years a revolutionary, non-Stalinist, leadership *led* a revolution that overturned capitalism—and right on the doorstep of the American imperialist colossus, no less. It was the beginning of the end of the long detour. The Castro team led the struggle through to victory over the objections of and in opposition to the Stalinists. The Cuban Stalinists were simply bypassed. This was extremely important because it gave us the opportunity to participate in the political process unfolding in

Cuba, and win young revolutionary forces in other countries who looked to Cuba for example and inspiration. It gave us the opportunity to influence events, not just comment on them. We responded as revolutionists, not sectarians.

We were not interested in being sideline critics. As Joe Hansen put it, for us it was a "fight for the soul of the Cuban revolution." (*Dynamics of the Cuban Revolution*, by Joseph Hansen, [New York: Pathfinder Press, 1978], p. 125 [2010 printing].)

We had no fatalistic conception that the degeneration of the revolution was inevitable because the Trotskyist forces were too small, the revolution too weak and isolated, and the Castro leadership not Marxist enough to prevent it. In politics, fatalism is a cover for cowardice, an excuse for inaction. By the active role we played in fighting to defend and to extend the revolution, and through what we said and wrote, we fought to prevent the development of a crystallized bureaucratic caste, to block the Stalinization of the Cuban revolution. That is the course we have maintained to this day.

Cuba in world context

Fourth, we always placed the Cuban revolution in the context of the world class struggle. Developments in Cuba could not be understood by looking at that island in isolation.

The unfolding Cuban revolution could only be understood by seeing it in relation to American imperialism, which had sucked the blood of the workers, peasants, and exploited middle classes for more than sixty years and was determined to crush the revolution.

Moreover, the revolution had to be placed in the framework of the existence of the Russian and Chinese workers states, where the planned economies conquered by the workers survive despite the counterrevolutionary character of the Stalinist castes that exercize power in those countries. Without the aid of the existing workers states, the Cuban revolution could not have survived.

We recognized that the Cuban revolution took place within a new relationship of class forces on a world scale, with imperialism more and more on the defensive. Nineteen fifty-nine was not 1919, when Soviet power in Russia was hanging by a thread, barely able to survive the imperialist onslaught, the blockade, and civil war.

Nineteen fifty-nine was not 1939, in the wake of the great defeats of the working class in Germany and Spain, the spread of fascism, and the imminence of World War II.

The Cuban revolution took place in the context of the victory of the Soviet Union in World War II and the tremendous advance of the colonial revolution in the postwar period, including the victory of the Chinese revolution. A few years later it would be the Vietnamese revolution that would give the Cubans a breathing space, diverting the resources of American imperialism. As the Castro leadership was the first to appreciate, were it not for the heroic resistance of the Vietnamese people the napalm that seared Vietnam might well have fallen on Cuba.

And the Cuban revolution itself was a factor contributing to the new rise of struggles in the imperialist centers as well.

Our responsibility

Finally, and most importantly, our starting point has always been our responsibility to defend the Cuban revolution against American imperialism. We knew that if we wanted to advance the revolution, to help it overcome its weaknesses, and to fight for its extension, then we had to begin by defending that revolution—not just in words, but in *action*—against Yankee imperialism. We knew that you couldn't begin to solve the problems confronting the Cuban revolution without throwing yourself into combat against the greatest threat—the aggression of American imperialism. If you didn't start there, you couldn't understand anything that was happening in Cuba. And nobody worth anything in Cuba would listen to you if you defaulted on the most elementary of internationalist duties.

Our movement stood in the front ranks of the forces defending the Cuban revolution. We set an example of how revolutionists stand up to their own imperialist government. We stretched our limited resources as far as we could, using our press, our election campaigns, and helping to build united-front actions to mobilize opposition to imperialism's campaign against Cuba. We distributed far and wide the speeches of the Cuban leadership, and the truth about Cuba.

There is no prouder chapter in the history of our party.

WHAT HAPPENED IN CUBA

The character and implications of the differences in the Socialist Workers Party and Fourth International today only become clear if we start—as we did twenty years ago—with the facts about Cuba.

The forces that later became the July 26 Movement began to come together in political opposition to Batista's military coup in 1952. Fidel Castro and other liberal and radical petty-bourgeois and bourgeois figures opposed the dictatorship and attempted to expose it by first taking action within the "legal" framework. But when all of the existing organizations and currents—including the Stalinist—defaulted and failed to seriously act against the dictatorship, Castro struck out to blaze his own path.

Fidel organized the unsuccessful raid on the Moncada army barracks on July 26, 1953. Many were killed. Fidel survived and was captured. Defending himself before Batista's judges, he outlined his program for raising the standard of living of every man, woman, and child in Cuba. While he was still in prison, the famous "History Will Absolve Me" speech was published and circulated throughout the island.

The July 26 Movement itself was born as the leaders of Moncada were released from the Isle of Pines two years later. Fidel publicly broke his last ties to the bourgeois Ortodoxo Party. They began organizing in Cuba and among Cuban exiles in Mexico and elsewhere to launch a guerrilla band in the Sierra Maestra mountains.

What was remarkable about the leaders of the Rebel Army was not their brilliance as military tacticians. There were a good many fiascos along the way, including some of the most famous events, such as the botched landing of the *Granma* on the shores of Oriente province in December 1956. But they understood that revolutionary strategy is above all political, not military. Thus, several months in advance Castro announced to the world that their expedition would land in Cuba before the end of 1956, knowing full well that he was increasing the risks militarily. He understood that the political impact of the announcement far outweighed the military disadvantages it created.

What was decisive for the victory of the Rebel Army was their systematic campaign of revolutionary propaganda aimed at the entire Cuban population, including the troops of Batista's army.

Led by figures from petty-bourgeois backgrounds, the Castro grouping was a revolutionary current built around a radical bourgeois-democratic program. They demanded an end to the tyranny and the torture of the Batista dictatorship. The program affirmed the goal of national independence, breaking the political and economic control of imperialism. Very importantly, they called for sweeping land reform. They projected plans for industrialization, advances in housing, health care, education. In short, their goal was to radically transform Cuban society.

They publicized the goals for which they were fighting far and wide. As the Rebel Army established itself in the Sierras and proved they could survive, they began to implement their land reform program in the territory they controlled. As a result, support grew among the peasantry for the land reform and the Rebel Army.

An active July 26 underground also existed and functioned in the cities. Funds were raised and supplies organized for the Rebel Army. Acts of sabotage were carried out. Propaganda was distributed. However, the political movement in the cities was up against very difficult odds. The repression made functioning hazardous. The trade-union officialdom, totally corrupted and in the pay of Batista, maintained a stranglehold on the organized labor movement. The Stalinists denounced the July 26 Movement as "petty-bourgeois adventurers" and fought the movement every inch of the way. Divisions within the July 26 Movement itself also emerged, with the more moderate wing blocking attempts to mobilize revolutionary opposition to the dictatorship. The Stalinists and the right wing of the July 26 Movement sabotaged a general strike called for April 1958.

But the Batista regime was so corrupt and increasingly discredited that these obstacles did not prevent the advance of the guerrilla movement. By mid-1958, the rebel columns were able to significantly expand their operations as their support grew and Batista proved incapable of fighting effectively—despite the best arms, training, and supplies Uncle Sam could furnish. In the summer of 1958, Batista's army, numbering tens of thousands, was incapable of defeating the Rebel

Army, consisting of only several hundred *barbudos*. Finally, and without a single major conventional military engagement, the discipline of Batista's officer corps simply disintegrated. The ranks of the army wouldn't fight. A growing number deserted, some going over to the Rebel Army. The support for the July 26 Movement in the cities and in the countryside became overwhelming. Batista fled in the early hours of January 1, 1959, and the Rebel Army marched into Havana, greeted by a general strike called by the July 26 Movement.

A coalition government in power

What distinguished the July 26 Movement from every previous radical petty-bourgeois formation, endemic to Cuban politics, was that the Fidelistas meant what they said. Once in power, they set out to implement their program and mobilize the masses of Cuban people in support of the measures they took.

Having learned the lessons of the 1954 CIA-organized coup against the Arbenz regime in Guatemala, the rebel leaders moved immediately to disband the Batista army and police. They put some of the most notorious police torturers on trial, and executed some 600 of them with swift justice—although most of these butchers had escaped to Miami. The public trials were used to educate and mobilize the masses.

It was this mass determination to establish revolutionary justice that provoked the initial howls of pain and hypocritical outrage from Washington about the "reign of terror" taking place in Cuba.

A coalition government was set up. While it included leaders of the July 26 Movement, the most important posts went to bourgeois figures. Castro took no post to begin with. Manuel Urrutia was named president. He had voted, as a judge, against the convictions of some of the rebel fighters who had been captured by Batista's police. José Miró Cardona, who was the president of the Havana Bar Association, was named prime minister.

This bourgeois coalition government then proceeded to implement some of the measures that had been promised and fought for by the July 26 Movement and the Rebel Army. Fissures within the government and within the July 26 Movement itself immediately began to appear.

The cutting edge of the revolution was the radical agrarian reform law adopted May 17, 1959. Prior to the revolution, 75 percent of the land had been owned by 8 percent of the population. Seven of the ten largest *latifundios* were American-owned, as was 40 percent of Cuban sugar production.

The agrarian reform law invoked the provisions of the 1940 constitution forbidding the holding of more than a thousand acres in a single property. Holdings beyond that were expropriated and distributed among the 700,000 landless peasants and agricultural workers, with priority to any tenants, sharecroppers, or squatters living on the land in question. Each family was guaranteed a minimum of sixty-six acres free, with the right to buy another hundred acres, which could be passed on through inheritance, but not sold. All cane land belonging to the giant sugar mills was expropriated, along with all land owned by non-Cubans. All land was to be compensated for by long-term government bonds.

The National Institute of Agrarian Reform (INRA) was established to oversee the implementation of the program, which provoked growing dismay and hostility in Washington and among the wealthy Cuban landowners. This in turn deepened the split within the government.

INRA and the Rebel Army, backed by the workers and poor peasants, acted more and more as a "dual power" to the moderate elements in the government.

Other measures were implemented. Government corruption was literally wiped out. Home and apartment rents were reduced by 30 to 50 percent. Mortgage rates for small homeowners were lowered. The national lottery was converted to provide funds for a government home-building program. Havana, which for decades had been used as a gambling den and brothel by the Yankees, was transformed. The private homes and clubs of the wealthy who had fled were confiscated and turned into schools and dormitories. Taxes were reduced by two-thirds for most citizens, while those who had previously evaded all taxes found themselves pursued by zealous collectors correcting years of fraudulent tax evasion. Gas, electricity, and telephone rates were reduced after committees of workers opened the books of the giant American-owned utilities and documented the criminal price gouging. Currency and import controls were introduced.

Rather than slowing down or retreating, as fissures within the July 26 Movement and the coalition government deepened, the Fidelistas moved further and further to the left, relying more and more on massive revolutionary mobilizations in the cities as well as the countryside. In turn, the Castro team itself was further transformed as it more and more reflected and responded to the deepening radicalization of the toiling masses of Cuba. The masses entered directly into the political process, initiating factory "interventions," putting their stamp of approval on, and consolidating, the revolutionary measures taken.

One by one the bourgeois ministers resigned from their posts. Huge mass mobilizations played a decisive role in driving key bourgeois forces out of top posts, and in strengthening the Fidelista forces. In February, Miró Cardona stepped down and Castro became Prime Minister. In July, Urrutia was replaced by Osvaldo Dorticós as President. By November 1959, when Che Guevara became head of the national bank, virtually all of the remaining bourgeois figures had been removed from the government.

Workers and farmers government

It was clear by then that a point of qualitative change in the nature of the government had occurred, and a workers and farmers government was in the saddle.

As Joe Hansen explained at the time, "By recognizing the new Cuban government as a workers' and farmers' government . . . we indicate its radical petty-bourgeois background and composition and its origin in a popular mass movement, its tendency to respond to popular pressures for action against the bourgeoisie and their agents, and its capacity, for whatever immediate reasons and with whatever hesitancy, to undertake measures against bourgeois political power and against bourgeois property relations." (*Dynamics of the Cuban Revolution*, p. 91.)

Among the most significant steps taken by this government was the organization of a workers and peasants militia of a quarter of a million people.

But the dominant property relations remained bourgeois. The capitalist class had not yet been expropriated. It still hung on to positions of power in the economy, and therefore a position from which it could work to regain the initiative and use its power to roll back the gains of the revolutionary upsurge. In other words, Cuba was not yet a workers state.

In July of 1960 Joe Hansen wrote: "What has been established is a highly contradictory and highly unstable regime, subject to pressures and impulses that can move it forward or backward." There remained the contradiction between the workers and peasants government and the economic power of the native capitalists and their imperialist senior partners. What was needed was "to carry the revolution forward to its culmination by toppling bourgeois economic and social relations . . ." (*Dynamics of the Cuban Revolution*, p. 90.)

This was the key challenge. And it was met decisively by the Castro leadership. Under the impetus of, and facing the escalating threats and offensive moves by Washington, the Castro government itself initiated the next steps and mobilized the Cuban workers to carry them through. They used the governmental power to organize and lead the masses in expropriating the bourgeoisie and opening the door to a planned economy, thus bringing about a revolutionary transformation of the class character of the state.

The nature of this revolutionary government can be seen from the way it responded to the major moves of the imperialists.

Following the promulgation of the first agrarian reform law, the imperialists escalated their preparation for a counterrevolutionary offensive. They charged that there had been a Red takeover in Havana. They began to complain that there were no free elections, although they had never complained about the lack of free elections under Batista.

They waxed indignant over the provisions for compensation in the agrarian reform law, which, they whined, weren't fair because the value of the land was assessed at the value listed for tax purposes by the landowners under the Batista regime! The White House grumbled that nothing was working the way it ought to, the new officials in the government wouldn't even take bribes. The imperialists denounced Fidel as a demagogue because he talked on television for so long. Of course, they never reported the content of what he said.

A campaign was launched in Congress and

in the capitalist press to cut Cuba's sugar quota. In January 1960, Eisenhower announced that he would seek authority to reduce the sugar quota. Havana responded by denouncing this as blackmail and announcing that Cuba would sell sugar elsewhere in the world market.

The next month Soviet First Deputy Premier Anastas Mikoyan visited Havana and signed an agreement for the Soviet Union to buy Cuban sugar. The government began to prepare a law to expropriate the sugar mills. Fidel announced: "As they cut our sugar quota pound by pound, we will seize their mills one by one." Hand-painted posters went up in the windows of houses throughout the island: "Sin cuota, pero sin bota." (Without the quota, but without the boot.)

The government passed a law authorizing the expropriation of American-owned property, stipulating that full compensation would be paid out of future income from sugar sold to the United States. No sugar sale, no compensation.

For some reason, that equitable arrangement made the American businessmen very angry.

Next came the refusal of the U.S.- and British-owned oil refineries to process Soviet crude oil. The response of the Castro government was to "intervene." If the foreign-owned monopolies wouldn't produce according to the needs of the Cuban people, the workers themselves should open the books, expose the lies concealed beneath the fraud of "business secrets," and establish workers control over production. "Intervention" in the oil refineries was a first step toward their expropriation.

Washington stepped up the financing and arming of counterrevolutionaries. Planes from Florida began bombing canefields and setting them afire. On August 6, 1960, taking the occasion of the first Latin American Youth Congress meeting in Havana, Fidel Castro announced the nationalization of all the American-owned sugar mills, oil refineries, the power and telephone companies. Again, compensation would be paid out of future revenues from sugar sold to the United States.

'. . . down to the nails in their shoes'

And this was followed by further expropriations, including of the holdings of the Cuban national bourgeoisie. Castro put it: "We will nationalize them down to the nails in their shoes." By the end of October, 1960, virtually every major capitalist holding had become public property. With the expropriations came state control over foreign trade and the expansion of economic planning.

These expropriations were not merely administrative acts, easily reversed at a future date. Each step was explained to the Cuban workers, and they were mobilized in actions that consolidated and carried through the expropriation of an entire ruling class. The trade unions, the local militia units, and other proletarian organizations acted directly to drive through these expropriations. The transformation of property relations was correctly seen as a conquest by the masses and for the masses.

This represented a qualitative change in the class character of the state. The workers and farmers government had used its power to advance the mobilization of the workers to expropriate the bourgeoisie. Capitalist property relations were thus overturned and the hold of the bourgeoisie on the economic levers of power was definitively broken. By the fall of 1960, a workers state had been born in the first "free territory of the Americas."

This was the opening of the socialist revolution in Latin America, right under the nose of Yankee imperialism, the despised colossus to the north. It was an event that was cheered and celebrated by the masses of people around the world. Here in the United States it was hailed by socialist workers, by a significant layer of the Black and Latino populations, and by radicalizing youth, who responded with enormous enthusiasm.

For the first time since 1917, a socialist revolution had succeeded *because* of, not *in spite* of, its leadership. That has a lot to do with our attitude to the Castro leadership today. The team around Castro earned the leadership of the Cuban masses by leading. They didn't try to stifle and sit on the mass mobilizations, or run ahead of them in order to divert their course. They inspired and organized them. From the start they saw that the only hope of survival was in the growing political consciousness, understanding, and support of the poorest and most oppressed and exploited layers of the population.

They saw that the revolution's only hope of survival was in winning international support and extending the revolution.

And they charted their course accordingly. That

was the beginning. But they have not abandoned that course over twenty hard years of unrelenting pressure from two sources.

First and foremost has been the brutal determination of American imperialism to crush the Cuban revolution by any means necessary—economic pressure, armed invasion, assassination, sabotage. If it can't be rapidly crushed, imperialism has stated its willingness to purchase the soul of the revolution if Cuba will only give up its support for anti-imperialist struggles around the globe and keep its internationalist army at home.

Second has been the inexorable pressure from the counterrevolutionary bureaucratic caste that holds power in the Soviet Union. Without aid from the Soviet workers state, the Cuban revolution could not have survived. But that has come with conditions. This dual nature of the Soviet aid is a crucial factor in evaluating the twenty-year history of the Cuban revolution and the policies of its leadership today.

Precisely because the fires of the October revolution have not been extinguished in the Soviet Union, because the publicly owned and planned economy established by the revolution has not been overturned, the Kremlin was obliged to come to the aid of Cuba in its own self-defense. Their purpose was to gain bargaining chips in the international game of détente. All aid has been with strings attached, with pressure on the Cuban leadership to uncritically support the domestic and foreign policies of the Kremlin.

What is remarkable is not the errors and concessions the Cuban leadership has made, subjected to the double pressures of Washington and Moscow. On the contrary, what stands out is the twenty-year record of refusal to bow to the pressures of imperialism or carry out the counterrevolutionary world strategy of the Kremlin.

Most of the differences being discussed in the Socialist Workers Party and Fourth International today center on an evaluation of precisely these points: Some comrades believe the Cuban revolution has degenerated. That it has become a Stalinist satellite of the Kremlin. That the search for peaceful coexistence with American imperialism does guide its foreign policy. That a privileged bureaucratic caste has crystallized inside Cuba.

Before taking up the arguments offered in defense of the view that Cuba is today a deformed or degenerated workers state, however, it is useful to first take up the theory that a socialist revolution never occurred in Cuba at all, that the social and economic measures just described were the policies of a new "state-capitalist" class.

THE 'STATE-CAPITALIST' THEORY

The comrades in the SWP who hold that Cuba is a state-capitalist country believe the Soviet Union is state-capitalist also. These comrades start from the political conclusion that there is nothing left of the October revolution to defend against imperialism today. From the standpoint of the world working class and its tasks, they see no qualitative difference between the Soviet Union and the United States. They believe the Soviet section of the Fourth International should be for the defeat of the Soviet Union in a war with imperialism. This is the political difference they have with Trotskyism.

It is a fundamental difference, with many political ramifications.

A corollary of this political stance is a basic disagreement with the position of the Trotskyist movement on the characteristics of a workers state. These comrades hold that a workers state exists if, and only if, the working class directly exercises political rule through democratic proletarian forms. If the working class does not exercise direct rule through its own democratic forms, it is not a workers state. They do not agree that the class character of a state is determined by the property relations it defends.

To back up this view they quote extensively from Marx and Lenin's predictions about what the proletarian dictatorship would look like, and what they urged the workers to fight for. They correctly point out that proletarian democracy is necessary to achieve the transition to socialism. Then they show that the Soviet Union deviates from that norm of a workers state—that the Stalinist bureaucracy has usurped political power, that the proletariat is disenfranchised and oppressed.

They argue that the Soviet Union ceased being a workers state around 1939, not because of any change in the relations of production or in property relations—which remained the same—but because of changes in the party and government. The purges of the old Bolsheviks, they say, severed the last living links to the October revolution. In other words, the class character of the state is determined not by the property relations that the state defends but by whether the political forms correspond to the programmatic norms laid out by Marx, Lenin, and Trotsky and defended by our movement.

We think these comrades use incorrect criteria for defining a workers state. Their error flows from the wrong political position of abandoning the fight to defend the economic conquests of the Bolshevik revolution before the decisive battle on that front has been fought.

But the position these comrades hold on the Soviet Union does not directly prove anything about the class character of Cuba. You can hold that the Soviet Union is state capitalist, but it doesn't automatically follow that Cuba is state capitalist. The Cuban revolution has its own dynamic—its own course of development that is quite different from the course of events in the Soviet Union. So we have to look at Cuba, not at the Soviet Union, to decide the class nature of the Cuban state and our political stance toward it. It's one thing to say that the Soviet Union, which had a proletarian revolution in 1917, degenerated to the point where the workers state was overturned. That's wrong. That's not a small mistake—it's a very big mistake—but it's not a new one.

It's quite another thing to say that there was never a workers state in Cuba, that there was never a social revolution in Cuba. Because if you can't recognize the socialist revolution in Cuba, it's doubtful that you could recognize one anywhere. And a leadership that can't recognize a revolution, can't lead one.

Healy's sectarian line

The original proponent in our movement of the point of view that Cuba remained capitalist was Gerry Healy, then a leader of the British section of the international, who refused to recognize the socialist nature of the revolution. He didn't think it was state capitalist—just capitalist. In his view, not much had changed in Cuba. He stood outside of and in opposition to the revolutionary process, and therefore avoided the necessity of throwing himself into the struggle to defend it against imperialist threats and attacks and to advance that revolution.

In the case of Healy, this sectarian stance toward the Cuban revolution went hand in hand with sectarian opposition to the process of reunification of the divided Fourth International. Agreement on Cuba was a key part of the political convergence that was taking place in the early 1960s, and gave a big impetus to the process of reunification. Healy's main interest was in using the Cuban revolution—which he didn't give a damn about—as a factional issue to block reunification.

The National Committee of Healy's Socialist Labour League wrote: "Does the dictatorship of the proletariat exist in Cuba? We reply categorically NO! The absence of a party squarely based on the workers and poor peasants makes it impossible to set up and maintain such a dictatorship. But what is even more significant is the absence of what the SWP euphemistically terms 'the institutions of proletarian democracy' or what we prefer to call soviets or organs of workers' *power.*"

According to Healy, and the comrades in the SWP who agreed with him, Cuba remained capitalist. Why? Because the Cuban revolution was not under the leadership of a recognized section or duly chartered sympathizing group of the Fourth International: "Cuba can and will be defined as a workers' state only when a revolutionary party based on the programme of the Fourth International has successfully overthrown the capitalist state. . . ." That was the Healyite position.

The comrades who today believe that Cuba is state-capitalist don't share Healy's political position. But they make a similar error by refusing to recognize the importance of property relations in defining the class character of a state.

Contradictions of 'state-capitalism'

The political problem with the state-capitalist view of Cuba is elementary. If all the gains and conquests of the Cuban revolution are possible under *capitalism*, then two things follow. First, we must say that this opens up the perspective of a whole new era of progress for humanity under capitalism, at least in the semicolonial world; and second, we must defend that kind of capitalism as a better kind of capitalism than that which existed under Batista or the capitalism that exists in the other Latin American countries today.

In other words, all of Marxism goes out the window.

Let's look at the tasks of the bourgeois-democratic revolution in the colonial world, which we know can only be carried out, in the imperialist epoch, under the leadership of the proletariat.

We can start with the land reform. There was a sweeping, radical land reform in Cuba. Unlike Stalin's bureaucratic and brutal forced collectivization, it had the overwhelming support of the peasants, rural poor, and agricultural workers. The result of this key advance was the consolidation of the political alliance between the Cuban workers and the Cuban peasants, an alliance that remains solid today.

Do we politically support this land reform? Should we have advocated it at the time? If not, how would our program have differed from the one actually carried out?

What about national independence? Cuba was a colony of the United States in everything but name. American capital owned great parts of Cuba's wealth. Batista was a Wall Street puppet. Havana was a cesspool of American gamblers, racketeers, drug dealers, and pimps.

That has been totally changed. Not a single piece of imperialist-owned property, machinery, land, or anything exists in Cuba today—with the exception of Guantánamo Bay base held by American imperialism through military force. The degradation and exploitation by American imperialism has ended. Cuba is the only country in all of Latin America that is truly independent from U.S. imperialism. Are we for this or against it? Was kicking out the imperialists a good thing? Could it have been done better or more thoroughly by a workers state than a "state-capitalist state"?

The Cubans carried out this task pretty well. And not because the Yankees willingly let go. Wall Street fought hard. U.S. imperialism mobilized its economic and political power against Cuba. When that failed, it organized an invasion. And the invasion was beaten back! At the Bay of Pigs.

Then in 1962, the imperialists began preparing for a second, more determined invasion. The Cubans knew it was coming. To head this off, Castro got nuclear arms from the Soviet Union and used them to call Kennedy's hand. This was a bold move, but the alternative was to allow an invasion to take place and go down fighting against vastly superior military forces. And it worked; the invasion plans were shelved, and the United States has had to keep them on the shelf ever since.

Castro's decision to obtain nuclear weapons thus prevented the Yankee military occupation of Cuba, a step that would have bathed Cuba in blood and rolled back the first socialist revolution in the Americas. Had the imperialists succeeded, it would have significantly shifted the world relationship of class forces against the workers and peasants. And the negative consequences for the world revolution would have been felt everywhere—in Vietnam, in Africa, and throughout Latin America.

Were we for Cuba and against the Yankee aggression? Obviously we have no differences on this. We were for Cuba. But how could we explain that *capitalist* Cuba stood off U.S. imperialism?

Moreover, the Cuban revolution has continued to defy Uncle Sam internationally. For twenty years it has refused to bow down to the demands of Yankee imperialism. And it has done more. In Angola—not in Latin America, but in *Africa*—Cuban troops played a decisive role in the defeat of the invading South African imperialist army. How could you explain *capitalist* Cuba sending troops to Africa to stand up to imperialism?

In another area of bourgeois-democratic tasks, along with land reform and national independence, we should add that the revolution made gigantic strides in ending the oppression of Blacks in Cuba, a key aspect of the national question. The job is not finished, but the Cubans have made greater progress on this front than any other country in the world.

The Cuban revolution put an end to Batista's torture chambers, his firing squads, his secret police. It turned his barracks into schools.

The political problems of the state-capitalist position don't stop with the tasks of the bourgeois-democratic revolution, because the Cuban revolution didn't stop with the bourgeois-democratic tasks. It has gone on to eliminate unemployment—eliminate the industrial reserve army, one of the preconditions for capitalism. It has advanced the standing of women in society; qualitatively raised the standards of education, of health care, of housing, of culture. Every measure of the standard of living and the quality of life of the Cuban masses has been qualitatively improved.

This is absolutely indisputable. Obviously we

are in favor of these gains and defend them.

But where does that leave us?

If we say that Cuba is capitalist, then we have to say that something new has appeared in the world. A new kind of progressive capitalist class has developed. A variety of capitalism has emerged that is superior, at least from the standpoint of the Cuban workers and peasants, and African workers and peasants, to any capitalism they have ever known.

Are we for it or against it? The Cuban people are for it, no doubt about that. They know there is something qualitatively better about Cuban society today than pre-1959.

But if Cuban *capitalism* can carry through a radical land reform, can achieve national independence from American imperialism, can advance the level of human dignity—if Cuban *capitalism* can do all that, then what happens to the theory of the permanent revolution?

The laws of the class struggle in the imperialist epoch preclude the possibility that the national bourgeoisie can solve the unfinished tasks of the bourgeois-democratic revolution. Only a workers and peasants alliance against imperialism, led by the proletariat, going over to measures that are socialist in principle and carried out *against* the national bourgeoisie, can solve the postponed democratic tasks.

But if Cuba is capitalist shouldn't we tell the people of Latin America, Africa, and Asia, who are striving to follow the Cuban example, that the Fourth International says: "Struggle for socialism, but if you can't get that, at least struggle for state capitalism, because it too can solve most of the fundamental problems that you face"? Wouldn't we have to say that?

We would have to abandon Marxism, abandon a scientific analysis of class society and say that capitalism in our time can promise a better life, that capitalism can enter upon a new era of human development and economic and social progress, including in the superexploited, dependent countries.

STALINISM VS. CASTROISM

The overwhelming majority of comrades in the Socialist Workers Party and Fourth International recognize that a socialist revolution took place in Cuba and a workers state exists there today.

However, within that framework, various comrades disagree that Cuba is today a workers state with bureaucratic deformations, as the majority of the SWP National Committee contends. They judge it to be something qualitatively different.

Some believe that the Cuban workers state from its birth was bureaucratically deformed to such a degree that the only correct political stance was to have called for a political revolution against the Castro leadership from the very start.

Others believe that the Cuban workers state was not born deformed, but degenerated over the last twenty years. They hold that a Stalinist bureaucratic caste has emerged and consolidated its grip on Cuba, and we must now call for the overthrow of the Castro leadership. Some believe this qualitative change had taken place by 1961, others think it did not occur until the 1968–71 period.

Within the SWP, Comrade Tim Wohlforth has the distinction of having defended virtually all of these mutually exclusive positions at one time or another. One and only one consistent thread runs throughout his various positions: hostility to the Castro leadership. His latest position, presented to the December 1978 plenum, holds that a bureaucratic caste was consolidated between 1968 and 1971.

Before taking up the evidence presented by Comrade Wohlforth and others to substantiate the position that we must change our position and now call for political revolution in Cuba, we should be clear on the criteria to be used. What must be proven by the comrades who want to convince the party to change its position?

What must be proven?

To justify changing our political line and calling for a political revolution in Cuba, it would have to be shown that a hardened, bureaucratic caste rules that country. By a bureaucratic caste we mean a petty-bourgeois social layer with institutionalized, material privileges so far-reaching that the interests of the ruling stratum are in contradiction with the class interests of the toilers of Cuba.

It would have to be shown that, in defense of its own privileges, this caste rules through totalitarian methods, as in the degenerated and deformed workers states.

Further, it would have to be proven that this caste

consistently places its narrow interests ahead of those of the world revolution, implementing a counterrevolutionary foreign policy, seeking an alliance with imperialism to strangle anti-imperialist struggles of the masses and upsurges of the proletariat. Such a caste follows a policy of seeking to preserve the status quo on a world scale in order to protect its own privileged standing. It serves the imperialist power with which it is "peacefully coexisting" in the most brutal counterrevolutionary manner. Its central policy guideline, at home and abroad, is determined by its goal of "building socialism [that is, securing its own privileges] in one country." The name of this policy is class collaboration.

In other words, to justify a change in our line, we would have to be convinced that the Castro leadership has clearly become a Stalinist formation, whatever national peculiarities it might have due to its distinct history and evolution. We would have to conclude that a Stalinist caste—a petty-bourgeois social layer that is the oppressor of the Cuban toilers—has consolidated its power and rules Cuba today.

A mere listing of bureaucratic practices or instances where the Cuban leadership has taken wrong or even reactionary positions on world events is not sufficient to substantiate such a conclusion.

We all know that the Castro leadership is not Trotskyist. We know that there has never been a government of workers and peasants councils. There have been mistakes, errors and shortcomings from the beginning and we have analyzed them from the start.

There has been a problem of bureaucratism, of privileges, of corruption of individuals from the beginning. As early as 1961 the revolutionary government openly acknowledged and attacked these problems. But the same things existed even in the Soviet Union under Lenin and Trotsky. In 1921, Lenin referred to the Soviet Union as "a workers state with bureaucratic deformations." But this was not the same as the political triumph of the crystallized petty-bourgeois social layer led by Stalin—what we know as Thermidor.

So evidence of bureaucratic practices or elements of privilege are not enough to alter our overall assessment of the regime. Nor is it sufficient to point to the relatively recent establishment of government institutions, such as the constitution and elected assemblies, which juridically reflect the fact that workers councils are not the basis of the Cuban government. Even if we were to conclude that some or all of these institutions can't be reformed but have to be totally replaced, this would not make the case for a political revolution to overthrow the regime.

We would have to be convinced that a qualitative change, the Cuban Thermidor, has taken place. It would have to be shown how and when it took place. How the privileges are institutionalized and how they affect all major social strata in Cuba.

If this had occurred it would be reflected in the international as well as domestic policies of the Cuban government. Thus, comrades who propose a change in our political position would have to convince the party that the Castro team, because of its social character and material interests, has consistently failed to advance the revolution on the international arena. They would have to convince the party that we can confidently predict that the Cuban leadership, in response to revolutionary openings, will act as all Stalinist castes do to derail and block a revolutionary victory. They will have to prove that we can now act on the conviction that any advance of the socialist revolution—in Asia, in Africa, in the Mideast, in Latin America—would not attract the Castro leadership nor win its support, but would be met with hostility from the Cuban government and the Cuban Communist Party. In short, they would have to convince the party that the guideline of Cuban foreign policy is class collaboration, the search for a peaceful-coexistence deal with American imperialism.

If these things can be demonstrated then obviously we would have to change our political line. We would then begin to work for the overthrow of the Castro government. We would proclaim to the world the need for a political revolution in Cuba.

It might seem that this is a heavy burden of proof to be shouldered by those who propose a fundamental change in our political line. It is a heavy burden. And it ought to be. It would not be a small decision for American revolutionists to call for the overthrow of the Cuban government. And we would want to be dead sure we were right before we made such a political move. We would want to be certain that the facts backing up this evaluation would convince any honest proletarian revolutionist or anti-imperialist fighter, in Cuba or elsewhere, who objectively examined them.

Unique character of the Castro leadership

The majority of the National Committee of the SWP is convinced that the evidence submitted by Comrade Wohlforth and others fails to meet this standard.

The Castro leadership does not have a consistent Leninist understanding of the proletariat's strategic line of march on a world scale, and for that reason they commit many political errors, including serious ones.

But the Castro leadership is a revolutionary, not a counterrevolutionary, current. They acted as revolutionists when they led the Cuban working class to power, and they remain revolutionists today.

Within the Cuban leadership as a whole there is a Castroist wing and a Stalinist wing, but it is the Castro wing that dominates fundamental policy decisions. Our stance has always been to support the revolutionists, the Castro current, against the Stalinists, to seek to influence, educate, and win the Castro leadership to a consistent understanding of revolutionary Marxism.

Their political limitations, combined with the colossal pressures of imperialism under which they live, often lead them to make political concessions to Stalinism. That is hardly surprising. What is remarkable, on the contrary, is the degree of independence they have maintained. Havana's foreign policy is decided in Havana, not Moscow. From Ethiopia to Vietnam, it is often at variance in practice with Moscow, and it stands as a powerful, though implicit, criticism of the Kremlin foreign policy.

For twenty-five years the errors of the Castro team have been remarkably consistent:

- their tendency to see armed struggle as the real dividing line between revolutionists and reformists, thus missing many key questions of revolutionary strategy and opening the door to class-collaborationist errors and adaptation to Stalinism;
- their failure to understand the class character and limits of petty-bourgeois anti-imperialist currents in the semicolonial world, thus failing to chart a proletarian course of united-front action while giving no political support to petty-bourgeois nationalist organizations, including those who have come to power;
- their failure to understand the need to build Leninist proletarian parties in opposition to such petty-bourgeois nationalist currents;
- their failure to understand the need for institutionalizing workers democracy by establishing soviets;
- their ignorance of revolutionary working-class strategy in the advanced capitalist countries, and lack of confidence in the revolutionary capacities of the proletariat of the imperialist countries.

At the same time, the revolutionary strengths of the Castro current have been just as consistent and unbending:

- their understanding of the need to politically motivate, explain, inspire, and lead the Cuban workers and peasants through every step of the revolution, educating and mobilizing them to meet the revolutionary responsibilities thrust on them by history;
- their commitment to proletarian internationalism as the guide to action; their bold, unyielding struggle to extend the revolution and refusal to bow to the pressures of imperialism;
- their determination to judge those who claim to be revolutionists by their *actions* in the class struggle, not by their words.

In short, Castroism stands counterposed to Stalinism, to building "socialism in one country." The strengths, weaknesses, and contradictions of Cuban policy are those of Castroism, not Stalinism.

Every argument advanced as proof of the Stalinization of the Castro current, upon closer examination proves the opposite.

Let's now take a look at the events that have been offered as evidence.

Stalinized by 1961?

In 1977 Comrade Wohlforth presented a document to the National Committee arguing that Castro's capitulation to Stalinism had been completed by 1961. (See "The Postwar Social Overturns and Marxist Theory," to be published in forthcoming SWP Discussion Bulletin.) According to Wohlforth, when the rift came with the national bourgeoisie and the pressure of imperialism was intensified, Castro rejected the course of "turn[ing] decisively to the working class and mobiliz[ing] this class through its own democratic organs . . ."

Instead, Wohlforth wrote, Castro chose the alternative of "turn[ing] to the Soviet Union for support and carry[ing] through a social transformation from on top, modelled after the East European pattern, fusing with the local Stalinists, and going over to Stalinism in the process."

First we should take a brief look at Cuban Stalinism in order to understand what it is Comrade Wohlforth believes the Fidelistas capitulated to in 1961.

The July 26 Movement was hardly ignorant of or naive about the Cuban Stalinists, who were organized in the Popular Socialist Party (PSP). The Stalinists were roundly hated and discredited in the Cuban working class for their popular-front alliance with Batista during the second world war (when they entered Batista's government), and their gangster tactics in the labor movement. With the beginning of the cold-war witchhunt, like their American counterparts, they found few defenders. From a highpoint of 87,000 members in 1942, they had declined to 20,000 by 1952. Only 7,000 remained by the beginning of 1959.

From the very first, the PSP had always been hostile opponents of the July 26 Movement. Following the July 26, 1953, raid on the Moncada barracks, the PSP issued a denunciation of the young rebels. They vilified the ill-fated but heroic July 26 raid as "a putschist attempt, a desperate form of adventurism, typical of petty-bourgeois circles lacking in principle and implicated in gangsterism."

Their political opposition to the Castro leadership and its revolutionary aims never wavered. However, under pressure of the growth of the July 26 Movement and the victories of the Rebel Army—pressure which affected their own ranks—the PSP was forced to change its tactical stance toward the Castroists. In mid-1958—only months before Batista's downfall, which by then appeared inevitable—the PSP sent an emissary to the Sierra Maestra to offer belated support to the July 26 Movement. Acting politically, Castro wisely accepted the offer.

However, the line of the Stalinists remained opposition to the program and practice of the Fidelistas. In May 1959—the very month the radical Agrarian Reform Law was decreed, signaling the opening of the direct conflict with the national bourgeoisie and its imperialist backers—the PSP urged restraint and warned against too radical a course.

"We are a small country, situated only a very short distance from the U.S.," they moaned. Cuba is "very dependent on imports. . . . In view of this, any leftist extremist tendency, any exaggerated measures . . . by the revolution and any attempt to disregard the realities and the concrete difficulties confronting the Cuban revolution must be rejected." Fortunately, it was their advice that was rejected.

In August 1960—on the very eve of the qualitative transformation of Cuba's economic and social structure—the PSP held a congress. Blas Roca gave the major report. In it, he explained: "The Cuban revolution is not a Communist revolution; it is anti-imperialist and antifeudal . . . patriotic and democratic . . . The social classes that are objectively interested in the fulfillment of these historic tasks are the workers, the peasants, the urban middle classes, *and the national bourgeoisie.*" (Emphasis added.) As Roca was speaking to the Stalinist faithful, the Cuban masses were outside in the streets, putting the national bourgeoisie out of business.

And Che was announcing to the Latin American Youth Congress in session at the Blanquita Theater in Havana that it was necessary to call things by their right names: The Cuban revolution was a socialist revolution.

Fusion of July 26 Movement and PSP

A year later, on July 26, 1961, Castro announced the merger of three organizations: the July 26 Movement, the Revolutionary Directorate (the student group that had supported the revolutionary struggle against Batista), and the PSP. The new formation was first called the Integrated Revolutionary Organizations, then became the United Party of the Socialist Revolution, and in 1965 became the Communist Party of Cuba.

In his 1977 contribution, Comrade Wohlforth branded this 1961 fusion as a sign of Castro's capitulation to Stalinism. But the opposite is true.

The Stalinist leadership of the PSP, along with the entire world Stalinist movement, was dealt a devastating blow by the Cuban revolution. The revolution had been made over their objections by a group they viewed as a bitter opponent. It shattered the myth promulgated by world Stalinism that only *they* could be at the head of a revolution. It also demolished their justification for reformism in Latin America: that no revolutionary mobilization was possible because the all-powerful Yankees would intervene to block any real advance by the masses.

The ranks of the PSP, which included some revolutionary-minded militants who had found their way into the Stalinist party by mistake, were attracted to and influenced by the revolutionary government and its leadership. Many were deeply affected by the gigantic events that were transforming their country. The ranks divided. Many became Fidelistas; others remained Stalinists.

The imperialist-backed invasion at the Bay of Pigs took place on April 17, 1961. Castro correctly saw the need to maximize the unity of all forces committed to defending the revolution in the face of the intensifying pressure from imperialism, the tightening of the blockade, and the ominous threat of a second U.S.-backed invasion. He saw the need to draw into the revolution all working-class cadres, including those of the PSP who were committed to the revolution.

The fusion was a correct political move. It advanced the defense of the revolution. Far from demonstrating Castro's "capitulation" to Stalinism, it highlights his capacities as a revolutionary politician. Wouldn't we have done exactly the same thing?

There never was any doubt that the decisions on policy would continue to be made by the Fidelistas, not the Stalinists of the PSP. In fact it is clear that one of the conditions of the fusion was recognition of the leadership of the Castro team. In 1965, when the fused formation became the Communist Party of Cuba, 80 percent of the 100-person Central Committee were either former members of the 26th of July Movement or other non-PSPers. There were no PSPers on the eight-person Politboro. It doesn't add up to a conversion to Stalinism.

Stalinization through trade and aid?

Wohlforth argues further in his 1977 document that the decision by the Cubans to turn to the Soviet Union for trade and military aid was an integral part of the process of Castro's capitulation.

Faced with the cutoff of the U.S. sugar quota, the ever-tightening noose of the economic blockade, and growing military threats, the Cubans turned to the only country in the world that could give them sufficient aid to survive. This didn't show that the Castroists had gone over to Stalinism; it showed that they were revolutionary fighters living in the real world of class combat.

Soviet aid was possible because of the existence of the proletarian state; because the 1917 victory of the Bolshevik revolution remains alive in the Soviet Union today despite the Stalinist bureaucracy.

In giving this aid—inadequate though it was—the Soviet bureaucracy exacted, and continues to exact, a political price from the Cubans. Every shipment of arms, of oil, of machinery is accompanied by an invoice demanding political payment. The Stalinists in Moscow insist that the Castro leadership remain silent and go along with Kremlin policy whether they agree or not.

The Cubans could have decided not to ask Khrushchev for the antiaircraft guns and tanks and oil that they needed to keep going, or refused to pay the price. They could have gone under with their honor intact, their principles untarnished—and their devastated island once again a colony of Yankee imperialism. Had they chosen that route, the subsequent course of the world revolution would have been different. If the Cuban revolution had been crushed what would that have meant for Vietnam? What would it have meant for Angola, for Ethiopia, for southern Africa? For Iran? For us?

No, we think it was correct for the Cubans to have turned to the Soviet Union for aid despite the political price tag.

Comrade Wohlforth's mistake is to aim at the wrong target—which means that he doesn't hit the right target. Our fire for the political concessions demanded from the Cubans by the Kremlin is aimed first of all at Moscow. Whatever criticisms we make of Castro's positions, the concessions he made, and how he made them must be within that framework.

The same is true of domestic policies as well. Stalinism in Cuba is a deadly danger. The leverage of the Stalinists inside the Cuban Communist Party is increased because of the role played by the Kremlin. But we can't advance the fight to strengthen the Castroist wing against the Stalinists if we lump the Castro leadership in with them and fail to see the counterposed lines.

The first Escalante affair

The notion that after 1961 Castro was a Stalinist, Moscow's man in Havana, flies in the face of every event of political significance. For example, the sequence of developments leading up to the first Escalante affair in which a layer of the Stalinist old guard was purged from the new organization for bureaucratic abuses—only eight months after the fusion.

In January 1962, *Pravda* ran an interview with Castro. However, the interview had been "edited," Stalinist-style. The censors had deleted entire paragraphs about the need for revolutionary struggle. The speech came out making Castro sound like Khrushchev. Four days later, in Havana, *Revolución* published the entire unexpurgated interview. Among the passages restored were: "No coexistence is possible between the exploited masses of Latin America and the Yankee monopolies."

A few days later, a million people turned out in Havana to protest the U.S.-engineered move to expel Cuba from the Organization of American States—a move that was part of the preparation for stepped-up military action against Cuba. The assembly gave thunderous approval to "The Second Declaration of Havana," a stirring call to revolutionary struggle by the workers and peasants of Latin America.

This declaration was aimed squarely at the imperialists, who exploit and oppress Latin America, and at those who try to divert the struggle against imperialism. The now famous injunction, "It is the duty of every revolutionist to make the revolution," was directed at those who claimed to be revolutionists, but came up with a hundred and one reasons for not engaging in the revolutionary struggle against imperialism.

The conclusion of the manifesto is worth quoting:

> It is the duty of every revolutionist to make the revolution. It is known that the revolution will triumph in America and throughout the world, but it is not for revolutionists to sit in the doorways of their houses waiting for the corpse of imperialism to pass by. The role of Job doesn't suit a revolutionist. Each year that the liberation of America is speeded up will mean the lives of millions of children saved, millions of intellects saved for culture, an infinite quantity of pain spared the people. Even if the Yankee imperialists prepare a bloody drama for America, they will not succeed in crushing the peoples' struggles, they will only arouse universal hatred against themselves. And such a drama will also mark the death of their greedy and carnivorous system. . . .
>
> This epic before us is going to be written by the hungry Indian masses, the peasants without land, the exploited workers. It is going to be written by the progressive masses, the honest and brilliant intellectuals, who so greatly abound in our suffering Latin American countries. Struggles of masses and ideas. An epic which will be carried forward by our people. . . .
>
> Already they can be seen armed with stones, sticks, machetes, in one direction and another, each day, occupying lands, sinking hooks into the land which belongs to them and defending it with their lives. They can be seen carrying signs, slogans, flags; letting them flap in the mountain or prairie winds. And the wave of anger, of demands for justice, of claims for rights, which is beginning to sweep the lands of Latin America, will not stop. That wave will swell with every passing day. For that wave is composed of the greatest number, the majorities in every respect, those whose labor amasses the wealth and turns the wheels of history. Now they are awakening from the long, brutalizing sleep to which they had been subjected.
>
> *For this great mass of humanity has said, "enough!"*

The "Second Declaration of Havana" was not exactly a Stalinist speech.

A few weeks later, in March 1962, Castro laid bare, in a public speech, the bureaucratic maneuvering of PSP hack Aníbal Escalante. He sharply pulled the rug out from under Escalante's schemes to turn the fused organization, the Integrated Revolutionary Organizations, into a replica of Stalin's bureaucratized Communist Party. He denounced Escalante's machine, administered by Stalinist gauleiters rather than working-class militants. He called for a struggle against the problems of bureaucratic abuse, of privileged layers seizing control of the state apparatus for their own purposes.

Comrade Wohlforth discounts the importance of the denunciation and removal of Escalante, saying this "was not a move against the whole of the Stalinist group which had fused with Castro but only a small section of it. The rest of the Stalinists played it safe and supported Castro against Escalante."

But that was Castro's goal! To split the former PSPers and drive out the most unregenerate Moscow hacks who thought the new organization was and should be *Stalinist*, not revolutionary.

Cuba's solidarity with Vietnam

Let's look at Cuba's foreign policy. If the Castro leadership was Stalinist from 1961 on, it is hard to explain their line on some rather important issues.

The Cuban leadership responded to Washington's brutal destruction of Vietnam by doing everything they could to aid the Vietnamese revolution. They saw that the war in Vietnam tied the hands of American imperialism, and gave Cuba a breathing space within which to battle the devastating effects of the economic blockade and cope with the problems it accentuated. The Cuban response to American aggression in Vietnam was qualitatively different from the response of Moscow or Peking. Guevara's famous call for "two, three, many Vietnams" summed this up. The Cubans offered to send troops to fight in Vietnam, but this move was rejected by the Vietnamese Stalinist leadership.

From their own experiences on the vulnerable front lines of the world revolution, the Cubans knew that only decisive action and a united front between the Soviet Union and China could prevent the imperialists from waging their war of devastation against the people of Indochina. They repeatedly demanded this of Moscow and Peking.

In March 1965, right after the U.S. began intensive bombing of North Vietnam, Fidel made a speech at the University of Havana, later published under the title, "Division in the Face of the Enemy Was Never a Revolutionary or Intelligent Strategy." In it, he explained Cuba's view on the Vietnamese revolution, and the treachery of both Moscow and Peking in the face of the imperialist escalation of the war:

> This enemy, not here, but thousands of miles from here, is attacking other countries as it is criminally attacking the people of North Vietnam and the revolutionary people of South Vietnam.
>
> This enemy is intervening in the Congo. It sends its ships, its marines, and its planes to any corner of the world. It takes advantage of divisions among the revolutionaries, of the lamentable divisions that exist in the socialist camp. Unfortunately they calculate, analyze, and take advantage of everything that can weaken the revolutionary front.
>
> That is to say that circumstances exist that involve dangers for us all, for us and for other nations in other parts of the world that fight for their independence and freedom. Dangers are not lacking.
>
> I am not going to speak at length about the problems related to the differences and divisions in the socialist camp. We don't even know when we may have to speak of this at length, because the problem is not to speak for the sake of speaking; the problem is to speak in order to say something, the problem now is to speak when, by speaking or talking or saying something, there is a positive and useful result and not a result that is positive and useful only to imperialism and the enemies of the peoples.
>
> We'd rather not have to face such bitter circumstances. As far as talk is concerned, enough and more than enough has been said already. As far as division is concerned, unfortunately, enough and more than is necessary has been said, more than suits the interests of the peoples and what, unfortunately, is useful to the interests of the enemies of the peoples.
>
> But for us, small countries, that do not base ourselves on the strength of armies of millions of men, or on the strength of atomic power, small countries like Vietnam and Cuba, we have enough instinct to see with serenity and to understand that these divisions and differences that weaken the strength of the socialist camp hurt no one more than us who are in special situations: here, ninety

miles from the Yankee empire; there, attacked by Yankee planes.

Here it's not a question of analyzing the problems under dispute theoretically or philosophically, but of recognizing the great truth: that in the face of an enemy that attacks, in the face of an enemy that becomes more and more aggressive, there is no justification for division; division doesn't make sense, there is no reason for division. . . .

And we ask ourselves whether imperialism has disappeared; we ask ourselves if the imperialists are not attacking North Vietnam; we ask ourselves whether in North Vietnam men and women of the people are not dying.

And who can be made to think or to believe that division is proper or useful? Perhaps it's not seen that the imperialists are advancing in North Vietnam? Perhaps it's not seen that the tactic the imperialists are following there is to smash the revolutionary movement in South Vietnam, attacking North Vietnam first under the pretext of the attacks being in reprisal, later arrogating to themselves the right to attack whenever they want to, and continuing to use masses of planes against the fighters of South Vietnam? . . .

And they don't hesitate in the least to declare that they propose to continue all that because even the attacks on North Vietnam have not had the effect of overcoming the divisions within the socialist family. And who doubts that this division encourages the imperialists? Who doubts that to face the enemy with a united front would make them hesitate, make them pause and think before launching their adventurous attacks and their barefaced intervention in that part of the world? Who is to be convinced of this? With what reason, with what logic? And who benefit from this? The imperialists! And who are the victims? The Vietnamese! And what suffers? The prestige of socialism, the prestige of the international communist movement, of the international revolutionary movement! And this truly hurts us! Because for us the liberation movement is not a demagogic word but a slogan that we have always felt deeply!

Because we are a small country that does not aspire to become the navel of the world; because we are a small country that does not aspire to become the revolutionary center of the world. And when we speak of these problems, we speak with absolute sincerity and we speak disinterestedly. We did not win revolutionary power in bourgeois elections but fighting weapons in hand; we speak in the name of a people who for six years irrevocably and unhesitatingly resisted the ambushes and the threats of imperialism.

We speak in the name of a people who for the sake of the strength of the revolutionary movement, for the sake of the strength of the socialist camp, for the sake of the firmness and the determination to defend the revolution against the imperialists, did not hesitate. A people who did not hesitate to risk the danger of thermonuclear war, of a nuclear attack, when in our country and on our territory—with the full and absolute right that we have never abjured, an absolutely legitimate act that we will never regret—we agreed to the installation of thermonuclear strategic missiles on our territory. And, not only did we agree that they should be brought here but we disagreed that they should be taken away. And I think that this is no secret for anyone. . . .

We don't act, as perhaps some think, as perhaps above all the imperialists think, on the basis of "when you see your neighbor's house on fire, you throw water on your own roof"—in reality, the way we act is, when we see our neighbor's house on fire, we want to share this difficulty.

We are not people to be frightened by these events; rather we are kindled to action by them. And we have one position. We are in favor of giving Vietnam all the aid that may be necessary, we are in favor of this aid being arms and men, we are in favor of the socialist camp running the risks that may be necessary for Vietnam.

We are quite aware of the fact that in case of any serious international complication we will be one of the first targets of imperialism, but this does not worry us and has never worried us. And we don't keep quiet or act like simpletons in order that our lives be spared.

This is, in all frankness and all sincerity, our reasoned, dispassionate stand, emanating from our legitimate and inviolable right to take measures and to act in the way we believe most correct and most revolutionary and let no one harbor the illusion that they can give us lessons on revolution.

I hope that errors of underestimation not be made, ignoring the peculiarities of our people, because Yankee imperialism has committed lots of errors of this kind. One of its characteristics was disdain for others, disdain for and underestimation of small nations. And imperialism has committed great colossal errors of underestimation in respect to our revolutionary people. It would be regrettable if others committed similar errors. Our sincere policy has been, and is that of uniting, because we are not and will never be satellites of anyone. And in this whole problem we have taken a very dispassionate, very honest, and very sincere position.

Is that the line of counterrevolution? Of a bureaucratic caste building "socialism in one country?"

Cuban and Latin America

Second, let's look at the Cuban policy in Latin America leading up to the 1967 defeat in Bolivia and the death of Che Guevara. The objective of the Cuban leadership was to extend the Cuban revolution onto the Latin American continent. This was their concept and their goal. In January 1959, the month of the triumph over Batista, Che Guevara declared, "The revolution is not limited to the Cuban nation . . . let this be the first step toward the victory of America." This leadership was internationalist from the beginning.

This internationalism was the heart of the Second Declaration of Havana. It was the reason for the creation of the Organization of Latin American Solidarity (OLAS).

Moreover, the Castroist line was not the Stalinist line of "two-stage revolution"—i.e., one-stage counterrevolution. Castro explained this very eloquently in a discussion with some Chileans in 1966:

> . . . We explained to them that to make a revolution it is first necessary to confront imperialism: that to make a revolution, although it may not be a socialist but a bourgeois-democratic revolution, a nationalist revolution, they had to confront imperialism and they had to confront the national oligarchy.

So far, this could have been said by any Stalinist talking left. But Fidel goes on to explain:

> I told them also that I did not think that conditions in Chile permitted a revolution of that type [i.e. bourgeois-democratic] and that in the conditions of Chile, if a revolution was desired, it would necessarily have to be a socialist revolution, and I explained why.
>
> Because an underdeveloped country, burdened with debts as Chile is, a country where large masses of the population live in the worst conditions, would necessarily have to strike a blow against the interests of imperialism, of the oligarchy, of big industry, of the import-export trade, and of the Bank if something was to be done, to give something to the peasant masses and to the masses of workers in the country.
>
> And also that to wage a battle against the oligarchy and against imperialism, the support of the worker and peasant masses was necessary to confront imperialism; and . . . that the masses of workers and peasants would not lend support to any bourgeois revolution, because the workers and peasants would not be willing to collaborate to serve the interests of an exploiting class.

Is that a Stalinist speaking? Is that the Menshevik line of the two-stage revolution?

There is no question that the Cuban leadership attempted to extend the revolution in Latin America. They waged a bitter factional struggle in the Latin American Communist parties against those who refused to take the revolutionary road. This culminated at the 1967 OLAS conference with Castro's condemnation of the Venezuelan CP.

The Castroists did not propose the Leninist strategy of party-building. They did not know about the method of the Transitional Program. To the Stalinist line they counterposed the strategy of guerrilla warfare. But we were on the side of the Cubans against the Stalinists.

In a desperate attempt to solve the problem of leadership, they even sent Che Guevara personally to lead the guerrilla movement in Bolivia.

We have many criticisms of the Bolivian adventure. These are political criticisms, not technical ones. They are spelled out in Joe Hansen's book under the title "The Seven Errors Made by Che Guevara." (See *Dynamics of the Cuban Revolution*, pp. 306–314.) But whatever criticisms you want to make of the Bolivian adventure, it is rather difficult to characterize it as an exercise in peaceful coexistence. That, it was not.

If anything, you can say that Cuban policy in Bolivia and elsewhere in Latin America was an attempt to repeat the process that had occurred in Cuba itself. That is, an attempt by the Cuban leadership to duplicate the revolution they themselves had made—to do it the way they had done it. Unfortunately, the circumstances were not favorable for that.

This is a mistaken policy. The Cuban revolution can't be repeated today without a higher level of consciousness than existed in the July 26 Movement. The imperialists learned lessons from the Cuban revolution also. A more powerful instrument, a Leninist party, is needed in order to bring about the overturn of capitalist property relations.

But there is quite a difference between a leadership that tries to extend the revolution using insufficient methods, and a class-collaborationist leadership that consciously tries to strangle and crush proletarian revolution to curry favor with imperialism. All the difference in the world. Our criticism of Stalinism is not that it doesn't defend the workers' interests consistently, or that it can't be relied on, or that it uses wrong methods for the right goals. No. Our opposition to Stalinism is based on different grounds.

History has spoken unambiguously: Stalinism is counterrevolutionary through and through. The Stalinists try to block and smash revolutionary initiatives, mass upsurges, anything that goes beyond the bounds of class collaboration. *Counterrevolutionary through and through*. Is that an accurate description of Che's adventure in Bolivia? Cuba's stand on Vietnam in 1965 or in 1979?

And if we say the Cuban line is Stalinist, then we have to, among other things, pretty up Stalinism. True, Stalinists can wage guerrilla war—or regular war under certain circumstances. The Red Army beat the German Nazis in a big war. In response to mass pressure in very special circumstances, they can even take the lead of revolutionary mobilizations—against their desires, in order to control them. But was there a great mass upsurge in Bolivia? Where was the pressure forcing the Cubans to wage guerrilla war in order to be able to head off and destroy a revolutionary mobilization? This is nonsense. Bolivia was an attempt to export the Cuban revolution. The methods used were mistaken. But it wasn't Stalinism.

1968: A TURNING POINT?

By the time of the December 1978 SWP plenum, Comrade Wohlforth was no longer defending his 1977 position that the degeneration of the Cuban revolution occurred in the early 1960s. He had shifted his ground and argued instead that the qualitative change set in around 1968.

According to Wohlforth: "Starting in late 1968 Castro abandoned his independent role. In foreign policy he endorsed the main outlines of peaceful coexistence and Stalinism. Internally he led the way in the consolidation of the Cuban bureaucratic caste. He is now its representative. The CCP Congress in 1975 represented the final juridical recognition of the consolidation of this caste and the establishment of the single totalitarian Stalinist party as the ruler of Cuba in the interests of this caste."

This is a point of view that has been put forward by a number of other comrades in the Fourth International, as well as many others on the left. It is based on a subjective and impressionistic reading of events. It is false.

Che Guevara was murdered in Bolivia in October 1967. The defeat of the guerrilla strategy in Bolivia and elsewhere signalled the end—for the time being—of banking everything on large-scale support by the Cubans for guerrilla war. This strategy had led to a dead end, and the Cubans pulled back from it without, however, publicly drawing the fundamental political lessons. For radicals who had become entranced with guerrillaism, and falsely equated it with revolutionary strategy, this amounted to a betrayal by the Cubans. A mood of disillusionment with the Cuban revolution spread among sections of the petty-bourgeois left.

This mood was reinforced by the Cubans' response to three major events that occurred in 1968: the prerevolutionary upsurge that shook France in May–June; the Kremlin's invasion of Czechoslovakia, to crush the incipient political revolution in August; and the bloody massacre of Mexican students by the Mexican bourgeois government in October. A series of negative signs inside Cuba in the next couple of years led many who viewed Cuba impressionistically to feel that a point of qualitative change had been reached, that the Cuban revolution had succumbed to Stalinism. This sentiment was felt most strongly by those who had held naive illusions in Castroism and who had overlooked the numerous wrong policies the Cubans had followed from the beginning. In their mood of disappointment, these radicals also became vulnerable to the incessant barrage of anti-Cuban propaganda emanating from the centers of world imperialism, and transmitted through the "radical" academic and other petty-bourgeois milieus.

Let's take a closer look at what actually happened in 1968.

When the May–June events rocked France, the Cubans expressed little interest in this historic event. French students who identified with the Cuban revolution and marched under portraits of Che Guevara felt betrayed. The Cubans didn't hail their struggle and enthusiastically defend the student radicals against the reactionary line of the French CP, intent on isolating the student movement from the working class and ending the general strike.

But the default of the Castro leadership on the May–June events didn't signal anything new. The Cuban revolutionaries had never had an understanding of or interest in the class struggle in the advanced capitalist countries. They had always been inclined toward the view that the working class in the imperialist countries would play a revolutionary role only after the revolutionary masses of the semicolonial world had defeated imperialism. From the start they repeatedly ignored openings to use their prestige and influence in the labor movement in the United States—where they could have the greatest impact. Lacking an understanding of the Leninist strategy of party building, they had no idea what revolutionists in the imperialist countries should do aside from aid guerrilla fighters in the semicolonial countries. This was one of the weaknesses that we criticized consistently from the beginning. Their wrong line on France was the continuation of an erroneous orientation—not a change in policy.

Invasion of Czechoslovakia

In August 1968 the Soviet army invaded Czechoslovakia. Castro made a speech that, while containing sharp criticisms of Kremlin policies on a number of questions, apologized for what he himself termed the "flagrant violation of Czech sovereignty." In Castro's view the invasion was an unfortunate necessity to checkmate counterrevolutionary moves by imperialism. Thus he provided left cover to the Stalinist crushing of the "Prague Spring."

But that is not all there is to be said on this point. First, we have to note that nothing about this wrong stand confirms the thesis of a qualitative change beginning in 1968. If the Soviets had invaded Czechoslovakia earlier—in 1967, or 1965, or 1964—is there any reason to think the Cuban line would have been different?

Second, Castro's speech must be placed in the context of the confrontation with the Soviet Union that had just occurred a few months previously around the second Escalante affair.

In 1962 Escalante had been sent into exile in Prague. When he returned in 1964 he was given a job on a state farm, from whence he proceeded to organize according to his custom as a hardened Stalinist hack.

In January 1968 a special three-day meeting of the Central Committee of the Communist Party expelled Escalante. He and thirty-five others were turned over to the courts for prosecution and given long prison terms.

It was not a very democratic procedure, either from the viewpoint of the norms of Leninist party democracy or Cuban law, which does not ban factional activity. This was criticized by supporters of the Cuban revolution.

But of interest to us here is the question, What was the second Escalante affair all about? He was already so discredited, it is hard to believe he constituted a significant threat. Something far more serious was involved: Soviet attempts to build their own reliable Stalinist base inside the Cuban CP. A second secretary of the Soviet embassy was charged with involvement in the Escalante "microfaction" and expelled from Cuba.

In retaliation for the Escalante affair, the Soviet Union in early 1968 reduced its aid commitments to Cuba—at a time when the economic effects of the imperialist blockade and errors in planning were taking a heavier and heavier toll on the Cuban population.

This also coincided with the dispute over "armed struggle" versus "peaceful road" in Latin America, in which Moscow and Havana were the main antagonists.

Is it credible to believe that six months after this showdown with the Kremlin over attempts to organize inside the Cuban party, Castro had abandoned his previous course and become a Stalinist?

Third, any nagging doubts on this score can be eliminated with a careful reading of the speech Castro made to explain the Cuban leadership's position on the invasion of Czechoslovakia.

After acknowledging that—even with his critical support for the invasion—"some of the things that we are going to state here . . . will constitute serious risks for our country," Castro went on to passage after passage of open, blistering attacks on the kind of "socialism" that exists in the Eastern European countries, and on the "peaceful coexistence" policies of the Soviet Union.

To take but one of many examples, Castro explained to the Cuban people:

> In the socialist countries, peace has been incessantly and widely preached. And we ask ourselves, what are all these campaigns leading up to? Do we say this because we are in favor of war? Do we say this because we are the enemies of peace?
>
> We are not the enemies of peace; we are not in favor of wars; we do not advocate universal holocausts. I feel obliged to say this because when we analyze these questions, right away it always brings up the cliche, the schemata, the accusations of warmongering, of promoting war, of being irresponsible, and so on and so forth. . . .
>
> The real promoters of war, the real adventurers, are the imperialists. Now, then, these dangers are real; they are a reality. And this reality cannot be changed by simply preaching, in one's own house, an excessive desire for peace. . . .
>
> That is why we who at the beginning did so many foolish things out of ignorance or naivete, for a long time have not painted any signs around here saying "Long Live Peace," "Long Live This," "Long Live That."
>
> Because at the beginning, out of mimicry, by imitation, we repeated things as they arrived here, until we reached a point, well, what is the meaning of "Long Live Peace"? Let's put up that sign in New York: "Long Live Peace" in New York, "Long Live Peace" in Washington.

Is that a Stalinist talking? Is that proof of Castro's commitment to seek peaceful coexistence with American imperialism?

Is it any wonder that speech was never printed in Moscow?

The Tlatelolco massacre

You can't find in the events of 1968 evidence of a qualitative change in the positions of the Cuban leadership unless you gloss over the errors that came before 1968. Cuba's attitude toward the 1968 Tlatelolco massacre in Mexico is a clear example of this.

The line of the Castro leadership toward the Mexican bourgeois regime was the same in 1968 as it had been since 1960. When the hangman's noose of the imperialist blockade was being pulled tighter and tighter around Cuba, the Mexican government refused to break diplomatic and trade relations. Mexico became the only country in Latin America that maintained ties with revolutionary Cuba.

The Cuban leadership never publicly criticized the Mexican government. They subordinated public denunciation of violations of democratic rights and other questions to maintaining their link with Mexico. We could debate whether or not they could have found some way out of this uncomfortable dilemma in the early 1960s, but it would be hard to characterize this general diplomatic stance as counterrevolutionary.

The greater problem comes from the fact that the Cubans have never differentiated between government-to-government diplomatic relations—and positions taken by the Cuban Communist Party or the party's individual leaders. Thus Castro serves both as prime minister and the head of the party. Seeing no need to distinguish between diplomatic needs and political positions, the Cubans in effect expressed political confidence in Mexico's capitalist government. In 1978 they made a similar error in relation to the Spanish government, which our comrades in Spain were correct in criticizing.

The Cuban leadership's silence on the 1968 massacre was an error, a continuation of that incorrect policy. It was not a new departure.

Negative developments inside Cuba

The international events of 1968 were followed by some negative developments inside Cuba. In the face of worsening economic conditions, social tensions were on the rise. First and foremost the problems were the result of the economic blockade, not the mistakes of the Castro leadership.

The most stunning thing about Comrade Wohlforth's report for the NC minority to the December 1978 plenum is that he failed to *mention* the imperialist blockade *even one time*, let alone fit it into his analysis of the economic or political problems or development of the Cuban revolution. This omission speaks volumes about Wohlforth's approach to the Cuban revolution, and why his frame of reference is so badly bent.

We start with the effects of imperialism's war against Cuba. We add to it the Soviet refusal to provide aid without limit and without restrictions, something clearly within its resources to do.

These problems were compounded by errors of the Castro leadership boldly but desperately seeking to leap over more rapidly than feasible the legacy of economic backwardness created by imperialism. One of the mistakes with the most far-reaching repercussions in this period was the campaign to harvest 10 million tons of sugar in 1970, which failed badly and produced dislocations throughout the economy.

As a result, inside Cuba there were increasing economic difficulties. Lines at stores got longer. Rations had to be cut. Things did not seem to be moving forward.

It was in this context that the scandalous Padilla affair took place.

Heberto Padilla, one of Cuba's best-known poets, was jailed in March 1971, on unspecified charges. A few weeks later, a debasing self-criticism appeared in his name, denouncing his own work. Artists and intellectuals who had supported the revolution were shocked at this violation of the norms of artistic freedom that the Cuban revolution had established. Many spoke up to condemn the treatment of Padilla. Castro himself lashed out at them, calling them enemies of the revolution.

The acute economic problems of the years 1968–71 coincided with the decision by the Castro leadership to pull back from the fiasco of the guerrilla strategy for extending the revolution. But it was not until the victory of the Vietnamese liberation forces and the collapse of the Portuguese empire in Africa brought about a significant shift in the relationship of class forces on a world scale and important new openings to advance the world revolution that the Cuban masses could see a new path of action along which to move. When that happened the Castro leadership, in typical fashion, moved decisively into the breach. As Castro said, the role of Job doesn't suit a revolutionist.

The lack of perspective reinforced negative trends in Cuba toward seeking individual solutions rather than collectively fighting to extend the revolution. The pressures of more than a decade of revolutionary struggle against heavy odds had taken an inevitable toll. Conservatism and bureaucratism, constant enemies of the revolution, gained impetus. This is not a mystical process. Daily existence for the masses in Cuba is rough. It was rougher in 1968–71. If the perspective of breaking out of the imperialist encirclement, of extending the revolution seems to be pushed off to the indefinite future, degenerative pressures are accelerated. People can get demoralized. They can turn toward thinking simply about their own future and that of their family above everything else. They can worry about getting a good position for their children. These things affect revolutionaries as well. We've seen that ourselves in the revolutionary movement. Even in our own party we've seen what happens when there don't seem to be a lot of openings, when there is no clear perspective for how to move forward.

But we can say sharply and definitively that whatever the negative trends and pressures were in Cuba in those years, they did not become dominant. There is simply no evidence that they gave rise to a massive growth and institutionalization of bureaucratic privilege such as exists in every other workers state.

That there are privileges and abuses is incontestable. But that is not the same thing as a crystallized bureaucratic caste that places the securing and expansion of its material benefits in the arena of consumption ahead of the interests of the Cuban masses. What the Cuban masses need more than anything is the extension of the world socialist revolution. And their line of proletarian internationalism, not peace and security and détente, is what sets the Cuban leadership off from all others in the workers states.

There have been no purges of the old guard revolutionary leadership, as indeed there must be if a counterrevolutionary caste is to establish its preeminence in Cuba.

Events like the Padilla affair have not been repeated. No Stalinist-style regime of thought control and brutal repression has been installed. The Cuban leadership has never openly acknowledged any errors in relation to the Padilla case, but it is clear that the Padilla episode did not signal the beginning of a wave of repression and intimidation of artists and intellectuals.

AFRICA: A DECISIVE TEST

The imperialists hoped to transform the Cubans' pause for reflection on the international arena into a right turn to "peaceful coexistence." They hoped that Castro would be tamed. They hoped they could bring Cuba into the framework of détente, exchanging improved trade and diplomatic relations, an end to the blockade, for Cuba's abandonment of the attempt to extend the revolution. But the imperialists have not succeeded.

When the new opportunity presented itself—in Africa—the response of the Cuban leadership was to seize it with both hands, to *act* to push forward the revolution in Black Africa. Far from responding like Stalinists, the Castro leadership gave unambiguous evidence of their continued revolutionary perspectives, audacity and intransigence.

In 1974, direct talks began in secret between the United States and Cuba. Washington made a significant concession as bait. They lifted part of the trade embargo, allowing subsidiaries of U.S. corporations abroad to trade with Cuba. They held out the promise of normalization of relations, which would mean above all an end to the blockade. All they wanted was for the Cubans to abandon their independent course and, like the counterrevolutionary regimes in Moscow and Peking, join in détente.

But the Cubans didn't buy it. They took the initiative to send troops to Angola to bloody the nose of the U.S.-backed South African imperialist army. They refused to retreat from their support for the Puerto Rican independence movement—a major concern of Washington.

In November 1975, Washington told the Cubans point blank, in private, that continuation of their revolutionary activities in Africa would put an end to the "normalization" talks. The Cubans told the Yankees we won't deal.

In response, President Ford stated publicly that Cuban actions in Africa and their continued support for the Puerto Rican independence movement "precluded any improvement in relations with Cuba and ended any efforts to have friendlier relations with Cuba." Washington's military threats against Cuba escalated. Castro reaffirmed in response that revolutionary Cuba would never negotiate away its right as a sovereign nation to pursue its own policies and to advance the revolutionary struggle against imperialism as Cuba saw fit. The Cubans had made a revolution so that they wouldn't be subjected to the dictates of Washington and they didn't see any reason to trade away what they had shed their blood to win.

As Castro explained to American journalist Barbara Walters in a long discussion-interview in 1977, "In actual fact, we feel very free, very free. We have no economic ties with the United States; we have the blockade on top of us; and, really, we have no reason to wonder if any part of our international policy is agreeable to the United States or not."

To many who had impressionistically concluded that Havana was heading down the road to détente, the refusal of the Cuban leadership to abandon their Africa policy and cooperate with the U.S.

came as something of a surprise. For several years comrades David Keil and Scott Cooper in the SWP, for example, have been submitting contributions to the internal discussion bulletin predicting Havana's imminent formal capitulation to Washington.

In August 1975, these comrades wrote: The blockade is "being dismantled" and the "Castro leadership [is] putting its faith in Ford, Kissinger and Company." (SWP DB, Vol. 33, No. 14.) This was just before the U.S.-Cuban talks broke off.

That fall, in October 1975, they asserted again, "Cuba is now in the process of completing a long diplomatic process of semi-negotiation, soon to become direct negotiation, with the U.S. imperialists, which will likely end up leaving no doubt about the Stalinist nature of the Cuban leadership." (International Internal Discussion Bulletin, Vol. XII, No. 5.) This prediction turned out to be 100 percent wrong.

In July 1976, these comrades were forced to admit that their confident predictions had not been borne out. They wrote, "Hoping for a way to join the détente by apple-polishing, Castro praised Gerald Ford and Henry Kissinger as great peace-lovers in a 1974 interview . . . The civil war in Angola intervened, however, to put an end to the U.S.-Cuban diplomatic feelers."

What a delicate way to put it: "The civil war in Angola intervened." No. *Cuba* intervened to drive the South African army out of the civil war in Angola.

"Now," concluded Keil and Cooper, "the newspapers are reporting developments that indicate Castro and the U.S. will move toward friendlier terms . . . Now we will see if the U.S. is ready for detente with Cuba. Castro has always been ready for detente with the U.S."

More than two and a half years after "the newspapers" were predicting the United States and Cuba were on the verge of détente—we're still waiting. The very least that these comrades ought to do is to write a brief explanation of why they were so wrong, why they gave so much credence to the line "the newspapers" were peddling.

The African revolution began making big gains at a time when the legacy of Vietnam and the deepening radicalization of the American working class in this country increasingly limited the ability of U.S. imperialism to intervene directly. The Cubans correctly sized this up and moved decisively to advance the anti-imperialist struggle in Africa.

In January 1977, the Colombian author Gabriel García Márquez published a long article on the Cuban role in Angola, based on numerous interviews conducted in Cuba. His account of the factors weighed by the Cuban leadership and how they arrived at their decision to respond to the Angolan government's request, in late October 1975, for help to turn back the South African invasion, is instructive.

> The possibility that the United States might intervene openly, rather than through the mercenaries and South Africa as it had been doing for some time, was obviously one of the most disturbing unknowns. But a rapid analysis suggested that at least Washington would think twice about doing so:
> It had just freed itself from the morass of Vietnam and the Watergate scandal. It had a President no one had elected. The CIA was under fire in Congress and low-rated by public opinion. The United States needed to avoid seeming—not only in the eyes of African countries, but especially in the eyes of American blacks—to ally itself with racist South Africa. Beyond all this it was in the midst of an election campaign in its Bicentennial year.
> Furthermore, Cuba was sure it could count on solidarity and material aid from the Soviet Union and other Socialist countries, although it was also aware of the implications its action might hold for the policy of peaceful coexistence and international detente.
> It was a decision of irreversible consequences, too large and complex to be resolved in 24 hours. Nonetheless, the leadership of the Communist Party of Cuba had only 24 hours to decide, and it decided without flinching, in a large, calm meeting on Nov. 5. Far from what has so often been said, it was an independent and sovereign act of Cuba. Only after the decision was made, not before, was the Soviet Union informed. (See *Intercontinental Press*, Jan. 31, 1977.)

As in Latin America in the 1960s, the Cubans made a bold move. They took an initiative which carried a big chance of provoking U.S. reprisals against Cuba. They didn't know what Washington would do. They didn't know how far Washington would go in escalating its threats against Cuba. But that has never stopped the Cuban leadership from acting in accordance with their view of their responsibilities to the world revolution.

Castro spelled this out nearly fifteen years ago, on July 26, 1965:

> As the revolutionary movement develops in Latin America, the imperialists will blame us more and more. As the revolutionary movement develops in Latin America, the threats and dangers will increase. But we will not tell the peoples of Latin America because of that, 'Wait don't make the revolution, because it will endanger us.' No. We exhort the revolutionists of Latin America to struggle! We exhort the revolutionists of Latin America to follow our example, and we readily run the risk. We show the peoples of Latin America the possibility of Revolution, and the threats and the dangers and risks don't bother us.
>
> Naturally we don't want the fruit of our efforts destroyed, naturally. We have worked arduously for the wellbeing of our country, for the security of our country, for the future of our country, but we are not afraid of the danger because of that, we don't flee from the dangers because of that. Although Cuba runs a risk, although the imperialists menace us, we want the Revolution, we want the liberation of the peoples of Latin America; we don't stop to look at our triumphs in an egoistic way; we don't stop to enjoy our triumphs in an egoistic way; we want the peoples of Latin America to have the same triumphs as us; we want the peoples of Latin America to follow our example. . . .

The response of the Cuban leadership to the new openings in Africa a decade later in 1975 proved beyond a doubt that their attitude to extending the revolution had not changed.

The Cuban army made the decisive difference in driving the invading South African imperialist forces out of Angola. In doing so, Havana struck a blow not for a privileged caste in Cuba, but for the African revolution, for the world revolution, for the Cuban working masses. The defeat of the South African invasion helped spur the revolutionary struggle in southern Africa. And the Cubans' actions against the apartheid regime won support for the Cuban revolution among the African masses.

The revolution in Ethiopia

Within the framework of the African upsurge came the Ethiopian revolution. The feudal monarchy of Haile Selassie was overturned in 1974 as a result of massive mobilizations of workers, peasants, soldiers, and students. The Ethiopian revolution, a *social* revolution, registered historic gains: a far-reaching agrarian reform; a drive to eliminate all the hangovers of feudalism and slavery; a series of nationalizations—of credit, banking, public utilities, natural resources, and some industry; the separation of church and state; and the spread of primary education as part of the mass campaign against illiteracy.

The Cubans supported that revolution. They have exactly the same political stance that we do on the need to defend that revolution against any and all attempts by imperialism or its clients to stop it or to drive it back. And they *acted* on it. This was confirmed by the Cuban army's role in beating back the Somali regime's imperialist-backed invasion of the eastern part of the Ethiopian state.

Starting from the contending class forces on a world scale, the Cubans understood that the struggle for national and social liberation in Ethiopia and the Horn of Africa is a confrontation between the toiling masses of the region and world imperialism, which has enormous stakes in that strategic area, and indeed on the entire African continent.

The Cubans correctly sized up the invasion by the army of Somalia as a military thrust by the Siad Barre regime aimed not at liberating the Somali people of the Ogaden, nor at overthrowing the Dergue in the interests of the workers and peasants, but at reversing the Ethiopian revolution. They saw through the demagogic claims of Siad Barre that his goal was the "national liberation" of the Somali people.

The Somali regime claimed title to four provinces with a population of seven and a half million people, only one and a half million of them of the

Somali nationality. The Somalian army invaded provinces inhabited by a majority of non-Somalis. They attacked the predominantly non-Somali cities of Harar and Diredawa. Officers of the Western Somali Liberation Front, which was backed by and partially composed of regular Somali army troops, had announced their intention to drive to within a few miles of Addis Ababa, the Ethiopian capital—far beyond the Ogaden. The Somali invasion was not, by intention or objectively, a national liberation struggle. It was an action carried out by a semicolonial capitalist government in the interests of imperialism and with imperialist backing.

Had the Somali regime's army not been driven back with the decisive help of the Cuban armed forces, it would have been a setback not only to the Ethiopian revolution but to the Somali people—both in the Ogaden and in Somalia. This is the unavoidable fact: a victory for the Somali regime would have strengthened the hold of imperialism throughout the Horn of Africa—and it is imperialism that is the most potent enemy of national self-determination for the Somali people. It was not the Cuban soldiers who were "betraying" the Somali national liberation struggle, but the Somalian regime of Siad Barre, and the Western Somali Liberation Front which supported the invasion.

Only if the Ethiopian workers and peasants drive their revolution forward to a socialist transformation of society—only if Ethiopia follows the Cuban road—can the gains of the Ethiopian masses be consolidated and advanced.

Cuba and Eritrea

Comrades who hold that Havana's foreign policy is the same as that of the Kremlin have pointed to the Cubans' role in Eritrea as definitive proof. But this "proof" falls apart under examination.

In contrast to their military intervention in the Ethiopia-Somalia war, the Cubans decided not to use their troops in the Dergue's reactionary offensive against the Eritrean independence struggle. The bourgeois press has published numerous accusations that the Cuban troops were, in fact, involved in the Dergue's military campaign that began in the second half of 1978, and which led to a major military defeat for the Eritrean forces. The Dergue itself has tried to give that impression. However, the evidence is overwhelming that the Cuban troops did not take part.

The Cubans themselves have repeatedly denied any military involvement. Since they have not been bashful about openly proclaiming their military role in repelling the Somalian invasion, and earlier in Angola, there is no reason to doubt the truthfulness of their statements. When the mass military offensive began in mid-November, the Eritrean People's Liberation Front dropped all mention of Cuban involvement while sharply escalating its condemnation of Moscow's military role. Even the U.S. State Department admitted on November 30 that it had no evidence that Cubans were involved in the fighting in Eritrea.

Moreover, the Cubans have politically differentiated themselves from both Moscow and the Dergue on the question of Eritrea, insisting on a political, not military solution. Cuban Vice-president Carlos Rafael Rodríguez summed up the Cubans' political position in late 1978, saying, "We helped the Eritreans in their fight for self-determination from the time of Haile Selassie onward. We feel there has to be some political solution to the Eritrean problem and there have to be talks between Eritreans and the central government." While *Pravda* waxed euphoric over the Dergue's military successes in the recent offensive, the Cubans' *Granma* said not a word about them.

The decision by Havana to take a dramatically different stand toward Eritrea from that held by Moscow and the Dergue came despite immense pressure from the Kremlin—to whom the Cubans' stance is politically embarrassing—and from the Dergue, which hoped to dress up its reactionary policy with the revolutionary mantle of the Cuban revolution.

At the same time, however, the Cuban government has spoken out against the right of the Eritreans to establish an independent state. This position not only weakens the Ethiopian revolution—which can not move forward on the backs of the Eritrean masses—it also injures the Cuban revolution and the anti-imperialist objectives it is fighting for in Africa.

The Cubans' wrong line on Eritrea is closely related to their mistaken and harmful policy of giving almost uncritical political support to the Mengistu leadership of the Dergue. Whether or not they actually agree with all of the Dergue's policies, they publicly adulate Ethiopia's rulers, hailing Mengistu as a "great revolutionary." The Cubans made the same kind of political error in Angola. They give political support to the Neto regime there, although the MPLA government is capitalist and has brutally repressed all independent working class mobilization.

This erroneous political stance toward petty-bourgeois nationalist regimes under fire from imperialism is not some new departure. It goes back to the very origins of the Castro current as a petty-bourgeois nationalist movement themselves and the political weaknesses they have never overcome: their failure to understand the need for a united front in action against imperialism while at the same time maintaining political independence and a clear working-class political line.

What is involved here are the contradictions, limitations, and political errors of Castroism, which are an obstacle to the development of a consistent proletarian program and strategy for the revolutionary vanguard. But it is not the same thing as the counterrevolutionary policy of Stalinism.

Stalinists are not only enemies of the socialist revolution, they are also enemies of the anti-imperialist revolution because it upsets the status quo and poses a danger, to them, of passing over into the socialist revolution. They know that well. They hate uncontrolled forces in motion, especially workers and peasants. They bloc with the bourgeoisie in order to hold back the independent struggle of the workers and peasants, prevent them from passing over to socialist revolution.

The Cuban policy toward the Dergue and other similar regimes, on the other hand, while politically erroneous and extremely disorienting and dangerous, is not based on the thoroughly counterrevolutionary interests of a crystallized bureaucratic caste trying to block the extension of the revolution.

The difference between Castroism and Stalinism in Africa today can nowhere be seen more clearly than in the character and role of the Cuban army.

The world has never seen the Stalinist bureaucracy in Moscow use the Soviet army the way the Cubans are using theirs in Africa. Only forces trained and inspired to act as proletarian internationalists could do that. And there is nothing the Kremlin fears more. They use the Red Army only as a border guard to defend the base of their own privileges. The Cubans are doing exactly the opposite.

The gigantic test of Africa also tells us some things about what has been going on inside Cuba. For example, thousands of doctors and teachers are today serving in Africa. They are seen as the most exemplary of revolutionaries, to be emulated by every man, woman, and child.

What about the army? As Trotsky pointed out in the *Revolution Betrayed*, the "army is only a copy of social relations." Every enlisted soldier fighting in Africa is a reservist who volunteered to join the battle in response to appeals channeled through the neighborhood Committees for the Defense of the Revolution. Volunteers.

What is more, a majority of those volunteers are Black, going to Africa because they are willing to shed their blood to accomplish in Africa what the Cuban revolution accomplished in Cuba. That's what they are fighting for. The Castro regime has appealed to the Cuban masses to join this revolutionary struggle in Africa, to extend the revolution. It has placed special emphasis on the common heritage that Afro-Cubans have with their African brothers and sisters.

Is this characteristic of Stalinism? To appeal to the oppressed nationalities? To mobilize them to fight to extend the revolution? Can you imagine the Kremlin raising a volunteer army of Ukrainians, Tatars and Azerbaijanis? Stalin tightened the bureaucratic visegrip on Soviet society by appealing to Great-Russian chauvinism, as he appealed to every backward idea and prejudice he could find.

That is the opposite of what is happening in Cuba today.

IF NOT STALINIST, THEN CENTRIST?

In the course of the discussion on Cuba, some comrades who agree that the Castro leadership is not Stalinist have raised the question, "Wouldn't it be accurate to call them centrist?"

In a loose way, of course, we can say that the Castro current is somewhere between revolutionary Marxism and counterrevolutionary Stalinism. But that isn't very useful. It doesn't help orient us politically. As is usually the case, behind the question of terminology is not so much a theoretical debate as a question of political line.

In several decisive aspects, the term "centrist" does not fit the Cuban leadership. Most importantly, no centrist current that has ever existed could have done what the Castro team has done in Cuba: lead the workers and peasants to power, bring about a socialist transformation of society, politically and militarily checkmate the most powerful imperialist power the world has ever known, and fight to extend the revolution for twenty years.

Centrist groupings are unstable and usually short-lived. They are vulnerable to pressures that tear them apart as they are driven either from the camp of reformism in the direction of proletarian revolution; or, under pressure from imperialism, away from the revolutionary movement toward reformism. They fly apart under the conflicting pressures of where they are coming from and where they are going.

The Castro leadership team has been in power some twenty years. It was forged as a political current somewhat earlier. If we were to adopt the term centrist to describe them, we would have to say that it is a highly peculiar kind of centrism at best. The central core of the leadership team around Castro has remained remarkably stable. There have been no splits, no purges. With the exception of Che Guevara and Camilo Cienfuegos, both of whom were killed battling for the revolution, the central leadership team remains the same, virtually to a person. What is more important, as we have seen, their line has remained remarkably consistent. The same strengths and weaknesses, the same contradictory aspects that marked their line twenty years ago mark their line today.

This poses another problem. If we agree that centrists couldn't have led the Cuban working class to power, then we have to conclude that they at least began as revolutionists. But if there has been no break in the continuity of their positions, when did they cease being revolutionists and become centrists?

If we were to decide they are now centrists, we would have to go back and undo what we said and wrote about the Cuban revolution from the beginning and explain why we were wrong. Or we would have to try to pinpoint a qualitative change from revolutionary to centrist, which doesn't match the facts.

There is a second characteristic of centrism that doesn't fit. Trotsky explained that centrists use plenty of revolutionary phraseology and radical rhetoric, but they pull up short of revolutionary decisions and revolutionary action. They are, he said, willing to talk about mass revolutionary action, but their real arena remains the parliament. They don't take their stated revolutionary positions seriously enough to act on them. The practical conclusions for action are never drawn or implemented. This is what we mean when we say that centrists tend to "talk left and act right." It is what Trotsky was referring to when he said that centrists are characterized by "halfheartedness."

The last word you could use to describe the Cuban leadership is "halfhearted." It just doesn't fit. The Cubans *say* and *do* the same thing. They *act* on their stated program. We don't always agree with what they do, but they don't say one thing and then do another. That sets them off from almost any kind of centrists we can think of.

They take their ideas seriously. They are not afraid to act, or take the consequences of their actions. The men and women of Moncada, of the *Granma*, of the Sierra Maestra, of the Bay of Pigs, of the missile crisis, of Bolivia, of Africa—they are men and women of revolutionary action, the kind that Trotsky said we would have more and more of in our epoch.

The Cubans are also irreconcilable enemies of imperialism. They don't bend. They don't buckle. In twenty years they have not conceded an inch to U.S. imperialism. And that also is not characteristic of centrism—especially when you understand what it means to be in power in a small country subject to incredible pressure from the American colossus.

Our party, and the Fourth International as a whole, have from the beginning characterized the Cuban leaders not as centrists, but as revolutionaries.

For example, the theses "On the Nature of the Cuban Revolution" adopted by the International Secretariat in 1960, before reunification of the world movement, referred to the "genesis, training, formation, and coming to maturity of a new revolutionary leadership," and remarked that "the most original element, in a revolution that is nevertheless so original in many aspects, is that for the first time a capitalist regime has been overthrown by a movement whose leadership was not linked up with the traditional workers' parties or influenced by the Soviet bureaucracy." (IIDB, Vol. XIV, No. 5, May 1977.)

Likewise the "Draft Theses on the Cuban Revolution" adopted by the SWP National Committee in December 1960 repeatedly refer to the Castro current as a "revolutionary leadership." (*Dynamics of the Cuban Revolution*, p. 97.)

If we were wrong we should jettison that label, but we should do so consciously and explain that it represents a shift, not a continuity with our previous analyses.

In our opinion, the term revolutionary is more accurate, and a better political guide. We don't think that card-carrying members of the Fourth International are the only revolutionaries in the world. There are revolutionary currents that arise outside the Fourth International. Naturally, forces that arise outside of our ranks, like the Castroist current, will not begin as Leninists or Trotskyists. Our job is to strive to win them to revolutionary Marxism, to a consistently revolutionary policy.

The Bolsheviks dealt with the question when they were trying to assemble the forces for the Third International. They invited to the founding congresses of the Communist International delegations from currents such as the Industrial Workers of the World (the Wobblies), the Shop Stewards Movement in Britain, and similar groupings from other countries. Lenin and the other leaders of the Communist International quite consciously and deliberately referred to these as revolutionary currents. Lenin was not light-minded. He didn't disparage the importance of precise terminology. He deliberately referred to them as revolutionaries as a way of defining a political stance toward them. He sharply distinguished them from the centrists, against whom Lenin urged an all-out war, to draw the line sharply and definitively between Bolshevism and centrism.

The Wobblies shared some of the strengths and weaknesses displayed by the Cuban revolutionaries. Their great strength was that they were determined fighters, uncompromising foes of the capitalists, with nothing but contempt for their courts, political parties, and legislatures. But they made all sorts of political mistakes. They rejected Marxism for syndicalist and anarchist ideas. They adapted to all kinds of petty-bourgeois ideas under the influence of agrarian populist movements. They had a losing strategy. No one was under the illusion that the Wobblies were Marxists. But for Lenin, what was decisive was the possibility of influencing revolutionary fighters and winning the best of them to the Communist International.

Imagine what his attitude would have been to an independent current that, whatever its limitations and errors, actually led the workers and peasants to seize power and overthrow capitalism, then defended and fought to extend the revolution for 20 years?

A WORKERS STATE WITH BUREAUCRATIC DEFORMATIONS

In his report to the December 1978 plenum, Comrade Wohlforth said that the "majority owes the party a positive description of how they see Cuba today. They certainly, I hope, do not claim it is today exactly what it was 17 years ago." On this we can agree.

At the time we recognized that a workers state had been established in Cuba, we noted that this was true despite the absence of democratic institutions of proletarian rule. The lack of workers councils posed a gigantic challenge and a problem to the Cuban revolution. Only through institutions of proletarian democracy can the working class and the peasantry be mobilized effectively to defend the revolution against its enemies, and to grapple with the tremendous problems inherited from the era of imperialist domination. This is not a moral question. It would not simply be "nice" to have soviets in Cuba. It is essential to the successful defense and healthy development of the revolution that the power of the masses be brought to bear through democratic proletarian forms.

In selecting the terms to describe Cuba, we rejected use of "deformed workers state." There certainly were deformations of workers democracy in Cuba. But in the political dictionary of our movement the term "deformed workers state" is both descriptive and programmatic. It is synonymous with the recognition that the state is controlled by a crystallized bureaucratic caste that must be overthrown through a political revolution.

As Joe Hansen put it in his article, "What the

Discussion on Cuba is About," we qualify the designation of Cuba as a workers state by adding that it is "'one lacking as yet the forms of democratic proletarian rule,' meaning that while it is not 'deformed' in the sense of having Stalinists in power, the state is not under the democratic control of the workers and peasants. . . ." (*Dynamics of the Cuban Revolution,* p. 171.) Using the term "deformed workers state" would signify to the ranks of the Trotskyist movement around the world that we believe a political revolution in Cuba is necessary. That is why we rejected, and continue to reject, that designation.

In 1961, when we used the descriptive phrase, a workers state "lacking as yet the forms of democratic proletarian rule," the "as yet" indicated our assessment that such forms might emerge relatively quickly. Today, we have to modify that description. The "forms of democratic proletarian rule" still do not exist. But the "as yet" is out of date. A number of institutional structures have been set up. These include legislative bodies, organs of "popular power," the Communist Party of Cuba, and others. None of these institutions fill the gap. None of them are soviet bodies of proletarian democracy in the Leninist sense.

We have also seen negative danger signs, such as the introduction of ranks into the armed forces. However, as we have already discussed, there is no indication that the development and institutionalization of privileges has reached the point of a qualitative change.

For this reason, we think the most accurate description of Cuba today is: a workers state with bureaucratic deformations. This means that a political fight has to be waged against bureaucratism and privilege and for the institutionalization of proletarian democracy, but it does not imply the need to organize the workers of Cuba to forcibly overthrow the Castro leadership. Under the impact of revolutionary developments on a world scale, the door to reform remains open.

Building a revolutionary Marxist party

Finally, Comrade Wohlforth asks the question, "Concretely how do we see a section of the Fourth International constructed in Cuba? I understand the comrades favor construction of such a section. If this is more than mere words, they must have some idea of how such a section is to be built and what political approach it should take towards the single existing government party in Cuba, the CCP."

Comrade Wohlforth explains that he wants an answer to the tactical question of whether Cuban Trotskyists should seek to work as members of the Cuban CP or not. "We must have an answer to this vital question!" he exclaims.

It would be wise to separate the question into two parts, which are confused in Comrade Wohlforth's formulation. First, what is our political analysis and strategic line toward the Cuban CP? Second, what tactical advice can we offer to those in Cuba who agree with us on this?

Let's begin with the first part of Comrade Wohlforth's question. From the very beginning of the Cuban revolution we have been in favor of the formation of a revolutionary-socialist party, a Marxist party, a Fourth Internationalist party in Cuba. In his "Report for the Political Committee" to the NC plenum in 1961, Joe Hansen outlined the following tasks to be carried out "inside Cuba." "First, that we follow a policy aimed at expanding and developing the proletarian democracy. That's our Number One. Second, that we follow a policy aimed at building a revolutionary socialist party. In other words, that we follow a policy of deepening, extending the socialist consciousness which has already begun in Cuba. And that we follow a policy aimed at extending the Cuban revolution throughout Latin America. . . ." (*Dynamics of the Cuban Revolution*, p. 117.)

The Cuban Communist Party is not a Leninist party. It allows no democratic internal life in the Bolshevik sense. There are no organized tendencies and factions around programmatic points that could advance the clarity of discussion and contribute to solving the problems facing the Cuban revolution.

Moreover, to a certain degree the Cuban Communist Party is not a political party as we think of one, so much as a part of the administrative apparatus. It suffers from some of the same bureaucratic deformations as the rest of the governmental apparatus.

But there are different layers, and different wings within the party. At the top is the team around Castro; the Stalinists are in a minority.

Our strategic orientation today is the same as it has always been: to support and strengthen the Castro wing against the Stalinists. To support the revolutionary wing against the counterrevolutionary forces and pressures. Within this framework we explain our differences with the Castro current and fight to win as many as we can to the program of the Fourth International.

Under the impact of great revolutionary events in the world, sections of the leadership of the Cuban CP can be impelled toward the left, toward us. There is room for different estimates of how likely it is that we will be successful in winning them to our program, or how significant they will be. But as long as we don't preclude this possibility, then we must agree on the importance of the fight to maximize the chances of winning as many as possible.

Also inside the Cuban CP are thousands, tens of thousands of proletarian revolutionary fighters and militants. Many of the best and most determined Cuban workers and soldiers are there, nominated for the party by their comrades in recognition of their revolutionary capacities. We must strive to reach these revolutionary cadres who can be won to revolutionary Marxism, to the program of the Fourth International.

Within this framework, let's turn to the second part of Wohlforth's question: What tactical advice can we offer to those in Cuba who agree with us? The answer is, not much. It would certainly be foolish to say that Trotskyists should not seek to join the Cuban CP. But what other organizations should they work in? What factories, what cities, what arenas of activity should they orient toward? We obviously can't answer these questions. We are not qualified to be offering tactical suggestions for revolutionists in Cuba today. We would be foolish to try.

We have views on programmatic questions and strategic orientation, which we share with everyone who will listen. But we leave it to those in Cuba who can be won to such a perspective to think through how to implement it. This is a fundamental principle of the Fourth International, embodied in its statutes.

When we acquire a lot more knowledge we may have tactical opinions for Cuban revolutionists to consider. But it is pointless to debate tactics when what is really involved is a far-reaching difference over strategic line. The difference we have with Comrade Wohlforth is not over the *tactics* of how to win revolutionary cadres in Cuba today. The difference is over the fundamental line of approach to the Cuban revolution and its leadership.

Comrade Wohlforth insists that we should be trying to convince the workers and peasants of Cuba to fight to overthrow the Castro leadership. The majority of the National Committee believes, in contrast, that the Castro leadership deserves our support in the battle to continue and deepen the fundamentally revolutionary direction that has marked the Cuban revolution for twenty years. Along that road Cuban Trotskyism will grow.

These two counterposed lines could not coexist within the same party in Cuba today no matter what the tactics. A party with Comrade Wohlforth's line in Cuba would attract forces—but not revolutionary forces. The revolutionary workers and peasants would consider such a party their enemy. And they would be correct.

That is why the political stakes in the discussion we are beginning are so high. We are still fighting for the soul of the Cuban revolution, for the soul of the Socialist Workers Party, and for the soul of the Fourth International.

A Firsthand Account

CUBA IN THE TWENTIETH YEAR OF THE REVOLUTION
By José G. Pérez

In July and August 1979, I and nearly 200 other young Cubans living abroad conducted a month-long visit to our homeland, as part of the Antonio Maceo Brigade. Our contingent was named in memory of Carlos Muñiz Varela, a brigade leader assassinated in Puerto Rico last April by counterrevolutionary exiles.

This was the second such visit by young Cubans living abroad. The first, at the end of 1977 and beginning of 1978, played a major role in advancing the rapprochement between the Cuban government and the Cuban community abroad that has come to be known as the "Dialogue." As part of promoting a new relationship with Cubans abroad, the Cuban government is releasing all persons still imprisoned for crimes against the revolution. In addition, tens of thousands of Cubans abroad are being permitted to visit their homeland. (In September the U.S. government abruptly revoked the charter of the Panama-based airliner that was coordinating most of these return visits.)

The Dialogue represents a sharp reversal of the Cuban government's attitude toward the exiles. (For a more detailed analysis of the Dialogue and its significance, see "Meaning of the Dialogue—Cubans in the United States and the Cuban Revolution" by José G. Pérez, in *IP/I* Sept. 24, 1979, p. 907.)

While many in the Antonio Maceo Brigade are supporters of the revolution, this was not a requirement for participation in the contingent. To participate, *brigadistas* had to oppose the U.S. economic blockade, have left Cuba before the age of eighteen due to parental decision, and not have a hostile attitude toward the revolution.

During the months leading up to the trip, those who had been involved in the first contingent and were organizing the second made a conscious effort to involve a broad spectrum of young Cubans, including many who had little previous political experience or knowledge about the revolution.

Makeup of the brigade
The biggest part of the contingent came from the United States, since most Cubans abroad live there. Others came from Puerto Rico, Mexico, Venezuela, and Spain, where the brigade has groups. Individuals came from Peru and Canada.

Most brigadistas were not affiliated with left political organizations. The small percentage who were included members of the Puerto Rican Socialist Party, the U.S. Socialist Workers Party, the Social Democratic Partido Socialista Obrero Español, and pro-Moscow Communist parties.

In addition, some brigadistas had been activists in various social protest movements, such as the environmental, antinuclear, women's liberation, and gay rights movements. Some didn't consider themselves socialists, although most did.

The contingent's political diversity made it anything but a group predisposed to accept without question the positions and presentations of the Cuban government and leaders. On the contrary, many were not sure about, or disagreed with, various official positions. On a couple of occasions this led to lively exchanges. While most of us were inspired by what we saw in Cuba, some were unmoved and a few were downright disenchanted.

What we did
We heard talks on a variety of topics, ranging from economic development, culture, and education to the role of such organizations as the Federación de Mujeres Cubanas (FMC—Federation of Cuban Women), Asociación Nacional de Agricultores Pequeños (ANAP—National Association of Small

Farmers), and the Unión de Jóvenes Comunistas (UJC—Union of Young Communists).

The schedule organized by the Instituto Cubano de Amistad con los Pueblos (ICAP—Cuban Institute for Friendship with the Peoples), which organized the trip, was a heavy one. Nevertheless, there were several free days when we could take off on our own, go wherever we wanted, and talk to whomever we wished. There was no suggestion that we should limit our contacts to functionaries or officials. On the contrary, we were encouraged to meet the widest possible cross-section of the Cuban people.

Most brigade members still have relatives in Cuba and were able to spend several days visiting them. There were brigadistas who hadn't seen close relatives for nearly twenty years—and this also afforded many of us close contact with a wide sample of the Cuban population.

ICAP and the fifty-odd young people from Cuba who accompanied us throughout the entire four-week tour made no attempt to dissuade us from asking questions or expressing opinions. On the contrary, we were encouraged to raise our ideas and discuss all aspects of the Cuban revolution.

We worked for a week and a half building apartments with the workers of the Ariguanabo textile plant, located almost an hour by bus outside the city of Havana. In addition to Havana, the Brigade also visited the provinces of Holguín, Santiago de Cuba, Cienfuegos, and Pinar del Río as well as the Isle of Youth (formerly the Isle of Pines).

How Cubans view brigade

Given its composition and the unique role it has played in the Dialogue, the Antonio Maceo Brigade is held in high esteem throughout Cuba, both by government officials and most of the people. A feature-length documentary, *Fifty-five Brothers and Sisters*, was made about the brigade's first contingent. The Cuban news media prominently covered the visit of our Carlos Muñiz contingent. We were received everywhere like brothers and sisters in the struggle against the U.S. government's hostile policy toward Cuba.

The attitude toward us was captured in a phrase of Fidel, summarizing his meeting with the Brigade's first contingent a year and a half ago: "La patria ha crecido" (the homeland has grown).

I felt there was a special openness to discuss with us many problems and challenges still facing the revolution—a greater openness than there might have been with other visitors, especially from the United States. In addition, it was easy to simply take off on our own during free time and melt into the general population.

Much could be written about Cuba on the basis of such a trip. The accomplishments of the revolution show what can be done by the working people of other countries if they follow the Cuban road. This article, however, has a particular goal: to provide information that might help clarify the discussion on the character of the Cuban leadership and its policies.

Within the Fourth International, the world Trotskyist organization, this discussion centers around whether the Cuban leadership is revolutionary—as the Fourth International has maintained—or whether a hardened bureaucratic caste, like the one that exists in the Soviet Union, has emerged in Cuba with institutionalized material privileges. Is the Castro leadership following a course that is in the interests of the Cuban workers and peasants? Or does it defend its own material privileges at the expense of the Cuban workers and peasants?

This discussion is not limited to the Trotskyist movement. Many of the same questions were raised in classes held by the Antonio Maceo Brigade in New York in preparation for the trip, as well as by brigadistas while we were in Cuba. Many books and articles published in the United States and other countries have also focused on this question. In Cuba, I met people who are aware of and follow both the broader discussion and the debate within the Trotskyist movement.

Before I visited Cuba I had a definite opinion on the basic questions. Despite the differences of opinion I have with the Cuban leaders on a number of points, I was convinced that the Castro team is a revolutionary leadership that bases itself on the conscious, organized power of the Cuban working class in alliance with the peasantry.

While in Cuba, I made a special effort to look into a number of questions that are cited as key tests of the character of the government—the policy toward women, the peasantry, and Blacks; the use of material and moral incentives; policy toward homosexuals; cultural policy; the degree to which high government officials and other functionaries have institutionalized material privileges; whether privileges have tended to increase; and many others. What I saw confirmed my assessment—sometimes in unexpected ways. This article is a report on what I found.

'We are internationalists'

Internationalism isn't just official policy in Cuba. It is something felt and lived by the entire nation, as much a part of Cuba as the Sierra Maestra or the royal palms. No matter where you go or who you talk to, the profound internationalist spirit of the Cuban revolution is in evidence.

FSLN's daily *Barricada* reports on the Cuban desire to aid Nicaragua.

Everywhere billboards proclaim: "For Vietnam, even our own blood"; "We are internationalists"; and "Long live the Sandinista National Liberation Front."

Theatres show documentaries about Angola's struggle for independence and Cuba's aid to Ethiopia in beating back the imperialist-inspired Somali invasion. Top hit songs on the radio, such as the "Song of the Twentieth Anniversary," proclaim "the honor of being internationalists."

Despite Cuba's own pressing needs, more than 1,000 (out of 14,000) Cuban doctors are abroad helping countries such as Nicaragua, Angola, Ethiopia, South Yemen, and Mozambique. A thousand teachers are helping Angola carry out a literacy campaign. In addition, thousands of African students, from junior high school age up, are studying in Cuban schools.

We arrived in Cuba July 14, as the final offensive against the Somoza dictatorship in Nicaragua was nearing victory. People everywhere were talking about Nicaragua, passing on the latest news, breaking into Anti-Somoza chants and slogans. *Granma* and *Juventud Rebelde*, the two main newspapers, devoted most of their front pages every day to Nicaragua. As the Sandinista offensive advanced, the headlines got bigger and the tone of the coverage more enthusiastic: Somoza Flees! The last pockets of the Somozaist resistence have been crushed!

Celebrations erupted all over the island. As the days passed, and reports from Nicaragua indicated the FSLN was initiating far-reaching social programs in the interest of the working masses, the rejoicing spread. A former commander of the July 26 Movement's Rebel Army, who is now head of a government institute, explained the rejoicing to me: "We have been waiting for this for twenty years. Now we aren't alone."

The climax of the celebration was the July 26 rally in Holguín, a city in eastern Cuba. Surrounded by twenty-six commanders of the FSLN, Fidel gave a speech pledging that Cuba would do everything within its power to aid the Sandinista revolution.

This promise was enthusiastically greeted by the Cuban people. Every day *Granma*, *Juventud Rebelde*, and other news media would report how the staff of such and such a hospital had met and voted to support Fidel's call for aid to Nicaragua. During our month-long tour, the brigade visited several hospitals and I talked to many doctors. I asked them whether they were willing to go to Nicaragua. Everywhere I received the same response: Cuba should do anything and everything for any nation fighting for its liberation.

One answered my question with an anecdote about several young professionals who had wanted to go fight against the South African invasion of Angola. They volunteered to go but were turned down, given the surplus of volunteers and Cuba's needs for trained personnel. So they went to another town, trying to pass themselves off as unskilled workers, hoping they would get to go.

Aiding the African revolution

I met quite a few people who were veterans of the Angola and Ethiopia campaigns.

I had read the account by Colombian novelist Gabriel García Márquez explaining how Cuba received an urgent request for aid from the Angolan government when that country was invaded by South Africa. (See *Intercontinental Press*, January 31, 1977, Vol. 15, No. 3, p. 74. See also *Cuba and Angola* [New York: Pathfinder Press, 2013], p. 127 [2013 printing]). The Cuban leadership had less than twenty-four hours to decide, and did so at a November 5, 1975, meeting. By November 7 the first contingent of 650 troops was on its way to Angola by plane.

Justo Hernández, one of the people working with us in construction, was in one of the first contingents to go to Angola. He explained how the mobilization was carried out.

In the middle of the night a telegram was delivered to his apartment telling him to report to the local military committee. "When?" he asked the people who delivered the telegram. "Right now," they said. There was a jeep waiting for him downstairs.

When he got to the offices of the military committee, other members of the reserves of the Revolutionary Armed Forces were already there.

An officer explained the situation: Angola had been invaded by South Africa and had turned to Cuba for help. Nobody knew how much South Africa was willing to commit to the invasion, nor whether the United States would intervene openly with its own troops. No one knew how the United States would respond to Cuba's bold decision to aid the Angolans with military forces. But that didn't stop them.

Volunteers would leave directly from the military committee. For security reasons, they couldn't even notify their families. Relatives would be informed of the situation later by the military committee.

Justo reported that although most volunteered to go, there were some who felt they couldn't or simply didn't want to go. There was no attempt made to pressure anyone into volunteering—if you weren't sure, it was better that you stayed behind. As it was, there were many more volunteers than were needed.

Similar stories were told to me by people all over Cuba.

'Let them be like Che'

Che Guevara is the symbol of the internationalist spirit of the Cuban revolution. At any factory, farm, warehouse, school, or hospital, you can see portraits of Guevara. October 8, the day he fell in battle in Bolivia twelve years ago, is commemorated as the "Day of the Heroic Guerrilla."

This is not the kind of lifeless cult that is sometimes built up around a historical figure, the better to bury what that person really stood for. Guevara's books, speeches, and articles are widely read and used as texts in Cuban schools and in political education classes run by the Communist Party and Union of Young Communists.

A nine-volume collection of his works, published on the tenth anniversary of his death, is available for the equivalent of five dollars. Some of his major writings, such as *Episodes of the Revolutionary War, Guerrilla Warfare, Socialism and Man*, and *Message to the Tricontinental*, are also available as separate books or pamphlets.

In his eulogy of Guevara, Fidel Castro said:

> If we wish to express what we expect our revolutionary combatants, our militants, our men to be, we must say, without hesitation: 'Let them be like Che!'. . . If we wish to say how we want our children to be educated, we must say without hesitation: 'We want them to be educated in Che's spirit!'. . . If we wish to express what we want our children to be, we must say from our very hearts as vehement revolutionaries: 'We want them to be like Che!'

That pledge is being carried out in Cuba today.

Virtually all of Cuba's six to fourteen year-olds belong to the Pioneers, a government-sponsored youth organization.

Among the books the Pioneers read is one called *Che—Commander of the Dawn*. In her introduction, author Renée Méndez Capote states:

> The author hopes to give to the youth ... an idea of the great humanity of this Argentine who made of Cuba his second homeland; who went to die in Bolivia because for him, true communist, the homeland had no borders. The homeland is there where other brothers fight and sacrifice themselves, convinced that the struggle will always take them to victory, because if they fall there will be other hands to pick up their rifles and carry onward the uncontainable battle for freedom. ...
>
> The author wants the youth who read this book to keep always in their heart the reason for the oath of our Pioneers: 'Pioneers for Communism! We will be like Che!'

If you talk to the Pioneers, you will see that they are indeed being educated in Che's spirit. The second day we were in Cuba we were taken to the inauguration of the Main Pioneer Palace, which is located in Lenin Park in Havana. The overwhelming majority of the several thousand people present were Pioneers. We spent several hours talking with them, waiting for the ceremonies to begin.

I asked one boy what kinds of games Cuban children play.

"We play Sandinistas versus the National Guard."

"And how does it go?"

"Sometimes it's hard, nobody wants to be a National Guard. We all want to be Sandinistas."

I got into a conversation with a girl, perhaps ten years old, about life in the United States and what it was like. She knew quite a bit about it—the unemployment, having to pay for medicine or to go to school. But she still wanted firsthand testimony.

Then she asked me if I wanted to move to Cuba. I told her I wanted to stay in the United States and make a revolution there like the Cuban revolution.

She asked me if there were many revolutionaries in the United States, and I told her not enough, not so many as in Cuba. To which she responded that we should go ahead and start the revolution; Cuba would send us more revolutionaries to finish the job.

Cuban children identify completely with the revolution. When they speak of things the revolutionary government has done, they always speak of what *we* did, even if it happened before they were born.

During a visit to a Pioneer Palace in a rural area in Santiago de Cuba, a *pionero* gave us a guided tour. He showed us the different workshops where the Pioneers learn about everything from communications to agriculture. One of these was the workshop of the Revolutionary Armed Forces, which has a display case with several rifles, some of them obviously old and used, some of them brand new. The *pionero* explained:

"These," he said, pointing to the old rifles, "are some of the weapons we used to liberate our homeland.

"And these," he added, pointing to the new rifles, "are some of the weapons we use today to help liberate other homelands."

Moscow's foreign policy

The revolutionary internationalist foreign policy of the Cuban government contrasts sharply with Moscow's, which is based on reaching class-collaborationist diplomatic deals with imperialism to preserve the world status quo.

Nowhere has this difference been more obvious recently than in the responses by Havana and Moscow to the revolutionary process unleashed by the overthrow of Somoza. Far from the enthusiastic solidarity and calls for material aid I witnessed in Cuba, Moscow has so far come through with practically no assistance to help reconstruct Nicaragua. And Moscow-oriented Stalinist parties around the world have given only routine coverage to events in Nicaragua and have not thrown their often substantial influence and resources into a massive solidarity effort. The Stalinists know that U.S. imperialism is dead-set against the Nicaraguan revolution, and they don't want to endanger détente by stepping on Washington's toes.

In his July 26 speech, Fidel included an explicit reference to the Soviet Union in his call for an "emulation campaign to see who can do the most for Nicaragua."

"We invite the United States, we invite all the countries of Latin America, we invite all the countries of Europe, countries of the Third World, our sister socialist nations," Fidel said.

"This is our position, in order to make a really human, really constructive effort based on a spirit of emulation."

This contrast between the foreign policy of

Havana and Moscow has been shown time and again throughout the two decades of the Cuban revolution, especially around Cuba's unbending solidarity with Vietnam. On several occasions, the Cubans openly took Moscow to task for its inadequate aid to Vietnam. Usually, however, the Cuban leaders choose—as in the case of Nicaragua—to exert the power of their own example as a way to pressure Moscow into providing at least token aid and support.

People in Cuba feel tremendous gratitude toward the Soviet Union for the substantial aid without which Cuba would long ago have been crushed by U.S. imperialism. It is not unusual for Fidel and other Cuban leaders to express appreciation for aid from the "homeland of Lenin."

"Others may bite the hand that has given them generous aid," Fidel said during his speech on the revolution's twentieth anniversary last January. "Cuba and her sons and daughters of today and tomorrow will acknowledge and be eternally grateful for what the Soviet Union has meant to our people!"

The Castro leadership obviously feels that Cuba's relationship with the USSR limits its freedom to differentiate Cuba's own foreign policy from that of Moscow. So explicit criticisms are few and far between, and differences are muted.

Of course, it is generally accepted in Cuba that the two countries follow their own independent foreign policies, and this is freely acknowledged by the Cuban government. Castro repeatedly stressed this point, for example, in interviews with U.S. reporters in late September. "At times we coincide. We don't always coincide," Castro told CBS News correspondent Dan Rather. Castro cited the October 1962 missile crisis as an example where the Cuban and Soviet foreign policy views did not coincide. (See *IP/I*, Nov. 5, 1979, Vol. 17, No. 40, p. 1071.)

While the existence of these differences is generally recognized in Cuba, however, the way they are handled often leads to confusion and a lack of understanding among the Cuban people about the source and significance of these differences. This does not contribute to their education about Stalinism and its class-collaborationist role in undermining progressive struggles around the world.

During our tour, for example, we were given a presentation on Cuba's foreign policy. During the question and answer period, somebody asked what the Cuban leadership thought of the foreign policy of the USSR. The answer was that obviously the policies of the two countries were different if for no other reason than that the Soviet Union is one of the two greatest powers in the world. That was the entire explanation.

Later, in an informal discussion with a person who turned out to be an official of the Cuban Foreign Ministry (although I didn't know it at the time), I returned to the question, expressing my dissatisfaction with the earlier answer. His reply was:

> The world revolutionary movement is very complex. The socialist camp is very complex, and undoubtedly there have been mistakes, there have been problems, weaknesses. To the degree these situations persist—and if you look at China this is undoubtedly true, for example—to the degree problems exist, this is due to the fact that imperialism, that capitalism, still retains a certain strength. Our method is not to seek divisions within the revolutionary movement, to fight only the imperialists, and to the degree the imperialists are weakened, these problems will be overcome.

Privilege in Cuban society

Cuba's internationalist foreign policy is an extension of the proletarian policies followed by the Castro leadership on domestic questions.

Marxists who hold that the Cuban leadership is not revolutionary must demonstrate that a new, privileged ruling layer is consolidating or has consolidated itself, and that the Castroist leadership is based on and fights for policies that protect the interests of this privileged social stratum, rather than the interests of the workers and peasants.

Because this question of material privilege is central, I tried to find out as much as I could about the real standard of living of the working masses compared to that of government functionaries and administrators, and to determine whether differences that exist have tended to increase over the past decade.

From all accounts, the economic situation of Cuba has improved substantially since the late 1960s. The fruits of this growing productivity have not been distributed disproportionately to a thin,

"Che Guevara is the symbol of the internationalist spirit of the Cuban Revolution."

privileged stratum of the population, but have benefited society as a whole.

Many of the extreme shortages of consumer goods that existed in the late 1960s have eased. For example, unlike a decade ago, there is now quite a bit of clothing in the stores. Some of it is still rationed, and everyone gets the same bare minimum of rationed clothing at low prices, whether you are a peasant or the president of a government institute. But, in addition, much clothing is now sold without the need for ration coupons, although at higher prices.

Cuban wage scales nominally run from about 90 to 700 pesos a month. (Officially 1 peso equals US$1.40.) However, in practice, it is rare for anyone to earn less than 120 pesos, and the only people I heard of who earn more than 400 pesos are a few doctors who occupy special posts.

For example, at one warehouse I visited in the city of Havana, formerly owned by my father, wages range between 120 and 152 pesos a month. The salary of the top administrator is 163 pesos a month.

At the factory that produces sugarcane harvesting combines, production workers earn up to 154 pesos and the highest paid administrator receives 250 pesos.

This doesn't tell the whole story, however, because workers engaged in productive labor—but not administrators—are entitled to incentive pay for surpassing the production norms for their job. The rate of incentive pay is 100 percent—if you produce twice as much, you get paid twice as much. In addition, all the employees, in this case including administrators, are entitled to an additional bonus of 10 percent of all their earnings during a three-month period if their factory, warehouse, or farm meets all its goals for quantity produced, efficient use of raw materials, etc.

At the warehouse I visited in Havana, for example, the effect of these incentive pay plans was that many workers consistently had much higher take-home pay than the administrators. This has created a problem, in that many workers are unwilling to accept promotions to administrative posts because it would mean a cut in real income.

Disparities in the standard of living are further reduced because everyone in Cuba receives many essential goods and services either free or at subsidized prices. Health care and education are totally free. About two-thirds of the cost of child-care is subsidized, and fees are adjusted according to income, ranging from two pesos to forty pesos a month. Rent is no more than 10 percent of income, and usually is 6 percent, which represents a substantial subsidy. All workers get at least one meal, sometimes two meals, every day at their workplaces for fifty Cuban cents each, which also represents a subsidy.

The 'historic wage'

Since the early 1970s, there has been a big effort to eliminate one source of sizable wage disparities, the so-called historic, or carry over, wage.

In Cuba, a historic wage is what a person holding that position earned under capitalism. If before the revolution you had a position that paid extraordinarily well, you continued to receive that wage even though the wage that other workers would normally receive today might be substantially lower. The rationale for this policy was that these wages were often the result of struggles by the workers of a particular plant, and what the workers were able to win under capitalism through their struggles shouldn't be taken away by the socialist revolution. The revolution set the goal of reducing inequalities in the workforce by raising the standard of living of the worst-paid workers, rather than lowering the wages of the best-paid.

Those who benefited most from this policy were the skilled aristocracy of Cuban workers, as well as many professionals. Over time historic wages tended to get transferred as an individual moved from one job to another and new "historic wages" tended to be created for positions where they had not existed before. I was told by one administrator that historic wages showed a particular tendency to become attached to administrative posts. Often this was done legally; sometimes not.

The policy adopted in 1973 prohibits the creation of any new historic wages, either for individuals or for posts. The historic wages that exist are now strictly nontransferable—if you leave a job, you leave the wage, and if a new person takes a job that previously had a historic wage, the new person gets only the regular wage.

This has sharply reduced one big source of large (for Cuba) disparities that fostered bureaucratic abuses and influence peddling.

Other measures have been adopted to prevent the growth of special privileges for functionaries. For example, there is a big shortage of housing in Cuba, as well as an insufficient supply of TVs, refrigerators, and other consumer durables. After various experiments, the Castro leadership implemented a plan of distribution primarily through workplace assemblies. The workers vote on who, among those who don't have a particular item, are most deserving because of their work performance. They are entitled to buy the scarce items.

As Fidel explained in his speech to the 1973 Congress of the Central Organization of Cuban Trade Unions:

> The distribution of household electrical appliances is another problem we've discussed. We understand that the solutions you've come up with are good ones. Some contradictions have arisen in the process. A worker said it was usually the 'good guy,' the worker liked by everyone, who got the electrical appliance.

> Now, if a 'good guy' can fool the masses, what about the public official? If a public official, instead of the masses, is in charge of distribution, he makes a hundred mistakes for every one the masses made.

Castro added that, of course, it was preferable not to have shortages. But if there isn't enough to go around, the system of workplace distribution has an additional advantage:

> . . . we think that, as long as these electrical appliances are scarce, the workers should be the first ones to get them. It's a matter of having the workers come first in a nation of workers. Before, electrical appliances were sold to anybody who was willing to stand in a long waiting line in front of a store, and this method caused a lot of irritation.

Earlier in his speech Castro had referred to the problem that developed in the late 1960s, with many people, especially women, leaving the labor force. In Cuba, people told me one reason for this was that it took hours and hours of standing in line to obtain many items. Even worse, some people began to pay others to stand in line for them, meaning that those with higher incomes got preferential access to items in short supply.

I found that overall the official policies are followed in real life. Of course, there are more than a few individuals who use their positions to secure privileges for themselves and who are guilty of other abuses. In Cuba, these comfortable careerists are popularly referred to as the 'acomodados.'

But the policy of the Cuban leadership seeks to counter this process and is a real check on it. Being an administrator doesn't automatically bring preferential treatment. For example, the administrator of the warehouse in Havana that I visited had been without an apartment of his own since divorcing his wife two years before. He said that was because couples with children get priority for housing. (Workplace distribution applies only to newly built apartments.)

Relations on the job

Relations on the job also reflect the absence of a privileged ruling group alien to the Cuban workers and hostile to their interests. Cuba does not have a system of democratic workers and peasants councils and there is no democratic control by the workers over the national economic plan.

But assemblies of workers at each workplace vote on the economic plan proposed for that workplace. Worker representatives, elected by an assembly of the entire work force, participate in the management councils of all enterprises. Five-member commissions of workers elected by secret ballot handle all cases of discipline within a workplace. A worker cannot be fired by management; only the workers themselves have that right.

In capitalist countries such as the United States, labor discipline and productivity are maintained primarily through the punitive pressures of economic coercion supplemented by favoritism. Workers who don't behave to the bosses' satisfaction get tossed onto the unemployment lines.

In Cuba, everybody has a job. Virtually every workplace I visited reported that they had fewer workers than they should have. Even if a worker is fired from a job, the government still has the responsibility of finding that person another one.

Nevertheless, the revolution's leaders have said that they jumped ahead of themselves in the late 1960s, when the policy was to move away from economic rewards for high productivity, and goods and services were increasingly distributed free to the population.

It rapidly became apparent that, given Cuba's stage of development, free distribution created a tendency to waste things that do not exist in limitless supplies. An experiment at a large housing development, for example, demonstrated that those who received an unlimited quantity of water for free used four to five times as much as those who had to pay something for it. The policy that was finally adopted was to provide free of charge the amount considered adequate for an average family, and to charge for any amount over that.

Moreover, the shortages of consumer items, coupled with the very low prices and increasing free distribution meant that a large amount of money accumulated in the hands of individuals. This resulted in a growing problem of people leaving the workforce, especially women.

The revolution dealt with this problem by raising the prices of non-essential items such as liquor.

More important, the so-called "parallel market" was created. Many items that still are in short supply are available in modest quantities at very low prices through the rationing system. If there is a surplus, it is sold first-come, first-served, but at higher prices. An extreme example is cigarettes, which are still rationed. Each adult is entitled to eight packs a month at the equivalent of US$0.28 each. Additional packs cost more than US$2.

Through these techniques surplus money has been reabsorbed, and it has become possible to meaningfully reinstitute economic incentives. Norms (quotas) exist for every job, and pay is determined by fulfillment of these norms. The guiding principle is: From each according to their ability; to each according to their work.

Contrary to what some have claimed, this has not meant the abandonment of moral—that is, political—incentives, which continue to be viewed

Great strides have been taken in developing the countryside. Special efforts have been made to mechanize sugarcane cutting.

as fundamental elements in building socialism.

"We should never think we are going to solve with money the problems that only consciousness can solve," Castro said in his 1973 speech to the congress of the Cuban labor federation. "We must use material incentives intelligently and combine them with moral incentives, but we must not be deluded into thinking we are going to motivate the man of today, the socialist man, only through material incentives, because material incentives no longer have the validity they have under capitalism, in which everything—even life and death—requires money.

"That is why the contribution made by the consciousness of the workers, by the political culture of the workers and by their attitude becomes an irreplaceable element in socialism, since the workers' motivations are of a different character."

The goal of both the material and the moral incentive is to deepen social consciousness, to make each individual aware that his or her relationship to society is different from what exists under capitalism.

"Above all we want to create the consciousness that the material welfare of the individual is dependent on the economic development of the society as a whole," an official of JUCEPLAN, the central planning agency explained in a talk to members of the Antonio Maceo Brigade. "The harder we work, the more we produce, the more there will be for everyone."

Cuban Communist Party

The Cuban Communist Party (PCC) and Union of Young Communists (UJC) are not organizations composed primarily of careerists and privilege-seekers. I met scores of members of the two organizations in Cuba. They were distinguished above all by being what they claim to be—conscious and dedicated revolutionists. This was indicative, though hardly a scientific poll.

To become a member of the party, you must be nominated by your co-workers and ratified by the party nucleus that you are to join. The PCC leadership has stressed the need to maintain and strengthen the working-class composition of the party. The number of administrators and functionaries that are permitted to enter each year is deliberately limited.

A distinguishing mark of the PCC and UJC members I met was their enthusiastic support for Cuba's anti-imperialist foreign policy and their eagerness to take international assignments. They reminded me of the IWW rebels described by James P. Cannon, founder of the Socialist Workers Party, as the backbone of any revolutionary movement: "The shock troops of the movement were the foot-loose militants who moved around the country as the scene of the action shifted." Except that the Cuban revolutionaries have expanded the scope of their activities far beyond the boundaries of one country.

Women in Cuba

Among the most widely discussed social questions in Cuba today is the liberation of women. I found more ferment and motion around this than any other domestic political issue.

The Castro leadership has promoted the battle for women's equality since the first days of the revolution. For example, in a speech on February 6, 1959,—less than a month after the Rebel Army's triumphant entry into Havana—Fidel was already beginning the job of educating the Cuban people on this question:

> The evils that have been accumulating are many. . . .
>
> There is talk, for example, of racial discrimination and it is true. But there is no talk about sex discrimination, of the number of women that they try to exploit, of the way women are viewed more as objects of pleasure than as figures in society who are and can be at the same height as men.
>
> On one occasion when we decided to organize the battalions of women fighters [as part of the Rebel Army], I explained the social reasons for doing this. I found a great difficulty in the prejudices of many men, and I had to explain to them that women are one of the sectors most discriminated against. . . .
>
> Women form part of the accumulation of prejudices that the social life, the economic circumstances and conditions of our country, have created. . . .

Since 1959, tremendous strides have been made towards achieving full equality for women. Among the greatest beneficiaries of the literacy campaign carried out in the first years of the revolution were the women, since they suffered from a significantly higher rate of illiteracy than men. For twenty years women have benefited from real equality in education, both among the youth and in the educational campaigns carried out among the adult population.

These educational advances in turn have facilitated the growing integration of women into the labor force. Before the revolution there were less than 200,000 women employed, 70 percent of them as domestics. One of the first tasks undertaken by the revolution was to provide training for those women so that they could take productive jobs. Today, some 800,000 women are employed, nearly 30 percent of the work force. Both the absolute number of working women and the percentage of the labor force that is female is increasing every year.

Discrimination against women is a crime punishable by law. Women's right to control their own bodies has become a reality through abortion and contraception, which are free and available to women of all ages. Women have broken into many previously all-male preserves, such as the medical profession and many industrial jobs.

One of the priorities of the revolutionary government from the very first years has been to utilize even scarce resources to develop and constantly expand low-cost, high-quality child-care centers. Currently there are facilities for more than 90,000 children, and they are being expanded at a rate of more than 10,000 places a year.

The centers accept children from the age of forty-five days up to when they enter school. They are not just baby-sitting services, but provide education, health care, balanced diets, and even clothing for the infants. Some centers are open twenty-four hours a day for women who work at night or have rotating shifts.

In addition, the government has set up boarding schools for hundreds of thousands of junior high school and high school students, who return home only on weekends. These schools have proved immensely popular both with parents and young people.

For students who live at home, the government is now providing free lunches at most schools. In prerevolutionary Cuba, the virtually universal practice was that children went home for lunch, making it very difficult for mothers to hold an outside job.

Challenges ahead

Nevertheless—as the leaders of the revolution are the first to admit—full equality for women remains a goal yet to be achieved in Cuba.

The First Congress of the Cuban Communist Party, held at the end of 1975, adopted a thesis and a resolution on women's liberation.

These documents emphasize that the oppression of women has its roots in the rise of class society:

> Discrimination against women started many centuries ago, since when the primitive communities disintegrated and private property and the division of society into classes was established, men obtained economic supremacy and with it social predominance.
>
> Through the different regimes based on the exploitation of man by man, women were relegated to the reduced framework of the home, her possibilities for participating in social production were limited or she was ruthlessly exploited.
>
> These concepts, which prevailed in our country until the overthrow of capitalism, can have no place in the stage of the building of the new society.

The thesis then shows, with facts, figures, and numerous examples, both what was achieved in the first fifteen years of the revolution and the considerable ground still to be conquered. It singles out, for example, the relatively low percentage of women who occupied leading posts in organizations such as the trade unions and the Committees for the Defense of the Revolution, in the party, and in the administration of the economy.

The thesis cites several reasons for this situation. The first is simply the short time the revolution has been in power: fifteen or twenty years are but a minute when measured on the timepiece of the evolution of human societies. Another reason is Cuba's continuing economic backwardness. This makes it impossible, for example, for the government to simply build, overnight, all the child-care facilities, cafeterias, and laundries needed for women to participate equally in society.

The third factor cited by the document is prejudices against women. "*A fundamental battle has to be carried out in the field of consciousness, because there still exist many backward attitudes that we are dragging with us from the past"* (emphasis in original).

In a talk to members of the Antonio Maceo Brigade, two leaders of the Federation of Cuban Women (FMC) explained what further progress had been achieved in the past few years.

The number of places for children in child-care centers has jumped from 55,000 to 92,000 in the last three years. Many new boarding schools have been built. Progress has been made in eliminating entertainment and cultural presentations that depict women as sexual objects. For example, the selection of carnival queens, which the FMC leaders said were often no more than beauty contests with a socialist veneer, has been halted.

Protective legislation that forbade women from holding certain physically strenuous or dangerous jobs has been replaced with recommendations to women that they not seek such jobs. But the final decision is now up to the woman, and a woman who applies for any job opening she is qualified to hold cannot be denied that job because of her sex.

The percentage of party members who are women has increased from 13 to 19 percent since 1975. The percentage of leading posts occupied by women in organizations, the economy, and the government has also increased.

This continuing progress has not been without friction. For example, the representatives of the FMC said it took quite a "fight" with the Ministry of Labor to convince them to drop regulations that made it illegal for women to hold certain jobs.

The FMC sees its basic task as "the full integration of Cuban women into Cuban society on the basis of full equality, not only in the laws and in theory, but also in practice." For that reason, "we will have to exist until discrimination and all its vestiges have been totally eliminated."

Continuing, steady progress towards full equality for women has been accompanied by increasing formal and informal discussion on the role of women in society.

For example, a recent film released by the Cuban film industry, *Retrato de Teresa* (Portrait of Teresa), deals with this question.

HARRY RING/MILITANT
"For twenty years women have benefited from real equality in education, both among the youth and among the adult population."

The film is about a woman textile worker with three children who finds herself torn between her desire to escape the stultifying limits of domestic life and the demands placed on her by her husband.

She is involved in a cultural group sponsored by her union. The union wants her to keep participating in it, which she also wants to do. At the same time she has to do all the housework and her husband is constantly accusing her of neglecting the home. Needless to say, he does absolutely nothing to help with household chores, much less share them equally with his wife.

As a result of all the pressure, Teresa takes a leave of absence from her job. But immediately upon returning to work, the conflict breaks out again. Her husband moves out after a violent fight and has an affair. Teresa, relieved of the pressure from her husband, continues in the cultural group, which wins national recognition.

The movie ends with Teresa's husband trying to

patch things up with her. He asks her to forgive him, and she answers with a question: "What if I had walked out and had the affair?"

His response is automatic—"No es lo mismo,"—it's not the same. With that, Teresa turns her back on him and walks away.

The film, which premièred the week of July 26, has been the focus of intense discussions, because it portrays something very common in Cuban society. As increasing numbers of women have been able to move into the work force and achieve economic independence, the divorce rate has risen sharply.

A special screening of the film was arranged for the brigade in Santiago de Cuba, and the following day we had a long bus trip to Cienfuegos. We spent the whole morning on the bus in a discussion, at times quite sharp, over the issues raised in the film.

The discussion started when one of the male college students from Cuba accompanying us on the trip remarked, "Of course, it isn't the same." This immediately met with a rash of objections, primarily from the women, and a heated discussion got under way, lasting several hours. Later, the discussion was rekindled when someone dragged out a copy of the Cuban CP thesis on women's liberation, quoting a part that says:

> *There cannot exist one morality for women and another for men; this is contrary to Marxist-Leninist ideology and the principles of this Revolution.*
>
> It is wrong to judge women in a different way than men; what is socially acceptable for men should be equally socially acceptable for women. . . .
>
> Men and women should be equally free and responsible to determine their relations in the arena of sexual life (emphasis in original).

I was curious to see whether the discussion on the bus had been atypical of Cuban society. I therefore went to see *Retrato de Teresa* again during a free day in Havana, and afterward stood outside the theater talking to people.

The same discussions were repeated—about the double standard in morality, about the responsibility of men for the housework, caring for the children, and related matters. The discussions would break down into smaller groups, with clumps of people breaking off to go to Coppelia's, a big ice-cream establishment across the street. I went with two women in their twenties who had been particularly insistent on defending equality for women, and who, it turned out, were both members of the Union of Young Communists.

We continued on the same theme, waiting in line to buy ice cream and then eating it.

Cuban Family Code

They said that the discussion on the role of women in Cuban society had really gotten off the ground on a massive scale only a few years before, with the government's introduction of the Family Code, which was formally proclaimed law at the beginning of 1975.

I told them that some radicals in the United States have attacked the Family Code, claiming it reinforced the family as an institution of the oppression of women. Their reaction was utter disbelief.

> You have to understand where we are coming from. Twenty years ago, if a girl in my family went out with a boy without a chaperone, she would have been considered a whore. A woman's place was to have babies and do the housework and to keep quiet unless spoken to. Often your parents told you who to marry, and if the man cheated on you, you couldn't leave him, for how were you to survive. Contraception was considered an attack on a man's virility; abortion a crime punishable by law. Women were denied education, access to jobs—everything.

They explained that the revolution had changed all that, and that a good number of the changes were ratified by the Family Code.

"It says women are equal in marriage, that's the main thing." They described the various provisions—equal control of joint property; equal rights and responsibilities for raising the children; equal right to have a profession or a job and to participate in broad social activity; elimination of any distinction between "legitimate" and "natural" children; enumeration of the duties of the parents toward their children and of the rights of children, etc.

It even says that men should share the housework equally. They described the mass meetings that were organized in every neighborhood to discuss the Family Code.

"When it was done well, it was tremendous," explained one of the young women. "Everything would go along fine, everyone agreeing, until they got to the part about equal responsibility for the home and for raising the children, and when this was explained, things got hot. It provoked much discussion, at the meeting, and afterwards.

"Then came the film," she added, referring to a documentary about the discussions held on the code. "The *machistas* were made to look very bad in the film, and this provoked more discussion, and it's been going on. But it is a very long process, because it's not just changing someone's opinion on something, but changing the way people live."

Freedom of opinion

Contrary to the image presented in the capitalist news media, Cuba is not a police state where people can't express antigovernment opinions for fear of ending up in a forced labor camp. Quite the contrary. Although most people I met were supporters of the revolution, some disagreed with one or another measure, and a few frankly couldn't have cared less about the revolution. They weren't afraid to say so.

One young man explained to me that the revolution was terrible because of the censorship of music. I was surprised by his statement, since I had spoken to many people, including artists, and had been told that the cultural policy of the government remained what it had been from the beginning—anything goes as long as it's not advocacy of counterrevolution. So I asked him to explain.

He claimed that several musical groups that are very popular in the United States had been banned from Cuban radio because they had given concerts in Pinochet's Chile. He rattled off a half-dozen names. I had never heard of any of them.

In fact, American disco and rock music is quite popular in Cuba, and on certain Cuban radio stations you're as likely to end up listening to the Bee Gees as to a native Cuban artist.

So I asked him what records these groups had put out and what their hit songs were. He didn't know. To me, it sounded like a frame-up, and I told him so. He assured me it wasn't so—he'd heard this reported on Voice of America.

Later I got a chance to ask a member of the writers' and artists' union about songs being banned from the radio. He said he'd never heard of such a thing. (He also added that he didn't think a boycott of Pinochet's collaborators was such a bad idea, or a violation of artistic freedom.)

If there is one term that describes the prevailing attitude in Cuba on many social and cultural questions, it is tolerance. The operative word is "respect"—you respect someone's right to say something, do something, be a certain way, even if you, or the party, or the government, do not agree with it.

For example, there is complete freedom of religion in Cuba. If you want to go to church, you go. If you want to pray, you pray. In reality, most people, especially young people, don't have anything to do with churches. I passed by one Havana church while Sunday noon mass was in progress. A small congregation of maybe fifteen or twenty people were in the front pews, dwarfed by the huge building. They were mostly older women.

"We don't worry about religion," a member of the Communist Party told me. "In the old society it was a source of hope for those without any, and was kept up by the rich so that people would pray instead of fighting the exploiters. Now the people know where hope lies—in the revolution—because they have seen the promises kept. Some people still pray to god to go to heaven, but they know if they want to solve a problem down here, they should talk to their delegate in the People's Power."

If the pope visited Cuba today, he would certainly not find himself received as in Poland!

The same kind of tolerance and respect characterizes other social relations.

Cuba was a Latin American country strongly influenced by the Catholic Church, and many traces of that influence still remain. Pre-marital sex, for example, was to people of my parents' generation the gravest of sins.

There is no "party line" on whether young people should have sexual relations. But in schools sex education is provided, and contraception and abortion are freely available. If a young, unmarried woman has an abortion, her parents are informed only if she wants them to be. The government respects the privacy of the individuals.

The government has been moving toward a similar policy on homosexuality. Laws inherited from the capitalist past punishing homosexuality as a crime have been quietly eliminated in the last few years. In this case, government policy considers the heterosexual couple to be the norm—but what people do in their own homes is their affair. According to government officials we spoke with, the antihomosexuality propaganda campaigns carried out in earlier years have been abandoned.

While in Cuba, I happened to meet some homosexuals, including members of the UJC, and they confirmed that this is the case. At the same time, they pointed out that antihomosexual attitudes are deeply held by many Cubans, and that this can be a big problem, especially in the absence of any efforts by the government to combat these prejudices.

The situation of unmarried mothers is in some ways similar. Again, the government holds the heterosexual couple to be the norm, but a woman's decision to become a single mother is her own. In this case, equal rights for her and the child are specifically guaranteed by the Family Code.

Institutionalization

Among American radicals, one of the least understood changes in Cuban society in recent years has been the process known as "institutionalization," and in particular, the setting up of government bodies known as Assemblies of People's Power.

These assemblies function on three levels: local, provincial, and national. The members of the assemblies generally do not devote most of their time to its work. Often they are workers who continue with their regular jobs. If they devote full time to assembly tasks, they take a leave from their regular job and, while working for the assembly, get paid whatever they were previously earning.

Local assemblies are elected periodically by direct secret ballot. By law, there must be at least two candidates for every delegate's seat, and all candidates must live in the neighborhood or area from which they are elected. Nominations are made at neighborhood assemblies.

Cuban law forbids any organization, including the Communist Party, from presenting official candidates, slates, or endorsements. U.S.-style campaign hoopla is also outlawed, being considered—not without reason—as more appropriate for a carnival than for an election.

At the same time, however, this way of organizing elections deemphasizes discussion of issues and policies and make no provision for the election of candidates based on the political positions they hold on the issues facing the Cuban working people and their government.

The local Assemblies of People's Power run the schools and many other local services. They elect from their members an executive committee and full-time functionaries. The delegates from the neighborhoods play the role of ombudsman, and one of the major roles of the assemblies is to serve as a link between the locality and the various administrative branches of the central government and economy. The assemblies also play a role in formulating economic development plans for their area.

Every three or four months, the deputy from a neighborhood has to present before a neighborhood mass meeting an accounting of what he or she has been doing. If at any time the people of the neighborhood are dissatisfied, the delegate can be recalled either through petition or through vote at a neighborhood meeting. The final decision on whether a delegate stays or goes is by secret ballot. If the delegate is removed, a new election is then held. Although recalls aren't common, it's happened often enough in the few years the system has been in operation (about 100 times) that everyone knows it is not merely a formal provision, but one that can be readily exercised.

From my discussions with people in various parts of Cuba, I found that the role of the assemblies is pretty much as officially described, although there is unevenness from area to area and even within a given locality in how well and responsively the system functions. Often this depends on who the particular delegate happens to be.

In general, people I talked with thought that this system is far preferable to the previous practices, where lines of authority over local services were often unclear and where many decisions had to be referred to government ministries headquartered in Havana, at which point they often got lost in administrative red tape.

The provincial assemblies are elected by the local assemblies. Delegates to provincial assemblies can be members of the local assemblies, but most often are not. The National Assembly is elected by the provincial assemblies.

According to the Cuban Constitution, the National Assembly is the highest decision-making body. Since it meets only a few days each year, however, most of its responsibilities are delegated to the smaller committees it elects—the Council of Ministers and the Council of State. Given the degree of popular support for the policies of the revolution and for the central team of leaders around Fidel Castro—which is identified with the development and implementation of the revolution's line of march—the fact that the top government officials are now elected hasn't brought about many changes.

The establishment of the organs of People's Power is the centerpiece of institutionalization, but not its only aspect. It has been a broader process of establishing vehicles through which Cubans can express opinions on and, within limits, participate in running society.

As part of institutionalization, the unions have been virtually rebuilt and their role clarified. Among the tasks of the unions is to defend the interests of the workers, ensure good working conditions, and guarantee that workers receive the pay they are entitled to. Union assemblies also discuss and vote on the economic plan for a given workplace. If the workers differ with the planning authorities on the goals, part of the job of the union leadership is to discuss with the planners and come up with a revised proposal.

Local union officials are elected by secret direct ballot and can be removed from their posts by the members at any time. (This is generally true of the local officials of all the mass organizations sponsored by the government, such as the Federation of Cuban Women and the Committees for the Defense of the Revolution.)

Prospects and problems

The stated purpose of institutionalization was to overcome a number of problems that became evident in Cuba in 1970, with the revolution's failure to achieve the ten-million-ton sugar harvest that had been set as the central economic goal.

At that time, Fidel said that the problem hadn't

The failure to reach the ten-million-ton goal in the 1970 sugar harvest showed the leadership that workers needed more input in decision-making and spurred the process of institutionalization.

been the workers, but the leadership of the revolution, which had been out of touch with the masses. Many workers knew the plans in their sugar refinery were unrealistic or that the mobilizations for the harvest were disrupting production. Yet there was no vehicle for them to express these opinions and collectively affect policy decisions.

In essence, the task the Cuban government set

for itself was to come up with institutionalized ways of being better in touch with what the workers and peasants are thinking, what their problems are, and what to do about them.

In doing this, the Cubans felt there were no ready models available for consultation. The example of the first years of the Soviet Republic, under the leadership of Lenin and Trotsky, has been obscured by decades of purges, the Gulag Archipelago, monstrous glorification of supposedly infallible leaders, and other undemocratic measures needed by the Stalinist bureaucracy to preserve its privileges.

The new Cuban institutions are not of the same type as the councils of workers, peasants, and soldiers in the early years of the Russian revolution. Historically, they did not arise in the same way. The soviets were the mass struggle organs that brought down the tsar. The Bolsheviks fought to win the leadership of the soviets away from the reformists who wanted to preserve capitalism, and they strengthened these mass organizations in the fight to overthrow the bourgeoisie and establish the institutions for a new government.

As I've already described, this is not the origin of the assemblies in Cuba. And that fact, along with the gutting of soviet democracy in the Soviet Union, has had an impact on the character of the institutionalization measures in Cuba.

Based on what I learned during the brigade trip, I think that institutionalization in Cuba has helped slow down and in some cases reduced tendencies toward the growth of bureaucracy and bureaucratism there, and that it has opened the door to greater elements of workers democracy, not less. It is neither a conscious, direct step toward democratic councils of workers and peasants modeled on those that existed in the early Soviet Union, nor an attempt to prevent such a development.

Instead, institutionalization has meant an increase in the ability of the Cuban masses to participate in running the country, especially on the local level, and to discuss and influence decisions on overall policies of the revolution.

Nonetheless, there remain serious limitations. Questions concerning the fundamental policy and economic alternatives of the revolution aren't discussed through and acted on by the population as a whole in an organized way.

The reason for this weakness is not so much that the present institutions are totally unsuitable. They could readily be adapted to begin such discussions, and they could be modified or revamped over time as the need arose. The fundamental reason hampering the full discussion of such national decisions is that the Castro leadership opposes the organization of varying currents of opinion around political issues or alternative platforms within the framework of the revolution. The Cuban leadership views the formation of such organized currents of opinion as an obstacle to the unity necessary for a small, isolated, underdeveloped nation to survive against the permanent siege imposed by the imperialist colossus to its north.

This position of the Cuban leadership is reflected in many ways in Cuban society. One that most struck me was the fact that the rich political discussions that go on all the time in Cuba find very little reflection in the printed media, especially mass-circulation publications such as the daily *Granma* and the weekly *Bohemia*. I was told that articles expressing differing views on such questions continue to appear in specialized journals from time to time. However, these don't reach most Cubans, even those in the Communist Party.

The concern for safeguarding the revolution and achieving the greatest possible unity in the revolutionary movement is a legitimate one. Under the ferocious attack of the counterrevolution, the Bolsheviks had to take away political rights from those who conspired with the counterrevolution and to violate other democratic norms. Such measures were necessary to ensure that the revolution survived.

Nevertheless, at the moments of greatest danger—even when the Bolshevik Party temporarily banned organized factions in 1921—it continued to have a rich internal life marked by debate and organized discussion. At the very party congress where the ban was passed, Lenin stressed the need to continue a "more comprehensive exchange of opinion between Party members" and the election of delegates to party congresses on the basis of political platform when that was necessitated by "fundamental disagreements."

This is in fact what happened. Various currents in the Bolshevik Party continued to have lively debates and at times sharp polemics. The issues were the fundamental questions facing the revolution. And the exchange of views strengthened the revolution rather than weakening it.

Lenin, Trotsky, and the other central leaders of the Bolshevik Party encouraged such an internal regime because they believed that it led to the best decisions. Moreover, the political clarity and education gained from such discussions, and the generalized understanding of decisions arrived at democratically, helped ensure that they were carried out with maximum effectiveness and unity.

Like the Cuban leaders, the Bolsheviks understood the fundamental importance of consciousness in motivating people to carry out the tasks of the revolution. They relied heavily on the freest possible discussion as a tool to develop consciousness. The idea of a monolithic party was not Lenin's; it was Stalin's—the flip side of the cult of the infallible leader.

The tremendous educational value of the Bolsheviks' methods can be gauged from the writings of Lenin that continue to be basic educational material in the revolutionary movement today. And these don't date simply from the period before the October revolution.

In fact, in the last year before his death, Lenin formed a political bloc with Trotsky to fight the bureaucratization, encroachments against the rights of oppressed nationalities, and threats against the monopoly of foreign trade—all of which were policies fostered by Stalin as he exploited Lenin's serious illness to extend his control over the party and government apparatus.

So, while in my opinion the institutionalization process represents an advance both from the standpoint of increasing elements of workers democracy and combating bureaucratization in Cuba, I think that a further qualitative improvement remains to be achieved: finding forms through which organized discussion on competing viewpoints can be held, both in the vanguard party and in society as a whole.

Changes in the countryside

Nowhere has the impact of the Cuban revolution been as deep as in the countryside. The barebone facts of this transformation are fairly well known. The giant *latifundios* owned by the American monopolies or native landholders have been nationalized. Individual small farmers have been given title to the land they work. Schooling and medical care have been made available to the rural population. Illiteracy, which was most prevalent in the countryside, has been wiped out. There are no children with the swollen bellies of malnutrition that abound in the rural areas of other Latin American countries. Mechanization of agriculture is proceeding steadily, especially the mechanization of the back-breaking sugarcane harvest.

The magnitude of the advances registered by the Cuban rural population is not always fully appreciated by people who are unfamiliar with the conditions of the peasants in countries exploited by imperialism. We had the opportunity to visit rural areas that before the revolution had been sunk in almost feudal backwardness and to hear *campesinos* tell us their own story.

We visited one of the new towns being built by the government in the Escambray mountains, in the center of the island. Instead of dirt-floor straw huts, these people now have modem apartments, with electricity and running water. Every apartment has a TV set, a window on the world. This town of about 1,000 has a grammar school, a clinic, recreational center, store, and library.

One woman explained to me what moving to this town had meant to her. She said that before the revolution, she and her entire family had been illiterate. She had never even heard of electricity, much less had an opportunity to use it. The first time she saw an electric light bulb, she thought it was magic. She had never been to a town or city, visited a doctor, or seen a movie or play.

I said that it must be like a new life. She answered, "The revolution didn't give us a new life, it gave us our first life. Before the revolution, we didn't live. We were like animals. I come from a very large family of fourteen children. Only four lived long enough to have children of their own."

She said that when the revolution came, at first they were suspicious. "We had never needed to read before, we didn't know what reading was for. We just wanted to be left alone to grow our food and raise our children."

Even after she and her husband had learned to read, had access to medical care, and her children had gone off to school, she still lived in a hut—although one with a concrete floor, thanks to the revolution. Then officials of the National Association of Small Farmers (ANAP) came and told them about the new community that would be built in their zone.

> We didn't want to move. You have to understand what we were like. The only thing we had ever had, the only security, was that piece of land and our hut.

It took several years to convince them. No coercion was used, just the positive argument of example.

> At first, it was just a couple of the older people, whose children had all moved away, who were having difficulty supporting themselves, who moved. Then there were a few others.
> They would come back and tell us, 'This is the real life. No more walking to the stream with heavy buckets of water for cooking. No more working from sunrise to sunset until you drop from exhaustion.'

So finally they moved. Her husband now works at a state farm rather than on his own private plot. They are both studying in what is known as "the battle for the sixth grade"—the governmental program to assure that every adult Cuban has completed a grammar school education. When they conquer that, they plan to continue in "the battle for the ninth grade." She has one son who is a doctor; another an agricultural expert currently stationed in Ethiopia; a daughter who is studying to be a teacher.

A visit to Sandino

Many of the original residents of the Escambray mountains no longer live in that area. During the early years of the revolution, CIA-sponsored counterrevolutionary bands were active in those mountains and succeeded, for a time, in convincing some of the *campesinos* that the revolution meant their small plots would be taken away. The government was forced to uproot many families in the area, and later they were resettled in the westernmost tip of Cuba, in a municipality (an area roughly comparable to an American county) known as Sandino.

If you've ever read the things put out by counterrevolutionary Cuban exiles in the United States, you've heard about Sandino, the "slave city" and "forced labor camp," allegedly comparable only to Hitler's concentration camps.

We visited Sandino. Again, in addition to hearing officials describe the accomplishments of the revolution in the area, we were able—in fact, encouraged—to talk to the people who live there. I happened to find one of those who had been resettled from the Escambray mountains.

> Nobody wants to talk about it anymore. It was a thousand years ago. But I know what they say in the United States, I listen to the shortwave, about how we are all slaves here. I laugh when I hear that.

He explained that when the revolution first came to power, "I didn't understand, I was confused. I saw them take the land from the big landowners, from the powerful important people. I thought that if even the rich couldn't save themselves from the communists, then for sure they would take my land. They just hadn't gotten around to me yet."

He told me how he was arrested by the revolutionary government for cooperating with the CIA-sponsored bandits. "I'm not so ashamed of it anymore. I know now it could have happened to anyone, because of our ignorance, because we believed anything the priests and the 'good people,' the exploiters, told us.

> The Revolution understood that too. We weren't treated as criminals, but as a brother who had gone astray. We were given a chance to start a new life here. It was hard work, we had to earn our right to be part of this revolution, but so has everybody else in this country for twenty years.

He is now a member of the Communist Party and a leader of his community. I asked him if there were others in the party like him, who had been deceived by the bandits. "Oh yes, there must be quite a few. But we don't think about that, we don't worry about that now. Cuba then was like a different country. We have a new homeland now, and what we think about is the Cuba of today, the socialist homeland we are building."

The transformation of the Cuban countryside is something to behold. There are paved roads everywhere. New agricultural communities like those we visited in the Escambray mountains are springing up on all sides.

Collectivization

Of all the countries that have abolished capitalism, Cuban officials report, Cuba has the biggest state sector in agriculture. Fully 70 percent of the arable land became state property in the early 1960's, including the large sugar plantations that simply couldn't have functioned if they had been broken down into individual family plots. They were transformed into state farms.

The "schools in the countryside" program combines academic study with productive labor. These students also tend citrus fields.

Nevertheless, the family farm is still an important part of the Cuban economy. At the very beginning of the revolution, efforts were made to convince the peasants to amalgamate into cooperatives, but they were soon abandoned as premature.

Now, a new large-scale campaign is under way to persuade the family farmers that they'd be better off as part of larger and more productive units, such as state farms and cooperatives.

In a talk to members of the Antonio Maceo Brigade, Juan José León, vice-president of the National Association of Small Farmers, explained the evolution of the government's policies.

He said that, at first, the resources to develop the technology for more productive large-scale agriculture did not exist. Tractors and other machinery can make large-scale farming more economical. But Cuba lacked the tractors. They didn't have the irrigation works or the planes to spray large areas with pesticides, or the fertilizers. Over the years, Cuba has modernized her agricultural technology, making it available to the individual small farms as well as to the state sector. Now a big advance in productivity is possible through collectivizing the small farms.

A second reason for the previous policy of not aggressively encouraging collectivization, León explained, was political. The motor force of Cuba's revolution is the conscious alliance of the workers with other productive classes, most importantly, the peasantry. What the peasants wanted most from the revolutionary government was their own land, the security of fair, stable prices and of knowing, through their own experience, that no one could take these away from them. In the early years of the revolution, he said, suggestions that the peasants should now give up their land and become part of a cooperative provoked consternation among the small farmers.

But today, after two decades, the government is aggressively trying to convince peasants to abandon the small family farm methods, either by selling their land to the state and becoming agricultural workers, or by pooling their land with other small farmers to form a cooperative.

Unlike the Soviet Union under Stalin, where collectivization was carried out by force and the country reaped agricultural catastrophe as a result, the revolution has made an inviolable promise to the small producers that they will never be pressured or forced to abandon their farms. The decision to collectivize is up to the small farmers.

Instead of forcing them to give up their land, they are shown the advantages of shifting to modern large-scale agriculture. In addition, the government provides still other incentives to peasants to collectivize.

For example, given Cuba's limited resources, it is impossible to provide and maintain services such as running water and electricity for an isolated farm family far away from any population concentration. But when several dozen small farmers get together and form a cooperative, the government helps them build a small community. And because the population is now concentrated, it becomes possible to provide many services that aren't available to an isolated family.

León told us that the government would like to advance toward collectivization of the small farms as quickly as possible, but not at the cost of breaking its pledge to the small farmers. He said their policy was based on the program of the *Communist Manifesto*:

> The goal of the revolution is to eliminate the difference between the countryside and the city. The basic tool we are using right now is promotion of cooperatives, convincing the small farmer.
>
> We can't take any other measures except convincing the peasants. If we are incapable of convincing the Cuban farmer that collective production is better than individual production, that means we have failed politically. Forced measures would mean the political failure of our revolution.

'Schools in the countryside'

One element in the transformation of the rural areas is the tremendously successful program of "schools in the countryside."

A basic principle of Cuban education is the combination of study with productive labor. The revolutionary government believes that work is a fundamental part of education, giving young people an appreciation of the effort involved in keeping society going as well as a sense of self-esteem as productive members of society, full partners in the revolution. They point out this idea isn't original, but again is taken from Marx, Engels, and Martí.

"Schools in the countryside" involve young people from junior high school age and up. They are boarding schools, with the students spending the week at the school and returning home over the weekend. The typical school has 600 students, with half working in the morning and studying in the afternoon, and the other half following the reverse schedule. Each school has large orchards of citrus fruit and sometimes other crops surrounding it. The students tend to and harvest the fruit with the help of agricultural experts.

This program got under way in the early 1970s, as the large number of children from the baby boom that immediately followed the revolution approached junior high school age. By all accounts, it has been tremendously successful. The students like it because it gives them a chance to broaden their experiences—many view it as an adventure. The parents like it because it helps relieve them of some of the burdens of raising children and because they know the children will have everything they need—good food, plenty of exercise, medical care, clothing and recreation, as well as an education. And—of course—all this is provided absolutely free.

The "schools in the countryside" have had their biggest impact on an island off Cuba's southern coast that used to be known as the Isle of Pines, but today is called the Isle of Youth.

Before the revolution, the main feature of the Isle of Pines was a chamber of horrors known as the Model Prison, notorious for its terrible conditions, and the torture and murder of inmates. It was there that Fidel and other survivors were imprisoned after the July 26, 1953, raid on the Moncada barracks. Many members of the July 26 Movement were also incarcerated there during the revolutionary war. Today the prison is a museum, a grim reminder of the barbarism of the capitalist past.

The countryside of the Isle of Youth has been transformed by dozens of ESBECs, as the junior high schools in the countryside are called. Land that before was unused now has large, scientifically cultivated citrus groves, which are tended by the students.

We stayed at one of the schools for several days during our visit. Everywhere you drive on the Isle of Youth, you can see two, three, or four of these schools surrounded by their citrus groves.

In addition to students from the Isle of Youth and from Cuba's western provinces, there are thousands of Africans studying on the Isle of Youth. Their schools are fully bilingual, run by joint teams of educators from Cuba and their native countries. Every effort is made to instill in the young Africans a sense of pride in the culture and the history of struggles for liberation of their own people.

We spent an afternoon with African students from various countries at one of the African ESBECs. We met seventeen-year-old veterans of Angola's war for independence against the Portuguese; Namibian youth who in some cases were the only members of their families who had survived massacres carried out by the troops of the South African regime; young Ethiopians who until a few years ago had nothing to look forward to but a life of serfdom under the boot of feudal landowners.

One Namibian girl, barely into her teens, told me, "Cuba is more than another country, more than a place to study. We study hard, then we go back to make a revolution in Namibia as beautiful as the one here. Cuba is the symbol of what we are fighting for."

U.S. imperialist pressure

One point that was constantly driven home to me by being in Cuba is the tremendous pressure the revolution is under from U.S. imperialism. Cuba is still an island under siege. Imperialism even has the Guantánamo Naval Base, a military post within Cuba's national territory.

At every factory the workers organize guard duty. Although for the moment antisocial actions (yes, there is still some crime in Cuba) are more of a problem than saboteurs, everybody knows that the United States government might organize a resurgence of terrorist attacks at any time.

Less than a year ago, Cuba was forced to carry out major military mobilizations when dozens of American warships showed up unannounced just a few miles off the coast. Spy flights in violation of Cuba's air space were resumed at the same time. A few days later came the official explanation from the U.S. Department of Defense: just practicing.

U.S. imperialism's aggression against Cuba is not a thing of the past. Three years ago, CIA-sponsored counterrevolutionary terrorists blew up a Cubana de Aviacion plane in mid-air near Barbados, killing all seventy-three aboard. Just last April, these same outfits took credit for the cold-blooded assassination of Antonio Maceo Brigade leader Carlos Muñiz Varela. Although the assassination took place in broad daylight, in front of witnesses, the cops have failed to arrest those responsible.

While the brigade was in Cuba, we received the news of a new attack on the travel agency that Carlos Muñiz had headed, which dedicates itself exclusively to organizing visits to Cuba by Cubans living abroad. A bomb was placed at its offices. Fortunately, it was found before it exploded. As usual, no arrests. On October 27, a powerful bomb ripped apart the gate outside the Cuban mission to the UN in New York City. Once again, there have been no arrests.

Bombings, assassination attempts, and countless other crimes in New York, Miami, and other American cities, have been carried out with complete impunity. The U.S. government cynically claims that it cannot catch the terrorists—as if it had not recruited, trained, armed, and organized them in the first place.

More damaging than the terrorist attacks, however, has been a policy which the U.S. government openly admits to carrying out—the economic blockade of Cuba. Fidel calls it "a knife at Cuba's throat"—and justly so.

In Cuba, we saw firsthand the impact of the blockade. Virtually all of the industrial plant inherited from the capitalist past was built with U.S. technology. Because of the U.S. blockade, Cuba has to buy spare parts from third-party chiselers, when it can get them, or do without.

In the streets of Havana, you can still see the 1950s Detroit models puttering along. Cuban car mechanics are said to be the best in the world, probably because they have gotten the most practice, fixing cars without spare parts from the manufacturers. But think of the tremendous expenditure of time and effort on problems that could be solved in five minutes with the right parts.

Cuba is a small country heavily dependent on trade. The economic blockade closes off huge markets for Cuban products. I was told that Cuba could produce a lot more rum—the best in the world—and earn desperately needed foreign exchange. But the markets aren't available.

Cuba also has to import many things. Right now, most imports come thousands of miles from Western Europe, the other workers states, or Japan. Many items could be bought as cheaply, or more cheaply, from U.S. manufacturers—and shipping would be considerably less expensive.

Whether it's a technician at an old electrical generating plant, a warehouse administrator with a broomcloset full of broken typewriters, or a housewife who has somehow managed to keep a Hoover vacuum cleaner going, virtually everyone in Cuba can tell you stories of what the blockade has meant for them in time, effort, sacrifice.

End the blockade!

Why does the United States maintain the blockade? Carter spelled it out in a report to Congress at the end of 1978: Cuban troops in Africa, Cuba's support to Puerto Rican independence, Cuba's solidarity with the revolutionary struggle against Somoza in Nicaragua. In a word, Cuba's anti-imperialist foreign policy. Change that, Carter told Cuba, and we'll be the best of friends.

Carter didn't have to wait long for a reply—the same reply U.S. presidents have heard for two decades. "Cuba can't be pressured or intimidated or bribed or bought," Fidel Castro countered in his twentieth anniversary speech.

One of the first days I was in Cuba, a member of the Union of Young Communists who was traveling with us asked me what was my party's position on Cuba. I started to explain that while we might not agree with all the positions of the Castro leadership, we considered it to be a revolutionary current in the international workers movement.

"Yes, yes, of course," she interrupted, "but what is your position on the blockade?" I told her we were against it, and why; that we had been stepping up our activities and education against it, and that we would like to see a broad, united-front movement develop to force the U.S. government to abandon the blockade. We discussed various ideas I had on this: how to involve the unions, and the role young Cubans in the U.S. who support the revolution can play. Then we talked about the international debate among radicals about Cuba.

Later I asked her why she had brought up the blockade right away, as if she thought maybe our position could have been different.

"No," she answered. "I knew you were against it, otherwise you wouldn't be here. It's just that sometimes, in these discussions concerning us, you can forget about the main enemy. You can get so wrapped up debating the best way to fight that not much fighting takes place.

"You're lucky. You're right in the home of the enemy. You should take advantage of that."

THE CHARACTER OF THE CUBAN LEADERSHIP
by Alan Jones

In an article entitled "Cuba—Twenty Years of Revolution," which appeared in the February 19 issue of *Intercontinental Press/Inprecor*, Comrade Jack Barnes has set out an analysis concerning the character of the Cuban leadership. He asserts with the greatest possible emphasis that this is a *revolutionary* leadership—not merely in the past but also at the present time. He approvingly states that:

> At the 1961 convention of the SWP, Morris Stein, one of the experienced veteran leaders of the party, explained to a minority grouping inside the SWP that was opposed to recognizing the realities of Cuba that the Castro leadership team was superior to the Bolshevik leadership, once you leave aside Lenin, Trotsky, Sverdlov, and people like that.
> That was what we were dealing with historically, that is what our responsibilities were, and are.[1]
> The Cuban leaders were revolutionists of action. In one of Trotsky's discussions with members of our party at the end of the 1930s, he predicted that the next great revolutionary leaders would not be great theoreticians like Marx, writing things like *Capital*. We are in an epoch now where we will see great revolutionists of action come forward, and we must come forward and meet them.
> That's what we saw in Cuba: an installment on that promise by Trotsky.[2]

> We have never seen a revolutionary leadership in power for this length of time.[3]

Barnes also states that there exists only one basic divide with regard to Trotskyists, the Cuban leadership, and counterrevolutionaries:

> ... the real line to be drawn is the line between the revolutionists—meaning Castro and those around him, including us—and the counterrevolutionaries on the other side, including the Stalinists and the so-called "Third Camp" social democrats.[4]

The basic situation is therefore logically characterized as one of "the existence of a workers state with a revolutionary leadership."[5]

These characterizations are evidently of great importance. Not merely was the Cuban revolution one of the most important events in the history of the international class struggle, but the Castroist international policy, in particular in Africa, is a major element in world politics. Furthermore, if there existed in even one country, regardless of its numerical weight, a workers state with an authentically *revolutionary* leadership, then this would be a fact around which revolutionists would have to organize their entire view of the world. A decisive, probably *the* decisive, task would be that of united anti-imperialist struggle, a united anticapitalist and antibureaucratic struggle, and the fight for the creation of a common revolutionary party with this current.

---

1. "Cuba—Twenty Years of Revolution" by Jack Barnes, in *Intercontinental Press/Inprecor*, February 19, 1979, p. 158. See also *Selected Speeches of Fidel Castro*, Education for Socialists (New York: Pathfinder Press, 1979), p. 8 [2014 printing].

2. Barnes, p. 158. See also *Selected Speeches of Fidel Castro*, p. 8.

3. Barnes, p. 155. See also *Selected Speeches of Fidel Castro*, p. 3.

4. Barnes, p. 157. See also *Selected Speeches of Fidel Castro*, p. 7.

5. Barnes, p. 159. See also *Selected Speeches of Fidel Castro*, p. 10.

Unfortunately, however, the characterizations and the argumentation given by Comrade Barnes are seriously wrong and could dangerously disorient revolutionists. We will look in this article at some of the theoretical and political issues involved.

The theoretical issues

The first theoretical question raised by Comrade Barnes's analysis is obviously whether there can be revolutionary forces that are non-Trotskyist—for obviously whatever its nature the Castroist leadership is not a Trotskyist one. The answer to this is undoubtedly that there can be revolutionists who are not Trotskyists and that this was the position of Trotsky himself.

Of course, in noting this Trotsky refused to characterize any current as revolutionary merely because it itself claimed to be so. Currents that existed at the time Trotsky wrote in the late 1930s—for example the Independent Labour Party in Britain, the POUM[6] in Spain, the London Bureau[7]—might well claim to be revolutionary forces but in reality they supported collaboration with bourgeois parties in Popular Fronts, refused to come out against Stalinist repression in the USSR, capitulated before imperialist wars, etc. They were not revolutionary but *centrist* forces. In this situation Trotsky did not hesitate to state of the initial Trotskyist forces in the Fourth International that "outside of these cadres there does not exist a single revolutionary current on this planet really meriting the name."[8]

However, this absolutely correct statement by Trotsky concerning the situation in 1938 did not mean that he considered that there could not be in other places and at other times authentically revolutionary forces which were not Trotskyist. On the contrary, he explicitly held the opposite position. He wrote: "The Fourth International will not be composed only of Bolshevik-Leninists [the name Trotskyists gave themselves at this time.]."[9] He stated: "The Bolshevik-Leninists consider themselves a faction of the International which is being built. They are completely ready to work hand in hand with other truly revolutionary factions."[10]

The reason why Trotsky held such a position is no mystery to anyone who has studied the history of the Marxist movement. Trotsky knew not merely from theory but from the experience of the Bolsheviks and the Comintern, in its revolutionary period, that any serious revolutionary party and International will inevitably have different ideological and political currents and trends within it. Even inside the Bolsheviks there had been different trends on certain questions, with "left" and "right" currents existing. On an international scale, Bolshevism had undoubtedly constituted the most consistently revolutionary trend in the workers movement. But that did not prevent there being other currents, which, while less consistently correct than the Bolsheviks, nevertheless were *authentically* revolutionary. Indeed, such currents could even be correct against Lenin on a number of questions. For example, Rosa Luxemburg was not a Leninist; she was precisely a "Luxemburgist." But that did not at all mean that she was not one of the greatest of all working-class leaders and actually correct against Lenin on certain issues. As Trotsky wrote:

> If one were to take the disagreements between Lenin and Rosa Luxemburg in their entirety, then historical correctness is unconditionally on Lenin's side. But this does not exclude the fact that on certain questions and during

---

6. Partido Obrero de Unificación Marxista (Workers Party of Marxist Unification), a left-centrist socialist organization that participated in the Popular Front government during the Spanish Civil War.—*IP/I.*

7. A loose association of centrist parties in the early 1930s which were not affiliated with either the Second or Third Internationals, but were opposed to the formation of a Fourth International. Among its members were the POUM of Spain and the SAP (Socialist Workers Party) of Germany.—*IP/I.*

8. Trotsky, *The Transitional Program for Socialist Revolution* (New York: Pathfinder Press, 1973), p. 196 [2014 printing]. Trotsky is here of course using "revolutionary" in its serious sense and not in the misleading way in which "revolutionary left" is sometimes used to mean all those organizations *claiming* to be revolutionary. This latter term is used in a false way that lumps together organizations that *are* revolutionary with those that are centrist. The term revolutionary throughout this article is used in this strict sense of organizations

that are proletarian in political position and not centrist.

9. Trotsky, *Writings of Leon Trotsky (1935–36)* (New York: Pathfinder Press, 1970, 1977), p. 195 {2012 printing}.

10. Trotsky, *The Crisis of the French Section (1935–36)* (New York: Pathfinder Press, 1977), p. 58 [2011 printing].

definite periods Rosa Luxemburg was correct as against Lenin.[11]

When Stalin, on the basis of particular issues on which she was wrong, attempted to claim that Luxemburg was not a revolutionist because she had not been a Leninist, Trotsky denounced this as nonsense. He wrote: "This great revolutionist is enrolled by Stalin into the camp of Centrism!"[12] He said that although Luxemburg was obviously not a Leninist, "the disagreements [between Luxemburg and Lenin], despite their importance and at times their extreme sharpness, developed on the basis of revolutionary proletarian policies common to them both."[13] Lenin completely shared this assessment:

> Rosa Luxemburg was mistaken on the question of the independence of Poland; she was mistaken in 1903 in her appraisal of Menshevism; she was mistaken in July 1914, when, together with Plekhanov, Vandervelde, Kautsky and others, she advocated unity between the Bolsheviks and Mensheviks; she was mistaken in what she wrote in prison in 1918 (she corrected most of these mistakes at the end of 1918 and the beginning of 1919 after she was released). But in spite of her mistakes she was—and remains for us—an eagle. And not only will Communists all over the world cherish her memory, but her biography and her *complete* works (the publication of which the German Communists are inordinately delaying, which can only be partly excused by the tremendous losses they are suffering in their severe struggle) will serve as useful manuals for training many generations of Communists all over the world.[14]

Furthermore, after the formation of the Communist International, and even after its degeneration, Trotsky was clear that not all revolutionary forces were Leninists—or that only Trotskyists could be revolutionaries. Thus, for example, Trotsky noted of one such case that: "The so-called left faction of the Italian Communists (Prometeo group or Bordigists) has its own traditions which are sharply distinguished from the traditions of the Bolshevik-Leninists."[15]

However, despite the fact that unity with these Bordigists was obviously not possible in the framework of a faction, which is what at that time of 1932 the Trotskyists defined themselves as, nevertheless Trotsky specifically stated that "the Bordigists represent a serious revolutionary group."[16] Although in this particular case, in the unfavorable conditions of the 1930s, the Bordigists underwent a rapid degeneration, and no one would any longer consider them revolutionary; nevertheless, once again this shows that Trotsky did not at all consider that *only* Trotskyists could be revolutionists. James P. Cannon was therefore perfectly following Trotsky's position, and drawing the organizational conclusions that Trotsky had drawn, when he wrote in 1961 that:

> Trotsky never envisaged the Fourth International as a monolithic, purely Trotskyist organization, but as a broad revolutionary movement in which we, orthodox Trotskyists, might possibly, under certain conditions and for certain periods, be a minority. He stated this explicitly in one of his letters prior to the Founding Congress in 1938. He proposed that Chen Tu-hsiu, who at that time was in sharp conflict with our Chinese section over some important questions, should be invited to be a member of the International Executive Committee.
>
> The internal regime of our international movement during the lifetime of Trotsky never tried to enforce monolithism. . . . The Discussion Bulletins of our international movement throughout this period show that differences of opinion on the most important questions arose again and again and were freely discussed. A large part of our education

---

11. Trotsky, *Writings of Leon Trotsky (1932)* (New York: Pathfinder Press, 1973), p. 180 [2011 printing].

12. Ibid., p. 172.

13. Ibid., p. 180.

14. Lenin, *Collected Works* (Moscow: Progress Publishers, 1966) Vol. 33, p. 210.

15. Trotsky, *Writings of Leon Trotsky (1932–33)* (New York: Pathfinder Press, 1972), p. 73 [2012 printing].

16. Ibid., p. 33.

in fact was derived from these discussions.

The recognition of the Soviet Union as a workers state, and of the obligation to defend it against imperialist attack, was a central principle of our international movement all the time. This characterization and this attitude was challenged time and again, year after year, and freely discussed without expulsions or threats of expulsion.

In the classic battle of 1939–40 with the Burnham-Shachtman faction, they were about as wrong as it was possible for a faction to be in America under conditions of that time. Shachtman thought we were engaged in a 'polemic' and conducted himself like a high school debater scoring points. He didn't really know that he was dealing with a question of a revolution and that it was dangerous to play with such a question. He didn't know it because he didn't feel it.

It was a red hot question for us at that time, just as the Cuban Revolution is at present, because public opinion was being mobilized every day by all the imperialist agencies against the Soviet Union. It was particularly reprehensible for Shachtman to choose that period to wash his hands of it. But despite this deep and terrible difference on such a burning question as one's attitude toward a revolution in existence, Trotsky did not advocate a split, not even if we should turn out to be a minority in the Convention struggle. The split followed only after the minority refused to accept the Convention decision.

That is still not the end of the story. *Seven years later* we conducted serious negotiations for unity with the Shachtmanites, despite the fact that they had not changed their position on the Soviet Union in the meantime. Those who may be playing with the idea of a 'monolithic' party and a monolithic international will have a hard time finding any support for it in the teachings and practice of the Old Man [Trotsky].[17]

Flowing from his characterization of the Cuban leadership as revolutionary, and from Trotsky's method of approach, Cannon also drew the necessary organizational conclusions. Talking of the discussion in Cuba on a new constitution after the declaration of the socialist character of the revolution, Cannon wrote:

> . . . the projected new constitution should provide for a representative workers' government based on workers' organizations or councils.
>
> Second, stemming also from the May Day declaration, our Cuban resolution should declare that this representative workers' government has to be led by a mass revolutionary party, formally organized and open to the most conscious and active revolutionary fighters.
>
> Third, the leadership of this party at its formal organization cannot be any other than that of the present leadership of the revolution and the defence of the country against the invasion.
>
> Fourth, the new constitution should provide for a regime of genuine workers' democracy, in which all tendencies supporting the revolution have full freedom of expression and association.
>
> Fifth, the Trotskyists, organized as a propaganda group, representing the tradition and unbroken continuation of revolutionary theory and practice will take their place as a definite tendency, like all other tendencies supporting the revolution, within the new revolutionary party.[18]

This position of Cannon's flowed logically from his characterization of the Cuban leadership. From the fact that they constituted a *revolutionary* current flowed the demand for unification in a single party based on internal democracy. From the fact that they were less consistently revolutionary in their positions than the Trotskyists flowed the rejection of the liquidation of Trotskyist forces, but instead their constitution as a definite organized tendency within the united party.

This conclusion of fighting for a perspective of

---

17. Cannon, in a May 22, 1961, letter to the SWP Political Committee, in *Trotskyism versus Revisionism* (London: New Park Publications, 1974) vol. 3, p. 80.

18. Ibid., p. 75.

organizational unification and tendency discussion obviously also applied to the international field. As Joseph Hansen pointed out, and against Healyite views to the contrary, the fact that a non-Trotskyist current could overthrow capitalism in a particular country in no way invalidated the need to build the Fourth International or for Trotskyists to participate as a tendency in the party of that country. As always, the character of a force, and its necessity or otherwise, had to be considered not from the national but from the world character of the class struggle:

> Now when we talk about a party, we mean an international party, one that is commensurate with tremendous international goals. We mean a party that is capable of taking the world working class and leading it forward to overthrow capitalism, which is an international system. From then on, leading the world out of capitalism to the socialist world of the future. That's what we mean by a revolutionary socialist party. A tremendous thing. One that is of the greatest historic importance. It's probably the greatest task that has faced humanity, the building of such a party.
>
> Now let me say right now that such a party has never been built yet. Marx didn't build one. Lenin didn't build one. They started the core of it. Their aim was absolutely clear—where they were headed. But they never conceived this party as simply a narrow, national party. They conceived it as an international one, one that is capable of the greatest task that has faced humanity, taking us from capitalism to socialism.
>
> When we say that capitalism is rotten-ripe for revolution, we also say that the conditions on an international scale are rotten-ripe for the construction of such a party, a tremendous international party that has all the knowledge and capacity, both political and theoretical, for accomplishing these great tasks. How are we going to build such a party? Will it be built in advance of the revolution? It would be very good if it could be—at least that's what the Cubans themselves say now—it would be good to have such a party in advance. The fact is that such a party has got to be built in the very process of revolution as revolutions occur with varying degrees of success. That's the fact that faces us. In some countries I think we will be able to build national sections of the party before the revolution occurs, and in some countries, like ours, I think that is an absolute condition for success. In other countries the revolution forges forward faster than the party. That's an evident fact of politics now. So, when we say a revolutionary party, a revolutionary socialist party, we don't just mean a revolutionary socialist party in little Cuba or in little Guatemala or in little Costa Rica or in little Nicaragua. Those will be important sections of it. We are thinking of an international party on a major scale, in which these are component parts.
>
> Thus we come to the conclusion that there is great unevenness in the growth and development of this party. Great unevenness. Some countries can forge forward faster than others. In some cases the action can transcend the political consciousness of it. Given this great unevenness in the development of an international party, we have to ask ourselves this question: Does this signify that it is impossible for the masses to overthrow a capitalist power in certain countries until the international party appears in full force and completeness? That's the question that faces us. We probably wouldn't even have asked this question if we hadn't already gotten certain answers. The answers are that in certain countries it is possible. Yugoslavia, China, and Cuba. That's the fact sheet. We have to look at it and say that's what it is. I would say that in the light of those three facts, we would have to conclude that it is possible in certain situations, in certain countries, under certain conditions—it is possible for the masses to go as far forward as establishing a workers' state.
>
> Having said that, we immediately come to the question of limitations. These are tremendous. Let's just take the case of Cuba. First of all, there were great and costly errors committed in the Cuban revolution. Great and costly ones. The revolution established a coalition government with bourgeois demo-

crats. That didn't help the revolution any. It led to a very ragged differentiation between the revolutionary forces and those that were counterrevolutionary—a process that's still proceeding in Cuba. That's the reason for all these "defections" that take place in Cuba; it's the flight of the counterrevolutionaries.

There was a great error made in the relations between the Cuban revolution and the American workers. One of the first things they did down there was to immediately break off all connections with the trade union movement in the United States. And George Meany said, "Thank you." He couldn't have asked for anything better than such an error on the part of the Cuban revolutionaries. Cut off their relations with the American trade unions.

They've made considerable errors in the extension of their revolution in Latin America. They realized the general importance and need of it, but so far as actually carrying it out in a coordinated, organized way, it has been very, very slipshod, with any number of errors. We can see that in a practical way in our experience with the Fair Play for Cuba Committee. The thing never seemed to get off the ground. It operates in a way that is completely alien to all our concepts—not only our concepts, but alien to the needs of the Cuban revolution. That's one of the problems that has arisen because of the lack of a revolutionary party in Cuba.

Take it from the economic side. Look at the delays that occurred down there in the process of the revolution, in expropriating the properties; they had to wait until they were pushed into it by American imperialism, slapped around, then there was a response, a defensive reflex to these blows struck by American imperialism. They were stumbling, fumbling, losing all kinds of valuable time which the bourgeoisie in the United States utilized in order to prepare the ground psychologically for their counterrevolution. Two years of time—a year and a half at least—was wasted almost, while the bourgeoisie in the United States, step by step, got prepared psychologically for the counterrevolution.

Finally, we come to this big error in the Cuban revolution, its big limitation; and that is the lack of the development of democratic forms of rule. To any Trotskyist, any revolutionary socialist, it jumps out before your eyes, the weakness of the revolution on that side. And that weakness derives primarily from the weakness of the leadership, of its consciousness. All these things tell us the limitations of this workers' state that has appeared in Cuba. And this side is just as important as the other side. That is, the recognition of what is positive about that revolution.

So, a success like the one in Cuba demonstrates not that a party has become superfluous—instead, what it demonstrates is just the opposite. It brings forward with new imperativeness the need for an international party of the kind I've tried to indicate in just a few sentences. That is, the need it has demonstrated is the need for Marxist political consciousness that takes the organized form of a party.[19]

These positions of Cannon and Hansen are, as we have seen, those of Trotsky himself. Comrade Barnes is therefore entirely within Trotsky's own framework in considering both that there can be authentically revolutionary forces that are not Trotskyist, and in rejecting any view that this leads to the liquidation of the Fourth International or the struggle for the specifically Trotskyist program.

However, this setting of the framework of analysis, while important, does not by itself solve the question of whether in the actual case of the Castroist forces we are confronted with an example of a non-Trotskyist revolutionary current. To determine this we have to look more closely at the issues involved and at the specific political character of the Cuban leadership.

How to judge revolutionists

The first thing we can note is that prima facie Comrade Barnes's characterization of the Cuban leadership as revolutionary does not make sense even by his own statements concerning their analysis and

---

19. Hansen, "Cuban Question: Report for the Political Committee (January 14, 1961)," in *Dynamics of the Cuban Revolution*, p. 104.

Eritrean guerilla fighters advancing on Ethiopia position.

line. Comrade Barnes affirms:

that the Cuban leaders "do not believe it is possible to think seriously about victorious revolutions in France, Britain, West Germany, Japan, or the United States. They do not believe it is possible in their lifetimes, or their children's lifetimes";

that "from the beginning, they would remain silent about reactionary actions of some governments, such as Mexico's, that maintained friendly diplomatic relations with Cuba. They have often taken an uncritical stance toward governments that take some anti-imperialist stands or actions, as in Chile under Allende and Peru under Velasco";

that "the Cuban revolution occurred without the creation of large-scale democratic committees of the working masses—what the Russians call red 'Soviets'.... The party and the government got all mixed up together as a result";

that "the Cuban leadership never developed a Leninist-type organization, with the right of minorities to argue for their point of view in front of the entire membership";

and that, in a considerable understatement by Comrade Barnes, the Cuban leaders "fail to understand and take the right line on questions like the Eritrean national liberation struggle."[20]

This, it must be said, is a pretty important list of objections to characterizing the Cuban leadership as revolutionary. It is somewhat hard to conceive of a revolutionary force, in the serious sense, which does not think that it is seriously possible to think about revolution in the imperialist countries, that takes an uncritical attitude to left-bourgeois governments, and that does not understand the need for socialist democracy or the construction of Leninist-type parties!

Nevertheless, we would agree with Comrade Barnes that the theoretical attitude of the Cubans on these questions cannot be the *finally* decisive criterion. Contrary to the views of various idiotic sects, one cannot judge the government of a workers state by utterly utopian, abstract norms according to which any deviation from "ideal line" determined by some individual immediately transforms those who wander into "counterrevolutionaries." Furthermore, we agree with Comrade Barnes that:

> It was inevitable, given the relationship of forces, that the Cubans would be forced to pay a political price. Some price would have to be paid by the best and most conscious revolutionary leadership.[21]

Anyone who has seriously studied the history of the Bolsheviks after the revolution knows that even they took a number of positions that were not exactly of total clarity, and that the method of

---

20. Barnes, p. 156. See also *Selected Speeches of Fidel Castro*, p. 6.

21. Barnes, p. 156. See also *Selected Speeches of Fidel Castro*, p. 5.

judging any revolution and its leadership by comparing it to textbook norms is hopeless.

In the final analysis, it is not any *theoretical* political position of a current that is decisive in defining its character; the ultimate determinant is its relation to the real *material* clash of class forces. When Marx defined those who were revolutionists he did not say that they were those who held such and such a theoretical position but that the Communists "have no interests separate and apart from those of the proletariat as a whole."[22] Or, as Engels put it, "Communism . . . proceeds not from principles but from *facts*."[23] Therefore, significant as the theoretical errors of the Cubans may be, they cannot be the finally decisive issue. The crucial question is the relation of the Cuban leadership to the clash of class forces.

It is this attitude that determined the fundamental *revolutionary* character of the Bolsheviks. Theoretical lack of clarity, or even straightforward confusion, over revolutionary prospects and the character of a particular regime is something even authentic revolutionists can commit. Lenin, for example, continued with confused formulations on the class character of coming revolutions in the colonial countries right up to the second congress of the Comintern, and the policy of the Bolsheviks with regard to the regimes in Turkey, Iran, and Afghanistan following the 1917 revolution, for example, was not at all free from errors. But the fundamental question was what happened when such errors collided with the real revolutionary movement of the masses.

The revolutionary character of the Bolsheviks was seen in the fact that no matter what theoretical lack of clarity might have sometimes existed, there is no doubt that when it came to the key clashes of the masses against any regime, the Bolsheviks supported the progressive struggles of the workers and peasants. It was Stalin who instead began not merely to systematize theoretical confusions into wholesale revisions of Marxist theory, but also began to place tactical relations to regimes above the revolutionary mobilizations of the masses. This is the clear difference between particular theoretical confusions made even by the Bolsheviks and cases such as China in 1926–27, not to speak of later examples, where the fundamental element of policy was not relations with the working-class and peasant masses but instead support to allegedly "progressive" currents, governments, etc. It is therefore to this relation of political line to the real clash of material forces that we have to turn if we want to characterize finally the nature of the Cuban leadership. As Joe Hansen put it on Cuba:

> In the school of Leon Trotsky and James P. Cannon—which is also the school of Lenin—I was taught that important as the books are and for all the time that must be put into mastering them, what is decisive is the revolution itself.[24]

The international class struggle
In evaluating the character of a current by its relations to the real material clash of class forces, however, a further crucial criterion must be observed. *The class struggle by its nature is international. Therefore the criteria for determining the character of a current are also international.* When Marx wrote the Communists "have no interests separate and apart from those of the proletariat as a whole. They do not set up any sectarian principles of their own, by which to shape and mould the proletarian movement,"[25] he therefore also clearly defined this on an international terrain.

> The Communists are distinguished from the other working class parties by this only: 1. In the national struggles of the proletarians of the different countries, they point out and bring to the front the common interests of the entire proletariat, independently of all nationality. 2. In the various stages of development which the struggle of the

---

22. Marx and Engels, *The Communist Manifesto* (New York: Pathfinder Press, 1970, 2008), p. 47 [2013 printing].

23. Engels, "The Communists and Karl Heinzen," in *Marx and Engels Collected Works* (New York: International Publishers, 1976) vol. 6, p. 303.

24. Hansen, *Dynamics of the Cuban Revolution*, p. 241. For further discussion on the question of the decisive role of materialist criteria in judging the class character of a force, see "Healy's Rejection of Dialectical Materialism," by Alan Jones, in *Intercontinental Press/Inprecor*, August 28, 1978, p. 966.

25. *The Communist Manifesto*, p. 47.

working class against the bourgeoisie has to pass through, they always and everywhere represent the interests of the movement as a whole.[26]

It is therefore on this terrain of *international* class struggle that the class character of a current can finally be determined. *More precisely, in relation to the question of the Cuban leadership, the fact that a current can take power on a national terrain does not make it revolutionary on a world scale* and, like all characterizations, the nature of the Cuban leadership cannot be determined solely from its orientation on the terrain of Cuba itself but only from its positions on the most fundamental issues of *world* politics.

Indeed, comrade Barnes himself has dealt quite correctly with the theoretical issues involved in characterizing a current. He pointed out against forces disoriented by events following the Second World War that "they failed to see how petty-bourgeois parties, including Stalinist parties, for the first time in history could stand at the head of revolutions that led to the establishment of workers states, but at the same time could not become, in a historical sense, a substitute for the Leninist party on a world scale as well as in their own countries."[27]

This position is entirely that of Trotsky himself, who noted that:

> The depth of disintegration of the enemy camp, its political demoralization, the worthlessness of its leaders, can assure decisive superiority to the proletariat for a certain time even if its own leadership is weak. But in the first place, there is nothing to guarantee such a "fortunate" coincidence of circumstances; it represents the exception rather than the rule.

> . . . To weaken the struggle against Stalinism on the grounds that under *certain* conditions even the Stalinist leaderships would prove unable to prevent the victory of the proletariat . . . would be to stand all of Marxist politics on its head.[28]

Furthermore, Trotsky did not confine this possibility of victory in particular countries merely to Stalinists but extended it to other nonrevolutionary, more particularly centrist, leaderships as well. Thus, for example, he noted that:

> . . . under *certain* historical circumstances the proletariat can conquer even under a left-centrist leadership. . . . The strategy of the party is an exceedingly important element of the proletarian revolution. But it is by no means the only factor. With an exceptionally favorable relation of forces the proletariat can come to power even under a non-Marxist leadership.[29]

And that "in some situations victory is possible even with a very bad policy."[30]

We therefore reject, as does comrade Barnes, any argument of the type that runs either that "this party made a revolution in a particular country, therefore it cannot be a Stalinist party," or that "this particular Stalinist party overthrew capitalism in a specific country, therefore Stalinism on a world scale is not counterrevolutionary." It has never been the case, as the above quotations from Trotsky show, that the position of Trotskyism on Stalinism is that it is counterrevolutionary because it cannot overthrow capitalism in some particular country. On the contrary, even when Trotsky was alive Stalinism did smash capitalism in particular instances—the transformations in eastern Poland in 1939–40 being the best-known case. The rejection by Trotsky, and Trotskyism, of Stalinism is because it cannot overthrow capitalism on a *world* scale, and indeed constitutes a counterrevolu-

---

26. Ibid., p. 47.

27. Barnes, "The Unfolding New World Situation," in *Dynamics of World Revolution Today* (New York: Pathfinder, 1974) p. 106. In order to bring out the issue at stake in the discussion on Cuba more clearly we deal in this article only with the chief characteristics of the line of the Cuban leadership in respect to that one area, the colonial world, where their line might most readily be thought revolutionary. It is obvious that the case could be made even more strongly by dealing with their line on the imperialist countries or their positions on the Soviet bureaucracy itself—for example, the Cuban position on the invasion of Czechoslovakia.

---

28. Trotsky, *Writings of Leon Trotsky (1932–33)*, pp. 43–44.

29. Ibid., p. 43.

30. Trotsky, *Writings of Leon Trotsky (1930–31)* (New York: Pathfinder Press, 1973), p. 381 [2011 printing].

tionary obstacle to this task. The fact that it can overthrow capitalism in *particular* countries in no way alters that fundamental character. All basic characterizations are derived from positions and character on a world scale. On that we have fundamental agreement with Comrade Barnes in the comments of his quoted above.

But what applies to the method of characterizing Stalinism applies to *all* currents. The character of the Cuban leadership *cannot* be derived from the fact that it overthrew capitalism in a particular country, by some equation of the type "making a revolution in Cuba, therefore character is revolutionary." To understand the nature of the Cuban leadership it is necessary to understand its international positions. These show it is *false* to characterize the Cuban leadership, particularly today, as revolutionary. What is involved with the Cubans is not particular mistakes of the type that even the most revolutionary leaderships would inevitably make, but a fundamental false line that does not correspond to the interests of the international working class and that on a whole number of questions is in conflict with it.

Attitude to the Cubans

Furthermore, we would note that the actual position expressed by Comrade Barnes on the Cubans is absolutely wrong, even if his own characterization of them were correct. What Trotsky said in relation to centrists applies also to a revolutionary leadership that was merely making grave mistakes:

> The theoretical possibility of a victory under centrist leadership must be understood, besides, not mechanically but dialectically. Neither the official party as a whole nor even its apparatus represents something immovable and unchangeable. . . . At the same time, it is completely indisputable that in the party's change of position the decisive role was played by the Left Opposition, if only through the fact that it posed the problem of fascism clearly and sharply before the working class. To change this course of ours, to adapt ourselves to the prejudices of the Stalinists instead of appealing to the judgment of the Communists, would mean to imitate the desperate centrists of the SAP[31]. . . . To blur our differences with centrism in the name of facilitating "unity" would mean not only to commit political suicide, but also to cover up, strengthen, and nourish all the negative features of bureaucratic centrism, and by that fact alone help the reactionary currents within it against the revolutionary tendencies.[32]

Even if we considered that the Cuban leadership were an authentically revolutionary leadership making mistakes, our task would not be to cover up these errors but on the contrary to clearly criticize them. Any other course, as Trotsky put it, would be to "help the reactionary currents within it against the revolutionary tendencies."

Unfortunately, however, Comrade Barnes takes the opposite course when it comes to certain key events. Instead of fundamentally criticizing the wrong positions of the Cubans he blurs over their line. This is most obvious with respect to one of the central pillars of Cuban foreign policy—their relations with the Ethiopian regime. Here Comrade Barnes states: "Fortunately, the Cubans have sharply differentiated themselves from the all-out support offered by the Kremlin to the Dergue's war against the Eritreans. However, they have failed to come out in favor of the right of Eritrea to independence."[33]

Bluntly put, we consider this statement totally false. What in fact is occurring in Eritrea, and the Cuban leadership has perfectly enough people in Ethiopia to be absolutely clear as to what is taking place, is one of the most bloody counterrevolutionary wars we have seen, even in the colonial world.[34] To root out liberation movements that have the almost total support of the Eritrean people, the Dergue and its backers have necessarily been forced to utilize methods qualitatively no different

---

31. See footnote 7.—*IP/I*

32. Trotsky, *Writings of Leon Trotsky (1932–33)*, p. 45.

33. Barnes, p. 156. See also *Selected Speeches of Fidel Castro*, p. 6.

34. For the more extended discussion of Cuban policy in Ethiopia and Eritrea on which this section draws heavily, see the excellent article "Eritrea: The Guilty and the Silent," by Richard Carver, in *Socialist Challenge*, January 25, 1979 [Reprinted following this article—*IP/I*].

from those adopted by the Americans in Vietnam. Around a third of the Eritrean population have been made refugees. Famine and depopulation have become key tools, and effects, of the offensive—with, to take merely one example, the population of Asmara falling from 250,000 to 100,000 following its capture by the Ethiopians. Among the chief weapons used by the regime are Napalm B, cluster bombs, and defoliant poisons. As the Ethiopian regime is absolutely aware it has no way of winning over the Eritrean people, its only aim is to pulverize and atomize the population to a point where its society is disintegrated and incapable of further resistance. The almost genocidal character of this conflict is not accidental or an "excess" but flows inevitably from the degree to which the Eritrean people have demonstrated their virtually unanimous demand for independence in the long war against the various Ethiopian regimes.

The role played by the Cubans here has been to fall in behind the war waged by the Mengistu leadership of the Dergue. Far from having "sharply differentiated themselves from the all-out support offered by the Kremlin to the Dergue's war," the Cubans are in fact a key cornerstone of that war effort. Without the Cuban military training, weapons, and support work, the Ethiopian forces would be totally unable to undertake their offensive. Furthermore, although even if they were nowhere near the front line Cuban agreement would still be indispensable for the war, reports indicate that Cuban units and advisers are directly participating in the fighting—in particular in the specialized forces such as the air force and artillery.[35] And on the key question of political support to the major policies of the Ethiopian regime, the Cuban press is full of constant declarations of the revolutionary character of the leadership of Mengistu and the Dergue.

Of course, we do not doubt that the Cubans had some differences with Mengistu on tactics for dealing with Eritrea. With their considerable experience of popular guerrilla war, we think it is likely that the Cubans feared that what is in fact happening would be the inevitable result of any attempt to settle the Eritrean question by force—i.e., that the Ethiopian regime would find itself in a totally bloody conflict in which it would still not be totally victorious and which would sap its forces over a long period. Furthermore, the Cubans were in a somewhat embarrassing political position because of their previous support for the Eritrean struggle and because of the consequences that would flow from their involvement in a totally counterrevolutionary war. Finally, perhaps even the Cubans genuinely supported the Eritrean people, or were opposed to war against them.

But no matter what the niceties or psychology involved, the Cubans have *never* shifted on the fundamental position of support to the Dergue and therefore to rejecting the sole solution to Eritrea that is in the interests of the international working class, the Eritrean people, and the Ethiopian revolution itself. Right at the time of Castro's visit to Addis Ababa in September of last year, the joint communiqué issued made clear that the "Cuban side also reaffirmed its absolute opposition to any kind of secession and expressed its firm belief that Ethiopia would solve all its problems in line with the principles of Marxism-Leninism." Once the secession of Eritrea is rejected, then in fact the kind of ferocious counterrevolutionary war that is taking place was inevitable. All history shows that there is no other way to try to fight a movement so massively supported by a people as in Eritrea except by the type of means the Ethiopians have in fact used.

There is in fact no doubt concerning the character of the Cuban policy in Ethiopia. It does not matter about the psychological motivation of their position. The root of the Cuban line in Eritrea lies in total failure to distinguish that support to the Ethiopian revolution is not the same thing as support to the Dergue, and that in fact that the two are incompatible. The *objective* character of the Cuban policy in Ethiopia is not qualitatively different in politics, although doubtless more audacious in tactics, than the general one of building "progressive" bourgeois and petty-bourgeois regimes that doubtless cause some important temporary annoyance to imperialism but whose fundamental historical character is clearly *capitalist*.

The Cuban policy furthermore is not different in the other African states from its nature in Ethiopia.

---

35. For this and the quotations given below, see the article by Richard Carver.

A particularly clear case is that of Angola. Here the Cubans intervened militarily, following the collapse of the Portuguese empire and the start of the Angolan civil war, to prevent the formation of a puppet regime of South African and U.S. imperialism. We totally support and hail that military intervention—although we would also point out,

We consider the Cuban international line centrist, not counterrevolutionary . . .

against any illusions to the contrary, that it could not have been sustained without the agreement of the Russians.

Once the military victory was achieved, however, the Cubans took no steps whatever—quite the reverse—to encourage the overthrow of capitalism in Angola. And this is no academic point when, with the prestige of their intervention and their great military weight, there is no doubt that a Cuban call for the overthrow of bourgeois rule in Angola would have had every chance of succeeding. Instead, the Cubans have constantly upheld the regime of Neto and backed it in all fundamental questions. These have included the smashing of the mass movements and organizations opposed to the leadership of the MPLA,[36] the covert agreement with the imperialists to end the incursions into Zaïre aimed at overthrowing Mobutu, and the rebuilding of key links with imperialist firms and regimes that can, or could, operate in Angola. The consolidation of a left-bourgeois regime, and not the overthrow of capitalism, has been the constant thread of Cuban policy in Angola just as in Ethiopia. This line has been repeated in the other African states in which the Cubans have a serious involvement.[37]

Furthermore, we may note that this policy in Africa, while by far the most audacious tactically and militarily of the Cubans' interventions, is not distinct in its political line from their intervention in other parts of the world. Already at the Havana Conference of Communist Parties of Latin America of June 1975 the Cubans affirmed their support for a bloc with the so-called national bourgeoisie. Chapter 6 of the declaration unanimously adopted at the conference is clear. It states that:

> . . . without abandoning the struggle for democratic rights and for the conquest of new structures in our countries . . . we communists are prepared to support the positions of Latin American governments that can stand for the defense of our national resources or can assert their will to put an end to the attempts of the multinational corporations to preserve and increase their control of our economies every day.
>
> This historical reality does not at all mean that there do not exist sectors within the Latin American bourgeoisie that because of the contradiction between their interests and those of imperialism adopt certain positions analogous to those of the proletariat, peasantry, and other noncapitalist layers of the population in struggle against imperialism and for the conquest of economic independence and complete national sovereignty.
>
> Consequently, these bourgeois sectors can contribute to the unity of democratic and anti-imperialist action jointly with the popular forces.
>
> The CPs and all other anti-imperialist fighters . . . accord great importance to this possibility . . . which constitutes an indispensable factor in this complex and multifaceted struggle.
>
> The incorporation into the broad anti-imperialist and anti-oligarchic struggle front of forces and organizations that represent sectors of the bourgeoisie is of great importance.

To leave absolutely no ambiguity as to what such a policy means, specific reference is made to the Popular Front decisions of the Comintern in lauding the attempts of the Latin American CPs before and during the Second World War "to form national, antifascist, and anti-imperialist fronts." The declaration states that "the resolutions of the Seventh Congress of the Communist International (1935) played an important role in this sense."[38]

---

36. Movimento Popular de Libertação de Angola (People's Movement for the Liberation of Angola).

37. See the article by Claude Gabriel, "Cuba's Role in Africa," in *Intercontinental Press/Inprecor*, February 19, p. 148.

38. Cited by Pablo Rojas, "Havana Conference of Latin American Communist Parties: Apology for Defeat," in *Inprecor*,

Such a policy is, of course, in complete accord with the attitude taken not only to Allende and Velasco but also to Neto and Mengistu. It is furthermore carried out in the Caribbean in relation to the government of Manley. *In short, the present policy of the Cubans in Africa toward the left-bourgeois regimes of that continent is not some accident based on lack of information but rests clearly on the international line of the Cuban leadership.* That line *cannot* be characterized as revolutionary—unless of course someone is proposing a startling revision of Marxism whereby the supporting of left-bourgeois regimes, and the opposing of the creation of workers states, has now become the hallmark of a revolutionary line.

There is of course no doubt that the practical means utilized to pursue this Cuban policy have sometimes been very audacious. It may well be the case that the Cubans have given Brezhnev some sleepless nights, and even heart attacks, with the tactical pursuit of their line. Whatever are the telephone conversations and secret discussions in which the Russians lay down the qualitative limits of what they will accept, we think it probable that the Cubans generally take the most left leeway they can grab and probably add a few surprises of their own that Brezhnev accepts only after the event. We think it quite likely that the Cubans may have their own reasons, which are not simply those of collaboration with imperialism, for not seeking the overthrow of capitalism in the African states. It is possible that the Cubans have drawn from the balance sheet of the blockade they have suffered, and the limits placed by material reliance on the Russians, that a more practical policy for some other states is not to break totally with capitalism and therefore suffer the inevitable toted imperialist counterattack.

But whatever the reasons and tactical disputes, this does not alter the *qualitative* character of Cuban policy in Africa. That policy is *not* to overthrow capitalism and establish workers states but to build and sustain left-bourgeois regimes that will, objectively, finally collide with and oppose the working class and the construction of workers states. It is also for this reason, incidentally, that no matter what their differences over practical means, there is *no* evidence of a *qualitative* clash between the Cubans and the Russians over policy in Africa—and it would in fact be very easy to see if this existed. Brezhnev has his own inimitable means, such as a few cargoes of oil turning up late in Havana, to let the Cubans know of his displeasure. However, all the evidence is that far from a qualitative rift between Castro and the Russians, the Soviet bureaucracy is providing the material means that are allowing Cuban policy in Africa to be carried out. All reports concur that the Russians have stepped up supply of heavy cargo planes to the Cubans for the practical execution of their African policy, and Russian pilots have been supplied for the defense of Cuba, to replace the Cuban pilots in Africa.

Of course, we stress that pursuing a policy that does not clash on qualitative questions with that of the Russians is not the same as the Cubans being Stalinists. The policy of Brezhnev is not fundamentally based on ideology or political line but on the existence in the USSR of a hardened privileged caste with material interests qualitatively different from those of the Soviet or international working class. That is, among other reasons, why the Soviet regime, and those of Eastern Europe, can maintain itself in political power only by police terror and ruthless suppression of the masses. There is no *serious* evidence, aside from the mouthings of sectarians, that such a hardened caste exists in Cuba in any way qualitatively comparable to the USSR, China, and so forth. The regime, far from ruling by terror, by all analyses enjoys mass popular support and would be overwhelmingly supported against any intervention and in any elections based on workers democracy—which makes it all the worse that the Cuban leadership has resolutely opposed any such system in the country and thereby reinforced the conditions for the major *quantitative* growth of bureaucracy that has taken place. It is for this reason that we consider the line of the Cubans internationally as a *centrist* one and not that of a counterrevolutionary bureaucratic caste.

But the reasons for the Cuban policy do not alter its objective character. Extremely audacious tactics and lack of aversion to utilization of violence do not constitute revolutionary politics by themselves. It is the *political line* that is decisive. *The international policy of the Cuban leadership today is not a revolutionary one.* Comrade Barnes's analysis and characterization is false.

November 20, 1975, p. 30.

The nature of the Cuban leadership

Finally, therefore, what is the character of the Cuban leadership? Comrade Barnes unfortunately gives us a theoretical framework within which it is impossible to solve the problem. He provides very clear evidence that the Cuban leadership cannot be characterized as Stalinist if that term, for the sake of argument, is defined as constituting a crystallized and hardened bureaucratic caste with clear material interests differing from those of the working class.[39] Indeed, there is no serious, as opposed to purely demagogic, evidence that such a crystallized caste exists in Cuba in any way that is qualitatively comparable to the USSR, China, North Korea, Vietnam, etc. We therefore, with Comrade Barnes, reject the slogan of political revolution in Cuba. This latter call would flow not from a situation where a wrong line is being pursued, even of an extremely serious type that disqualifies a force from being considered revolutionary, but where these positions are rooted in the existence of a caste with *material interests* separate from and opposed to those of the working class.

However, having demonstrated the non-Stalinist character of the Cuban leadership, Comrade Barnes then goes on to state, as we have seen, that "the real line to be drawn is the line between the revolutionists—meaning Castro and those around him, including us—and the counterrevolutionaries on the other side, including the Stalinists and the so-called 'Third Camp' social democrats." But the categories of "revolutionary" and "counterrevolutionary" do not at all exhaust all the phenomena in the workers movement. It is therefore *false* to pose things in the framework provided by Comrade Barnes. By ascertaining that the Cuban leadership is not Stalinist, let alone "Third Camp" social democratic, we do not thereby determine that the situation in Cuba must be characterized as "the existence of a workers state with a revolutionary leadership." There is within the workers movement not merely revolution and counterrevolution but also *centrism*. Or, put in the analogies of the Russian revolution, there exist not merely the situation of 1917–1923 with the existence of a revolutionary leadership, and that of a post-1933 where the call for a political revolution was needed, but also that of 1923–33—i.e., a period of transition in which the leadership of the Soviet state was not revolutionary but where the slogan of political revolution was still not the correct one.[40]

This is the situation faced today in respect to Cuba. Although a crystallized bureaucratic caste, with not merely wrong political positions but *material interests* which are different from those of the working class, has not been hardened out, nevertheless a false international and domestic policy *is* being pursued. Lack of socialist democracy provides a permanent situation in which conditions for the crystallization of such a bureaucracy exist. *Rejection of the slogan of political revolution does not lead to the conclusion that the Cuban leadership is a revolutionary one.* Comrade Barnes's analysis and characterizations should be rejected. Without this being done political disorientation and later even sectarian disillusion will occur both with regard to Cuba's current policy and in the face of new turns that will take place in the future—including quite possibly new orientations not merely with respect to colonial states and the Stalinist bureaucracy but also in relation to imperialist powers.

APRIL 7, 1979

---

39. By this we do not necessarily mean that this is in itself a sufficient criterion for a party to be Stalinist. However, for the present purposes the really key question is whether such a crystallized bureaucracy with distinct social interests exists or not in Cuba and therefore we do not object to the use of the term "Stalinist" in the present context to indicate the existence of such a layer. By saying that we do not consider the Cuban leadership Stalinist we indicate we do not believe it is based on such a layer qualitatively comparable to that of the USSR. The semantic dispute of whether this is a correct definition of Stalinism, or whether that term must include that a particular party is not merely bureaucratized in the qualitative sense but also tied to the Kremlin, can be left on one side here provided there is agreement on the substance of what is involved.

40. This analogy should not of course be stretched too far and be taken, in particular, as applying to the origins of the Cuban workers state. It is not necessary here to enter into the discussion of whether the Castro leadership was always centrist in character. We may merely note that the fact that it made a revolution in Cuba settles nothing either way on this issue. As we have seen, Trotsky specifically allowed for the possibility that in particular countries the working class could conquer power even under a centrist leadership; this flows inevitably from the correct understanding that forces can only be correctly characterized by their position in relation to the *international* class struggle.

Discussion on Cuba

THE REVOLUTIONARY CHARACTER OF THE CASTRO LEADERSHIP
By David Frankel and Larry Seigle

I. What the Discussion Is About

Are Fidel Castro and the other men and women who led the struggle against the Batista dictatorship, who led the Cuban working class in the process of establishing a workers state, and who have led the defense of that revolution against imperialism for the last twenty years, centrists?

Alan Jones answers this question "yes" in his discussion article, "The Character of the Cuban Leadership" in the July 2 *Intercontinental Press/Inprecor*.

Comrade Jones's article raises issues that are at the heart of the discussion now beginning within the world Trotskyist movement on what *political line* we should follow in relation to the Cuban revolution and its leadership. Comrade Jones's contribution has advanced the discussion by clarifying some points and helping to put in sharper focus the differences that exist on others.

He correctly stresses broad areas of agreement that serve as the framework for discussing the points in dispute.

Most importantly, Comrade Jones agrees that the Fourth International must "reject the slogan of political revolution in Cuba" (p. 97, col. 1). He states that calling for a political revolution could only be supported by proof of "the existence of a caste with *material interests* separate from and opposed to those of the working class" (p. 97, col. 1, emphasis in original).

And he concludes forcefully,

> There is no *serious* evidence, aside from the mouthings of sectarians, that such a hardened caste exists in Cuba in any way qualitatively comparable to the USSR, China, and so forth. The regime, far from ruling by terror, by all analyses enjoys mass popular support. . . ." [P. 96, col. 2.]

The rejection of any call for political revolution registers important progress in the discussion. Prior to the present debate, a number of comrades in the Fourth International were beginning to slip into a stance in favor of calling for a political revolution. If the discussion we are having on Cuba accomplishes nothing else, it will be worthwhile if it convinces comrades to pull back from casually adopting such a stance—a position that would amount to political suicide for any revolutionary internationalist organization.

Comrade Jones also agrees that it is possible for "authentically revolutionary" leaders and currents that are not Trotskyists to arise. When that happens the Fourth International must recognize them as fellow revolutionists, defend them and reach out to them, and try to draw them closer to our program and our banner. He adds, correctly, that recognizing and acting on this reality in no way "leads to the liquidation of the Fourth International or the struggle for the specifically Trotskyist program" (p. 89, col. 2). To the contrary it is an irreplaceable part of building the revolutionary workers international.

Further, Comrade Jones agrees,

> Contrary to the views of various idiotic sects, one cannot judge the government of a workers state by utterly utopian, abstract norms according to which any deviation from "ideal line" determined by some individual imme-

diately transforms those who wander into "counterrevolutionaries." [P. 90, col. 1.]

Finally, Comrade Jones states his agreement with the point made by Jack Barnes, in his speech on the twentieth anniversary of the Cuban revolution, that:

> It was inevitable, given the relationship of forces, that the Cubans would be forced to pay a political price [for Soviet economic and military aid]. Some price would have to have been paid by the best and most conscious revolutionary leadership. [*Intercontinental Press/Inprecor,* February 19, 1979, p. 156, col. 2.]

However, Comrade Jones considers the Castro leadership to be centrist, not revolutionary. As he states it:

> There is within the workers movement not merely revolution and counterrevolution but also *centrism*. Or, put in the analogies of the Russian revolution, there exist not merely the situation of 1917–1923 with the existence of a revolutionary leadership, and that of a post-1933 where the call for a political revolution was needed, but also that of 1923–33—i.e., a period of transition in which the leadership of the Soviet state was not revolutionary but where the slogan of political revolution was still not the correct one.

> This is the situation faced today in respect to Cuba. [P. 97, col. 2.]

In order to bring into sharp focus the debate over whether Castroism is a centrist current, we have to make a distinction between two stages in the history of the Cuban revolution and the Castro leadership.

The first question we must deal with is whether or not the Castro current was centrist from the time it emerged in the mid-1950s. A petty-bourgeois grouping with a radical bourgeois-democratic program, it was the dominant and decisive component of the July 26 Movement.

The second question is what has happened since the establishment of the Cuban workers state. The Castroist leadership has been the dominant and decisive component of the government and the party in Cuba for twenty years. In answering the question of whether Castroism is centrist *today* we must, as Comrade Jones correctly explains, turn to the analogy of the Soviet Union from 1923 to 1933. A centrist current that holds governmental power in a workers state is clearly a very specific kind of centrism. Here the precise question we must ask is whether Castroism is a form of *bureaucratic centrism*, the term Trotsky used to define the Stalinist leadership during the period it was consolidating its power, basing itself on the privileged bureaucracy.

By making this distinction between two periods in the development of the Castroist current, we can clarify the issues under discussion, and narrow in on the differences that exist.

II. Was Leadership of July 26 Movement Centrist or Revolutionary?

When the Cuban revolution occurred, it was seen as a breakthrough by the world Trotskyist movement as a whole. For the first time since the Russian revolution of 1917, a non-Stalinist leadership had come to power and led the working class in the establishment of a workers state.

The Cuban revolution signalled the opening of the socialist revolution in the Western hemisphere.

It also represented a powerful blow against the stranglehold of Stalinism on the international workers movement.

In the world political resolution adopted by the 1961 party convention, the Socialist Workers Party pointed to the far-reaching significance of the Cuban revolution for the struggle against Stalinism:

A completely new force must now be taken into account—the Cuban revolution and its leadership. Havana wields immense independent influence throughout Latin America. . . .

The Cuban revolution gave every Communist party in the world, and above all the Cuban Communist party [the Popular Socialist Party], something to ponder. A handful of determined revolutionaries demonstrated that the masses can be mobilized and power won without Moscow's approval. They demonstrated it without the help and even against the opposition of a strong Communist party. The bypassing of the Communist party opened up a new vista throughout the world on the possibilities of overcoming the obstacle of Stalinism in constructing revolutionary parties. [Published in the *International Socialist Review*, Summer 1961, p. 97.]

Revolutionary minded youth throughout Latin America were inspired by the Cuban revolution and they sought to bypass the Stalinized Communist parties as Castro and his comrades had done.

In assessing the Cuban leaders at the time, Joseph Hansen wrote in "The Theory of the Cuban Revolution" that Castro and the team around him "have convincingly demonstrated that they really meant it when they said they were prepared to carry the revolution through to its necessary conclusion no matter where it took them" (*Dynamics of the Cuban Revolution*, p. 265).

Hansen concluded, "Up to now the Cuban leaders have appeared as great revolutionists of action" (Ibid., p. 266).

This was also the view of Ernest Mandel. In his pamphlet *Marxism Vs. Utraleftism* (Paris: The Fourth International, 1967), Mandel wrote that "in no revolution of the twentieth century was the agrarian problem solved as radically, as completely and as quickly as in the Cuban revolution under the leadership of Fidel Castro" (p. 31).

Answering sectarian opponents of the Cuban leadership, Mandel talked of ". . . Fidel Castro, marching at the head of all the toiling masses of his country, mobilising them continually, crushing the bourgeois state machine through class action, arming the workers and peasants and expropriating the bourgeoisie and breaking the grip of world imperialism . . ." (p. 41).

Mandel hailed ". . . Castro and the Fidelista current, who fought, not without success, for a socialist revolution in Cuba and who, against the Soviet bureaucracy and its Cuban agents, have maintained their orientation towards a socialist revolution in the rest of Latin America!" (p. 49).

Agreement on what line to take toward the Cuban revolution and a common assessment of its leadership was a key point in the process leading to the reunification of the Fourth International in 1963. "The Dynamics of World Revolution Today," one of the documents approved by the Reunification Congress, described the importance of the Cuban revolution, saying:

CUBAN NATIONAL INSTITUTE OF AGRARIAN REFORM
Cuban farmer receives land title under Agrarian Reform.

The victory in Cuba marked the beginning of a new epoch in the history of the world revolution; for, aside from the Soviet Union, this is the first workers state established outside the bounds of the Stalinist apparatus. [*Fourth International*, October–December 1963, pp. 11–12.]

Another document adopted at the 1963 Reunification Congress, "The International Situation and Our Tasks," said of the Cuban revolution:

> It marks also the arrival in power, for the first time since October 1917, of a revolutionary leadership which, in relation to objective necessity and its own conscious understanding, has systematically sought the international extension of the socialist revolution, at least throughout Latin America. [Ibid., p. 36.)

Nowhere in the documents of the Fourth International in this period or in articles by its leaders, is the Castro team referred to as centrist. At least through the fifth year of the Cuban revolution, the world movement as a whole agreed that the Fidelistas were a revolutionary current.

The recognition of the revolutionary character of the July 26 Movement leadership was essential to understanding the Cuban revolution and adopting a line of action aimed at deepening it, defending it, and extending its impact.

Origins of the July 26 Movement

Why did the Fourth International consider the Castro current to be revolutionary? We can answer this by taking a brief look at some of the decisive turning points in its history and evolution.

The July 26 Movement began as a petty-bourgeois formation with a radical democratic, anti-imperialist, and nationalist program. It was organized in opposition to the Stalinists and the bourgeois liberal opponents of Batista.

In December 1955, Fidel Castro wrote of these bankrupt forces:

> The political business of opposition is fully discredited and decadent. First they demanded a neutral government and immediate general elections. Then they stopped at demanding only general elections in 1956. They are no longer talking about a particular year. They will end by taking off their last fig leaf and accepting *any* arrangement with the dictator. [Robert Taber, *M-26: The Biography of a Revolution* (New York: Lyle Stuart, 1961), p. 50.]

Stubbornly refusing to compromise with either the dictatorship or the bourgeois opposition, Castro declared, "The names of those who impede the task of liberating their country should be recorded in the same place of infamy and shame as the names of those who oppress it" (Ibid., p. 51).

Breaking publicly with the bourgeois Ortodoxo Party in March 1956, Castro said the July 26 Movement would be a movement "without sugar barons, without stock-market speculators, without magnates of industry and commerce, without lawyers for big interests, without provincial *caciques* [political bosses], without small-time politicians of any kind."

Instead, Castro insisted, the July 26 Movement would be "the revolutionary movement of the humble, the hope of redemption of the Cuban working class, the hope of land for the peasants who live like pariahs in the country that their grandfathers liberated, the hope of bread for the hungry and justice for the forgotten" (Ibid., pp. 50–51).

All this, as the Castro leadership team was to prove, was not merely revolutionary rhetoric of the centrist variety.

The program of the July 26 Movement included a thoroughgoing land reform, abolition of the dictatorship, elimination of corruption, lower rents, improvement of housing, and increased employment through public works.

Castro and his comrades sought to achieve this program by revolutionary means, mobilizing the Cuban toilers independently of both the impotent bourgeois opposition and the treacherous Stalinist and other petty-bourgeois reformists who subordinated themselves to imperialism and the Cuban bourgeoisie.

The intransigence and iron-willed determination of this revolutionary leadership was graphically demonstrated by the struggle they waged in the Sierra Maestra Mountains and in towns and cities across Cuba. At each turning point, when less revolutionary leaders would have capitulated outright to bourgeois and imperialist pressure, or at least vacillated, the Castro team stood firm.

Denouncing the 'Miami Pact'

In late 1957, when the Rebel Army forces in the Sierra Maestra were making gains and the more far-sighted bourgeois figures could see the beginning of the end for Batista, a "Pact of Unity" was made public in Miami. It was signed by a number of Cuban bourgeois opposition groups and, purportedly, by the July 26 Movement.

In fact, however, this pact of unity with bourgeois forces, on their terms, was completely at odds with the revolutionary perspective of the Fidelistas. When the Castro leadership in the Sierras learned that representatives of the July 26 Movement in the United States had gone along with this sell-out, they did not hesitate to publicly, and in the strongest language, repudiate the "Miami Pact."

In explaining the position of the central leadership of the July 26 Movement, Fidel Castro reaffirmed their unbending revolutionary determination to carry the struggle through to its conclusion. A review of the position of the July 26 Movement at this critical juncture in the Cuban revolution is particularly timely because of the lessons it offers to those in Nicaragua today who want to take the Cuban road.

In a public letter to the organizations who had signed the "Pact of Unity" Castro declared:

> No matter how desperate our situation may be, or how many thousand soldiers are sent against us by the Dictatorship in its present design to annihilate us . . . we will never accept the sacrifice of certain principles that are cardinal to our understanding of the Cuban Revolution. [The text of this declaration is published, in a translation by the author, in Mario Llerena, *The Unsuspected Revolution* (Ithaca: Cornell University Press. 1978), pp. 257–70.]

First, Castro denounced the Miami Pact for its failure to include "the express declaration that foreign intervention of any kind in the internal affairs of Cuba is rejected [which] shows a very lukewarm kind of patriotism and unparalleled cowardice."

Are we, Fidel asked, "so mediocre that we do not know how to say a word on this matter? How, then, can we call ourselves revolutionaries. . . ?"

Second, he denounced the pact for omitting a declaration rejecting any type of military junta—no matter how patriotic, democratic, or even "revolutionary"—to replace Batista. Fidel knew that some of the bourgeois forces were looking for ways to hang on to at least shreds of Batistaism without Batista. He denounced the "false illusion that Cuba's problem can be solved simply by the Dictator's absence."

> Let me tell you then that we are making it perfectly clear that, should a Military Junta take Batista's place, the 26 of July Movement will resolutely continue fighting its war of liberation.

Third, he denounced the provision, contained in the Miami Pact, that after the overthrow of Batista, the armed revolutionary forces should be merged with the "regular armed forces of the Republic." Fidel reminded the leaders of the bourgeois opposition that the July 26 Movement "is the only organization having organized and disciplined militias throughout the country, as well as an army in the field. . . ."

He declared flatly and unequivocally: "The 26 of July Movement demands for itself the function of maintaining law and order and of reorganizing the armed forces of the Republic."

Finally, Fidel denounced all the compromisers and halfhearted opponents of the dictatorship:

> Our victories are there, and nothing can cause them to be forgotten. Our men, firmer than ever, are prepared to fight till the last drop of blood. Defeat is for those who have denied to us all assistance; for those who, having given us their word at the beginning, then left us alone; . . . for those who, having the arms, hid them away like cowards at the hour of action. They are the ones who are wrong—not we.
>
> One thing we can assert with all certainty: had we seen other Cubans fighting for freedom, persecuted and about to be exterminated; had we seen them resist day after day without giving up or weakening in their attempt, we would not have hesitated one min-

ute in going to their help and dying with them if necessary. For we are Cubans, and Cubans do not remain impassive when others are fighting for liberty—even if it is in a different American country. Do the Dominicans gather on some islet with the intent of liberating their country? For each Dominican, ten Cubans assemble. Do Somoza's henchmen invade Costa Rica? There go the Cubans to fight. . . .

Fidel concluded by warning:

> . . . let nobody try to conduct from Miami a revolution that is being carried out in every town and hamlet throughout the island, with fighting, agitation, sabotage, strikes, and the thousand other ways of revolutionary action that are included in the strategy of the July 26 Movement.

By denouncing the "Miami Pact" the Castroists reaffirmed their revolutionary course and rejected the road of conciliation.

After January 1, 1959

This same revolutionary character marked the Castroist leadership in power after the overthrow of Batista.

Yankee imperialism and its Cuban protégés were trying to block the social advances promised by the July 26 Movement and demanded by the Cuban masses. The Castroists began to base themselves more and more on mass mobilizations of the workers and poor peasants. As Castro put it in his speech on the twentieth anniversary of the revolution, "Before January [1959], a vanguard was the main protagonist in events; since that January, the main protagonist has been the people."

This process of relying increasingly on the mobilization of the workers and peasants, and being drawn to the left by them, began even before the Rebel Army reached Havana, when ruling class figures tried to form a "responsible" government to replace Batista, who had fled to the Dominican Republic. Here's how it looked to *New York Times* correspondent R. Hart Phillips, whose book *Cuba: Island of Paradox* (New York: McDowell, Obolensky), appeared in 1960:

> Fidel Castro declared that his insurgents would remain on a "war footing" and would not accept the designation of Dr. Carlos Piedra as President. . . .
>
> The people responded to the call from Fidel Castro for a general strike. Commerce and industry had not opened on New Year's Day of course and restaurants, hotels, cafés and other establishments which usually operate on holidays closed their doors. International and domestic plane service was suspended at the José Marti International Airport. Vessels arriving in Havana were unable to dock due to the fact no port workers were working. Some 2,000 American tourists were caught. [P. 399.]

Fidel Castro and his rebels arrived in Havana on January 8, 1959. Never in the history of Cuba has anyone received such a welcome. The ovation was of such magnitude that it was a little frightening. The majority of Havana's one million inhabitants must have turned out. [P. 404.]

Phillips went into some detail to document her fear that Castro was selling out—to the working masses.

> Many of the reforms of Castro, such as the promise of honesty in administration, the suppression of illegal gambling, the campaign against prostitution, narcotics traffic and other vices, have been applauded by the public. . . . However, when Castro then stated that all land which the government considers as not being efficiently cultivated would also be seized, and that a limit would be placed on the amount of land any individual or company could own, cane planters, tobacco plantation owners, and cattle ranchers expressed their concern.
>
> The reduction of rents by 30% to 50% is considered just by the tenants but unreasonable by the owners of property. . . .
>
> The owners of vacant lots in all towns have been ordered to sell them to anyone who wants to build a home. . . . But the statement by Fidel Castro that no land in the island is

worth more than four dollars per *vara* (33" x 33"—the old Spanish measurement) caused not only the wealthy but the middle class to regard their investments with concern....

Dr. Fidel Castro has promised the workers they will receive higher wages and that living costs will be reduced. This has resulted in a wave of labor demands in every industry....

The imposition by the revolutionary government of currency controls and restrictions of imports—for the first time in the history of Cuba—has further disturbed and handicapped commerce and industry. [P. 411–13]

Nationalized U.S.-owned electric company. Sign says: "This building is the property of and is occupied by workers who are ready to give their lives for national sovereignty. We support nationalization!"

Phillips felt it necessary to sternly remind Castro that his measures against the wealthy few were taking on "an ominous overtone. Many of these people inherited their properties or obtained them by their own hard work and frugality" (P. 413).

On the foreign policy front, Phillips complained,

> The constant whipping up by Fidel Castro of an extreme nationalistic spirit is regarded by many Cubans as ill advised in an island which depends on exports for its economic life and must import the greater part of its food. "Economic independence" has been a catchword of politicians in Cuba since the dawn of the Republic, but the majority of Cubans realize that it is an impossible dream, since Cuba is inevitably tied economically to the United States—its best customer and largest supplier. [P. 413.]

But what distinguished the July 26 Movement from every previous radical petty-bourgeois formation and demagogic politician was that the Fidelistas *meant what they said*. Once in power, they set out to implement their program and to mobilize the masses of Cuban people in support of the measures they took.

Having learned the lessons of the 1954 CIA-organized coup against the Arbenz regime in Guatemala, the rebel leaders moved immediately to disband the Batista army and police. They put some of the most notorious police torturers on public trial, and executed some 600 of them with revolutionary justice—although most of these butchers, rapists, torturers, and hangmen had escaped to Miami. The public trials were used to educate and mobilize the working people.

The cutting edge of the revolution in the early months was the radical agrarian reform law promulgated on May 17, 1959. Holdings beyond 1,000 acres were expropriated and distributed among the 700,000 landless peasants and agricultural workers, with priority given to any tenants, sharecroppers, or squatters living on the land in question. All cane-growing land belonging to the giant sugar mills was seized, along with all land owned by non-Cubans.

To carry through the land reform, the National Institute of Agrarian Reform (INRA) was established. Soon INRA and the Rebel Army, backed by the workers and poor peasants, were acting more and more as a "dual power" to the moderate figures in the bourgeois coalition government.

When the imperialists and their Cuban helpers began to escalate their campaign of threats, pressure, and pleas for "moderation," the coalition government began breaking apart and fissures appeared within the July 26 Movement. Rather than retreating or even slowing down, the Castro leadership moved further and further to the left, relying more and more on massive revolutionary mobilizations in the cities, as well as the countryside. In turn, the Castro team itself was further transformed as it increasingly reflected and responded to the deepening radicalization of the toiling masses of Cuba. The working class, supported by the poor peasantry, entered directly into the political process, initiating factory "interventions," putting their stamp of approval on, and consolidating, the revolutionary measures taken.

Meanwhile, in Washington, a campaign was launched in Congress and in the capitalist press to cut the quota for Cuban sugar allowed to enter the United States. In January 1960, President Eisenhower announced that he would seek authority to reduce the quota. Havana responded by denouncing this as blackmail and announcing that Cuba would sell sugar elsewhere in the world market.

The next month the Soviet Union agreed to purchase Cuban sugar. The Cuban government began to prepare a law to expropriate the sugar mills. Fidel announced: "As they cut our sugar quota pound by pound, we will seize their mills one by one." Hand-painted posters went up in the windows of houses throughout the island: "Sin cuota, pero sin bota." (Without the quota, but without the boot.)

Washington stepped up the financing and arming of counterrevolutionaries. Planes from Florida began bombing cane-fields and setting them afire. On August 6, 1960, addressing the first Latin American Youth Congress meeting in Havana, Castro announced the nationalization of all the American-owned sugar mills, oil refineries, and the power and telephone companies.

This was followed by further expropriations, including of the holdings of the Cuban capitalists. Castro put it: "We will nationalize them down to the nails in their shoes."

No hesitating. No vacillating. No halfhearted measures. As the pressure built up, and the revolutionary process deepened, the Castro leadership responded by turning toward the workers and exploited peasants and leading them in revolutionary combat.

And they didn't knuckle under to U.S. imperialism either. As Castro recalled when he addressed the United Nations in September 1960:

> Notes from the State Department rained on Cuba. They never asked us about our problems, not even out of a desire to express condolence or commiseration, or because of the hand that they had in causing the problems. They never asked us how many died of starvation in our country, how many were suffering from tuberculosis, how many were unemployed. . . . They demanded three things: speedy, efficient, and just payment. Do you understand that language? Speedy, efficient, and just payment? That means, "Pay right now, in dollars, and whatever we ask for our lands." [Taber, p. 320.]

Notes weren't the only thing that rained down on Cuba. Backed by the CIA, Florida-based counterrevolutionaries began a steady campaign of armed attacks, including the use of incendiary bombs against the cane fields.

Threats from Wall Street, economic sabotage, and armed attacks failed to stop Castro. Instead, the Fidelistas created and armed a mass popular militia. Finally, in August–October 1960, they led the workers in the expropriation of the capitalists and the transformation of Cuba into the first workers state in the Western Hemisphere.

Watching this evolution, the Fourth International as a whole came to the conclusion that we were dealing not only with revolutionists, but with a grouping that by relying on the working class, mobilizing the masses, and going on to establish a workers state had in the process themselves been transformed into proletarian revolutionists, although not Trotskyists.

To our knowledge, no one in the Fourth International at the time proposed that this grouping of great revolutionaries of action should be labelled "centrists." The term was too incompatible with everything that the leaders of the July 26 Movement were showing in practice.

Furthermore, labelling the leadership of the Cuban revolution "centrist," however the term may have been qualified by adjectives, would have been an obstacle to carrying out the line of action adopted by the Fourth International. This line, which was agreed on by both public factions of the international that existed at the time, included turning toward the Cuban revolution and its leadership; seeking ways to collaborate with them as fellow revolutionaries; and taking advantage of the anti-Stalinist character and course of the revolution to win a new hearing for revolutionary Marxism in Cuba and among all those throughout Latin America and around the world who were positively influenced by that revolution.

IWW's Big Bill Haywood

This approach was summed up by James P. Cannon, a leader of the SWP and one of the founding leaders of the Fourth International. In May 1961, in a letter to the Political Committee of the SWP, Cannon wrote:

> The only *revolutionary* policy for [the Fourth International in regard to] Cuba is to *recognize* the revolution there, as it is and as it is developing as a *socialist* revolution—and to *identify* ourselves with it, and to act as a part of it, not as scholastic wiseacres standing outside the living movement. [Cannon's emphasis.]

In another letter along the same lines (other parts of which are quoted by Jones) Cannon went on to develop this point:

> Fortunately, the problem now under discussion is not academic. It centers, at the moment, on Cuba and the Cuban Revolution and the leaders of this revolution. In exceptional circumstances, these people have changed Cuba and changed themselves. They have carried through a genuine socialist revolution, and armed the working population, and defended the revolution successfully against an imperialist-backed invasion. And now they openly proclaim themselves socialist. . . .
>
> In my opinion, that's pretty good for a start—and I am talking here about the leaders as well as the masses who support them. If such people are not considered as rightful participants in a discussion, and possible collaborators in a new party and a new international—where will we find better candidates?
>
> Trotsky, in the middle Thirties initiated extensive discussion and collaboration with left-centrists who only talked about the revolution, and even that not very convincingly. The Cuban revolutionists have done more than talk, and they are not the only ones on trial from now on. We are also on trial. What would our talk about revolution be worth if we couldn't recognize a revolution when we see it?

If the Fourth International had not reached out to the Castroists and sought to collaborate with them as fellow revolutionists, the international would have been bankrupt, a lifeless sect.

Lessons from the Comintern

By following Jim Cannon's advice to approach the Castroists as fellow revolutionaries, not as either centrists or opponents of some other stripe, the Fourth International was applying the lessons learned from Lenin and Trotsky. After 1917, even though they held state power in the Soviet Union, the Bolsheviks recognized there were revolutionary currents in numerous countries who would not be immediately won to Leninism. They sought to win them to the side of the Russian Revolution and the revolutionary international.

In considering how well the name tag "centrist" fits the Castro current, it is instructive to take a look at the kinds of forces Lenin and Trotsky considered revolutionists, not centrists, and why.

One example was the Industrial Workers of the World, the "Wobblies." The IWW was neither Marxist nor Leninist—politically it represented anarcho-syndicalism of a sectarian variety. In relation to the needs of the working class, its political weaknesses were greater than those of Castroism.

It was certainly not capable of leading the working class forward to either mass industrial unionism or construction of a revolutionary Marxist party—to say nothing of making a socialist revolution in the United States. The IWW had no program for advancing the socialist revolution internationally.

Within the United States, although the IWW proclaimed and popularized the idea of uniting the working class into one big industrial union, its sectarianism made it incapable of advancing this idea in practice. At the IWW's second convention in 1906, the Western Federation of Miners, the only strongly organized union affiliated with the IWW, was driven out of the organization because its leaders weren't revolutionaries.

This same confusion between the tasks of a political party and the role of a trade union, which prevented the Wobblies from consolidating an effective trade-union organization, also turned the IWW into an obstacle to the building of a revolutionary socialist party in the United States.

The IWW had a bad case of anarcho-syndicalist ultraleftism. It opposed running in elections on principle. In many cases it adopted a policy of "silent defense"—that is, of refusing to speak in the capitalist courts. Castro's famous "History Will Absolve Me" courtroom speech compares rather favorably to that.

And unlike the Fidelistas, the IWW proved incapable of learning the lessons of experience. The majority of its leading cadres did not come over to the Communist Party after the Russian Revolution.

Nevertheless, the Communist International, under the leadership of Lenin and Trotsky, recognized that the IWW was an organization of revolutionary class-struggle fighters. The IWW was specified in the Communist International's first manifesto as one of the organizations invited to join.

In his opening address to the Second Congress of the Communist International, which was attended by delegates of the IWW, Zinoviev declared his solidarity with "the workers who are in the ranks of the Communists or the ranks of the IWW or other revolutionary organizations following the same path as the Communist International" (*The Second Congress of the Communist International* [London: New Park Publications, 1977], vol. 1, p. 6. See also *Workers of the World and Oppressed Peoples, Unite!*, vol. 1 [New York: Pathfinder Press, 1991], p. 133 [2013 printing]).

The Bolsheviks recognized the IWW for what it was—an organization of revolutionary fighters with an incorrect program. The Wobblies were revolutionists of action. They were for uncompromising struggle against the capitalist class and its cops, courts, political parties, parliaments, wars, and exploitation.

The Comintern took the same attitude to the British Shop Stewards movement, which was also represented at the Second Congress of the Communist International, and to syndicalist currents in other countries.

Malcolm X: revolutionary or centrist?

Another, more contemporary, example is also relevant: Malcolm X.

Like the Castroists, Malcolm X did not come out of the workers movement. He was a revolutionary nationalist, fighting for the rights of the oppressed Black population in the United States. He was an uncompromising opponent of racism, of the imperialist government, and of the two capitalist parties in the United States.

He was greeted by the Socialist Workers Party as a fellow revolutionist. In fact, the SWP recognized him as one of the greatest revolutionary mass leaders produced by the American working class. We sought to collaborate with him and to influence his thinking within that framework. In the words of SWP leader George Breitman, Malcolm "was a revolutionary—increasingly anti-capitalist and pro-socialist as well as anti-imperialist. These labels fitted, even though he did not apply them to himself" (George Breitman, *The Last Year of Malcolm X: The Evolution of a Revolutionary* [New York: Pathfinder Press, 1967], p. 40 [2013 printing].)

Malcolm X was not a Trotskyist. Some of his political mistakes were similar to those of the Castroists. Like the Fidelistas, Malcolm was not clear about the need to distinguish between giving support to bourgeois regimes in the semicolonial countries in their conflicts with imperialism, and expressing political confidence in, or giving a political endorsement to, such regimes.

For example, this is how Malcolm described the "highlights" of his trip to Africa in 1965:

> During that trip I had audiences with President Nasser of Egypt, President Nyerere of Tanzania, President Jomo Kenyatta (who was then Prime Minister) of Kenya, Prime Minister Milton Obote of Uganda, President Azikiwe of Nigeria, President Nkrumah of Ghana, and President Sekou Toure of Guinea. . . . I was impressed by their analysis of the problem, and many of the suggestions they gave went a long way toward broadening my own outlook. [Interview in *Young Socialist*, March–April 1965, p. 3. See also *Malcolm X, Black Liberation, and the Road to Workers Power* (New York: Pathfinder Press, 2009), p. 49 (2012 printing).]

Like Castro, Malcolm did not see the socialist revolution in the United States as a realistic perspective. As George Breitman put it, Malcolm was "not yet a Marxist. He saw the white workers only as they were (politically immature, lacking in independence, blinded by prejudice), and not as they might or would become under different conditions" (*The Last Year of Malcolm X*, p. 71).

Breitman also points out that Malcolm was a devout Muslim until his death. But all this didn't stop the SWP and the Fourth International from recognizing Malcolm as an uncompromising fighter and revolutionary politician.

In fact, we were in a better position to work out our line in regard to this promising development in the mid-1960s because of what we had learned from events and from the discussion in the SWP and in the international several years earlier on the question of the Cuban revolution and its leadership. We were more receptive, and responded more quickly, to Malcolm's evolution than we would have been if we had not experienced and learned from the Cuban events.

It is also worth noting that sectarian opponents of the Cuban revolution, especially Gerry Healy in Britain and his miniatures inside the Socialist Workers Party in the United States, were as virulently anti-Malcolm as they were anti-Castro—and for the same reasons.

As with the Castroists, we could not have followed a correct line toward Malcolm if we had considered him to be a centrist. This is not a question of terminology but of political stance and intervention by revolutionary politicians. How different the real political line of Breitman's book would be if he had decided to call it: *The Last Year of Malcolm X: The Evolution of a Centrist*!

The parallels between Malcolm X and the central leadership team of the July 26 Movement can be extended further. Both the Castroists and Malcolm X began as revolutionary nationalist fighters. They did not begin as socialists or conscious partisans of the working class. Their political origins were not in the organized workers movement, but in the struggles of an oppressed nation. Because of their uncompromising commitment to improving the

Malcolm X addressing a June 1963 rally in Harlem. A "centrist" or one of greatest revolutionary mass leaders created by the American working class?

lives of their people, they evolved into prosocialist and anticapitalist fighters. The Castroists became proletarian revolutionists, basing themselves on the toiling masses and mobilizing them to overthrow capitalism. Malcolm was gunned down by the forces of reaction precisely because he too was moving in that direction.

The development of revolutionary currents that did not begin as part of the workers movement was the subject of some discussion at the Second Congress of the Communist International in 1920. In the colonial world especially, where the proletariat itself was small and the workers movement weak, the Bolsheviks were convinced that they would see the emergence and development of such revolutionary and anti-imperialist forces.

In his report from the Commission on the National and the Colonial Questions delivered to the Second Congress, Lenin explained that the commission had decided to "speak of the national-revolutionary movement rather than of the 'bourgeois-democratic' movement" in the colonial world (Lenin, *Collected Works* [Moscow, Progress Publishers, 1966], vol. 31, p. 241).

Giving the reasons for this change in terminology, Lenin explained:

> . . . if we speak of the bourgeois-democratic movement, we shall be obliterating all distinctions between the reformist and the revolutionary movements. Yet that distinction has been very clearly revealed of late in the backward and colonial countries, since the imperialist bourgeoisie is doing everything in its power to implant a reformist movement among the oppressed nations too. [Ibid., p. 242.]

The "Supplementary Theses on the National and Colonial Question," which were adopted at that Congress, put special emphasis on the importance of orienting toward these revolutionary forces.

> 1. One of the most important questions that faces the Second Congress of the Communist International is to establish exactly the mutual relations between the Communist International and the revolutionary movement in the politically oppressed countries dominated by their own capitalist system, like India and China. . . .
>
> 4. . . . The Communist International must enter into much closer connection with the revolutionary forces that are at present participating in the overthrow of imperialism in the politically and economically oppressed countries. [*The Second Congress of the Communist International*, New Park. Now available from Pathfinder, *Workers of the World and Oppressed Peoples, Unite!*, pp. 280–81.]

The reporter on the "Supplementary Theses," M.N. Roy, gave an example of the kind of revolutionary forces the theses were referring to:

> In recent years there has been a new movement among the exploited masses in India that has spread very quickly and expressed itself in mighty strike waves. . . . One can say of this mass movement that it is at all events revolutionary, although no-one would say that the workers and peasants who form this movement are also clearly class-conscious. [Ibid., p. 286.]

Doesn't the July 26 Movement fit into this category of movements of oppressed nations and nationalities that are "at all events revolutionary" despite the fact that they are not under the leadership of revolutionary Marxists?

Aside from the decisive fact that the Castroists displayed none of the concrete characteristics of centrism enumerated by Trotsky—such as vacillation, conciliation, revolutionary rhetoric and reformist deeds, halfheartedness, or cowardice—they were not, in the beginning, even part of the workers movement or its periphery.

Schematically, we often view the workers movement as represented by a semicircle, with the camp of reformism (Stalinist and Social Democratic) at one end, and the camp of revolutionary Marxism at the other. The centrists are somewhere in between—left centrists closer to the revolutionary pole and right centrists closer to reformism. Moreover, these groupings are invariably in motion—either away from reformism and toward revolutionary Marxism or in the opposite direction.

But "national revolutionary" or "revolutionary liberation" movements (to use the language of the Second Congress) don't fit into this two-dimensional schema. The July 26 Movement did not become part of the proletarian movement until after the downfall of Batista, when it led the Cuban masses in the establishment of a workers and farmers government and the construction of a workers state and transformed itself in the process. It did not start from the camp of reformism, pass through a centrist stage, and arrive at revolutionary positions. It followed a different trajectory altogether.

The Fourth International was correct in recognizing the Castroists as a revolutionary leadership, despite their mistakes and inadequacies. In doing so, we followed the same political approach as that taken by Lenin and Trotsky in dealing with revolutionary non-Marxist currents in the workers movement, such as the IWW, and with revolutionary currents in the colonial world arising outside the workers movement.

For the Fourth International, a correct approach to such revolutionary groupings is a matter of life and death.

In general, our forces represent a tiny vanguard. In no country have we succeeded in building a mass party, or even a small revolutionary party of a few tens of thousands. Nowhere have we won hegemony within the vanguard of the working class. In many countries, no organized forces identified with the Fourth International exist at all.

At the same time, the decay of world capitalism is pushing new forces onto the road of revolution. We see this process beginning among the young workers inside the imperialist countries. The process is especially apparent in the colonial and semicolonial countries.

New leaderships are thrown up by these struggles. We must be able to recognize revolutionary currents when they arise, or we will never win them to Marxism.

Kautsky, Luxemburg, and Trotsky

Because centrist formations lack an independent social foundation, they react sharply to the pressure of the workers at one time and of the capitalists at another. This is the source of their vacillation, hesitation, halfheartedness, inability to act decisively, and reliance on radical-sounding talk but timidity when it comes to action.

Lenin first used the term "centrism" to describe Karl Kautsky after Kautsky—despite his reputation as an upholder of orthodox Marxism—failed a decisive test. He capitulated to the imperialist ruling class in his own country in World War I. Later, Kautsky refused to defend the Russian revolution—while mouthing Marxist-sounding "criticisms."

Kautsky's centrism consisted of his refusal to act as a revolutionary, his failure to identify with a real revolution when it occurred. As Lenin put it, Kautsky's centrism was "a blend of loyalty to Marxism in word and subordination to opportunism in deed" (Lenin, *Collected Works*, vol. 28, p. 230).

Centrism was a term used to describe those forces in the workers movement that refused to come over to the side of the October revolution, whatever their radical verbiage or "orthodox" Marxist stance. But Lenin and Trotsky did not use it as an epithet against revolutionaries merely because they weren't Leninists.

As Comrade Jones correctly points out, neither Lenin nor Trotsky ever approached Luxemburg as a centrist, or "labelled" her as such. Luxemburg opposed the building of a Leninist-type party. She opposed the right of oppressed nations to separate and form their own state. She opposed some of the revolutionary measures the Bolsheviks took in the aftermath of the October revolution.

ROSA LUXEMBURG: A revolutionist, but not a Leninist.

But when the decisive test of the victorious Bolshevik revolution drew a line of blood through the workers movement on an international scale, Luxemburg was on the side of the Bolsheviks. In her pamphlet, *The Russian Revolution*, she wrote:

> Only a party which knows how to lead, that is, to advance things, wins support in stormy times. The determination with which, at the

decisive moment, Lenin and his comrades offered the only solution which could advance things ("all power in the hands of the proletariat and peasantry"), transformed them almost overnight from a persecuted, slandered, outlawed minority whose leader had to hide like Marat in cellars, into the absolute master of the situation....

Whatever a party could offer of courage, revolutionary farsightedness and consistency in a historic hour, Lenin, Trotsky and the other comrades have given in good measure. All the revolutionary honor and capacity which western social democracy lacked were represented by the Bolsheviks. Their October uprising was not only the actual salvation of the Russian Revolution; it was also the salvation of the honor of international socialism. [*Rosa Luxemburg Speaks* (New York: Pathfinder Press, 1970), p. 538 (2013 printing).]

In 1932, Trotsky wrote:

> ... some of Rosa Luxemburg's political mistakes may be with sufficient theoretical justification characterized as left centrist. One could go still further and say that the majority of divergences between Rosa Luxemburg and Lenin represented a stronger or weaker leaning toward centrism. But only the idiots and ignoramuses and charlatans of the Comintern bureaucracy are capable of placing Luxemburgism, as an historical tendency, in the category of centrism. It goes without saying that the present "leaders" of the Comintern, from Stalin down, politically, theoretically, and morally do not come up to the knees of the great woman and revolutionist. [Leon Trotsky, *The Struggle Against Fascism in Germany* (New York: Pathfinder Press, 1971), p. 275 (2013 printing).]

In fact, one might even point out that Trotsky himself, before 1917, was not a Leninist, that he hesitated and vacillated between Bolshevism and Menshevism. This point has been made before—by Trotsky himself. In an article entitled "Our Differences," written in November 1924, Trotsky reviewed his own political evolution. Trotsky explained that, in the years before 1917, he

> ... held an attitude toward Menshevism that differed fundamentally from Lenin's. I thought it was necessary to fight for the unification of the Bolsheviks and Mensheviks within a single party. Lenin thought it necessary to deepen the split with the Mensheviks in order to cleanse the party of the main sources of bourgeois influence upon the proletariat....
>
> ... my "conciliationism" led me at many sharp turns in the road into hostile clashes with Bolshevism. Lenin's struggle against Menshevism was inevitably supplemented by a struggle against "conciliationism," which was often given the name "Trotskyism."
>
> ... It would never even enter my head now, long after the fact, to dispute the correctness in principle and the colossal historical farsightedness of Lenin's critique of Russian "conciliationism," which in its essential features was akin to the international current of centrism. [Leon Trotsky, *The Challenge of the Left Opposition (1923–25)* (New York: Pathfinder Press, 1975), pp. 338–39 (2013 printing).]

But only the most schematic of formalists could entertain the thought of labelling Trotsky before 1917 as a centrist. Trotsky was an unbending revolutionist, though not yet a Leninist. Trotsky recalled:

> I came to Bolshevism by a long and complicated road. Along this road I had no interests other than those of the revolution and the proletariat. I fought against Leninism when I thought that it was wrongly dividing the working class. When I realized my mistake as a result of experience, I came over to Leninism....
>
> ... In May 1917 I returned from America and placed myself at the disposal of the Bolshevik Party.... If I came to Leninism later than many other comrades, nevertheless I came soon enough to take part as one of Lenin's closest coworkers in the July days, the October Revolution, the civil war, and the other work of the Soviet years. [Ibid., pp. 343–44.]

Trotsky and Luxemburg, the revolutionists, were driven by the Russian revolution *toward* Bolshevism. Kautsky was driven by the same events *away* from Bolshevism. That is the difference.

Centrism an obstacle to revolution

The closer centrists—including left centrists—get to an actual revolution, the more they reveal their role as an obstacle to the proletariat. In 1939, Trotsky wrote:

> Left centrism, especially under revolutionary conditions, is always ready to adopt in words the program of the socialist revolution. . . . But the fatal malady of centrism is not being capable of drawing courageous tactical and organizational conclusions from its general conceptions. [Leon Trotsky, *The Spanish Revolution (1931–39)* (New York: Pathfinder Press, 1973), pp. 421–22 (2014 printing).]

"A centrist party is carried away by events and is drowned in them," Trotsky wrote (Ibid., p. 339).

From this point of view, the Castroists were just the *opposite* of centrists. They rejected the label of Marxism—or even socialism—while boldly moving ahead with revolutionary policies. They certainly weren't drowned by the Cuban revolution.

An example of a left-centrist group tested in a revolution was the Spanish POUM, which was formed in 1935 by a fusion of Trotskyists with a group that had broken from the Spanish Communist Party over the ultraleft policies of the "third period."

Centrist POUM played a "fatal role in the development of the Spanish Revolution."

In one of his last articles, "The Class, the Party, and the Leadership," Trotsky said: "To the left of all the other parties in Spain stood the POUM. . . . But it was precisely this party that played a fatal role in the development of the Spanish revolution." Trotsky added that "a centrist party invariably acts as a brake upon the revolution, must each time smash its own head, and may bring about the collapse of the revolution" (Ibid., p. 446).

Was the Castroist current a brake on the Cuban revolution, an obstacle to the establishment of the workers state? On the contrary, the Castro leadership repeatedly called the masses into the streets, and mobilized them against imperialism and the Cuban capitalist class.

Trotsky, in a 1935 letter on the question of centrism, said:

> You have observed very well that the people from the SAP [a German centrist party] . . . made quite radical speeches in which they advanced our principles quite passably, in order all the better to snap their fingers at these same principles when the time for the adoption of decisions came around. You remark very aptly that this is indeed classical centrism itself. [*Writings of Leon Trotsky (1934–35)* (New York: Pathfinder Press, 1971, 1974), p. 315 (2011 printing).]

Speaking of the British Independent Labour Party, Trotsky refers to the "vacillating elements, the so-called centrists" (*Writings of Leon Trotsky (1935–36)*, p. 174). He points out the "countless vacillations to the right and to the left" of the Spanish "Left Communists" (*The Spanish Revolution (1931–39)*, p. 253).

Again, writing in 1937, he says, "The POUM's official position is shot through with ambivalence. It cannot be otherwise: ambivalence is the heart of centrism" (*The Spanish Revolution (1931–39)*, p. 319).

In the same article Trotsky characterizes the course of Andrés Nin, the POUM leader, as one that "permits him to avoid drawing practical conclusions from his radical arguments and to continue the policy of centrist vacillation" (Ibid., p. 320).

Later Trotsky writes of the POUM and "its halfway measures, its indecisiveness and evasiveness, in short . . . its centrism . . ." (Ibid., p. 390).

Susceptibility to opposing class pressures also results in the unstable and shortlived character of centrist groupings. They are invariably torn apart by big social crises, since at those times the conflicting pressures reach their most acute point.

In the United States, the Trotskyists fused with the centrist group around A.J. Muste in 1934, and within two years the Musteites had shattered. Some went over to the Stalinists, some dropped out of politics, and some came over to Trotskyism. Muste himself went back to the church.

Another example was the leftward-moving centrist tendency in the Socialist Party that participated in the formation of the American Socialist Workers Party in 1938. That centrist grouping began moving to the right again as imperialist pressure increased with the approach of World War II. In less than two years those who were not won to Trotskyism had left the SWP with Max Shachtman and James Burnham.

During the 1930s there were big centrist formations in Germany, Belgium, Britain, and Spain. They had far greater material resources and many more members than the Trotskyists, but none of them survived World War II in any meaningful form.

Compare this record to that of the Castroists. Although the July 26 Movement certainly did split as the Cuban revolution deepened, the central core of leaders who fought with Castro in the Sierra Maestra has remained remarkably stable for nearly twenty-five years.

Of course, it is correct to argue that a group can lack one or another of the "classical" attributes of centrism and still be centrist. But these characteristics should not be lightly tossed aside. They have been defined by decades of revolutionary experience. They are not secondary or peripheral features but, as Trotsky explained, the "very heart of centrism." They are the *concrete* manifestations of centrism in the heat of the class struggle.

And in the case of Castroism, *not a single one* of these characteristics fits. On the contrary, the Fidelistas charted an uncompromising course. They never hesitated or vacillated, and when they encountered unforeseen obstacles, they led the workers and peasants in marching right over them.

III. Is the Castro Leadership Today Bureaucratic Centrist?

Comrade Jones states: "It is not necessary here to enter into the discussion of whether the Castro leadership was always centrist in character" (p. 97, footnote 40). However, he doesn't explain why he thinks it is "not necessary" to deal with this question. Surely he would agree that in order to understand a complex phenomenon like Castroism it is necessary to look at its origin and development. And the fact that the Castroists led a socialist revolution ought at least to be taken into account.

Comrade Jones states: "The character of the Cuban leadership *cannot* be derived from the fact that it overthrew capitalism in a particular country..." (p. 93, col. 1). We don't dispute this point. Theoretically, there is no reason to rule out the possibility that, under certain extreme historical conditions, a centrist grouping could take power. We have already seen this with Stalinist formations. But this is totally beside the point. We have made, we think, a convincing case that the Castroists were a revolutionary, not a centrist, grouping when they led the Cuban workers and peasants to power. It is not a question of theoretical possibilities, but of historical facts.

The Fourth International's characterization of the Castro team as revolutionary was not an exercise in scholasticism. It was a political assessment integrally related to the tone and character of our *intervention*. It indicated an approach, a stance, by revolutionary politicians. It educated an entire generation of Trotskyist leaders. To be "agnostic" about this history, which was an important conquest for our movement, is not the mark of a serious proletarian revolutionist.

But let's put this question aside for the time being and, with Comrade Jones, examine the situation in Cuba today.

It is, of course, possible to hold the view that,

in spite of the revolutionary character of the July 26 Movement in the late 1950s and early 1960s, once the Castroists were in power, at the head of the Cuban workers state with a growing state bureaucracy, a process of degeneration took place. This position is held by some in the Fourth International today.

As Comrade Jones correctly points out there is an example of the degeneration of a revolutionary leadership of a workers state: the Soviet Union. He rejects the idea that a bureaucratic *caste* exists in Cuba today—a crystallized social formation that has institutionalized its privileges and consolidated its power to the point where a political revolution is needed to advance the interests of the working class. As a result, Comrade Jones narrows the analogy with the Soviet Union to the decade between 1923 and 1933—"a period of transition in which the leadership of the Soviet state was not revolutionary but where the slogan of political revolution was still not the correct one" (p. 97, col. 2).

We agree this is the only correct historical analogy to pursue in determining whether the Castro leadership is centrist today.

But, if we are to follow Trotsky's method, we must be concrete. The centrism of the Stalin faction in the period 1923–33 was a specific kind of centrism, what Trotsky called "bureaucratic centrism."

The emerging bureaucracy that was consolidating itself into a hardened caste in the Soviet workers state was centrist in the sense that it balanced between the pressure of the working class on one side and imperialism on the other, directing its blows against the workers while defending its social base, in its own way, against attempts at capitalist restoration.

It was also centrist in the political sense. Contrary to Comrade Jones, Stalin's center in those years was not "the leadership of the Soviet state." It was the dominant wing of the leadership. The Stalin faction balanced between the at times large left and right wings of the CP. Stalin's first target was the revolutionary left wing of the Bolshevik Party. But in time he was also compelled to suppress the right Bolsheviks. Stalin gained the allegiance of individual leaders from both right and left, and eventually murdered those who would not go along.

The revolutionary current was decisively defeated and exiled. Thus, it turned out that the bureaucratic centrist period was a stage in the degeneration of the Soviet Communist Party, giving way to Stalinist Bonapartism.

Trotsky explained, "As the bureaucracy becomes more independent, as more and more power is concentrated in the hands of a single person, the more does *bureaucratic centrism* turn into Bonapartism" ("The Workers' State, Thermidor and Bonapartism," in *Writings of Leon Trotsky (1934–35)*, pp. 289–90).

Stalinist Bonapartism still balances between the proletariat and world imperialism, but the balancing act no longer results in the kind of zigzags that were evident during the period in which it was consolidating its power.

Trotsky said in 1937:

> The interests of the Bonapartist bureaucracy can no longer be reconciled with centrist hesitation and vacillating. In search of reconciliation with the bourgeoisie, the Stalinist clique is capable of entering into alliance only with the most conservative groupings among the international labor aristocracy. This has acted to fix definitively the counterrevolutionary character of Stalinism on the international arena. [*The Spanish Revolution (1931–39)*, p. 382.]

What are its social roots?

Bureaucratic centrism is rooted in an emerging privileged bureaucracy, and represents the increasingly distinct interests of that bureaucracy. This distinguishes it from other kinds of centrism, which do not have an independent social foundation.

Trotsky developed this point in the section of "What Next?" subtitled "Centrism 'In General' and Centrism of the Stalinist Bureaucracy." Written in 1932, it sheds important light on the relationship between bureaucratic centrism and the rising bureaucratic caste. In it, Trotsky insists on basing the analysis of bureaucratic centrism on the material interests of the bureaucracy. He insisted that bureaucratic centrism could only be understood by asking: "What historical necessities does it meet? What are its social roots?" (*Struggle Against Fascism in Germany*, p. 271). Trotsky wrote:

Speaking formally and descriptively, centrism is composed of all those trends within the proletariat and on its periphery which are distributed between reformism and Marxism, and which most often represent various stages of evolution from reformism to Marxism—and vice versa. Both Marxism and reformism have a solid social support underlying them. Marxism expresses the historical interests of the proletariat. Reformism speaks for the privileged position of proletarian bureaucracy and aristocracy within the capitalist state. Centrism, as we have known it in the past, did not have and could not have an independent social foundation. . . .

Centrism within the workers' movement plays in a certain sense the same role as does petty-bourgeois ideology of all types in relation to bourgeois society as a whole. Centrism reflects the processes of the evolution of the proletariat, its political growth as well as its revolutionary setbacks conjoint with the pressure of all other classes of society upon the proletariat. No wonder that the palette of centrism is distinguished by such iridescence! From this it follows, however, not that one must give up trying to comprehend centrism but simply that one must discover the true nature of a given variety of centrism by means of a concrete and historical analysis in every individual instance.

The ruling faction of the Comintern does not represent centrism "in general" but a quite definite historical form, which has its social roots, rather recent but powerful. First of all, the matter concerns the *Soviet bureaucracy.* In the writings of the Stalinist theoreticians this social stratum does not exist at all. We are only told of "Leninism," of disembodied leadership, of the ideological tradition, of the spirit of Bolshevism, of the imponderable "general line"; but we never hear a word about the functionary, breathing and living, in flesh and bone, who manipulates the general line like a fireman his hose.

In the meantime this same functionary bears the least resemblance to an incorporeal spirit. He eats and guzzles and procreates and grows himself a respectable potbelly.

He lays down the law with a sonorous voice, handpicks from below people faithful to him, remains faithful to his superiors, prohibits others from criticizing himself, and sees in all this the gist of the general line. Of such functionaries there are a few million. A few million! Their number is greater than the number of industrial workers in the period of the October Revolution. The majority of these functionaries never participated in the class struggle, which is bound up with sacrifices, self-denials, and dangers. These people in their overwhelming mass began their political lives already in the category of a ruling layer. They are backed by the state power. It assures them their livelihood and raises them considerably above the surrounding masses. They know nothing of the dangers of unemployment, if they are gifted with the capacity to stand at attention. The grossest errors are forgiven them so long as they are ready to fulfill the role of the sacrificial scapegoat at the required moment, and thus remove the responsibility from the shoulders of their nearest superiors. Well, then, has this ruling stratum of many millions any social weight and political influence in the life of a country? Yes or no? [Ibid., p. 277.]

This social foundation gave bureaucratic centrism quite different characteristics from other kinds of centrism.

Whereas in capitalist countries, the centrist groupings are most often temporary or transitional in character, reflecting the evolution of certain workers' strata to the right or to the left, under the conditions of the Soviet republic centrism is equipped with a much more solid and organized base in the shape of a multimillioned bureaucracy. [Ibid., p. 280.]

Such was the material foundation of bureaucratic centrism in the Soviet Union. And such was Trotsky's insistence on rooting his analysis of the Stalinist bureaucratic centrists in material reality, in looking at its social roots.

Unfortunately, Comrades Jones—who himself has written, as he reminds us in a footnote to his article, on "the decisive role of materialist criteria in judging the class character of a force"—does not follow Trotsky's method in applying the concept of centrism to the Cuban leadership today.

To be consistent with Trotsky's approach, Comrade Jones would have to argue that the Castroist leadership bases itself on a developing privileged bureaucratic caste. He would have to show that—while it has not yet crystalized into a consistently counterrevolutionary caste that cannot be reformed but must be overthrown by political revolution—its policies represent the historical interests of this social layer and not those of the Cuban working class. Only then could the designation centrist, or to be precise, bureaucratic centrist, be applied to the Castro leadership today.

However, Comrade Jones makes no such case. To the contrary, in emphasizing the "mass popular support" for the regime, he seems to imply just the opposite; that the Cuban working class and poor peasantry remain the social base today of the Fidelista current.

Does the 1923–33 analogy hold?

Let's zero in on the analogy between Cuba today and the Soviet Union in the years after 1923. In important respects the comparison is meaningful.

In Cuba, a tremendous revolutionary upsurge began in 1959. Mobilizations of the masses of workers and peasants swept capitalism aside, inaugurated a workers state, and defeated the imperialists' attempts—culminating in the Bay of Pigs invasion in April 1961 and the missile crisis in October 1962—to reverse the revolutionary victory.

But as the Cubans began to confront the problems of administering the economy, in the face of acute shortages and scarcity and under the pressure of the economic blockade imposed by imperialism, major problems of bureaucratism, based on material privilege, began to confront them.

As in the Soviet Union in the 1920s, a relatively large state bureaucracy grew up and exists in Cuba today. Many of its members enjoy certain material advantages and a significant number are inclined toward routinism and political conservatism.

As in the Soviet Union in the 1920s, divisions exist in the party and in the government in Cuba today. There is a right wing that fights for domestic and international policies that protect and strengthen the special privileges of sections of this bureaucracy. There is a left wing that bases itself on and fights to advance the historic interests of the toiling masses. And there is a centrist layer that wavers between them.

But while the analogy holds in many respects there is one crucial difference between Cuba today and the Soviet Union in the period we are talking about. *In the Soviet Union after 1923 the center, that is, the Stalin faction, was dominant. It defeated the revolutionary wing, absorbed the bulk of the right wing, and consolidated the bureaucracy's preeminence and power.*

In Cuba, the left, the Castroist leadership, remains to this day the dominant and decisive wing, preserving to itself the key policy decisions on domestic and foreign policy.

That does not mean the Stalinist right wing has been smashed. In fact, it commands considerable power and exercises control over important aspects of state and party administration. Its influence is broadly felt in the political life of the country. This can be seen, for instance, in the Communist Party of Cuba, which is not identical with the Castroist leadership. The CPC incorporates, in its membership as well as its leadership, the revolutionary left wing, the right wing, and centrist forces. Organizationally, it does not function as a Leninist party. Polemics and organized debates between different tendencies are not presented to the entire membership of the party. For these reasons, we cannot consider the CPC as a party to be revolutionary in the sense that the Castroist current is.[1]

But in Cuba today, the right wing is not in the saddle. It does not openly challenge the Castroist left wing, which enjoys to this day tremendous authority with the masses.

The right wing is compelled to go along with major policy decisions. These include such moves as the liberalization of internal cultural policies and the refusal to buy into détente, which would mean abandoning Cuba's revolutionary foreign policy, toning down Cuba's active support for the Puerto Rican independence struggle, and giving

---

1. Just as it is not accurate to equate the Castro current with the CPC, it is incorrect to equate the Castro leadership with every grouping in Latin America that considers itself Castroist. Some of these undoubtedly are centrist.

up the bold and aggressive use of internationalist forces to aid the anti-imperialist struggle in Africa in a way not paralleled by a workers state since the days when the Soviet Red Army was led by Lenin and Trotsky.

Is this conflict between the Castroist wing and the Stalinist right wing something new? The answer is no. In 1962 the Castroists and the Stalinists clashed sharply and the conflict burst into public. The dangers posed by privilege and bureaucracy were explained at the time by Fidel Castro himself, who not only threw the full weight of his prestige into the fight against bureaucratism, but mobilized the Castroist current for this fight and opened it up to any young revolutionary, no matter what political background she or he came from.

In a speech given in March 1962, Castro declared:

> No privileges should be forthcoming! War against privilege! War against all manifestations of weakness, against all self-seeking! ("The Revolution Must Be a School of Unfettered Thought," in *Selected Speeches of Fidel Castro*, Education for Socialists [New York: Pathfinder Press, 1979], p. 69 [2014 printing].)

Shortly after that speech, the Castroists pulled the rug out from under Aníbal Escalante and his chums, old-time Stalinist hacks who were building for themselves a bureaucratic machine in the newly formed ORI, the Integrated Revolutionary Organizations (forerunner of today's Communist Party).

In a television speech to the entire country, Castro revealed what had been going on:

> In every province the general secretary of the |Stalinist| PSP was made general secretary of the ORI; ... in every municipality, the general secretary of the PSP was made general secretary of the ORI; in every nucleus, the general secretary—the member of the PSP—was made general secretary of the nucleus. Is that what you would call integration? Compañero Aníbal Escalante is responsible for that policy. ["Against Bureaucracy and Sectarianism," in Ibid., p. 92.]

With particular disgust, Castro recalled a recent visit to a factory. He found that the party cell there included the director, the director's secretary, and the director's brother-in-law.

> We went there to exchange a few opinions with the members of the nucleus and out came the head of personnel, in a work center like that one, which is filled with workers dressed in sweat shirts and overalls smeared with grease, a head of personnel wearing a "cute" shirt with loud colors and a pair of white pants. And he was a member of the nucleus! What the blazes! They were completely separated from the masses. [Ibid., p. 94.]

This confrontation with the problem and pressures from a privileged bureaucracy has been a constant fact of political life in Cuba. In March 1967, the newspaper *Granma*, in an editorial entitled "The Struggle Against Bureaucratism: A Decisive Task," said:

> As long as the state exists as an institution and as long as organization, administration and policy are not all fully of a communist nature, the danger will continue to exist that a special stratum of citizens will form in the heart of the bureaucratic apparatus ... which can convert bureaucratic posts into comfortable, stagnant or privileged positions.

In this conflict between the Castroist left wing and the Stalinist right wing, we have never been, and must not be neutral—or defeatist. The outcome of this prolonged battle for the soul of the Cuban revolution will have major ramifications for the world revolution. The stakes are high. Our strategic orientation today must be the same as it has always been: to support and strengthen the Castro wing against the Stalinists. We identify with and back the revolutionary wing against the counterrevolutionary forces and pressures and the centrist vacillators. It is only within this framework that we can effectively explain the differences we have with the Castro current and fight to win Cuban revolutionaries to the program of the Fourth International.

As Jim Cannon stressed, *if we are to influence them*, we have to recognize the revolutionary leadership in Cuba and identify with it, in order "to act as a part of it, not as scholastic wiseacres standing outside the living movement."

What is happening in Cuba today?

Is this assessment of the different currents in the Cuban leadership, and their relative weight, accurate? Let us examine what is actually going on in Cuba today and compare it to the course of events in the Soviet Union from 1923 to 1933. If the left wing were not still dominant in Cuba, if bureaucratic centrists—in whatever combination of vacillators and Stalinists—were in command, we would expect to see some parallels in the key areas. Instead, what we find are glaring contrasts.

First, let's recall what was happening in the Soviet Union during the years when the bureaucracy was consolidating its hold, when the bureaucratic-centrist wing, not the revolutionary wing, dominated major policy decisions and administration domestically and internationally.

A fierce, open faction fight was raging in the ranks of the party and state apparatus. Beginning in 1927, thousands of revolutionists were systematically imprisoned, exiled, and—in the case of Joffe, for example—driven to suicide. The country was run by a police regime that cultivated an atmosphere of fear. Even though a few courageous public protests occurred, "The party mass is terrorized," Trotsky wrote in July 1928. (*The Third International After Lenin* [New York: Pathfinder Press, 1936, 1996], p. 333 [2013 printing].) Rigorous censorship was increasingly imposed. The history of the Bolshevik Party and of the Russian revolution was systematically falsified.

Poet Heberto Padilla: His arrest in 1971 rightly drew wide criticism. There have been no further such incidents.

Material privileges for the bureaucracy were expanding and being institutionalized by the ruling group. Special stores and rationing privileges were being established for state and party functionaries, along with access to special housing, schools, vacation resorts, and so on.

The gains made by the oppressed nationalities and women were being reversed. As early as 1922, Lenin was attacking Stalin for his bureaucratic chauvinism toward the oppressed nations of the Soviet Republic. There was an open revival of anti-Semitism as early as the mid-1920s. To justify the retreat from the Bolsheviks' goal of socializing the responsibilities of the family, the household drudgery of women was being glorified.

In the field of culture, the regime had already embarked on the road that led to the Stalinist straitjacket of socialist realism and the "party line" in art.

By the late 1920s, the dominant faction had initiated the forced collectivization of agriculture, which in the next few years would lead to the death of millions. This was a savage blow to the alliance between the workers and the poor peasants that the Soviet state was built on. It took decades for agriculture to recover.

How does this compare to what's happening today in Cuba, twenty years after the overthrow of Batista, seventeen years after Castro's 1962 appeal for "war" against privilege and bureaucracy?

Oppressed nationalities and women are generally among the first to feel the blows of reaction, but there is no evidence that these specially oppressed sectors are losing ground in Cuba. Even bourgeois observers are forced to admit this.

Joe Nicholson Jr., a reporter who spent six weeks in Cuba in 1973, said in his book, *Inside Cuba* (New York: Sheed and Ward, 1974):

> The Revolution's success in upgrading women's status has been phenomenal. Fifteen years ago, who would have believed ingrained social customs could be changed so rapidly any place in Latin America? No other Latin country has attempted it.... The Cuban gov-

ernment continues to combat pockets of resistance to the woman's new role—resistance that persists among some women as well as men. [p. 99.]

Nicholson says,

I had made a point during my first several weeks in Cuba to interview dozens of blacks because I had been incredulous about the Revolution's claim to have eliminated all racial discrimination. The blacks were virtually unanimous in saying racial discrimination was a thing of the past. [p. 107.]

Although Nicholson was highly critical of the treatment of homosexuals, he noted that rather than getting more repressive, the atmosphere was improving.

An indication of the general climate in Cuba was the publication in 1978 of a book called *Contra Viento y Marea*. The book is composed of interviews with fifty young Cubans in the United States who describe how they came to identify with and support the revolution. Criticisms and questions on the treatment of women and gays are included, and some passages are obviously written with the 1971 arrest and persecution of the poet Heberto Padilla in mind.

Casa de las Americas, one of the most important Cuban publishing houses, not only printed, circulated, and promoted the book in Cuba, but also gave it a special prize!

Although the disgraceful Padilla affair was widely publicized at the time, and rightfully drew wide criticism—including from the Trotskyist movement—we should note that there have been no repetitions. A survey of the cultural scene in Cuba by Peter Winn—a professor at Columbia and Yale—was published in the June 10 *New York Times Book Review*. After interviewing dozens of Cuban poets and writers, including friends of Padilla, Winn's main conclusion was to stress the variety and vitality of literary art in Cuba today. A Cuban publishing house has just published a book of Padilla's translations of English poets.

"Indeed," *Christian Science Monitor* correspondent James Goodsell reported January 31, "there is much more freedom of expression these days in Havana than at anytime in this reporter's memory of the 20 years that Dr. Castro has been in power."

There is no indication that special stores, accessible only to Cuban bureaucrats, have been established. This is a striking contrast to the Soviet Union in the late 1920s.

And what about the political prisoners? Are there growing numbers imprisoned for their political ideas? In a bold political move, the Castro leadership has in the last year released virtually every political prisoner on the island. Even Amnesty International has conceded that there were no "prisoners of conscience" in Cuba. Political prisoners were all people convicted for counterrevolutionary *acts*. Nonetheless, the Cuban government has taken an action that has effectively rammed Carter's human-rights hypocrisy right down his throat.

What a contrast to the decade of retreat, reac-

No compulsion is used to get Cuban farmers to join cooperative and collective farms. Alliance of Cuban workers and peasants remains firm.

tion, and growing repression in the Soviet Union between 1923 and 1933, when the "Gulag Archipelago" was being constructed!

In contrast to the offensive of the ruling Stalinist faction against the revolutionary generation of 1917, in contrast to the reign of terror against the Left Opposition, including the expulsion of Trotsky in 1928, those who *led* the socialist revolution are not being driven out of power, as they must be if a political counterrevolution is to eventually triumph. Fidel Castro could accurately state in his speech on the occasion of the twentieth anniversary of the victory over Batista:

> Our Revolution has always been characterized by its unbending steadfastness, its loyalty to principles and its deeply humane spirit. It has never devoured any of its sons and daughters, because there has been no cult of the personality, no gods thirsting for blood. [*Selected Speeches of Fidel Castro*, p. 181.]

An extremely important indication of social relations is the question of the alliance between the proletariat and the poor peasantry, on which the workers state is based. In the Soviet Union, this alliance was severely weakened by Stalin's forced collectivizations. Nothing of this type has occurred in Cuba. Nothing. The alliance is as firm as ever, if not firmer. Agriculture is one of the key policy areas which the Castro wing keeps closely under its control.

An article in the June 1 *Christian Science Monitor* described how the Cubans encourage collectivization—"small farmers living outside the city who agreed to lease their land to the state, leave their thatched cabins, and join collective farms were given refrigerators and color televisions when they moved into furnished apartments or duplexes."

'Socialism in one country'?

One of the very first signs of the defeat of the revolutionary wing of the Bolshevik Party and the domination of foreign policy by the bureaucratic centrists was the retreat from revolutionary internationalism. Stalin formulated his theory of "socialism in one country" in 1924.

Have we seen any such retreat by the Castroist current in Cuba?

Peter Osnos, the foreign editor of the *Washington Post* and its former Moscow correspondent, described the view he got of Cuban foreign policy during a recent trip to Cuba in a March 11 article. Osnos said:

> Perhaps the most significant difference between Cuba and its Soviet bloc allies that I sensed is ideological zeal—the impulse that assures popular support for shipping thousands of troops off to Africa (Havana teenagers wear T-shirts with pictures of Angola's Agostinho Neto) and tolerance of serious shortages in consumer goods.
>
> Cubans are proud that they are able to send doctors and teachers, as well as soldiers, to Angola and Ethiopia—even if that means, as it does, sacrifices in their own development. There is a messianic quality to this, underwritten by Castro's exhortations. . . .
>
> Cuba is by no means democratic in the sense that we regard the term. Yet there is an almost palpable atmosphere of public participation in matters great and small. . . .
>
> Take the mobilizing of support for Vietnam against China. In his speech and other statement, Castro skillfully blended Hanoi's victory over the United States with his own long defiance of *Yanquis* and the new *Yanqui* courtship of China into an argument that made the interests of Cuba and distant Vietnam seem parallel. . . .
>
> "We have shed our blood in Angola and Ethiopia," a banner at the Havana rally said. "We are prepared to do so in Vietnam." The record shows that on this score, Cubans mean what they say.

If Cuba today were in the midst of spreading reaction, experiencing the process of the consolidation of the dominant political hold of a privileged bureaucratic social layer within the state and party apparatus, wouldn't we see a widespread increase in social tension, tightening repression, growing intolerance of cultural freedom, purges and expulsions in the party—especially on the left—a turning inward, loss of faith in the possibility of extension of the revolution, depoliticization of the working class, qualitative widening of the gap between the privileged layers and the rest of the population, an increase in antagonism between Blacks and whites, forced retreat for women, increased oppression of youth—and more?

But we see no such thing. And Comrade Jones makes no attempt to provide evidence of any such developments.

Maybe it's a left turn

It might be argued that although things are not moving to the right in Cuba—there may even be a loosening up domestically and a reversal of some of the negative developments that occurred earlier around the time of the Padilla persecution—and although Cuba's foreign policy, especially in its confrontation with imperialism in Africa, may even be closer to a revolutionary line than in the past, nonetheless these trends are totally consistent with the domination of a centrist bureaucracy. After all, as Trotsky explained, bureaucratic centrism was marked by zigzags, including left turns.

Might not the current phase of the Castroist leadership be a left turn comparable to the "left turn" Stalin began in 1928?

This argument overlooks the fact that the ultraleft course of the so-called "Third Period" was in no way a move toward proletarian internationalism. It was a move *away* from it. It wasn't any "better" than the opportunist period of 1924–27, nor was it preferable to the Popular Front line that replaced it by 1935.

"Third Period" ultraleftism was marked by an insanely sectarian and adventuristic line for the CPs abroad, including a policy of splitting the union movement and building "red" trade unions; characterizing workers in the Social Democratic parties as "social fascists" with whom no united front was possible, thus paving the way for the victory of Hitler; and physically attacking other currents in the workers movement. In the Soviet Union itself it was marked by the terror of the forced collectivization of agriculture and an escalation of the police-state methods of the Stalin faction.

The "Third Period" did *not* include a greater cultural diversity, increased political debate in the Soviet working class, heightened international consciousness, or anything like it. In fact, the "Third Period," like other sharp policy reversals, appeared inconsistent and irrational. Each was actually a necessary part of the consolidation of the monolithic power of the Stalinist bureaucracy. As Trotsky explained in *The Revolution Betrayed* (New York: Pathfinder Press, 1937, 1972) [2013 printing]:

> From the point of view of socialist forms of society, the policy of the bureaucracy is striking in its contradictions and inconsistencies. But the same policy appears very consistent from the standpoint of strengthening the power of the new commanding stratum.
>
> The state support of the kulak (1923–28) contained a mortal danger for the socialist future. But then, with the help of the petty bourgeoisie the bureaucracy succeeded in binding the proletarian vanguard hand and foot, and suppressing the Bolshevik Opposition. This "mistake" from the point of view of socialism was a pure gain from the point of view of the bureaucracy. When the kulak began directly to threaten the bureaucracy itself, it turned its weapons against the kulak. The panic of aggression against the kulak, spreading also to the middle peasant, was no less costly to the economy than a foreign invasion. But the bureaucracy had defended its positions. [pp. 283–84.]

This was the roots and character of the left and right turns of the bureaucratic centrists—it is not of the Castro leadership.

Is there anything at all about the social foundation, policies, or evolution of the Castro current that points in the direction that the Soviet bureaucratic centrists were moving between 1923 and 1933? We see no such thing.

The problems and deformations of bureaucratic developments exist. But the revolutionary wing that led the Cuban workers to power remains dominant in the key areas of foreign and domestic policy. And that remains decisive for us in assessing our attitude to the Cuban leadership today.

There is the possibility of degeneration of these revolutionists, especially if the extension of the socialist revolution is held off, imperialism is strengthened, and if Leninists are not capable over time of acting in such a way to gain the confidence of and influence the Cuban revolutionaries. But that possibility is not the fact today.

IV. Cuba's Policy in Africa

Comrade Jones bases his case for the bureaucratic-centrist character of the Castro leadership on its political positions internationally. In fact, he argues that this is the only valid criterion:

> *The class struggle by its nature is international. Therefore the criteria for determining the character of a current are also international. . . .*
>
> *. . . in relation to the question of the Cuban leadership, the fact that a current can take power on a national terrain does not make it revolutionary on a world scale* and, like all characterizations, the nature of the Cuban leadership cannot be determined solely from its orientation on the terrain of Cuba itself but only from its positions on the most fundamental issues of *world* politics. [Emphasis in original, p. 92.]

Perhaps this confused idea is why Comrade Jones makes no attempt to examine what is happening in Cuba today. He disregards the fact that foreign policy is an extension of domestic policy, not vice versa.

More importantly, however, he seems to be arguing that only those with a consistently revolutionary line on all fundamental questions of world politics can be considered revolutionaries. Such a definition would effectively negate his earlier agreement that there are revolutionary currents that are not Leninist.

Certainly no one but the Fourth International even comes close to a consistently revolutionary line on all questions of the international class struggle. And if that is the criterion, there are no revolutionaries outside the Fourth International.

We prefer Jim Cannon's approach. Those who *lead* the workers of their own country to "take power on a national terrain"—there is no other way to take power—should be recognized as revolutionists, even if their program might be inadequate, and they fall short of Leninism in practice.

But let's examine Comrade Jones's case against the Castro leadership's policies internationally.

He argues that the role of Cuba in Angola and Ethiopia does not provide evidence of the revolutionary character of the Castro leadership. To the contrary, he states, it demonstrates that the Cuban "policy is *not* to overthrow capitalism and establish workers states but to build and sustain left-bourgeois regimes that will, objectively, finally collide with and oppose the working class and the construction of workers states" (p. 96, col. 1).

Referring to the key role of Cuban forces in driving back the South African invasion of Angola, Comrade Jones says, "We totally support and hail that military intervention . . ." (p. 95, col. 1).

But he states,

> Once the military victory was achieved, however, the Cubans took no steps whatever—quite the reverse—to encourage the overthrow of capitalism in Angola. And this is no academic point when, with the prestige of their intervention and their great military weight, there is no doubt that a Cuban call for the overthrow of bourgeois rule in Angola would have had every chance of succeeding. [Ibid.]

Comrade Jones is correct in criticizing Castro's political endorsement of the Neto regime in Angola. As they have done in other cases, the Castro leadership fails to note any contradiction between those anti-imperialist policies and social programs that all revolutionists would support, and the anti-working class character of the bourgeois regime in Angola. But Comrade Jones's idea of what the Cubans could—and should—do to help advance the class struggle in Angola must be more carefully considered.

By driving back the South African invasion of Angola the Cubans brought decisive aid to the toiling masses of Angola. They helped establish a framework in which the workers movement can develop on more advantageous terms than if it had to contend with an imperialist-imposed regime. Moreover, the Cubans helped to move forward the liberation struggle throughout southern Africa by stopping the South African imperialists. The defeat of the imperialist army in Angola was one of the inspirations for the Soweto uprisings.

But Jones seems to hold the mistaken view that the South African imperialist threat is no longer a pressing concern for Angola. This does not square with the facts.

The June 1979 issue of *Southern Africa* magazine reported:

> ... throughout this spring South African forces have been particularly active along the Namibian border.... Through the first half of March alone, the Angolan Defense Ministry reported 70 South African flights over Angolan air space, 13 regions bombed, 132 tons of bombs dropped, 12 dead, and 30 injured....
>
> And since then the South African raids have not abated. "The war with South Africa never ended," said Defense Minister Iko Carreira recently.

Working closely with the South African military is the formerly anti-imperialist National Union for the Total Independence of Angola (UNITA).

UNITA leader Jonas Savimbi claimed in a June 18 interview in *Time* magazine that the "intention of the Cubans is to control the border with Namibia so that they can help SWAPO [the South West Africa People's Organisation—the liberation movement fighting South African control of Namibia]."

Savimbi bragged, "Today they [the Cubans] fear to come into this area. We control most of the south."

Although Savimbi's claims are doubtless inflated, UNITA actions, combined with continuing South African and Rhodesian raids, represent a continuing threat to the Angolan workers and peasants.

From this point of view, the continued Cuban military role in Angola is progressive and the Trotskyist movement should support it wholeheartedly. Furthermore, the Cuban forces in Angola are also aiding the liberation struggles in Zimbabwe and Namibia, giving training and other assistance to fighters from those countries.

Along with military aid against imperialism, the Cubans have sent teachers, doctors, agricultural experts, technicians, construction workers, and others to help the workers and peasants of Angola overcome the legacy of colonialism and the destruction left behind by the South African invasion.

Wouldn't any revolutionary government do exactly the same thing?

Would it be a more revolutionary policy to refuse material aid to a beleaguered former colony such as Angola because the workers and peasants had not yet conquered power? By extending this aid, are the Cubans taking responsibility for the policies of the Neto government? Should they cut off that aid? Is that what the Fourth International should be advocating?

By their unselfish help to Angola and other countries that are trying to overcome the legacy of colonialism and continuing imperialist domination, the Cubans are strengthening the anti-imperialist forces. Even with Cuba's own extremely limited material resources, their revolutionary aid has made a decided difference in countries like Angola and Ethiopia.

But this aid is more than material solidarity, it is bold political action. The Cubans *give* their aid, they don't sell it to be repaid at interest, or to be

South African troops on maneuvers near the Angolan border.

paid for with political concessions. This constitutes a clear, though implicit, contrast to the "aid" given by countries with vastly more extensive resources. Isn't it in striking contrast to the policy followed by the Kremlin—a policy the Cubans are familiar with from bitter personal experience? Isn't it in striking contrast to the policy followed by the imperialist countries, who talk of "human rights" while they continue to pillage and rape the colonial and semicolonial world?

We are, as we have seen, in agreement with Comrade Jones that the Cubans are wrong in so far as they lend their *political* endorsement to the Neto regime, which is the class enemy of the Angolan workers and peasants. The Cuban leaders do not make the necessary distinction between the policy the Cuban government follows toward Angola's government (maintaining relations and extending material aid) and the policy that ought to be followed by the Cuban Communist Party (explaining to the Angolan workers and peasants that only by taking the Cuban road and overthrowing capitalism can they guarantee the defeat of imperialism and the advance of their own revolution).

However, we are in complete *disagreement* with the policy Comrade Jones seems to be recommending to the Cubans.

He states that "with the prestige of their intervention and their great military weight, there is no doubt that a Cuban call for the overthrow of bourgeois rule in Angola would have had every chance of succeeding" (p. 95, col. 1).

Should the Cuban forces in Angola try to organize and lead the overthrow of the Neto regime? This seems to be what Comrade Jones is suggesting. Such a policy, or anything approaching it, would be an unmitigated, ultraleft adventure. Who would the Cubans replace Neto with? It is the Angolan workers and peasants who must overthrow capitalism in Angola—not the Cubans. Were the Cubans, with "their great military weight," to try to substitute for that force, it would be a total disaster. For the Fourth International to call on them to do so would be wild adventurism that could only isolate the Trotskyist movement from any serious working class forces in Angola as well as in Cuba.

Cuba and Eritrea

Although Comrade Jones argues that a "particularly clear case" of Castro's centrism is Cuba's policy in Angola, he spends more time on the question of Eritrea. He highly recommends Comrade Richard Carver's analysis of events in Eritrea and bases his own account on an article by Carver entitled "Eritrea—the Guilty and the Silent" (reprinted in *Intercontinental Press/Inprecor*, July 2, p. 671).

Before turning to Carver's article, let's look at the key paragraph in Comrade Jones's indictment of the Cuban policy in Eritrea. He says:

> The role played by the Cubans here has been to fall in behind the war waged by the Mengistu leadership of the Dergue. Far from having "sharply differentiated themselves from the all-out support offered by the Kremlin to the Dergue's war," the Cubans are in fact a key cornerstone of that war effort. [P. 94, col. 1.]

Comrade Jones goes on in the same paragraph to list several reasons why he thinks the Cubans have fallen in behind the Dergue's war in Eritrea, and why they "are in fact a key cornerstone of that war effort."

He argues first, "Without the Cuban military training, weapons, and support work, the Ethiopian forces would be totally unable to undertake their offensive."

Cuban military aid to Ethiopia began in a substantial way in December 1977. By March 1978, these Cuban forces had helped defeat the imperialist-backed invasion of the Somalian army. That invasion was aimed at weakening and rolling back the Ethiopian *revolution*, which was driven forward by one of the deepest and most far-reaching mass mobilizations ever in Black Africa. Without "Cuban military training, weapons, and support work," it is possible that the imperialist-backed forces would have been successful in replacing the Dergue with a pro-imperialist regime. This would have helped neither the Ethiopian workers and peasants, the Eritrean workers and peasants, nor the Somalian workers and peasants.

The fact that the Cubans helped Ethiopia beat back an imperialist-inspired attack is to their

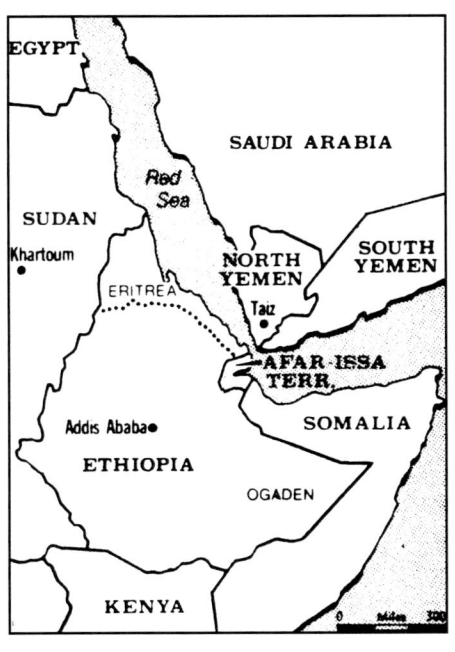

credit. And in Ethiopia, as in Angola, the imperialist threat is a continuing one.

Reading Comrade Jones's article, one would never know that a vast social revolution had occurred in Ethiopia in the last five years, a development imperialism is not favorably disposed toward. Nor would one have any idea why Cuban troops were sent to Ethiopia in the first place.

Does he agree that the Cubans played a progressive role in helping to drive back the Somalian army?

Does he agree that the character and scope of the Ethiopian revolution must be the starting point for understanding the class forces in motion throughout the region? Does he agree that imperialist pressure against the Ethiopian revolution is continuing and that the Cubans are right to support Ethiopia against these imperialist-inspired threats?

If he does agree with these points, then Comrade Jones cannot logically complain about "military training, weapons, and support work" provided by Cuba to the Ethiopian armed forces. If he does not agree, he should say so explicitly and explain his reasons.

In any case, the Cubans have repeatedly stated that their internationalist aid to Ethiopia is designed to counter such imperialist attacks and is not directed against the Eritrean national liberation forces.

Speaking at the University of Chicago December 2, 1978, Raul Roa-Kouri, Cuba's permanent representative to the United Nations, declared that the Eritrean question was "separate from the Ogaden completely," and that Cuban military personnel "have not and will not" participate in the conflict.

Does Comrade Jones propose that the Cubans should have withheld their military aid in the war against the Somalian invasion on the grounds that, because of that aid, the Dergue might have been able to shift more supplies and troops to the Eritrean battlefields? Does Comrade Jones think that, as some have argued, the Cubans are complicit in the slaughter of Eritreans because they defended, arms in hand, the Ethiopian revolution against the invasion by the Siad Barre regime? *If they followed such sectarian reasoning, the Cubans would be compelled to stand aside from every struggle against imperialism not under the leadership of revolutionary-Marxist forces.* Fortunately, they do not follow such an ultraleft abstentionist policy.

However, Comrade Jones does not rest his whole case on this guilt-by-association indictment. He also seeks to produce "the smoking gun." But this is a total frameup.

He states:

> Furthermore, although even if they were nowhere near the front line Cuban agreement would still be indispensable for the war, reports indicate that Cuban units and advisers are directly participating in the fighting—in particular in the specialized forces such as the air force and artillery. [P. 94, col. 1.]

Two points should be taken up here. First is Comrade Jones's claim that Cuban agreement is indispensable for the Dergue to carry out its war in Eritrea.

What is the basis for such a claim? The Dergue was fighting in Eritrea before any Cubans were in Ethiopia at all. It does not follow orders from Havana.

A question of fact

Second is the question of fact. Comrade Jones says nothing about the specific "reports" he is relying on. In a footnote, he recommends the article by Richard Carver for further documentation.

In his entire article, Comrade Carver offers only *two* specific sources for the charge that Cuban troops took part in the Ethiopian military campaign against the Eritrean liberation struggle.

Carver's first source is statements by the Eritrean People's Liberation Front: "EPLF communiques repeatedly point to Soviet and Cuban officering as the explanation" for Ethiopian gains in the war.

What Carver neglects to mention is that statements from other Eritrean liberation sources have contradicted the charges levelled against Cuba by the EPLF spokespeople. The Eritrean Liberation Front, the other main group in Eritrea, has frequently *denied* that Cubans were involved in the fighting against them.

Even the statements by EPLF representatives have been inconsistent. At times they have claimed Cuban involvement in the fighting, at times said nothing about Cubans, and at times admitted that there was *no evidence* of a direct Cuban role.

Eritrean fighter guards captured Ethiopian troops. There is no evidence that Cubans have been involved in Eritrean fighting.

One of the few journalists to have actually been in Eritrea and toured the battle areas with the EPLF is Dan Connell, a Reuters correspondent whom Carver cites. He is a supporter of the EPLF and also writes for the U.S. radical weekly, the *Guardian*. In a major series on the Eritrean war in that paper, Connell pointedly did not charge that the Cubans were involved in the war there.

The wisdom of uncritically accepting "facts" reported by the EPLF in the war may be judged by Carver's report that "the EPLF also says Soviet warships have been bombarding the coastline and landing troops and supplies." Really? A Soviet naval bombardment in the Red Sea? And no one said anything but the EPLF? Washington did not even make a diplomatic protest over this first Soviet naval bombardment of an African country? This is a patent absurdity.

Carver's second source is refugee accounts. He says:

> Many refugees report the presence of Cuban troops operating the Ethiopian artillery and flying their MIG-19s, 21s, and 23s. One of them told Dan Connell of Reuters:
> "We saw white men with the Ethiopians. Most of them were Cubans. . . . I saw them firing. The Ethiopian militia was in front, and the whites were behind them firing the big weapons which were on heavy trucks."

How this eyewitness was able to tell that "the whites" behind the Ethiopian militia were Cuban is unclear. Did this witness overhear them speaking Spanish? Were they carrying pictures of Ché Guevara? Smoking Havana cigars?

Were Afro-Cubans excluded and only "white" Cubans included?

Even Carver has to concede that such "reports are not definitive proof." But they are not corroborated by even a single bit of solid evidence. The fact is that no such evidence exists. No captured Cubans. No photographs, no bodies, no nothing.

Yet even all this does not prevent Comrade Jones from basing his factual case entirely on these "reports." It is nothing but a rotten frame-up.

Even the U.S. State Department had to admit on November 30, 1978—after the most recent massive Ethiopian military offensive against the Eritrean liberation forces had already begun—that it had no evidence the Cubans were involved in the Eritrean fighting.

The Cubans themselves have, as previously noted, repeatedly denied any military involvement in Eritrea. Their general policy has been to openly take credit for such interventions where they are real—in Angola, in the Ogaden, and elsewhere.

Lacking any substantial evidence that the Cubans are lying about their policy in regards to Eritrea, we have no reason to support the accusations against them. It is more likely that the charges are false. The wisdom of this appraoch is indicated by the fact that in late 1977 the White House approved a covert CIA program to discredit the Cubans on the question of Eritrea. It had the direct blessing of Carter and of his Special Coordinating Committee, a cabinet-level body headed by National Security Adviser Zbigniew Brzezinski that oversees clandestine operations.

Citing "well-placed sources," *New York Times* correspondent Seymour Hersh revealed three of these programs in a report in the June 1, 1978, edition. Two of the operations involved sending clandestine radio and other communications gear to the Egyptian and Sudanese governments.

"In addition," Hersh continued, "the C.I.A. organized an *anti-Cuban propaganda operation* during intensified fighting between Ethiopia and insurgents in Eritrea. . . ." (emphasis added.)

Could that be one of the sources of the strangely persistent reports in the bourgeois press of Cuban military involvement against the Eritreans? Everything points in that direction.

Cuba and the Dergue

Comrade Jones's final argument on Eritrea is that since the Cubans lend political credence to the Dergue in general, therefore they must take responsibility for its policy in Eritrea. As he puts it, "on the key question of political support to the major policies of the Ethiopian regime, the Cuban press is full of constant declarations of the revolutionary character of the leadership of Mengistu and the Dergue" (p. 94, col. 1).

Pointing to the fact that the Cuban leadership opposes the right of Eritrea to declare its independence from Ethiopia, Comrade Jones says, "Once the secession of Eritrea is rejected, then in fact the kind of ferocious counterrevolutionary war that is taking place was inevitable" (p. 94 col. 2).

In other words, no matter what the Cubans actually say and do in relation to the Eritrean struggle, so long as they refuse to support secession, they bear moral and political responsibility for the genocical war. This makes no sense, logically or politically.

The Cuban line on Eritrea is dead wrong. They do not support the right of the Eritrean people to establish their own independent state. The Fourth International has repeatedly pointed out why this stance endangers not only the Ethiopian revolution but poses an obstacle to the defense and advancement of the Cuban revolution too. However, nothing is gained by painting the Cuban line as *worse* than it actually is, or insisting that their line is the same as the Dergue's or Brezhnev's, which it is not.

The inescapable fact is that whatever the errors of their line, the *political* attitude of the Cubans toward the struggle in Eritrea has *differed* sharply from that of both Moscow and the Dergue. In contrast to their role in fighting off the Somalian invasion, the Cubans have consistently avoided falling in behind the Dergue's reactionary drive in Eritrea. They have repeatedly insisted that a political solution to the conflict is in order, not a military one.

Cuban Vice-president Carlos Rafael Rodríguez summarized this stand late in 1978 when he said, "We helped the Eritreans in their fight for self-determination from the time of Haile Selassie onward. We feel there has to be some political solution to the Eritrean problem and there have to be talks between Eritreans and the central government."

Raul Roa-Kouri, in the speech cited above, stated that "the solution is not separation, but a non-military, political solution respecting Eritrean nationality and autonomy within the larger Ethiopian revolutionary state." Referring to the Eritreans, he claimed that "elements of the national liberation movement support the Cuban position."

While *Pravda* effusively hailed the Dergue's military advances in Eritrea, *Granma*, the newspaper of the Cuban Communist Party said *not a single word about them*.

What is involved here is not a penny-ante difference. A shooting war is going on. Both Moscow and the Dergue put heavy pressure on the Cubans to back the war. The Cubans have refused.

A 'convergence' with Moscow?

The Cuban workers state, led by the Castro current that continues to be based on the workers and peasants of that country, has a consistently anti-imperialist foreign policy. The Soviet workers state is led by a regime that is based on the privileged bureaucratic caste of the USSR and is the enemy of the Soviet workers and peasants. It does not have an anti-imperialist foreign policy. To the contrary, unlike Havana, Moscow subordinates everything to seeking accommodation with and protection from, imperialism. The difference is as simple as that.

Does the policy of the Castro leadership at times converge with the interests of the Soviet bureaucracy? Yes, at times it does. Both Havana and Moscow favored Ethiopia in its war with Somalia. They both supported Angola in its war with South Africa. And there are other examples. But this convergence of interests doesn't prove that Cuba's line is the same as that of the Kremlin.

After all, doesn't our line at times converge with the interests of Moscow? Didn't we also support Angola against the South African imperialist invasion?

Didn't we have a "convergence" with Moscow in Vietnam, where we both backed the Vietnamese side in the war against American imperialism? And don't we also have a "convergence" with Moscow in defending the Soviet Union itself against imperialism—albeit with different methods? Does the fact that we defend the Soviet Union against imperialism make us closet-Stalinists ourselves?

No, the "convergence" doesn't prove anything except that the Soviet bureaucracy remains the ruling caste in a workers state at constant war with imperialism, despite the Kremlin's futile efforts to seek permanent accommodation through détente.

Because the Cubans do not have a Leninist program, they make mistakes—sometimes bad ones. But it would be a suicidal error for the Fourth International to miss the internationalist, anti-imperialist, revolutionary *axis* of Cuba's foreign policy.

As Castro said in his speech on the twentieth anniversary of the revolution,

> Of course we won't bow our heads—in this hemisphere, in Africa or anywhere else in the world.
>
> The United States insists on maintaining its criminal blockade as an instrument for exerting pressure on and expressing its demands with regard to Cuba, but Cuba can't be pressured or intimidated or bribed or bought. Cuba isn't China or Egypt. [*Selected Speeches of Fidel Castro*, p. 179.]

V. What Is at Stake?

When serious disputes erupt on questions of terminology, political factors are always involved. These don't always reflect fundamental differences, but they invariably are rooted in disagreements over how to approach and intervene in political developments.

That is what is involved in the discussion over whether we should now, after nearly two decades, abandon our recognition of the Castro leadership as revolutionary, though not Leninist, and decide to label it "centrist."

If we were to adopt the approach proposed by Comrade Jones we would call the Castroists "bureaucratic centrists." It would be possible, of course, to add some adjectives to qualify this label. We might call them "left bureaucratic centrists." It might even be suggested that Castroism is bureaucratic centrism *sui generis*. But nothing fundamental would be changed by such refinements.

By adopting this terminology we would be invoking the historical parallel of the defeat of the revolutionary wing of the Bolshevik Party by the bureaucratic centrists and their domination of the policies of the Soviet workers state in the period from 1923 to 1933. We would be saying that the role of the Castroist leadership today is equivalent politically to the role played by the Stalin faction, at least in the 1920s.

What would this mean politically? We would have to adopt a stance parallel to the approach of the Left Opposition in the 1920s. We would abandon our policy of consistently seeking to strengthen the Castroist wing against the Stalinists in Cuba, and within that framework present our Leninist program. That would no longer be our axis.

Instead, the axis of our analysis, our writing and speaking, our intervention would be one of trying to expose the betrayals of the revolution by Castro and his bureaucratic faction as they zig-zag along. And even when we support a concrete action they take, we would warn insistently that the general line along which the ruling Castroist wing is advancing constitutes a deadly threat to the Cuban revolution and to the interests of the toilers in Cuba and around the world. We would follow this policy inside of Cuba as well as internationally.

Would such a line attract forces to the banner of the Fourth International in Cuba? We believe it would—*but what kind of forces?* They would be *sectarian opponents* of the revolution, not proletarian fighters.

Such a step would set the entire Fourth International on a sectarian course that would head toward destroying our revolutionary fiber. It would place us in opposition to the one revolutionary leadership in power in the world, whatever its deficiencies, mistakes, and wrong policies. It would prevent us from *affecting* the course of events in Cuba in the most positive way, as part of the revolutionary current in opposition to the Stalinist right wing. It would reverse the course our world movement has always followed in approaching the Castroists, Malcolm X, and other revolutionary forces outside the Fourth International.

Worst of all, if we couldn't recognize a revolutionary leadership when we saw one we would be incapable of *practicing*—as opposed to merely talking about—the art of revolutionary politics. If not corrected, this step would lead us toward the "scholastic wiseacres" and sterile sectarians that Jim Cannon warned against.

JULY 26, 1979

ETHIOPIA, SOMALIA, AND THE AFRICAN REVOLUTION

By Eric Flint, Morgantown Branch; and Bruce Levine, Lower Manhattan Branch, New York Local

The full-scale war which occurred in the Ogaden during 1977 and 1978 played a critical role in the development of the class and national struggle in north Africa. For this reason, and because the war raises important questions about the way Marxists should approach national-democratic conflicts in general, it is necessary that the Fourth International and the Socialist Workers Party of the U.S. orient themselves correctly here.

We have not done so to date. The international as such does not have a formal position on the Ogaden war. The draft resolution adopted by the United Secretariat ("The World Political Situation and the Tasks of the Fourth International," [IIDB Vol. XV, No. 5]) is evasive (to say the least) on this score, but implicitly supports Ethiopia against the Somalis—a position we consider seriously mistaken. The (U.S.) Socialist Workers Party makes its support to Ethiopia very explicit and has mounted a literary propaganda campaign in defense of its position.

The present discussion article, on the contrary, defends the view that the world Trotskyist movement should have given military-technical support to the Somali forces in the Ogaden war. The clearest and most completely elaborated case for supporting Ethiopia is contained in a pamphlet by Ernest Harsch of the SWP entitled *The Ethiopian Revolution* (Pathfinder Press, November 1978).[1] Our arguments will therefore take the form of a debate with comrade Harsch.

The original position of the SWP

When the Ogaden war broke out, the Socialist Workers Party did not hold to the pro-Ethiopian position which it was later to adopt. In fact, during the entire course of the war, the SWP supported the Somalis. Only once the war was over did the majority of the party leadership reconsider its position and reject it in favor of the one outlined in the Harsch pamphlet.

We think the original position of the SWP was fundamentally correct. Likewise, we believe that the articles which comrade Harsch wrote in *IP/I* in defense of the SWP's *original* position constituted in general a factually accurate, methodologically sound, and programmatically correct approach to the war and the issues which it raised.

Let us review the original SWP position, particularly as elaborated in comrade Harsch's earlier articles.

The foundation of the entire analysis was the belief that the revolution in the Horn of Africa would best be served by the victory of the oppressed Somalis against the oppressors of the Ethiopian empire.

Ethiopia as it exists today is a neocolonial creation which rules over a semifeudal society, oppressing workers, peasants, women, and numerous national minorities. It is a classic prisonhouse of nations.

The Ethiopian revolution's strategic line of march necessarily leads through the mobilization of all these oppressed and exploited sectors in defense of their rights. This requires the destruction of the chief obstacle which exists in Ethiopia to this revolutionary mobilization—the Ethiopian bourgeois state apparatus ruled over by the Dergue military junta.

With respect specifically to the Somalis, it was understood that:

1. The Ethiopians (Amharas) have been the historic oppressors of the Somali people for the past one hundred years and have performed this task in the objective interests and with the active collaboration of the western imperialist powers.

2. The Somali people, who were dispersed among five separate political-states and colonies at the hands of Ethiopia and western imperialism, constitute a single nation whose ongoing struggle for national liberation and national reunification is just and progressive.

3. This struggle has deep historical roots reaching back over the better part of a century. It has often taken the form of major rebellions and wars, such as the struggle of the "dervishes" against Ethiopia, Italy, and Britain during the first two decades of the twentieth century; the struggle of the Somali peasants during the early 1960s against Haile Selassie in Bale and the Ogaden; the 1963–64 war between Somalia and Ethiopia over the Ogaden; and the struggle of the Western Somali Liberation Front against both Selassie and the Dergue during the 1970s.

4. The war between Somalia and Ethiopia in 1977–78 was a direct and organic continuation of the Somali struggle for national liberation and unification.

5. The Somali population of the Ogaden perceived the 1977–78 war precisely in this way and therefore supported, in its vast majority, the Somalian forces against the Ethiopians.

6. Siad Barre's motives for pursuing this war did not include a genuine interest in the national liberation of the Somali people. Siad Barre's actions reflected a narrow desire simply to increase the power of his own regime at the expense of an historic enemy, on the one hand, and to appease the demands of the Somali masses (both in Somalia proper and elsewhere) for a national liberation struggle. The objective significance of this war, however, was determined not by Siad Barre's subjective outlook and petty calculations but by its actual contribution to the region-wide struggle of oppressed workers and peasants against the Ethiopian state.

7. A victory by the combined forces of the Somalian state and the WSLF would constitute a powerful blow on behalf of the Ethiopian revolution. It would (a) advance the struggle for Somali national liberation, a powerful democratic struggle in the course of which the conservative government of Siad Barre could itself be brought down; (b) aid—perhaps decisively—the Eritrean struggle for self-determination by tying down and demoralizing substantial sections of the Dergue's armed forces on the eastern front; (c) encourage other oppressed nationalities in Ethiopia, like the Sidamos and Oromos, to step up their own struggles against Amharic national oppression; (d) deal a major blow against the already tottering Ethiopian state apparatus and the military-bonapartist Dergue which is desperately trying to keep that state machine intact in the face of the popular mobilizations; (e) give a mighty impulse, both subjectively and objectively, to the struggles against the Dergue by workers, peasants, and women in the Amharic heartland; (f) undercut the ability of bourgeois regimes in neighboring countries (such as Djibouti, Kenya, Uganda, and the Sudan) to maintain their own domination over oppressed nations currently trapped within their borders; and, indeed, (g) inspire struggles of nationally oppressed peoples throughout Africa and the semicolonial world as a whole.

8. For a number of reasons, U.S. imperialism was unwilling and unable to transform the Somali struggle into a passive instrument of its own counterrevolutionary goals. At no time, therefore, were the subjective hopes, fears, calculations, etc., of the western imperialists decisive in determining the objective character and significance of the Somali struggle.

The change of line and its defense

We repeat: the analysis outlined above is as correct today as when it was first elaborated. Unfortunately, it has been abandoned in favor of thoroughly confused and mistaken position. The new position can be outlined as follows:

1. As before, Marxists support the right of self-determination for the Somalis of the Ogaden.

2. The Ogaden war of 1977–78, however, did not revolve around this question. Instead, the Somali camp objectively represented a mortal threat to the Ethiopian revolution as a whole.

The unprogressive, counterrevolutionary significance of the Somalian camp is proven by the fact that (a) much of its military power came not from within the Ogaden proper but from the Somalian state—making the Somali struggle not a genuine national uprising but a foreign invasion; (b) the Somalian government was not a consistent champion of Somali national rights (e. g., in Kenya and Djibouti); (c) the Somalian government sought the backing of western imperialism for its campaign in the Ogaden; (d) the Somalian government had designs on territory within Ethiopia where the population was not, in its majority, Somali; (e) western imperialism, thoroughly hostile to the Ethiopian revolution and its Russian and Cuban allies, directed and encouraged the Somalian invasion.

As comrade Harsch now sees it, the Somali struggle was decisively shaped by the reactionary goals of Siad Barre and Jimmy Carter. He writes, "Throughout much of 1977 and into early 1978 Washington's most important attempt to strike out at the Ethiopian revolution focused around the Somalian invasion of the Ogaden desert and other regions in the eastern part of the Ethiopian state."

3. Since this was in reality a war between defenders and enemies of the Ethiopian revolution, the correct orientation for Marxists was (a) to support the Dergue and its Cuban and Russian allies against Siad Barre and the WSLF while (b) opposing the suppression of the Ogaden Somalis' national rights by the Dergue and its forces.

Below we will show that comrade Harsch's second, current position is factually mistaken, methodologically un-Marxist, and programmatically disastrous for the revolution in north Africa.

Invasion or national struggle: a false dichotomy

Comrade Harsch's attempt to define the national question out of the Ogaden war is clearest in the following passage:

> At the time [i.e., originally], we overestimated the scope of the Somali national struggle in the Ogaden, presenting it as the major element in the conflict and minimizing the other questions involved. Our assessment has since changed. In reviewing the facts, it is fairly clear that the imperialist-backed Somalian invasion was the overriding aspect of the war, both in its actual extent and its political thrust.
>
> . . . The Somalis in Ethiopia and Kenya remain oppressed nationalities within those states, and have from time to time struggled against their oppression. Leninists support those struggles and support their right to self-determination—that is, their right to decide for themselves what kind of state form they want to live under. But that is their decision to make, not the Somalian regime's.
>
> In recent years, however, the struggle in the Ogaden has never reached anything like the level of the Eritrean mobilizations. This is not to denigrate it; it is just a fact that needs to be noted. And the leadership, the Western Somali Liberation Front, has been traditionally dependent on the backing of the Somalian regime.
>
> . . . There was little nationalist activity in the Ogaden through most of the Ethiopian revolution. In fact, there were few signs of struggles by the Somalis in the Ogaden until the Somalian regime itself decided to send in its army. Thus the Somalian military thrust was clearly not in response to any upsurge of the Somali masses. (*The Ethiopian Revolution*, pp. 28–29.)

Harsch's purpose here is to impose a rigid demarcation between the Somali national struggle in the Ogaden and the invasion of the Ogaden territory by the army of the Somalian state. Apparently, the only legitimate form of national struggle in the Ogaden would be one conducted solely by residents of the Ogaden. Presumably the same yardstick applies to national struggles by the Somalis imprisoned in Kenya and Djibouti. Only indigenously Kenyan-Somali or Djibouti-Somali movements can be considered legitimate national struggles worthy of our support. We cannot support a Somali national struggle when its main strength comes from the Somali state.

This argument and the schema upon which it is based has no connection with reality. There is not now and never has been an "Ogaden national question" (or a "northern Kenya national question" or a "Djibouti national question") which is separate and apart from the overall *Somali* national question.

The Somalis are a single nationality judged by every single criterion ever advanced by Leninists—historical development, common territory, common language, common culture and religion, etc. During this century, the Somali people and their territory have been divided up and parceled out into five separate entities: British Somaliland, Italian Somaliland, Kenya, Ethiopia, and French Somaliland (now Djibouti).

The Somali struggle for self-determination has therefore always necessarily been at the same time a struggle for national reunification. Comrade Harsch's first articles illustrated this fact quite well. Thus he quoted one of the major Somali nationalist groups based in Italian Somaliland in 1948 as follows: "We wish our country to be amalgamated with the other Somalilands and to form one political, administrative and economic unit with them. We Somalis are one in every way. We are the same racially and geographically, we have the same culture, we have the same language and the same religion. There is no future for us except as part of a Greater Somalia." (*IP/I*, Feb. 20, 1978, p. 218.)

Comrade Harsch himself continued: "These aspirations were also reflected in a meeting in Mogadishu, now the capital of Somalia, in August, 1959, at which Somali delegates from Somalia, Djibouti, the Northern District of Kenya, and the Ogaden and Haud regions of Ethiopia organized a pan-Somali movement aimed at unifying all Somalis within one state."

On June 26, 1960, British Somaliland became fully independent. Five days later, Italian Somaliland also became independent. The two former colonies immediately fused to become what is now known as Somalia. At the same time, the new nation proclaimed that its ultimate goal was the reunification of *all* Somalis into a "Greater Somalia."

"In fact," as comrade Harsch noted, "this goal was written into the first Somalian constitution. The Somalian flag includes a five-pointed star, representing the former British and Italian colonies now incorporated into Somalia, as well as the three 'lost territories.'" (There is more historical background of this kind in another of comrade Harsch's excellent early articles, "Somali Rebels Gain in Ethiopia," *Intercontinental Press*, September 12, 1977.)

The attempt to rigidly demarcate the Somali struggle in the Ogaden from initiatives on the part of the Somalian state to regain Somali territory is clearly impossible. Somalia *per se* has since its founding been viewed by the other Somalis as liberated territory and has been the center and staging area for the Somali struggle as a whole.

In this respect we are not dealing with something in the Ogaden which is in any way strange, unique, or exotic. It is an example of a common form of national struggle known as irredentism.

The classic case of irredentism in the modern world is Ireland. British imperialism arbitrarily cut Irish land and the Irish nation in two in order to best resist the power of the Irish national struggle. "Northern Ireland" is an artificial entity; the Catholic population there irresistibly presses forward toward their liberation from oppression at the hands of the British and their Ulster colonial-settler cops and to restore Ireland as a whole to its previous unity.

What is our attitude toward this goal? What would we do if the Republic of Ireland sent an "invading" army northward to force the issue of reunification? Wouldn't we consider this progressive? Or would we tell the Catholics in the North that, while we would support their right to national self-determination, we cannot support a struggle based in or led by their compatriots to the South?

The answer should be obvious. One of the most damning things we say about the "Green" bourgeoisie and their parties is that they do *not* do this sort of thing but rather acquiesce in the continued dismemberment of the Irish nation. Other examples of the same general phenomenon can easily be produced: the liberation and unification of Germany and Italy in the nineteenth century, of Vietnam in the twentieth, and so on.

To ignore this dynamic—and to counterpose to it a formal distinction between domestic rebellions and foreign invasions—is not simply a logical error. It means accepting the fundamental terms of the national oppression imposed upon the Somalis (or the Irish—or the Vietnamese until 1975). It accepts the borders imposed on the oppressed as the proper basis for judging whether their struggle is legitimate or illegitimate. It rejects the whole history of struggle for liberation and unification on the part of the Somali people themselves.

To defend his new position, comrade Harsch is forced to deny the unitary character of the Somalian national struggle and to forget everything he once knew about the historical roots of that struggle. In the new revision, it often seems as if Siad Barre cooked up the whole issue of the Ogaden in 1977 or 1978 ("In fact, there were few signs of struggle by the Somalis in the Ogaden until the Somalian regime itself decided to send in its army").

Harsch stretches this point the furthest when he implies that the Somalian attempt to wrest the Ogaden away from Ethiopia had no support from the Ogaden's Somali population. We support the fight of the Ogaden Somalis for national self-determination, he says, "But that is their decision to make, not the Somalian regime's."

His problem, of course, is that the Somalis of the Ogaden made their decision before the eyes of the entire world. They greeted the Somalian army with open arms. In his pamphlet, comrade Harsch himself grudgingly grants that "There were some reports that the Somali population in the Ogaden generally favored the Somalian military actions, especially since they were viewed as being directed against the Somalis' traditional oppressors." (*Ethiopian Revolution*, p. 32.)

In fact, as comrade Harsch once observed, not merely "some" but *all* reports from the Ogaden during the war revealed that population's overwhelming, spirited, and active support for the Somalian forces. The Somalis of the Ogaden fought side by side with the Somalian army against the Ethiopians and the Cubans, often enough armed only with sticks and stones.

The troops of the Dergue, on the other hand, showed little morale or fighting spirit—reflecting accurately the moral and political relationship of forces in that conflict. As comrade Harsch told us in February 1978:

> Reporters visiting the Somali-held areas described seeing arms caches and heavy equipment, such as tanks and artillery, that had been left behind during the Ethiopians' hasty retreats. By September, the Dergue's forces had been driven back to the immediate areas around Harar and Diredawa, the two major cities in the region. Toward the end of the year, Harar came under heavy Somali attack.
>
> Western correspondents who toured the Ogaden also reported massive support for the WSLF troops from the Somali population. One journalist said in an August 24, 1977, Agence-France-Presse dispatch, 'The visitors were often greeted by noisy but disciplined crowds shouting hatred for the Ethiopian government and its leader, Col. Mengistu Haile Mariam.' And Graham Hancock reported in the September 18, 1977, London *Sunday Times*, 'I did not see one village, nor one nomadic Somali group, that was not armed and angry, ready and willing to fight again at any time. The entire population seemed intoxicated with victory, in total support of the guerrillas and very able to defend itself.' (*IP/I*, February 20, 1978, p. 219.)

In the face of evidence like this, what counterevidence has been presented? In his entire pamphlet, comrade Harsch is only able to advance one "fact" intended to suggest that the Ogaden Somalis withheld support from the Somalian army. Here it is:

"Diredawa has one of the larger industrial bases in Ethiopia, with a working class of about 20,000, composed half of Oromos and half of Somalis. Both the Oromos and the Somalis had to flee from the Somalian invasion." Harsch concludes, ". . . the response of the Somali workers in Diredawa indicates that support for the Somalian invasion among the Somalis was at least not universal." (*Ethiopian Revolution*, pp. 31–32.)

Really, you blink your eyes after reading this.

Diredawa at this time was the scene of intense fighting between Ethiopian and Somalian forces. In the course of the fighting, the Somalian army began shelling the city. The civilian population, including the Somalis, fled . . . not from "the Somalian invasion" but from artillery shells. What were they supposed to do? Gather in the town square in parade formation, waiting to be blown to bits? Just to prove to skeptical foreign observers that they did, indeed, wish to be liberated from Ethiopian domination?

There is a familiar ring to this argument, incidentally. During the Vietnam war, refugees from battle zones swelled the population of imperialist-ruled Saigon. Imperialist apologists cited this as evidence that Vietnamese support for the NLF "was at least not universal." Revolutionaries never had any trouble exposing such arguments.

The most remarkable thing about this little story is that it is the *only* one which comrade Harsch has managed to dredge up to support his claim that Somali support for the Somalian troops was "at least not universal."

In sum, all the evidence at hand indicates that the attack by the Somalian army constituted an armed struggle of the Somali people in support of their national liberation and reunification. The main instrument of that struggle was the Somalian army, which is in simple fact the most powerful military force at the disposal of the Somali nation. This is precisely why the oppressed Ogaden Somalis viewed these troops not as invaders but as liberators.

Siad Barre: his plans, hopes, and class

The historical facts here are pretty clear and intractible. To read the Ogaden war out of the ranks of national liberation struggles, comrade Harsch is therefore forced to emphasize not objective facts but the presumed subjective viewpoint of Somalian President Siad Barre. By proving that this man is not at all our ideal of a national liberation fighter, Harsch believes he has proven the struggle which Siad's troops waged to be utterly reactionary. Comrade Harsch writes:

> But why then did General Siad choose to go in, and why at that particular time? He claims he wanted only to aid the liberation of the oppressed Somalis. But the regime's real attitude on this score became clear after the war, when one of its [Somalia's] officials actually tried to cover up for the oppression of the Somalis living in Kenya. . . . The Somalis in Kenya are faced with just as much national oppression as those in the Ogaden. They have faced severe repression over the years. What *is* different between Kenya and Ethiopia is that in Kenya there is no revolution going on, and the regime is a close American ally. (*Ethiopian Revolution*, p. 29.)

Two issues are here collapsed into one. Let us examine them separately.

First is comrade Harsch's belief that the timing of the Somalian invasion—coinciding as it did with the fall of Selassie and the growing disintegration of the Ethiopian state apparatus under the pressure of the Ethiopian revolution—in itself indicates something sinister about the whole enterprise.

This is a very odd notion. Of course the invasion occurred at this point. The oppressed and exploited naturally press forward most energetically when they see that their enemy is preoccupied, weakened, or paralyzed. The February revolution in 1917 gave the go-ahead for oppressed nationalities throughout the Russian empire to do just this.

More recently, the fall of the shah and Bakhtiar have encouraged Iran's Kurdish and other oppressed minorities to take advantage of Khomeini-Bazargan's weakened position to raise their own national demands. As a young Kurdish nationalist explained recently, "The central Government is very weak, so now is the best time to enforce our demands." (*New York Times*, March 1, 1979.)

Should we consider the Kurdish national movement in Iran somehow artificial or suspicious because it is escalating "at this particular time"—that is, when the state is extremely weak and U.S. imperialism's relations with the government are unprecedentedly strained? Of course not.

Comrade Harsch once understood the correct way to understand the not-so-strange timing of the Ogaden war. Then he wrote,

> The downfall of Selassie in 1974 and the significant advances made by the Eritrean freedom fighters inspired the Somalis to once again press forward with their struggle. The WSLF was reorganized. In an interview in the August 1977 *New African Development*, WSLF leader Abdullahi Hassan Mahmoud

explained, 'The dethroning of Haile Selassie has opened the way before all oppressed nationalities in Ethiopia to move.' (*IP/I*, February 20, 1978, p. 219.)

This brings us to the second point which comrade Harsch was trying to make in the passage we quoted earlier. That is, that Siad Barre and the Somalian ruling class is not genuinely interested in winning national liberation for their oppressed compatriots in other countries. Not only have they in the past sought to dampen the struggle of the Ogaden Somalis but even after invading Ethiopia they sought to paint up the situation of the Somalis oppressed by Kenya. By the same token, Siad sought backing from U.S. imperialism for his enterprise in pursuit of which he today says "relatively little about the oppression of the Somalis in Ethiopia, concentrating more on condemning the presence of Cuban troops and appealing to Washington to halt the spread of 'communism.'" (*Ethiopian Revolution*, pp. 29–30.) Comrade Harsch also suspects the Somalians of planning to annex large parts of Ethiopia which do not have predominantly Somali populations.

Much of what comrade Harsch has to say about Siad is accurate. It is also beside the point. Siad Barre is a typical leader of a bourgeois government in a semicolonial country. Like the rest of the colonial and semicolonial bourgeoisie, he is treacherous, conservative, chauvinistic, narrowminded, and always eager to strike a deal with imperialism. There is a world of difference between the way the colonial bourgeoisie leads (or misleads) national struggles and the approach of Marxists. As Lenin wrote,

> The bourgeoisie of the oppressed nations persistently utilize the slogans of national liberation to deceive the workers; in their internal policy they use these slogans for reactionary agreements with the bourgeoisie of the dominant nation . . . ; in their foreign policy they strive to come to terms with one of the rival imperialist powers for the sake of implementing their predatory plans (the policy of the small Balkan nations, etc.). ("The Socialist Revolution and the Right of Nations to Self-Determination," *Collected Works*, Vol. 22, p. 148.)

Addressing the same subject on another occasion, Lenin explained, "What every bourgeoisie is out for in the national question is either privileges for its own nation, or exceptional advantages for it. . . . The proletariat is opposed to all privileges, to all exclusiveness."

But does this mean that we may never support struggles episodically led by the colonial bourgeoisie? Of course not. It means only that the proletariat must distinguish its own goals, program, and methods from those of the colonial bourgeoisie in the course of that struggle.

Lenin, once again, argued that "the proletariat's policy in the national question (as in all others) supports the bourgeoisie only in a certain direction, but it never coincides with the bourgeoisie's policy. The working class supports the bourgeoisie only in order to secure national peace (which the bourgeoisie cannot bring about completely and which can be achieved only with *complete* democracy), in order to secure equal rights and to create the best conditions for the class struggle." It is precisely because we approach the same national struggle with different ends in mind that the workers "always give the bourgeoisie *only conditional* support." ("The Right of Nations to Self-Determination," *Collected Works*, Vol. 20, p. 409.)

Trying to decide whether to support any movement primarily or even mainly by examining the motives and subjective goals of its leaders is not Marxist, it is idealist and sectarian. It is the tried and true method, for example, of the Spartacist League, using which they have succeeded in outlawing virtually every important struggle for national (or any other) rights on the face of the planet.

It is an idealist method because it *assumes* that what is in the head of the leadership must determine the objective significance of the struggle itself. It leaves completely out of account the objective logic of the struggle and, in particular, the way in which the oppressed and exploited masses look upon, relate to, and are affected by this struggle.

The real significance of the Somali military campaign in 1977–78 was determined by objective, historically rooted factors—by the oppression of the Somalis by the Ethiopian state, by the integral role played by all the national struggles in the development of the Ethiopian revolution, by this struggle's relationship to the Eritrean struggle going on simultaneously. Quite apart, therefore, from what Siad Barre may or may not have been planning, hoping, scheming, or praying for at the time, the decision to send Somalian troops into the Ogaden had an objectively progressive character.

This is precisely why it received the wholehearted support of the Somali workers and peasants within Somalia proper as well as in the Ogaden. The Somali masses could see perfectly clearly that the time was ripe to press forward against their historic oppressor. Indeed, for Siad to pass up this golden opportunity would have been to court popular hatred at home. Comrade Harsch saw this a year ago, noting:

> Siad Barre, in fact, has little option but to support the Somali struggle in the Ogaden and elsewhere. He pointed out in an interview in the June 13, 1977, issue of the Paris fortnightly *Afrique-Asie* that 'no government, no regime, no Somalian leader could survive in this country if he moved to abandon the policy of recovering the territories that are still colonized by foreign occupiers.' (*IP/I*, February 20, 1978, p. 219.)

The Eritreans, too, grasped the real significance of the Ogaden war. They therefore viewed the Somali cause as progressive and inseparably tied to their own.

Siad Barre is not the first unsavory character to whom Marxists have given military support in the course of a national struggle, is he? Marx and Engels supported the Prussians in their war with France in 1870–1871, despite the fact that the Prussian prime minister was a dyed-in-the-wool reactionary, Otto von Bismarck.

Bismarck was no friend of the German working class. He sought to unify fragmented Germany in a reactionary manner to serve reactionary ends of his own. Although eventually compelled to fight Louis Bonaparte in the interests of German national independence, Bismarck had himself recently "conspired with that very same Louis Bonaparte for the purpose of crushing popular opposition at home," as Marx pointed out. ("First Address on the Franco-Prussian War," *On the Paris Commune*, Moscow: Progress, 1971, p. 37.)

Despite all this, Marx and Engels recognized the *essentially* progressive character of the Prussian military campaign and therefore supported it conditionally. Engels wrote, "Bismarck . . . is doing a bit of our work, in his own way and without meaning to, but all the same he is doing it. He is clearing the decks for us better than before." (Marx and Engels, *Selected Correspondence*, Moscow: Progress, 1965, p. 242.)

What about the Sino-Japanese War in the 1930s and '40s? Japan's attempt to transform China into a protectorate brought it into conflict with Chiang Kai-shek. In this conflict, the Fourth International gave military-technical support to Chiang.

We did so despite a number of facts: (1) Chiang was the notorious butcher of the Chinese workers; the blood of Shanghai's slaughtered proletarians was still fresh on his hands. (2) Chiang's resistance to Japan was halfhearted at best. Until the end of the decade, Chiang preferred to fight the CP instead of the Japanese army. (3) Chiang's principal strategy against Japan was to enlist the massive aid of one of Japan's imperialist rivals (the U.S.) in his own support. (4) Chiang had a chauvinist-expansionist concept of China's national rights—i.e., the "return" of China's ancient boundaries and the absorption of much territory since occupied by independent nations. One of Chiang's chief foreign-policy goals, according to a former "old China hand" in the U.S. State Department, was "the restoration of China's 'traditional' frontiers—interpreted ever since the establishment of the Republic as being those fixed by the robust Manchu conquerors." (O. Edmund Clubb, *Twentieth Century China*, N. Y.: Columbia University Press, 1967, p. 158.)

The Fourth International's policy in that war was based on an understanding of the *objective* role played by Chiang's troops insofar as they fought against the Japanese forces.

Despite his expansionist ambitions; despite his past, present, and future crimes and betrayals; despite his ties to U.S. and European imperialism, Chiang was compelled to resist China's complete subordination to Japan. This resistance was progressive, even if Chiang carried it out in a reactionary and desultory way and for his own reasons. Trotsky wrote,

> We need have no illusions about Chiang Kai-shek, his party or the whole ruling class in China . . . Chiang Kai-shek is the executioner of the Chinese workers and peasants. But today, he is forced, despite himself, to struggle against

Japan for the remainder of the independence of China. Tomorrow he may again betray. It is possible. It is probable. It is even inevitable. But today he is struggling. Only cowards, scoundrels, or complete imbeciles can refuse to participate in that struggle." ("On the Sino-Japanese War," *Leon Trotsky on China* [New York: Pathfinder Press, 1976], p. 723 [2012 printing].)

Historical examples of this type are plentiful, including our support for Haile Selassie himself when Ethiopian independence came under attack from imperialist Italy.

The question of non-Somali territory

Before moving on, let us take a closer look at the question of Siad Barre's territorial ambitions. In his pamphlet, comrade Harsch points out that Somalian troops struck beyond the Ogaden, and that the WSLF laid claim to territory that was not populated primarily by Somalis. "These facts alone," he says, "show that the Somalian army was not waging a 'national liberation struggle.'" (p. 31.)

In our opinion, "these facts alone" show no such thing. The military occupation of non-Somali territory by the Somalian army was not impermissible in principle.

Since when do Marxists insist that, during an armed struggle, progressive forces are duty-bound never to advance beyond the borders of their own territory? No army can observe such absurd rules of conduct. Once hostilities have begun, considerations of a purely strategic nature often dictate the deployment of one's forces. Indeed, it is usually to one's advantage to carry the battle lines beyond the bounds of the terrain which is being sought or defended.

Thus, during the Franco-Prussian War, Engels counseled German revolutionists to "join the national movement . . . insofar and for so long as it is limited to the defense of Germany." He immediately added, however, that a war's defensive character "does not exclude an offensive, in certain circumstances, until peace is arrived at." (*Selected Correspondence*, p. 243.)

The Somalian siege of the cities of Diredawa and Harar is today cited as proof of the purely chauvinist-expansionist character of the Somali struggle. But all during the actual fighting, these cities were regularly described (by Harsch himself, among others) as necessary strategic targets if the Ogaden as a whole was to be held militarily.

There is another fact which is now suddenly being ignored. In their military offensive against the Dergue, the Somalian army was acting *in alliance* with liberation forces representing other (non-Somali) oppressed nations within the Ethiopian empire. Comrade Harsch himself once reported that the Oromo Liberation Front and the Afar Liberation Front "have begun to coordinate their own struggles with that of the WSLF." (*IP/I*, September 20, 1978, p. 219.) The same was true of other nationalist forces, such as the Somali Abo Liberation Front. (*New York Times*, December 27, 1978.) In view of this multinational alliance, one would *assume* that the insurgent forces would set out to liberate not merely Somali territory but the territory of their allies as well.

But for the sake of the discussion, let us assume the worst. We ignore the dictates of military-strategic considerations during wartime. We ignore the fact that the Somalians were allied and coordinated with other nationalist forces also fighting for their liberation from Ethiopian oppression. Let us assume that insofar as Siad Barre's troops occupied one inch of land beyond the borders of unquestionably Somali terrain they did so without any justification whatsoever.

That is, let us for a moment grant comrade Harsch everything which he has failed to prove.

Even granting all this, is it accurate to say that this "alone show[s] that the Somalian army was not waging a 'national liberation struggle'"? No, not at all. Not even when all this unproven speculation is taken as fact.

Why? Because whatever the merits of this individual issue, the fight over non-Somali territory was never, at no time, the crux, the pivot, the *essence* of the Somalian-Ethiopian war as a whole. On the contrary. With regard to the war as a whole, it occupied a purely secondary position. It is an error of the first magnitude to try to deduce the character of any war from its secondary features instead of its principal focus.

Let us return to the Franco-Prussian example. Engels judged that the essence of that war was Germany's just and progressive struggle against national oppression at France's hands. "Germany has been driven by [Bonaparte] into a war for her national existence," he wrote to Marx. It was on the basis of this judgment that he and Marx counseled provisional military-technical support to Bismarck.

At the same time, however, they took note of a secondary aspect of the same war. "Bismarck is now intimating an intention of annexing [Alsace and Lorraine] to Bavaria and Baden," Engels noted. This was unjustified. But it was a secondary, not the central, question in this war. That is why they continued to support Prussia. While supporting Prussia, they simply urged their supporters in Germany to "work against any annexation of Alsace and Lorraine." (*Selected Correspondence*, p. 243.)

Opposition to unjustified annexation occupied a *subordinate* position in the Marxist policy because the question of Alsace and Lorraine occupied a subordinate position in the war itself. Precisely the same is true of the war in the Ogaden.

If it were determined that the Somalians were out to make illegitimate annexations, our job would *not* have been to refuse to support the Somali struggle for the Somali Ogaden. We should simply have made opposition to additional annexations a part of our general policy of continuing support to the Somalis.

So concerned is comrade Harsch over the *possible* oppression of various peoples in a hypothetical future that he completely forgets that today and for at least a century past Ethiopia has been really oppressing not only the Somalis but also the Oromos, Sidamos, and others. In his flight of fancy, it is Somalia which has become the oppressor (despite the fact that it has only one-tenth Ethiopia's population). Simultaneously, Ethiopia (which has brutally oppressed non-Amharic peoples throughout the Horn of Africa for generation after generation) now appears as Somalia's victim . . . whose defense is necessary to defend the Oromos and Sidamos from Somali oppression!

> Consequently, the given war or revolt is not assessed on the strength of its *real* social content (the struggle of an oppressed nation for its liberation from the oppressor nation) but the possible exercise of the '*right* to oppress' by a bourgeoisie which is at present itself oppressed. (Lenin, "The Discussion on Self-Determination Summed Up," *Collected Works*, Vol. 22, p. 332.)

Imperialism and the Somali struggle

Thus far, we have examined (1) comrade Harsch's misunderstanding of the nature and significance of the Somali national struggle; (2) his consequently false distinction between struggles by Somalis "indigenous" to the Ogaden and by the Somalian state itself; (3) his irrelevant preoccupation with Siad Barre's unsavory record as a representative of the Somalian neocolonial ruling class; and (4) his attempt to make Somalia's alleged plans of chauvinist conquest of non-Somali peoples—plans, incidentally, which he never analyzes in any detail—the crux of the whole struggle in the Ogaden.

It is now time to turn to the last—and most important—of his arguments, namely, that the Somalian invasion was a sort of Trojan Horse manufactured in Washington, in essence simply the instrument through which U.S. imperialism "attempt[ed] to strike out at the Ethiopian revolution." We will see here again that the argument is based on a major distortion of the factual record and a fundamental departure from the method by which Marxists approach questions like this one. As he puts it,

> But the invasion by the regular troops of the Somalian army was not directed at liberating the Somalis in the Ogaden. It was carried out in the interests of American imperialism, with imperialist backing, and was directed at striking a serious blow against the Ethiopian revolution. [A Somalian victory] would have meant a further entrenchment of the imperialist stranglehold over everyone, including the Somalis. In this light, Siad's willingness to go along with Washington's schemes is a betrayal of the Somali masses. The WSLF's willingness to serve as a cover for the invasion was likewise a betrayal. (*Ethiopian Revolution*, p. 33.)

There are circumstances in which a given national struggle (which we might otherwise support) becomes submerged within a more powerful, more decisive and all-encompassing reactionary military campaign.

The classic case is that of Serbia in World War I. Previously, socialists had supported Serbia's national claims and struggles against the Austro-Hungarian Empire.

But with the opening of the war, the objective situation was transformed. As an ally of the Entente powers, the Serbian forces were absorbed into the unified forces of one of the imperialist camps. From that time forward, the Serbian-Austrian front became simply one of many fronts in an inter-imperialist war waged on both sides over division and redivision of the colonial and semi-colonial world. Concretely, it ceased to be possible in that war to support the just struggle of the Serbian people without at the same time allying oneself with those now actually commanding Serbia's army—i.e., French, British, and later U.S. imperialism. Lenin wrote,

> In the present war the national element is represented only by Serbia's war against Austria ... If this war were an isolated one, i.e., if it were not connected with the general European war, with the selfish and predatory aims of Britain, Russia, etc., it would have been the *duty* of all socialists to desire the success of the Serbian *bourgeoisie*—this is the only correct and absolutely inevitable conclusion to be drawn from the national element in the present war.

But the Serbian struggle had now ceased to be isolated; it was strongly, immediately, and obviously "connected" to the Entente armies. Socialists could therefore give it no support. "The national element in the Serbo-Austrian war is not, and cannot be, of *any* serious significance in the general European war. If Germany wins, she will throttle Belgium, one more part of Poland, perhaps part of France, etc. If Russia wins, she will throttle Galicia, one more part of Poland, Armenia, etc." ("The Collapse of the Second International," *Collected Works*, Vol. 21, pp. 235–236.) The imperialists, being in command of the "Serbian liberation forces" during the world war, would in fact dictate the terms of victory—to wit, the continued oppression of Serbs, Poles, Armenians, alike.

A more recent example of this type of situation occurred during the civil war in Angola. The intervention of South African troops on the side of the FNLA-UNITA forces qualitatively altered the nature of the war there. Prior to the arrival of Cuban troops, the South African armored column was without question the single most powerful military force in Angola. The weight of South Africa's direct military intervention was so great that *objectively* a war among different factions of the national liberation movement became transformed into a struggle pitting South Africa (and its Angolan hangers-on) against those defending the independence of Angola (led by the MPLA). In the event of a victory of the South African-FNLA-UNITA camp, it would have been the South African army which would occupy decisive positions in Angola. It would have been South Africa which would be *dominating* (not simply *influencing*) the situation.

Historically, we have always demanded clear proof that a given national liberation struggle really had been subsumed under an imperialist (or other reactionary) war effort before we withdrew our support from it. The mere fact, in and of itself, that an oppressed nation receives support or aid from an imperialist country in order to prosecute their struggle for national self-determination (against, say, the given imperialism's enemy) is not yet sufficient grounds for writing off that struggle as reactionary. It must be shown that aid and support has become domination and control.

A good statement on this subject was written by someone who is today a prominent supporter of the mistaken line on the Ogaden war, comrade David Frankel. He was explaining why revolutionists continued to support the national struggle of the Kurds against Iraq, despite the fact that both the Shah of Iran and the CIA supported and gave substantial material aid to the Kurdish forces for their own reasons. Comrade Frankel wrote:

> Does acceptance of arms from one or another imperialist power brand a struggle as reactionary? The question has come up once again in regard to the fight of the Kurds in Iraq for autonomy.
>
> It was widely known that the shah of Iran supplied the Kurdish rebels with arms until he reached an agreement with the Iraqi regime in March [1975]. Now ... it has been revealed that Richard Nixon ordered the CIA to send a shipment of arms worth several million dollars to the Kurds.
>
> Opponents of the Kurdish struggle used the fact that the fighters were receiving aid from the shah to smear it as proimperialist.

The most active role in this campaign was played by the pro-Moscow Stalinists.

Frankel answered the Stalinist smear with a lesson in orthodox Marxism:

> There is nothing new in national liberation movements turning to one or another imperialist power for material support. The Irish revolutionists, who led the famous Easter Rebellion of 1916, for example, turned to Germany for aid. A German submarine loaded with arms was sent, but was captured by the British. Had the arms arrived safely, would this have justified the dismissal of the Irish liberation struggle as a German imperialist plot? A similar example was the struggle of the Arab people for independence from the Ottoman Empire during World War I. A massive Arab rebellion was encouraged by British agent T. E. Lawrence ('Lawrence of Arabia'), and armed by British imperialism. Was the demand of the Arab masses for independence and their rebellion against the Ottoman Empire therefore a British plot, not deserving of support?
>
> The answer of revolutionary socialists is that the right of self-determination is an inviolable principle, and peoples denied this right by an oppressor nation are justified in fighting for it by any means necessary. This includes the right to take advantage of whatever contradictions may exist among the world powers and to accept arms from any source that will supply them.
>
> The question of who is leading the struggle, or of what other forces may seek to reap profit from it, is secondary to the main principle. ("The CIA and the Kurdish Struggle in Iran," *IP*, November 17, 1975.)

In advancing this position, comrade Frankel was doing no more than reiterating a point made frequently by Trotsky—for example in the article, "Learn to Think: A Friendly Suggestion to Certain Ultra-Leftists":

> Let us assume that rebellion breaks out tomorrow in the French colony of Algeria under the banner of national independence and that the Italian government, motivated by its own imperialist interests, prepares to send weapons to the rebels. What should the attitude of the Italian workers be in this case? I have purposely taken an example of rebellion against a *democratic* imperialism with intervention on the side of the rebels from a *fascist* imperialism. Should the Italian workers prevent the shipping of arms to the Algerians? Let any ultra-leftists dare answer this in the affirmative. Every revolutionist, together with the Italian workers and the rebellious Algerians, would spurn such an answer with indignation. (*Writings of Leon Trotsky (1937–38)* [New York: Pathfinder Press, 1970, 1976], pp. 434–35 [2012 printing].)

Our refusal to cancel our support to a national struggle before it has become clearly and materially subordinated to imperialism is probably best shown in the case of the Sino-Japanese War.

Following U.S. entry into World War II and the conclusion of the alliance between U.S. imperialism and Chiang Kai-shek's forces, Max Shachtman and his Workers Party and others concluded that it was time to withdraw support from China's struggle. The Chinese forces, Shachtman argued, had become merely another arm of Allied imperialism.

Proof? Shachtman pointed to the substantial amounts of money and materiel sent by the US to China, to the fact that in January 1942 the Allied command created a China-Burma-India Theatre of War with Chiang designated Commander-in-Chief of Allied forces in the China Theatre, and to the fact that American Lieutenant General Joseph Stilwell was simultaneously made Chiang's Chief of Staff and U.S. commander in this theater.

The Socialist Workers Party and the world Trotskyist movement rejected Shachtman's arguments. The Executive Committee of the Fourth International fully recognized the reactionary maneuvers of U.S. and Allied imperialism and what they were attempting to accomplish by latching onto the Chinese war effort, noting:

> American imperialism, pursuing its 'manifest destiny', is preparing to take over British Empire positions in the Far East, including China, and to bring about the defeat of its Japanese rival in the Pacific. Washington plans

to subdue Japan in war, to expel the Japanese imperialists from China, and to assume the overlordship of the Chinese people. Preparatory steps in this direction are the increased 'aid' given to Chiang Kai-shek in the form of loans and war supplies.

The International denounced imperialism's designs and the complicity in them of the Chiang regime. But we nevertheless concluded:

> This, however, will not prevent the revolutionists from continuing to stand for the victory of the Chinese armies over the Japanese invaders. The Washington-Chungking alliance and the flood of American material assistance to the Chiang Kai-shek regime will not erase the task of driving the Japanese imperialists from Chinese soil. ("American Intervention in China" in *Fourth International*, May 1941.)

SWP leader John G. Wright elaborated on this point in a polemic against Shachtman the following year. "What is the criterion," he asked, "whereby Marxists determine whether a colonial or semicolonial country is conducting a progressive struggle? We determine our position, first of all, on the basis of *fact*. Does this struggle play an *independent* role? If it does, we support it."

What about the imperialist maneuvers to take advantage of this national struggle? "The action of the imperialists are decisive only to the extent that the nationalist element of the struggle is destroyed by them or their agents. Any one who opposes support of China's war against Japan must first demonstrate that the nationalist element in China's war against Japan has no serious significance in comparison with the direct intervention of China's imperialist 'allies.'" He added:

> The imperialists in both camps cannot at will transform colonial and semicolonial struggles into their opposite. They have the will, but they lack the magic powers with which both Shachtman and Oehler endow them. As matters stand at present, all the imperialists who unquestionably intend to destroy nationalist struggles *if* given the opportunity, are not crushing these struggles but are involuntarily doing just the opposite in relation to China and India.

There is, in short, a gap between what the imperialists intend and hope for and what they are actually able to accomplish. Wright observed—and his words are extremely relevant to the more recent conflict in the Horn of Africa—"The intentions of the ruling classes by no means decide great issues." ("Why We Defend China," *Fourth International*, April 1942.)[2]

'On the basis of fact'

Against the background of this review, we can return to the specifics of the Somali-Ethiopian war. We have been reminded that the intentions or subjective plans of Jimmy Carter are not enough by themselves to determine the character of the Somali struggle. "The intentions of the ruling classes by no means decide great issues." We must determine, "on the basis of fact," to what degree U.S. imperialism actually did directly intervene in the Ogaden war and whether it was really the dominating, controlling element in that war.

Comrade Harsch insists that U.S. imperialism did play this kind of role, subordinating all other elements of this war to its own attempt to "strike out at the Ethiopian revolution"—and that, if victorious, Siad's drive "would have meant a further entrenchment of the imperialist stranglehold over everyone, including the Somalis." What proof does he offer?

Harsch shows us, first, that after the Kremlin withdrew its support from Somalian claims against Ethiopia in early 1977, the U.S. government offered economic and military assistance to Mogadishu, hoping to bring the latter within its own orbit. Siad Barre, for his part, was not at all averse to accepting such aid. Quite the contrary. (*Ethiopian Revolution*, p. 30.)

Thus far, there is nothing here to prove that the actual escalation of the fighting in the Ogaden occurred on the orders or under the control of U.S. imperialism. Siad Barre, taking advantage of the weakening of the Dergue's state apparatus, moved ahead to press long-standing claims to the Ogaden (justified claims, let us recall). To do so, he was prepared to accept aid from the U.S. just as he was previously happy to take it from the USSR.

So comrade Harsch tries to add to the evidence. He writes:

Secretary of State Cyrus Vance had given Siad another [?] go-ahead for his invasion during a July 4 speech, when he hinted broadly that American aid would be forthcoming. And on July 26, when the invasion was well underway, he announced specifically that Washington was willing to sell arms to Siad. (p. 30.)

Notice that all the material cited thus far refers to U.S. aid—not to speak of control—as something still off in the future. Now comrade Harsch quotes the London *Economist*: "The United States will not be the only country offering military aid to Somalia. Britain, France, Germany, Iran and Pakistan are also involved, and Saudi Arabia will be paying most of the bills." So it is still a question of what the U.S. *will* do. Harsch continues in the same tense: "Siad made a little publicized trip to Saudi Arabia, where government officials told him they were in contact with Washington and were ready to ship French and British arms immediately."

And now comes the concluding sentence of this paragraph. Read carefully; it is an important one: "The public American offer was later withdrawn, but the efforts to encourage Siad from behind the scenes continued." (*Ethiopian Revolution*, pp. 30–31.)

Two things should strike the reader's eye. First of all, all these "facts" add up to . . . "broad hints," "willingness to sell arms," "offers to sell arms" and being "ready to ship arms." That is to say, *no actual assistance is proven here*.

Secondly, while most of this passage is extremely detailed, the last sentence suddenly shrouds us in a mist. So "the public American offer was *later* withdrawn"? Exactly when was it withdrawn? Under what specific circumstances? And for what reasons? These are rather important questions. What are the answers?

Comrade Harsch gives us none. In a moment we will see why.

Even though the "public American offer" was withdrawn, we are told, "the efforts to encourage Siad from behind the scenes continued." What efforts? When were they made? By whom? Once again, silence.

Why this sudden vagueness? For one good and simple reason. Greater detail would explode comrade Harsch's entire case. It is true that *prior* to, and even to some extent during the very early stages of the invasion when the dimensions and success of the Somalian advance were yet unclear, Washington did indeed make *offers*, "in principle," of *some* military aid to Somalia.

But precisely when it became clear that Somalia was launching a major invasion of the Ogaden— and a very successful invasion, to boot—the United States government withdrew its offer of military aid and demanded that the invasion be terminated. Let us look at the factual specifics which comrade Harsch has chosen not to present:

Fact #1: On August 9, 1977, as the Somalian invasion was in full swing, the State Department told a Somali military aid mission that the arms earlier promised by Carter would not be supplied unless Somalia ended its invasion. (*New York Times*, June 2, 1978.)

Fact #2: On September 1, 1977—at the height of the success of the Somalian invasion—the State Department publicly announced it had withdrawn Carter's July offer of military assistance. A spokesman for the State Department stated, "We have decided that providing arms at this time would add fuel to a fire we are more interested in putting out." (Harsch, "Somali Rebels Gain," *IP/I*, September 12, 1977, p. 974.)

Fact #3: The Carter Administration then forbade U.S. allies to transfer U.S. arms to Somalia. (*New York Times*, June 2, 1978.)

Fact #4: In a lengthy article published in the October 2, 1977, issue of the *New York Times*, correspondent Richard Burt reviewed the record on this score. During the "early spring and summer," he wrote, "in reaction to growing Soviet influence and anti-Americanism in the regime of Lieutenant Col. Mengistu Haile Mariam in Addis Ababa, the United States moved to isolate Ethiopia diplomatically and tentatively agreed to begin arming Somalia.

> This move is generally judged to have been a mistake and to have created problems that should have been anticipated earlier. . . .
>
> After high level discussions between Mogadishu and Washington, the State Department in early July announced an agreement 'in principle' to supply Somalia with a limited quantity of 'defensive arms.'
>
> By this time, however, United States intelligence analysts already suspected that regular Somali forces were fighting with the Western

Somali Liberation Front in the Ogaden. By early August, their numbers were suspected to be in the thousands.

Embarrassed by Somalia's military advances and fearing that Somalia might begin to prosecute territorial claims against Kenya and newly independent Djibouti, the Administration decided in late August that it would not go ahead with the arms deal.

Fact #5: The editors of the *New York Times* editorialized on November 18, 1977: "The time may be right, therefore, for an American diplomatic approach to persuade Somalia to pull back from its dangerous adventure in exchange for defensive arms and needed development assistance."

Fact #6: As the Somalian invasion deepened, the Carter administration not only barred assistance to it but also maintained economic support to Ethiopia and made overtures for a resumption of closer U.S.-Ethiopian ties. (*IP/I,* February 20, 1978, and the *New York Times* of February 17, 1978.)

Fact #7: Following the withdrawal of the Carter offer of military aid, Somali officials publicly denounced the U.S. for betraying Somalia. (*New York Times,* October 3, 1977.)

Fact #8: In January 1978, the U.S. State Department once again rejected a Somalian request for military aid against Ethiopia. "We will not contribute to a conflict by pouring gasoline on it," said a State Department representative (UPI dispatch, *New York Times,* January 18, 1978.)

Fact #9: On January 21, 1978, the United States, France, Britain, West Germany, and Italy issued a joint statement pledging support to efforts by the Organization of African Unity to get a negotiated end of the war. (*New York Times,* January 22, 1978.) Correspondent John Darnton characterized the OAU's attitude toward the war as "all but taking Ethiopia's side." (*New York Times,* February 14, 1978.)

Fact #10: On February 11, 1978, the *Times* reported that "in stronger terms than any Administration official had used previously, Mr. Vance [U.S. Secretary of State] in effect demanded that Somalia withdraw its forces from the Ogaden region . . ."

Fact #11: In a news conference March 9, 1978, President Carter made clear that he supported the OAU's attitude toward the Ogaden war: "We stand ready to assist the Organization of African Unity in working out the basis for negotiations between Ethiopia and Somalia which would *ensure the territorial integrity of all countries in the region and the honoring of international boundaries."* (Emphasis added.)

Responding to questions at the same news conference, Carter added:

> We notified Somalia many months ago that as long as they were in occupied territory that there would be no consideration on our part for defensive arms of any kind. I think it would require a tangible demonstration of the carrying out of this commitment on the part of the Somalians [to withdraw] and also a renewed commitment not to dishonor the international boundaries of either Ethiopia or Kenya before we would be willing to discuss with them economic aid or defensive arms supplies. (*New York Times,* March 20, 1978.)

Fact #12: Ernest Harsch reported in *IP/I* of March 20, 1978, that Somalia had agreed to withdraw from the Ogaden and that:

"The editors of the *New York Times*, one of the most influential bourgeois dailies in the United States, likewise hailed the development. In an editorial March 10 entitled, 'Somalia Retreats, Everyone Gains,' they called the pledge to withdraw 'wise'." Harsch added that "According to unnamed administration officials cited by reporter Graham Hovey in the March 10 *New York Times*, Carter sent a personal letter to Siad Barre just a few days before the withdrawal announcement. 'The President's letter,' Hovey explained, 'was co-ordinated with other efforts by interested countries to persuade Somalia to withdraw, the officials said. They cited Saudi Arabia and Iran in particular as governments that had tried to press the American argument for withdrawal."

Fact #13: Only in June of 1978, months after the Somalian retreat before a Cuban-led counterattack in the Ogaden, did the U.S. renew its offer of military assistance to Somalia. Even now, however, its offer amounted to a relative pittance ($15 million) compared with the estimated one billion dollars worth of aid given by the USSR to Ethiopia—not to mention, of course, more than 20,000 Russian and Cuban troops.

Moreover, this U.S. offer was made dependent

upon assurances from Siad Barre that the weapons would not be used outside of Somalia's boundaries. The U.S. government reportedly demanded, as a precondition of sending arms now, that it could send a Pentagon inspection mission to Somalia to make certain that the weapons would not be used for another invasion of the Ogaden. (*Washington Post*, June 2, 1978.)

Fact #14: During the same month, an American military mission to Kenya recommended to the White House that U.S. military aid to that country be boosted to offset any possible threat of renewed Somalian attempts to seize Somali-inhabited territories outside Somalia's borders. (*New York Times*, June 7, 1978.) A staunch neocolonial ally of U.S. imperialism, Kenya had opposed the Somali invasion of the Ogaden from the start, fearing the spread of the Somali national struggle to its own territory. In February 1978, for example, Kenyan jet fighters forced down an Egyptian plane carrying military aid to Somalia. (*New York Times*, February 16, 1978.)

Fact #15: Despite a personal trip to Europe by Siad Barre in July of 1978, the governments of France, Great Britain, Italy, West Germany, and Holland refused to supply Somalia with any military assistance. (*Africa News*, September 25, 1978.)

Fact #16: As of February 1979, Carter was *still* refusing to make good even on his June 1978 offer to renew military aid to Somalia. Despite the protests of Siad, "the US has made arms supplies contingent on Somali repudiation of its campaign for self-determination for Somali-speakers in neighboring Ethiopia and Kenya." (*Africa News*, February 16, 1979.)

U.S. policy

Facts like these nowhere appear in comrade Harsch's pamphlet, although some of them did reach print in his earlier articles. Against the background of these facts, let us review the real outlines of U.S. policy, considerations, and intervention in the Ogaden war.

Undoubtedly, the Dergue's nationalization of land and industry, together with its pose as a Marxist-Leninist regime and its continually closer alliance with the USSR, deeply angered the U.S. ruling class. At the same time, the USSR's transfer of support from Somalia to the larger prize of Ethiopia made possible a renewal of U.S.-Somalian ties after years of estrangement.

To satisfy Siad Barre and to blackmail the Dergue, the White House floated "broad hints" and offers "in principle" of military aid to Somalia. It was doubtless hoped that this limited probe would serve to scare Mengistu back toward an alliance with the U.S.

But at no time did the U.S. encourage or anticipate the kind of full-scale invasion of the Ogaden which Siad Barre actually launched. For reasons which we will discuss in a moment, this invasion flew directly in the face of the key principles of U.S. policy in the Horn and, indeed, in Africa as a whole.

It is precisely because Washington did *not* actually support this invasion—much less dominate, control, and subordinate it to itself!—that comrade Harsch has to rest his case on such a flimsy factual foundation. He must grossly inflate the importance of "broad hints" and verbal promises which occurred *before* the invasion and completely ignore or evade imperialism's actual reaction to the invasion itself.

It is possible, of course, that Siad Barre misinterpreted Washington's policy and really believed that Carter would go the limit with him. Even if this were true (and it is pure speculation), it would be beside the point. What matters in the last analysis, as always for Marxists, is not what rulers or leaders want, wish, hope, or fear. What matters is what actually occurs and the occurrence's objective impact.

At no time during the course of the war did the Somalians receive any military assistance from the United States. We, at least, know of none, and Harsch has shown us none.

At no time during the course of the war were there any substantial numbers (possibly none at all) of U.S. or U.S.-allied troops or military advisers assisting the Somalis.

Once it became clear that the Somalis had definitely *lost* the struggle—primarily because of Russian and Cuban intervention on the side of the Dergue—*then* the U.S. promised and its allies gave modest amounts of military assistance to the Somalis. West Germany now gave Somalia $25 million, the French sent sixty tanks, Saudi Arabia kicked in forty-three helicopters, etc., comrade Harsch stresses. He even claims that this relative teaspoonful of military aid was given because "the imperialists had not given up entirely on the prospect of using the Somalian invasion [which had, remember, already been defeated!] as part of a broader attack" on the Ethiopian revolution. (*Ethiopian Revolution*, p. 36.)

Strange logic. During the late summer and fall of 1978, when Somalia was in fact winning the war, when it had *conquered 97 percent of the Ogaden*, the imperialists flatly refuse to give Siad Barre any military assistance. After he had clearly lost the war, after almost all the military equipment possessed by Somalia had been destroyed, after the USSR had poured in one billion dollars of assistance plus troops to Ethiopia, after the Cubans committed 17,000 combat troops, *then* the western imperialists offer a few million dollars, some tanks and helicopters . . .

. . . and this somehow proves that Washington not only supported but even dictated, dominated, and controlled the invasion?

Comrade Harsch thinks that the dispatch of two U.S. gunboats to the Red Sea in February 1978 is further ironclad proof of U.S. responsibility for the invasion itself. This, too, is strange logic. Armed with the most powerful navy in the world, capable of dispatching massive task forces built around nuclear aircraft carriers anywhere on the waters, U.S. imperialism proves its domination of the Somali invasion of the Ogaden by sending two gunboats (specifically, one destroyer and one frigate) to the Red Sea.

They did not join in the fighting; they did not aid the Somalis. *They did not measurably affect the course of the struggle in any way at all*, as a matter of fact. In evaluating the objective impact of imperialist intervention in the war, this last fact is the decisive one.[3]

Why, then, were the two ships sent? They were probably dispatched as a cheap and non-binding way to register opposition to the Russian and Cuban presence in the Horn and to discourage any attempt by the Ethiopians and their allies to mount a counterinvasion of Somalia.

Comrade Harsch himself involuntarily testifies to U.S. imperialism's general inability to act decisively or effectively in the war when he calls this impotent gesture involving the two ships, "the *most direct warning yet* of American imperialism's *desire* to move in against the Ethiopian revolution and against the Cuban presence in Africa," and then adds, "But *before* the imperialists could blink again, it was all over." (*Ethiopian Revolution*, p. 36, emphasis added.)

Problems of US imperialism

These are the facts. What lies behind them? If Carter hated the Dergue, wanted to crush the Ethiopian masses, dismember Ethiopia, and please Siad Barre, why didn't he simply do so? That is, why *didn't* the U.S. subordinate the Somalian forces to a larger and more powerful attack of its own—in the way, for example, that the Serbians became subordinated to the Triple Entente and the FNLA-UNITA forces became subordinated to the South Africans in Angola?

There is really no mystery here. Comrade Harsch knows the answers to these questions very well. He supplied them himself, not only in his early articles but to some degree even in his pamphlet.

First, why didn't the U.S. simply send in its own troops? Answer: because antiwar sentiment in the U.S. and anticolonialist sentiment in Africa and elsewhere made this much too risky. Thus Carter was from the outset restricted to indirect forms of involvement.

Why, then, did he not strongly encourage and materially support Siad Barre's invasion?

(1) Because this invasion *objectively abetted* the popular mobilizations underlying the Ethiopian revolution. Carter was unwilling to risk stimulating these plebeian forces any further, since he was in no position to keep them under his own direct control.

(2) This invasion was a clear and open violation of one of the key principles of the neocolonialist OAU—that is, that the state boundaries imposed upon Africa by colonial rule must not be tampered with, especially through armed force.

The defense of neocolonial borders is no abstract, pacifist, or legalistic fixation. The entire African continent is composed of states which exist only through the oppression and dismemberment of oppressed nations. It is a virtual tinderbox, as a result.

Somalia's attempt to redraw the map in greater conformity with genuine national rights, if successful, could have triggered parallel struggles in Kenya and Djibouti, first of all, but also from one end of Africa to the other. At the end of this kind of process lies the collapse of neocolonial regimes all over the continent.

As comrade Harsch correctly saw at one point, "The American imperialists have been concerned not so much with the Somali intervention in the Ogaden as with the threat that the Somali struggle for self-determination could pose to U.S. interests in the region. A successful struggle by the Somalis in the Ogaden for freedom from Ethiopian rule and unification with Somalia could have inspired oppressed peoples in other countries." (*IP/I*, March 20, 1978, p. 335.) This is why Kenya in particular and the OAU as a whole opposed Siad Barre's invasion, despite their dislike for the Dergue.

Marxist analysis vs. fanciful speculation

This brings us back to a recurring error in comrade Harsch's entire pamphlet. Unable to shape his case out of hard fact, he repeatedly turns to more pliable materials. These include misplaced emphasis on the goings-on in the heads of Siad Barre and Jimmy Carter. They also include the most fanciful speculation and conjecture about what the Ogaden war might eventually have been transformed into. His policy towards the actual war which occurred is then deduced from the hypothetical war which never did.

Here, for example, is how this imaginative method is used to "prove" (1) that the Somalian invasion was in fact a palpable threat against all Ethiopia and the Ethiopian revolution itself, and (2) that in mounting the invasion Siad Barre acted throughout merely as the agent of U.S. imperialism:

> If the Somalian troops had been successful in consolidating their position in Ethiopia, or at least in hanging on longer than they did, it would have provided an ideal opening for Washington and its allies to move in in much greater force. In fact, given the overall Somalian weakness in relation to the military might of the more powerful Ethiopian state, further Somalian advances would have been possible only with considerable outside backing. Siad Barre may have miscalculated, but he is not a total fool. He obviously believed, and with reason, that the backing would be available. (*Ethiopian Revolution*, p. 32.)

This is a classic case of circular reasoning. *If* Siad Barre aimed to make "further advances" into Ethiopia, he would have required "considerable outside backing." *Since* Siad planned on making "further advances," he must have been given guarantees of "considerable backing" for them from the U.S. Otherwise, his presumed plans of conquest would be those of "a total fool"—which Siad is not.

The two things comrade Harsch is obligated to prove (genuine plan of expansionist conquest and U.S. backing for it) are thus simply *assumed*, and each assumption is then used to "prove" the validity of the other assumption!

To put this another way—comrade Harsch begins by admitting that Somalia was simply incapable of doing more than capturing the Ogaden. Of course, he spurns the obvious conclusion—i.e., that the Somalis had no serious plans for doing more than that. Rather, he concludes triumphantly, the fact that they were *unable* to destroy the Ethiopian revolution proves precisely that they intended to do so . . . because the only way they could have done so was with full-scale support from Washington, which is what comrade Harsch told you all along.

So the final proof that Siad Barre's real goal was to destory the Ethiopian revolution is found in the obvious fact that he was objectively incapable of carrying out such a task. Whew! It reminds us of the gag, "If we had some bacon, we could have bacon and eggs. If we had some eggs."

Not surprisingly, comrade Harsch has by now long since abandoned the simple declarative tense in favor of the much more convenient subjunctive: "If the Somalian troops *had been* successful . . . it *would have* provided," "Somalian advances *would have* been possible," "Siad Barre *may have* miscalculated," etc., etc. And the whole elaborate edifice of guesswork and second-guesswork finally rests upon Harsch's surmises about the personal mental capacities of Somalia's dictator. Siad Barre is capable of miscalculating, but not of acting like a complete fool, which proves that he had secret knowledge of forthcoming U.S. support.

Well, Siad Barre may or may not have miscalculated, and he may or may not be a total fool, and he may or may not have believed, and he may or may not have had reason to believe, and to miscalculate, and, for that matter, to be a total fool.

In the meantime, however, all the facts at our collective disposal indicate that U.S. involvement in the war itself was limited to a few vague promises of military assistance before the invasion followed by the immediate withdrawal of these promises (much less the assistance itself) the moment the invasion really got underway.

But comrade Harsch proceeds. Having earlier insisted, against fact and logic, that the essence of the Somali cause in the Ogaden was to serve as "Washington's most important attempt to strike out at the Ethiopian revolution," he now begins his very next paragraph by lamely admitting that "From the imperialist viewpoint, the actual invasion may have been more of a probe against the Ethiopian revolution than an outright attempt to decisively defeat the Ethiopians then and there."

This is a rather startling switch, isn't it? Up until this point, the entire thrust of Harsch's presentation, and especially of his speculations, was to portray the invasion as an imperialist-spawned attempt to overturn the entire Ethiopian revolution. Suddenly, this elaborate if poorly constructed edifice is casually knocked flat and replaced with a totally different one. No longer discussing "Washington's most important attempt," we now find ourselves considering merely "a probe."

What is the significance of this switch? Does it admit that Washington wasn't really committed to—much less in control of—Siad's enterprise? That Siad himself may not have been trying to bring down the whole Ethiopian revolution "then and there"?

Yes; this is exactly the reality which comrade Harsch finally has to acknowledge, even if not clearly or frankly. Unwilling to draw the necessary political conclusions from this reality, however, he is forced even deeper into the realm of imagination. He continues:

> If the invasion had been more successful on the ground, and if the general political situation in the United States and abroad had been more favorable to Washington, it [i.e., the probe] would certainly have provided an opening wedge for a much more substantial attack. (p. 32.)

"If the invasion had been more successful"? It was successful. Within a matter of mere weeks, the Somalis had successfully liberated almost the whole of the Ogaden, capturing Jijiga and were laying siege to Harar and Diredawa.

What Harsch means, therefore, is: If the invasion had been more successful in the purpose *which I choose to assign to it*, namely of making a far more extensive military incursion into the rest of Ethiopia . . . In that speculative case, Siad's alleged allies would have been free to make "a much more substantial attack."

At least, they would have "if the general political situation in the United States and abroad had been more favorable to Washington." Which it was not! On the contrary. As comrade Harsch, among others, has noted repeatedly, the domestic and international political situation was not and is still not conducive to Washington's launching the kind of open and direct military campaigns which it would otherwise like to do.

And why is the international situation unfavorable to such attempts? This fact, too, has its history. (1) The legacy of the popular Vietnam antiwar movements have severely hampered the ability of the U.S. ruling class to intervene directly and massively with military force in the colonial and semicolonial world. (2) This is especially true in Africa because of the presence in the U.S., and especially its cities, proletariat, and *army*, of a Black population acutely sensitive to imperialist maneuvers in Africa.

So comrade Harsch's formula ultimately reduces itself to the following: *If* Siad Barre had succeeded in making the kind of massive military assault upon Ethiopia as a whole which I tell you he was planning (despite "the overall Somalian weakness in relation to the military might of the more powerful Ethiopian state"), and *if* the U.S. had not been driven out of Vietnam by the Vietnamese people and a massive antiwar movement at home, and *if* there were no Blacks strategically located in the U.S. economy and armed forces, *then* Washington would have had an "opening wedge" for a "much more substantial assault" (whose nature we still do not know) upon the Ethiopian revolution. We've returned to our bacon and eggs.

The most you can say about such an argument is that it really cannot be refuted categorically. Who can deny that, if the war in the Ogaden had been fought under historical circumstances completely different from the ones which actually existed, it might have had an equally different character and significance?

The method of Lenin and Trotsky

But on the other hand, who will openly say that we should deduce our policy toward an actual struggle from speculation about one which might have occurred in another place and time? Certainly not Lenin, who insisted that "The categorical requirement of Marxist theory in investigating any social question is that it be examined within *definite* historical limits . . ." ("The Right of Nations to Self-Determination," *Collected Works*, Vol. 20, p. 400.)

And certainly not Trotsky. "In order to determine in each given instance the historic and social character of a war, we must be guided not by impressions and conjectures but by a scientific analysis of the politics that preceded the war and conditioned it," he wrote.

To abandon this method is to lose oneself in a maze of personal prejudices and fancies.

> It is quite obvious that the proletariat must build its policy on the basis of a *given* war, as it is, i.e., as it has been conditioned by the whole preceding course of development, and not on hypothetical speculation over the possible strategic outcome of the war. In such speculations everyone will invariably choose that variant which best corresponds to his own desires, national sympathies, and antipathies. Obviously, such a policy would be not Marxist but subjective, not internationalist but chauvinist in character. ("A Fresh Lesson," *Writings of Leon Trotsky (1938–39)* [New York: Pathfinder Press, 1969, 1974], p. 77 [2012 printing].)

In momentary retreat from his hypothetical world devoid of anti-imperialist and antiwar sentiment and American Blacks, comrade Harsch only turns again to hunches (and speculations about hunches) regarding the goals of the alleged "probe." This guesswork reaches a deafening crescendo on page 32:

> As it was, the imperialists were trying to see what they could get away with. They were testing out a number of options. Would the Somalian invasion itself be sufficient to cripple the Ethiopian revolution, or could the occupation serve as a beachhead for further attacks? How useful and compliant was the Somalian regime? [So this was *not* known?] What kind of role could the Saudis or Iranians play? How directly could Washington go in, or Paris, or Bonn? How much would the invasion encourage the rightist guerrilla bands in Ethiopia? Could it increase the opportunities for a rightist coup in Addis Ababa?

This crescendo of questions serves only to conceal comrade Harsch's lack of answers. His problem is that he does not know and cannot explain just how the Somali struggle was supposed to smash the Ethiopian masses. All he knows is that Carter *wanted* to smash and was *looking* for ways to do so. Imperialism's *inability* to go from wish to action expresses itself even in this paragraph's closing sentence: "While the imperialists may not have had a completely thought out plan, their target was clear: the Ethiopian revolution." (P. 32.)

The real meaning of the war

The Somali struggle in the Ogaden, whatever may have been the narrow outlook of Siad Barre, was in fact the outcome of the whole history of Ethiopian oppression and the Somali struggle against it. The unification of the Somali people and their land is not the episodic whim of one dictator but expresses the long-standing aspiration of the Somali masses, for which they have organized and fought for decades. This has always been a progressive goal and a progressive fight; we support steps which lead in its direction, even when they are taken at the behest of a bonapartist bourgeois regime.

Of course, if it could be demonstrated on the basis of the facts that the Somali struggle actually did constitute, in its essence, an assault upon the Ethiopian *revolution*, that it had been dominated by and subordinated to imperialism, then Marxists would not support but oppose it. That, however, cannot be assumed. It must be proven. And that proof demands something far more substantial than the jerry-built structure which comrade Harsch has constructed out of factual inaccuracies and speculation about what might eventually have happened after this war, all balanced precariously upon pointless conjectures about what the world might look like if the history of the last few decades had been different from what it was.

Comrade Harsch's fundamental point of departure is the assumption that the Somali struggle and the needs of the revolution in Ethiopia were counterposed. Here he is radically wrong. The Somali liberation struggle is as legitimate and integral a part of the Ethiopian revolution as is the Eritrean struggle. The kinship of these two movements was obvious not only to the Eritreans and the Somalis but also to the opponents of both—i.e., to Mengistu, Castro, and the Kremlin bureaucracy.

Comrade Harsch denounces the Somali offensive in the name of the Ethiopian revolution. A Somali victory in the (Somali) Ogaden, he insists, would have constituted "a blow at the Ethiopian revolution."

His reasoning is based, however, on an impermissible equation. He is equating the interests of the Ethiopian *revolution* with those of the bourgeois Ethiopian *state and government*. In fact, however, these interests stand in contradiction with one another because the Ethiopian state is an immediate *barrier* to the genuine and complete development of the Ethiopian revolution.

It is certainly true that a Somali victory would have constituted a major blow by this oppressed nation at the military bonapartist regime and the Amharic oppressor state in Ethiopia. But how can this be construed as a blow against the Ethiopian revolution? On the contrary. It would have been a major blow on behalf of that revolution.

Comrade Harsch speculates that a Somali victory might have encouraged the rightist guerrilla bands in Ethiopia. What he completely neglects to consider is that even the initial victories of the Somalis did encourage the Eritreans. It also gave them practical military assistance by forcing the Dergue to fight a two-front war.

Comrade Harsch also speculates that a Somali victory *might* have increased "the opportunities for a rightist coup in Addis Ababa." What he completely neglects to consider is that even the initial victories of the Somalis—along with those of the Eritreans—did accelerate the demoralization and disintegration of the Ethiopian army. In other words, he fails to notice the fact that a Somali victory would have helped to undercut the very forces necessary to launch a successful rightist coup in the first place.

There is an unfortunate consistency in comrade Harsch's method. Throughout, he bases his position on speculations concerning the impact of a Somali victory on Carter's psychology, Siad Barre's ambitions, and on the most reactionary forces in Ethiopia. But at no point does he base his policy on a serious consideration of how a victory of the oppressed Somalis would have affected *the rest of the oppressed masses in the Horn of Africa.*

Yet it is precisely this consideration, first and foremost, on which a revolutionary policy should be based. A Somalian victory would have given a massive stimulus to the revolutionary mobilization of the masses throughout the region. This is precisely why such a victory was so dangerous from the standpoint of U.S. imperialism. This is the reason why Carter could toy with the aspirations of the Somali people but dared not actually unleash them.

First of all, a victory for the Somali struggle in the Ogaden would have advanced the larger struggle for Somali reunification. Comrade Harsch justly complains that the Somalian government has never consistently tried to carry through this struggle to the end. In particular, he points to Siad Barre's treacherous conciliationism toward Kenya and Djibouti. But isn't it clear that a Somali victory in the Ogaden would have undercut that conciliationism? Would have whet the appetite of all Somalis for further and more militant measures against their historic oppressors? The government of Kenya certainly thought so—and so did Jimmy Carter's advisers.

Thus a victory in the Ogaden would have laid the objective basis for a struggle by the insurgent Somali masses *against* Siad Barre and the compromising neocolonial ruling class which he represents. Siad would have been squeezed in a vise between a rising tide of Somali nationalism and the limitations of his own class position and policy. A correct policy on the part of revolutionary socialists in Somalia—giving the kind of military-technical support to Siad that Trotsky urged be given to Chiang against Japan—would have greatly increased the influence of Trotskyism among the Somali masses. We might add that *only* such a policy could possibly have done so; any other would have totally discredited a Trotskyist party in the eyes of the Somali workers and peasants.

Secondly, a Somali victory would have delivered a major blow in behalf of the Eritrean liberation struggle. Indeed, given the major advances which were then being registered by the Eritreans, an Ethiopian defeat in the Ogaden would very likely have ensured the final success of the Eritreans against the demoralized and defeated Ethiopian army.

Thirdly, a Somali victory would have stimulated all other national struggles in the Horn, inspiring all the other oppressed peoples of that region. Comrade Harsch fears the possible Somalian oppression of Oromos and/or Sidamos. But in earlier articles, he himself pointed out that Somali victories in the Ogaden strengthened the hand of the Oromo liberation movement. Even if Siad had wanted to suppress the Oromos and Sidamos, therefore, such ambitions would have run into a stepped-up resistance—a resistance inspired precisely by the victory of the oppressed Somalis!

Moreover, a Somalian victory would have constituted the first successful breach in the OAU's monolithic opposition to democratic struggles directed against the neocolonial system in Africa. To one degree or another, therefore, it would have encouraged such struggles throughout the continent.

Finally, a Somali victory would have struck a blow on behalf of the revolution within Ethiopia's Amhara heartland. The Dergue's ability to dominate the Amhara masses requires the stabilization of its power base as a whole—in particular its oppression and exploitation of subject peoples. The fundamental source of the Dergue's power, moreover, is the army. By cracking the morale and discipline of that army, a Somali victory would have given the Amhara masses much more room in which to organize and struggle in their own interests.

Comrade Harsch holds that the defeat of the Somalis was the best way to further the Ethiopian revolution. But his position does not flow from an assessment of the actual events or the actual context of the war. Rather, it derives from speculations about what might have happened—*assuming* (1) the passivity of the popular masses in general, and (2) an identity between the Dergue and the Ethiopian revolution as such.

As we have indicated, this approach was wrong from the beginning in its method as well as with regard to the concrete facts. Not only was it based on pure speculation, but it was based upon the most *pessimistic, conservative* kind of speculation.

It *assumed*, against all the evidence, that a Somali victory would be successfully employed by U.S. imperialism as an "opening wedge." It *assumed* that the Somali people as well as the American people would sit passively by and allow this to happen.

It assumed that Siad Barre would successfully walk the tightrope between incorporating the Somalis in the Ogaden into Somalia and squelching a parallel upheaval among the same people in Kenya and Djibouti. It assumed that Siad Barre would successfully retain his precarious balance atop the movement of the Somali people.

It assumed that a Somalian victory would not lay the basis for an Eritrean victory. It assumed that a Somalian victory plus an Eritrean victory could not provide an "opening wedge" for the Amhara masses themselves. It assumed that the Oromos, Sidamos, and other oppressed nationalities in Ethiopia would not be materially and psychologically bolstered in their own liberation struggles by the victory of the Somali people.

It assumed—and this is especially amazing in the light of subsequent developments in Iran—that U.S. imperialism's semicolonial allies in the region would be able to intervene in a major way in this war regardless of their own internal domestic problems. It assumed that right-wing elements in the Ethiopian ruling class would be able to depose Mengistu while at the same time suppressing the struggle of all the oppressed and exploited in the region. And on and on.

None of these assumptions were legitimate.

If we must speculate, let us at least project the *most* likely outcome of events, the outcome most closely adhering to the real rhythm of the revolutionary process. If we do this, we will see that a Somali victory in the Ogaden would have stimulated the revolutionary mobilization of the masses in opposition to the counterrevolutionary Dergue regime and to the power of U.S. imperialism throughout Africa.

The whole structure of neocolonialism, particularly clear in Africa, depends upon the existence of bourgeois governments in control of states which are to a large extent (and often enough completely) the artificial creation of western colonialism. One of the factors ensuring the collaboration of these semicolonial regimes with western imperialism is that these regimes depend upon the imperialists to maintain their undemocratic boundary-systems against the struggles of the oppressed nationalities trapped within them. This has been repeatedly demonstrated not only in Ethiopia, but also in Nigeria, Zaire, Lebanon, Chad, Iran, Iraq, Jordan, Turkey, India, Sudan, Kenya, Morocco, Mauritania, the Philippines, Indonesia, Sri Lanka, Pakistan, the Malagasy Republic, Malawi, Sierra Leone, Liberia, Ghana, and elsewhere.

National oppression within the semicolonial countries, in short, is one of the chief transmission belts for the national oppression of all the semicolonial countries by imperialism. In this case, Amhara oppression of Somalis, Eritreans, etc., plays a key role in bolstering imperialist oppression of Ethiopia as a whole.

These two levels of national oppression cannot in general be separated from one another, much less counterposed. The struggles of the oppressed nationalities against their neocolonial jailers is not some kind of separate or secondary factor in revolutions like the one in Ethiopia. They are, instead, concrete manifestations of the mass struggle against the system of neocolonialism as a whole.

This, in the final analysis, is the reason why revolutionary socialists should have supported Somalia against Ethiopia in the Ogaden war. Not for "moralistic" or "formalistic" reasons—although we certainly sympathize with the thoroughly just struggle of the Somalis for national freedom from their historic oppressor. This policy was the right one because a Somali victory would have constituted an important strategic blow against imperialist neocolonialism on behalf of the developing African revolution.

The test of events

The Ogaden war of 1977–1978 is a thing of the past. But the conflicts which produced that war persist, although the relationship of forces has been affected by the Dergue's victory.

The most important and immediate effect has been the major defeats suffered by the Eritrean liberation movement. It was the defeat of the Somalis in the Ogaden—and the leading role played in that defeat by Cuban troops—which rescued the Dergue's army and freed its troops for use against the people of Eritrea. The Somalian defeat not only removed one front of what had been a two-front war for Mengistu; it also enabled Mengistu to regain his grip on the ranks of the Ethiopian army and to intimidate not only the oppressed nationalities of Ethiopia but also the masses in the Amhara heartland.

This is the result of Mengistu's victory, the victory belatedly supported by the Socialist Workers Party. This result was quite predictable. No extravagant flights of fancy were needed to foresee it. The reactionary impact of the Dergue's victory provides a crushing verdict on the policy and analysis advanced in the pamphlet written by comrade Harsch.

Of course, the revolution in the Horn of Africa is by no means over. While the Eritrean freedom fighters have been driven back to the guerrilla tactics which they outgrew several years ago, their struggle nonetheless continues. Recent clashes in the Ogaden show that the Somali question is still posed. And while the Amhara masses in Addis Ababa and the highlands have been relatively quiescent during the past period, the sharpening contradictions of Ethiopian capitalism guarantee that the class struggle will soon revive here, too.

For this reason—as well as to avoid a serious miseducation of our cadres about how to approach the national question in general in a revolutionary situation—it is imperative for the Socialist Workers Party and the Fourth International to adopt a correct approach toward the Ogaden War.

MARCH 13, 1979

Notes

1. The material in this pamphlet originally appeared in the September 25 and October 2, 1978, issues of *Intercontinental Press/Inprecor*.

2. Incidentally, Shachtman also denounced the Chinese army for crossing the border into Burma in its war against Japan, citing this as further proof of the imperialist domination of the Chinese war effort. The editor of *Fourth International* replied, "A war of national defense, according to Shachtman's logic, can be fought

only by sticking within one's own frontiers; to sally out beyond them changes the character of the war. Of a Shachtman of his time who in a war of national defense disapproved an offensive into enemy territory Marx wrote that he 'confuses a defensive war with defensive military operations. So if a fellow falls upon me in the street I may only parry his blow but not knock him down, because then I should turn into an *aggressor*! The want of dialectic comes out in every word these people utter. . . .'" (Felix Morrow, "China in the War," *Fourth International*, August 1942.)

3. Contrast the above with Carter's rush delivery of $390 million in weapons in March to North Yemen plus an aircraft-carrier task force openly poised for an attack on South Yemen. (*New York Times*, March 7, March 11, 1978.)

THE ETHIOPIA-SOMALIA WAR, ERITREA, AND CUBA—
WHAT THE FACTS SHOW:
A Reply to Flint, Levine, Kramer, Wohlforth, and Keil

By Ernest Harsch and Larry Seigle

The Ethiopian revolution that began in 1974 was an upheaval of major historical importance, not only in the region of the Horn of Africa, but throughout Africa and the Middle East. The gains that the insurgent Ethiopian masses won weakened imperialism and were an inspiration for the entire world revolution.

Like all deep-going revolutions, the one in Ethiopia has set powerful social forces into motion. Peasants against their landlords, oppressed peoples against their national oppressors, workers against their capitalist bosses, soldiers against their officers.

And like all revolutions in the colonial and semicolonial world today the Ethiopian revolution has drawn the fire of the most reactionary forces, including the foremost imperialist power: Washington. In 1977–78, these counterrevolutionary assaults took the form of an American-encouraged and backed invasion of Ethiopia by the neighboring capitalist state of Somalia. The Ethiopian armed forces, with the decisive assistance of 17,000 Cuban volunteers, were eventually successful in repelling this reactionary attack.

The Somalian invasion was aimed at undermining and rolling back the gains of the Ethiopian revolution. Revolutionary socialists should have supported the Ethiopian side of the war, while continuing to defend the national rights of the Somalis and other oppressed peoples within Ethiopia, while fighting to maintain the political independence of the working class from the Ethiopian military junta, and while striving to deepen the revolution into a socialist one.

This position was advanced most extensively in two articles by Ernest Harsch in the September 25 and October 2, 1978, issues of *Intercontinental Press/Inprecor*, which were reprinted, slightly revised, in the pamphlet, *The Ethiopian Revolution* (New York: Pathfinder Press, 1978); and in an article by David Frankel in the July 7, 1978, *Militant*, which was included in the pamphlet *Upsurge in Africa* (New York: Pathfinder Press, 1978).

Several comrades have taken exception to the party's position on the Ethiopia-Somalia war, outlining their differences and views in four discussion articles: Tim Wohlforth in "Minority Report on Cuba," David Keil in "Our Choice in Cuba," Eric Flint and Bruce Levine in "Ethiopia, Somalia, and the African Revolution" (all published in *SWP Discussion Bulletin*, Vol. 36, No. 2, April 1979), and Flint, Levine, and Shelley Kramer in "The Cuban Revolution: A State Capitalist Analysis," based on a report by Kramer to an expanded meeting of the Political Committee in August 1978 (in *SWP Discussion Bulletin*, Vol. 36, No. 3, May 1979).

Despite their widely divergent views on many other questions, all of these comrades have a similar position on the Ethiopia-Somalia war and all approach the question in a similar manner. The views put forward by these comrades are diametrically opposed to those that the SWP holds. Because of their similar views, we will take up their arguments together, while concentrating, for the most part, on the article by Comrades Flint and Levine, which contains the most extensive arguments for reversing the party's position on the war. This article develops at some length the view capsulized in the report on Cuba given by Comrade Kramer that by opposing the Somalian regime's invasion, the party is "on the wrong side" (Flint, Levine, and Kramer, p. 26). According to this view, it "was progressive when Somalia sent its troops to aid the Somali national liberation struggle in the Ogaden" (Ibid., p. 29).

Comrade Wohlforth maintains the Somalian

regime's sending of its army into the Ogaden region of Ethiopia was "part of a national liberation struggle of the Somali population of the region" -(p. 11). He also asserts that the SWP, by opposing the Somalian invasion and calling for a victory for the Ethiopian side of the war, has changed its "traditional and principled position in favor of the right to self-determination in Africa . . ." (p. 10).

Like Wohlforth, Comrade Keil believes that "the Somalian intervention in the Ogaden war was a result of the nationalism of the oppressed" (p. 37).

Similarly, Flint and Levine assert that "the attack by the Somalian army constituted an armed struggle of the Somali people in support of their national liberation and reunification. The main instrument of that struggle was the Somalian army, which is in simple fact the most powerful military force at the disposal of the Somali nation" (p. 135 of this volume). Moreover, "a Somali victory would have constituted an important strategic blow against imperialist neocolonialism on behalf of the developing African revolution" (p. 152 of this volume). Therefore, we "should have given military-technical support to the Somali forces in the Ogaden war" (p. 130 of this volume).

In short, all these comrades favored a Somalian victory in the war and a defeat for the Ethiopian side. They oppose the decisive Cuban assistance to the Ethiopians in fighting off the invasion. In their view, a decisive defeat for Cuban troops in Ethiopia was the road to advancing "the developing African revolution."

Obviously, our differences are not of nuance or emphasis. They run to the very heart of how revolutionists seek to push forward the class struggle in the context of the mass upheavals that are taking place in the Horn of Africa. They involve which side we should have been on during the shooting war of 1977–78: fighting with the Ethiopian and Cuban forces against the imperialist-inspired attack, or lining up with the counterrevolutionary invasion.

At the time of the Ethiopia-Somalia war, the SWP took a position in our press that "tilted" toward Somalia. We argued that the national struggle of the Somali people was the most important element in this war.

However, when we reviewed the actual facts of the war, we discovered that the opposite was the case. We had reduced the class struggle to the national struggle. The facts indicated clearly that the element of the national struggle of the Somali people was not the dominant element in the war. A victory for Somalia would have been a victory for imperialism against the Ethiopian revolution, and therefore it would have set back the struggle of the working class and its allies, including the oppressed nationalities within Ethiopia's borders.

In mid-1978, analyzing the facts we had, we changed our position. Since then, even more factual evidence proves we were correct in changing our position. The facts show: (1) The Somalian invasion of Ethiopia was not preceded by or linked to any upsurge in national liberation struggles on the part of the Somali nationality in the Ogaden or in Somalia itself. (2) The imperialist powers, most notably the United States, actively encouraged and supported the Somalian invasion because they wanted to deal a blow to the Ethiopian revolution. (3) The area the Somalian government claimed title to and tried to occupy militarily is *populated overwhelmingly by non-Somali peoples*, particularly the Oromos and the Sidamos, who in fact had been in the very vanguard of the peasant struggles against the feudal landlords that were a major element of the Ethiopian revolution.

Therefore the defeat of the imperialist-inspired invasion by Somalia was progressive. The Cubans' decisive role in the military defeat of the Somalian army was likewise progressive. The defeat of the Somalian invasion shifted the relationship of class forces in favor of the working class and its allies in the Horn of Africa. It was to the advantage of the Eritrean independence fighters, who would have been among the first to suffer from a victory for pro-imperialist forces in Ethiopia. It strengthened the peasants in their struggle to prevent the rolling back of their victories over the feudal landlords. And, it put the working class in a better position to construct an alternative leadership to the petty-bourgeois Dergue, and to move forward in the fight to establish a workers and peasants government.

Now Comrades Kramer, Flint, Levine, Wohlforth and Keil are proposing to change our position on the war in the opposite direction. They think the invasion by the Somalian army was progressive. They think the party and the Fourth International should have backed the Somalian government, the

Western Somali Liberation Front (which is at least partially controlled by the Somalian government), and other groups fighting against the Ethiopian side. They think we should have done what we could to help those forces deal a decisive defeat to the Cuban internationalist fighters and the Ethiopians.

This would have put the party and the Fourth International on the side of the counterrevolutionary offensive instigated and encouraged by the imperialists and aimed at putting them in a better position to roll back the gains of the Ethiopian revolution.

Why do these comrades go so far off? One reason obviously is their extreme antipathy to the Castro leadership, which they consider to be counterrevolutionary through and through. Their drive to put as much distance as possible between the Castroists and the Fourth International impels them toward the wrong side in the Ethiopia-Somalia war. The position these comrades hold on Castroism and the Cuban revolution is analyzed in "In Defense of the Cuban Revolution: National Committee Majority Report," by Larry Seigle (in *SWP Discussion Bulletin*, Vol. 36, No. 1, April 1979).

In this article, we will deal with what the factual record actually shows about the Ethiopia-Somalia war, the Cuban role in Eritrea, and the mistakes the five comrades make in how they approach these questions.

Before examining these points in detail, let's set the record straight on one important point.

Comrades Flint and Levine claim that the SWP earlier had a "fundamentally correct" position on the war—that is, that the party's position was the same as the one they now put forward. That is false. Their statement of the "original SWP position" is in actuality a summary of *their* position (see pp. 13–14). Among the misstatements of our earlier position are two essential points.

1. Flint and Levine virtually ignore the Ethiopian revolution in the eight-point compilation they present as the "original SWP position" on the Ethiopia-Somalia war. The Ethiopian revolution was, and remains, the starting point for us in analyzing events in the Horn of Africa. The mistake the SWP made during the Ethiopia-Somalia war was *not* the mistake Flint and Levine make: totally leaving out of the picture the deepgoing social revolution in Ethiopia.

2. At the time of the war, the SWP did mistakenly view the national liberation struggle of the oppressed Somali people in the Ogaden as the overriding factor in the war. However, at no time did we believe, as do Flint and Levine, that "the attack by the Somalian army constituted an armed struggle of the Somali people" or that the army of capitalist Somalia was "at the disposal of the Somali nation."

As it was, the contradictions of our original analysis of the war soon became so apparent that we were impelled to reevaluate it. This led to a correct explanation of the war and of what political stance to take toward it. This was important, for it helped us not only to understand the dynamics of the Ethiopian revolution more clearly, but also to more easily avoid falling into similar pitfalls on other questions (the recent wars between China and Vietnam and between Tanzania and Uganda come to mind). The ability of the SWP to recognize and correct its errors on the Ethiopia-Somalia war is likewise testimony to the party's political vitality.

A revolution ignored

Any analysis of recent events in the Horn of Africa must begin with one incontrovertible fact: there has been a revolution in Ethiopia. Not just a military coup, not just a change of faces in the government, not just a shakeup of authority, but a deepgoing, *social* revolution, in which the old ruling classes were overthrown, dispossessed, and destroyed, in which a centuries-old monarchy was toppled, in which the workers, peasants, and oppressed nationalities have begun to rise up to fight for their rights and for a new social order that reflects their class interests.

Despite the depth and historic impact of that revolution, all five comrades do a thorough job of ignoring it.

The closest Comrade Wohlforth even comes to the revolution is when he states, "In the meantime [during the war in Angola] a left military government had come to power in Ethiopia. This government was and is capitalist. In addition to carrying out progressive actions against Haile Selassie's feudal holdings, the Dergue as it is called, also took actions against the militant students who had originally supported it" (p. 11). The massive upheavals of the Ethiopian workers and peasants disappear entirely in Wohlforth's version, to be replaced by nothing more than "progressive actions" carried out by a "left military government." Thus while denigrating the Ethiopian revolution, Wohlforth at the same time gives the Dergue more credit than it deserves for the changes that have been carried through.

Keil follows a simpler course. He omits mention of any "progressive actions" carried out by the Dergue.

Like Wohlforth, Comrades Flint and Levine refer to "the Dergue's nationalization of land and industry" (p. 145), without any mention of the massive demonstrations, strikes, and peasant uprisings that forced the Dergue to take those actions. At some points, they even seem to question whether a real revolution has taken place after all. They state, for instance, that "Ethiopia as it exists today is a neocolonial creation which rules over a semi*feudal* society, oppressing workers, peasants, women, and numerous national minorities" (p. 131, emphasis added). Do they think that the elimination of the feudalist landlord class has been a fraud? Do they think that the system of feudal property relations that existed under Emperor Haile Selassie has somehow survived the nationalization of all land and the seizure of the large feudal estates by the peasants who worked them?

The revolution in Ethiopia has been a central factor in the class struggle in that part of the world since 1974. No other fact—be it the Eritrean independence struggle, the Ethiopia-Somalia war, or the repressive policies of the Dergue—can be properly understood in isolation from that revolution.

Yet that is just how Comrades Wohlforth, Keil, Flint, Kramer, and Levine view the 1977–78 war. They of course make a few references to the revolution. But if it is not entirely ignored in their analysis, it is treated as a peripheral event, as an off-stage noise. That makes it easier for them to dismiss or minimize American imperialism's drive to halt the revolutionary process in Ethiopia. That makes it easier for them to deny that the Somalian military invasion was an attack directed against the Ethiopian revolution. That makes it easier for them to distort the reality of the war by ripping it out of its class struggle framework—in which the basic conflict was between the Ethiopian revolution and imperialist reaction.

So for the benefit of the discussion, let us briefly summarize the significance of the Ethiopian revolution and what it has accomplished.

The fall of the monarchy, the rise of the masses

Ethiopia under Haile Selassie was ruled by a monarchy based on a feudal landlord class. There were some Ethiopian capitalists, but their interests were so intimately intertwined with those of the aristocracy as to be virtually indistinguishable. The ruling class was largely Amhara in composition. In the south, where the largest feudal estates were located, its domination was based upon both class exploitation and national oppression; the peasants, who were tied to the land and obligated to provide labor, taxes, and tribute to the lords, were largely Oromos and Sidamos who had been conquered by the Amharas in the nineteenth century. Other peoples, too, were oppressed by this aristocracy: the Eritreans, who since the early 1960s have been fighting for their independence; the Afars in the northeast; the Somalis, a nomadic people in the eastern desert region known as the Ogaden; the Nilo-Saharans in the west, the Arussi and Kaffa in the south, etc. Amharic was the only legal language. Because capitalist productive relations had only begun to make a few inroads in the cities and in the coffee-growing agricultural areas, the Ethiopian working class was still very small.

One of the most important characteristics of Ethiopia under Selassie was that it was a semicolony of American imperialism, just as every other country in Africa—"independent" or not—is still under the domination of the imperialist powers. Much of Ethiopia's trade was with the United States. Washington had armed and trained the entire Ethiopian military. At one point during the 1960s, up to 4,000 American military personnel were stationed in Eritrea. The Selassie regime served as an important regional prop for American imperialism's domination over that corner of Africa.

The revolution that began in February 1974 changed all that.

Suddenly, unexpectedly (at least to Selassie and his American advisers), the urban masses rose up. Addis Ababa, Jimma, Asmara, Diredawa, and other cities were shaken by mammoth urban mobilizations, among the largest that have ever taken place anywhere in Africa. Taking into account the much smaller size of Ethiopia's urban population, these marches, demonstrations, and mass rallies were comparable to the urban upheavals in Iran.

And like the revolution in Iran, they touched virtually every sector of society. Workers, who numbered only a few hundred thousand in the entire country (out of a total population of 30 million), unleashed a series of strikes. Women demonstrated for their rights. Muslims (in one especially large march of 100,000) protested against religious discrimination. Townspeople, in particular in the southern city of Jimma, rose up and ousted local governments, in some cases taking power for a time through popularly chosen bodies. Soldiers rebelled and began arresting their officers, as well as prominent aristocrats and government officials. The Eritreans, whose own struggle for independence had been an important factor in weakening the Selassie regime in earlier years, responded to the Ethiopian revolution by mobilizing like never before to fight for their national rights. Most significantly, given the centrality of the land question in Ethiopia, the Oromo, Sidamo, Kaffa, and other peasants in the south rose up spontaneously, seized land, crops, and farming equipment, and drove out the landlords.

Under the impact of this powerful battering, the government apparatus and the military hierarchy started to crumble. The revolution, however, did not have any organized revolutionary political leadership. In this context, a group of junior military officers and lower-ranking soldiers, including some who were non-Amharas, seized power in the name of the revolution and deposed Selassie. They quickly set out to purge the state apparatus, while at the same time seeking to keep the masses in check. These junior and noncommissioned officers, who were organized within the Dergue, were largely petty-bourgeois nationalist in outlook. They were against the feudal aristocrats (scores of whom they executed) and wanted to develop Ethiopia economically. But the Dergue feared the independent power of the masses. So while coming to power on the crest of the revolutionary upheaval, the Dergue simultaneously sought to contain the revolution, to channel it in a "safe" direction, to prevent the workers and peasants from taking power in their own hands. The Dergue, however, was extremely weak and was itself rent by political and factional divisions. It consequently was unable to establish stable control over the masses.

Under considerable mass pressure, the Dergue enacted a series of sweeping revolutionary measures. It nationalized all banks, insurance companies, and credit institutions, in which imperialist interests had been heavily involved. It nationalized more than 100 companies, bringing under state control the bulk of the largest enterprises, including mining, utilities and transport, iron, steel, cement, and oil.

It promulgated a radical land reform, which was, in fact, the most radical yet carried out *anywhere in Africa*. All rural land was nationalized, all debts and obligations by tenant farmers and sharecroppers were cancelled, and a twenty-five-acre ceiling was placed on the size of farms cultivated by individual families. The previously existing capitalist farms were brought under direct state control and farming cooperatives were established. In many cases, the peasants had already begun to implement such measures on their own, but the legal adoption of the land reform measure extended and systematized the expropriation of the feudal lords throughout the country.

This marked the definitive overthrow of the feudal system. That is why we call the revolution in Ethiopia a *social* revolution, even though capitalism itself still survives.

There have been other important gains of the revolution as well. The church and state were separated, and institutionalized discrimination against Muslims was ended. A basic literacy campaign was launched and efforts were made to improve the abysmal health-care system. Urban land and surplus housing were nationalized, wiping out the big slumlords in the cities.

A few concessions were even made to the oppressed nationalities, despite the Dergue's continued military campaign against the Eritrean independence struggle and its unwillingness to grant the nationalities their right to self-determination. These concessions included recognition and increasing use of local languages, as well as promises (not yet carried out) of regional autonomy. The land reform itself, by removing the Amhara feudal lords from the southern provinces, ended the worst aspects of national oppression over the Sidamo, Oromo, Kaffa, and other peasants. For that reason, they have been among the strongest supporters of the revolution.

Even the national character of the government is no longer as exclusively Amhara as it was under Selassie. There has been stepped-up recruitment of non-Amharas into the administration and military, and the establishment of peasant and neighborhood committees has given people from other nationalities a greater voice in local affairs. Mengistu Haile Mariam, the head of the Dergue, is himself of Oromo and Nilo-Saharan background.

Comrades Flint and Levine, as part of their argument that the Somali struggle for national liberation and unification was the reason for the Somalian invasion, imply that the war was preceded by an upsurge of the Somali masses in the Ogaden. But the actual evidence (excluding the self-serving claims the Somalian regime made after the fact) indicates otherwise.

The Somalis in the Ogaden certainly had genuine and deeply felt grievances, but the fact remains that they were little affected by the mass mobilizations that were sweeping virtually every other corner of Ethiopia. This is partly ascribable to the fact that the vast bulk of them are nomads and therefore had little to directly gain from land reform. Their migratory life also meant that contact with government administrators, the most immediate source of friction with the central government, was relatively infrequent in this period. Finally, the Somalian regime dominated the political leadership of the Ogaden Somalis (which we will return to later) and was still at that time following its past policy of seeking to dampen the Somali national struggle within Ethiopia.

The failure of the Ethiopian revolution to really draw in the participation of the Somalis was a weakness, and made it easier for the imperialists and the Somalian regime to later launch their attack against the revolution in the name of the oppressed Somali masses.

In contrast to the situation in the Ogaden, Eritrea became a hotbed of the revolution. Despite the Dergue's brutal efforts to crush the Eritrean independence struggle, the Eritrean workers and peasants mobilized almost in their entirety. For a period of a few years the Eritreans successfully reduced the Ethiopian presence to a toehold of just a few cities.

Eritrea was symptomatic of the Dergue's general inability to immediately rein in the masses. Although it instituted a fierce repression against part of the left, in which hundreds were killed, it could not restore "order." Students pressed for democratic rights. Workers carried out sporadic strikes and demanded workers control of the nationalized industries. Conflicts occurred within the neighborhood committees (*kebeles*), peasant associations, and the government-backed trade-union federation between those who sought to use them as organizations of the struggling masses and those who were attempting to transform them into simply instruments for the implementation of government policy.

The pressures on the Dergue were intense. It was still too weak to turn openly against the masses. It had to continue riding with the upheaval. And because of the radicalization of the masses and the growing attractiveness of socialist ideas, it had to portray itself as "socialist," even "Marxist-Leninist," in order to retain some popularity. Notwithstanding its initial attempts to maintain close ties with American imperialism, the Dergue was forced to adopt an increasingly anti-imperialist stance, culminating with the expulsion of most of the remaining American personnel from Ethiopia in April 1977.

Ethiopia and the permanent revolution

The Ethiopian revolution has been a momentous event. It has struck a serious blow against imperialism on behalf of the masses of the entire colonial and semicolonial world, and ranks with other recent advances of the colonial revolution: the revolution in Iran, the revolution in Afghanistan, the winning of independence from Portuguese colonial rule by Angola and Mozambique, and the overthrow of Pol Pot in Kampuchea.

Marxists support such struggles and whatever gains they may achieve, even if the working class does not succeed in taking power and beginning to reorganize society along socialist lines. Any struggle that weakens imperialism, that loosens imperialism's grip and mobilizes the masses in struggles to win their demands helps advance the class struggle as a whole.

Marxists also understand the dynamic that democratic struggles in the colonial world have in this epoch of imperialism and of capitalism's decline as a world system. Since capitalism no longer plays a progressive role in humanity's social advancement, the bourgeoisie is unable to fully grant or carry through those democratic tasks that were historically part of the bourgeois democratic revolution in the days of capitalism's rise. In fact, it increasingly opposes democratic gains and seeks to constrict them every step of the way. Because of this, struggles for democratic rights often spill over into proletarian challenges to the very framework of capitalist property relations, and thus become part of the broader class struggle for the overthrow of capitalism and the establishment of socialism. In today's world, struggles for national liberation and other democratic advances can only be fully realized through the socialist revolution. That is one of the basic premises of Trotsky's theory of the permanent revolution.

This dynamic can be seen at work in Ethiopia today. Most of the demands that were raised during the early days of the revolution were of a democratic character: for an end to the monarchy, for land reform, for national liberation, for the elimination of religious discrimination, for equality for women, for an elected government. A few of those democratic demands have been partially realized through the mobilizations of the masses themselves. Others have yet to be won. But these changes in Ethiopia already point toward the socialist revolution. They cannot be fully completed or realized short of such a revolution. Realizing the need to move forward even further, workers in Addis Ababa and other cities have already raised the demand for a workers government. Especially telling is the growing popularity of socialist ideas, which has forced the Dergue not only to claim that it is socialist, but also to permit the widespread sale of works by Marx, Engels, and Lenin.

What has been lacking so far in Ethiopia has been a revolutionary workers party that would carry this process through to its logical and necessary conclusion. And if the revolution does not advance toward the overthrow of capitalism, it will slip backward. Many of the gains of the revolution will be whittled away.

Washington—no passive observer

Like us, the imperialists and other reactionary forces realize that situations like that in Ethiopia, under revolutionary leadership, can lead to the overthrow of capitalism. They have been taught by bitter experience.

Washington learned that lesson especially well in Cuba, where a revolution that was initiated around struggles for national independence, land reform, and an end to Batista's tyranny very quickly confronted the entrenched interests of American imperialism and the local capitalists; rather than capitulate to those interests, the revolutionary leadership around Castro instead mobilized the masses for the expropriation of the bourgeoisie itself.

Washington and the other imperialist powers deeply fear the dynamic of the colonial revolution. That is why they oppose democratic measures such as land reforms, nationalizations, the winning of national rights, or the ouster of dictatorships, especially when carried out as a result of mass upheavals. The whole history of the colonial revolution reveals that when the threat to the imperialists' interests has been deep enough and when antiwar sentiment at home has not placed too high a domestic political price on foreign military interventions, they have not hesitated to intervene. They do so directly, as when the U.S. sent troops to Korea, Vietnam, Lebanon, and the Dominican Republic. And they do so indirectly, when imperialist troops are not feasible or necessary; the CIA-engineered overthrows of Mossadegh in Iran, Arbenz in Guatemala, Lumumba in the Congo, Nkrumah in Ghana, and Allende in Chile are just a few of the more well-known examples. In 1961, the U.S. organized and equipped a small army of Cuban exiles to invade Cuba. To Washington's dismay, the invaders were smashed at the Bay of Pigs. A decade and a half later, the Cubans delivered other similar blows against imperialism, first in Angola, then in Ethiopia.

American imperialism has responded to the Ethiopian revolution as it has toward the numerous other upheavals in the colonial world—with active opposition.

From an "oasis of stability" in Africa, the revolution had transformed Ethiopia into a source of instability for capitalist order. Not only had Washington's direct stake in Ethiopia been greatly undermined, but the revolution threatened to upset imperialism's position in the entire region. If the revolution was to be checked, the White House had to act.

During the first two years or so of the Ethiopian revolution, American imperialism followed a two-sided course.

On the one hand, it sought to bolster the rightist forces within Ethiopia, in opposition to the Dergue, which was unreliable from Washington's point of view. It funneled money and other assistance, via West Germany, Saudi Arabia, Egypt, and the Sudan, to the reactionary Ethiopian Democratic Union (EDU), an armed force led by dispossessed landlords and aristocrats. The EDU carried out numerous attacks against government forces in the provinces of Tigre, Begemder, Godjam, and Wollo, and briefly managed to capture a few towns and cities in those areas.

Another similar rightist group, the Afar Liberation Front (ALF), was established in mid-1975. Led by dispossessed Afar landlords (foremost among them Sultan Ali Mirah and his son), the front had close ties with the EDU and received aid from the Saudi Arabian and *Somalian* regimes in its attacks against the Ethiopian revolution. (The ALF is a classic example of how reactionary class forces can adopt the guise of a "national liberation" movement. Comrades Flint, Kramer, Levine, Keil, and Wohlforth should take note of its ties to the Somalian regime, and of its later coordination of military actions with the Western Somali Liberation Front.

The other side of Washington's intervention involved efforts to subvert the revolution from within, and to try to transform the Dergue into a reliable instrument of counter-revolution. Instead of cutting off aid to the Dergue immediately after it came to power—and thus leaving it even more susceptible to pressures from the Ethiopian workers and peasants—Washington sought to keep channels open and to back the Dergue insofar as it tried to contain the revolution. That included the provision of tens of millions of dollars worth of military hardware, intended to strengthen the Dergue's hand against its leftist opposition and against the Eritrean independence struggle. Washington understood the contradictory character of the Dergue, and sought to bolster its most reactionary wing; certain Dergue figures had already shown themselves more amenable to imperialism's interests.

By 1976, it was clear that both prongs of this attack against the revolution were failing. The EDU suffered serious reverses at the hands of the Dergue's forces, as did the ALF. Washington's efforts to push forward the more conservative figures in the Dergue had likewise been frustrated by the execution in November 1974 of Gen. Aman Michael Andom, the first chairman of the Dergue, and in mid-1976 of Majors Sisay Habte and Kiros Alemayehn, both of whom were thought to have favored much closer American ties. (The elimination of the so-called "moderates" in the Dergue continued through 1977, when both Gen. Tafari Banti and Lt. Col. Atnafu Abate were executed, leaving Mengistu Haile Mariam the new chairman and dominant figure in the Dergue.)

Besides the Dergue's increasing anti-American pronouncements, Washington was worried about its inability to put any firm rein on the masses. Despite massive repression, the Eritreans continued to make gains and the leftist Ethiopian People's Revolutionary Party was able to survive for many months as a significant force in Addis Ababa, Dire-dawa, and other cities.

Washington's disaffection with the Dergue reached a decisive turning point in August 1976. In that month, Assistant Secretary of State for African Affairs William Schaufele described the Dergue as "unstable, prone to violations of human rights, incapable of managing Ethiopia's deteriorating economy, and beset by insurgencies and incipient insurgencies" (Colin Legum and Bill Lee, *Conflict in the Horn of Africa* [New York: Africana Publishing Company, 1977], p. 70.) Although some minimal ties were retained with the Dergue, Washington from that point onward began to curtail its assistance to the Ethiopian regime, reaching an almost complete break in direct ties by April 1977. By this point, Washington's unsuccessful efforts to transform the Dergue into an effective and stable obstacle to the Ethiopian revolution were replaced by stepped-up preparations for a more direct attack on the Ethiopian revolution—using the army of the Somalian regime of Gen. Mohammed Siad Barre.

It is surprising that Comrades Kramer, Flint, Levine, Wohlforth, and Keil have *not one word* to say about American imperialism's active opposition to the Ethiopian revolution during its first three years. It would be enlightening to know what they think Washington's policy was. Hands off? Had the imperialists written off the Horn of

Africa? Did their incapacity to directly militarily intervene mean they did nothing?

By the time the five comrades do get around to mentioning the role of American imperialism at all, in their discussion of the Ethiopia-Somalia war, it is not to put the spotlight on the danger emanating from Washington, but to dismiss Washington's interest and involvement as a peripheral factor.

Even then, Comrades Flint, Kramer, Levine, and Wohlforth think that Washington's alliance with Somalia had nothing to do with the imperialist offensive against the Ethiopian revolution. "It was a matter of restoring as best as possible a balance of power with the USSR," Wohlforth proclaims (p. 11). Similarly, Cuba's anti-imperialist response, defending the Ethiopian revolution arms in hand, is belittled by Wohlforth as "a matter of power politics. Ethiopia is bigger than Somalia" (p. 11). Absent from this approach is any assessment of the class forces involved.

While Wohlforth, Levine, Kramer, and Flint deny that the U.S. backing for Somalia played any role in the Somalian invasion, Comrade Keil goes further. He insists, "The U.S. *opposed* the Somalian side in the war" (p. 30, emphasis in original). As we will soon see, Washington did nothing of the kind.

The comrades' playing down of the active role of American imperialism in the Horn of Africa is connected with their relative unconcern about the overall gains and impact of the Ethiopian revolution. From their blindness to the basic conflict between the Ethiopian revolution and imperialist counterrevolution flows much of their mistaken perception of the Ethiopia-Somalia war itself.

Before examining in detail how Washington used the Somalian invasion to attack the Ethiopian revolution, it might be useful to first look at Flint and Levine's methodological errors, particularly as they relate to the national question.

A mistaken method

Flint and Levine make the mistake of trying to explain the forces involved in the Ethiopia-Somalia war by invoking the general concept of support to national liberation struggles. Once this supreme principle is invoked, with this method, it is no longer important to examine the concrete, specific struggle. The actual confrontation of class forces is submerged into an abstract concept.

Comrades Flint and Levine then rely on a series of quotations on national struggles from Marx, Lenin, and Trotsky—each of which refers to *specific and concrete* cases—to "prove" their view of the Somalian invasion is correct. But, as we will see, their use of these quotations bolsters only their abstract approach. They do not advance their argument on the concrete case under discussion. They thus make exactly the mistake that Marx, Lenin, and Trotsky warned against—they dissolve the concrete question into abstract formulas.

For Flint and Levine it is enough to characterize the Somalis as an oppressed people, and their struggle for self-determination as a legitimate one, to conclude that the Somalian invasion deserved the support of revolutionists. They view the national struggle of the Somalis as a timeless force divorced from the actual class struggle. Specifically, they minimize or ignore the class conflict in the Horn of Africa, in which the Ethiopian revolution is the dominant fact, and the international class conflict between the exploited masses of the Horn of Africa and imperialism.

They reinforce their mistake by relying on the public rationalizations given by the Somalian capitalist government for sending its troops into Ethiopia. They also lend credence to the public statements of the Carter administration, denying U.S. involvement on the side of Somalia, proclaiming Washington's "neutrality," vowing never to "dishonor" existing borders in Africa, and other patent nonsense. They then conclude by restating the premise with which they began: that the Somalian invasion of the Ogaden and other parts of Ethiopia was an expression of the Somali national liberation struggle and thus deserved our support.

By taking the question of national liberation in isolation, Flint and Levine elevate it into an absolute. They lose sight of why Marxists support such struggles and what place democratic demands such as the right to self-determination have in our program as a whole.

We begin from the understanding that oppression of all kinds, including national oppression, cannot be ended under capitalism. As long as the bourgeoisie rules, as long as imperialism maintains its stranglehold over the peoples of Africa, Asia, and Latin America, severe limits will be placed on any democratic gains that are won, both in the colonial world and within the imperialist countries themselves. Only when the working class takes power and prepares the way for the construction of a socialist society will it be possible to rid the planet of national oppression.

Within this framework, Marxists support struggles for the national self-determination of oppressed peoples as one way of helping to weaken imperialism and the capitalist class, and of giving an impetus to the broader class struggle. Because of their objectively revolutionary thrust, we don't make our support to anti-imperialist struggles conditional on our support to the particular leadership at a given time. We try to advance these struggles by proletarian means and to win the leadership away from the petty-bourgeois vacillators and betrayers. Only in that way can the struggles have a chance of success and open up greater opportunities for the class battle of the workers against the bourgeoisie.

We do not support every struggle that claims to be a national liberation struggle. And we do not automatically support everything those fighting for national liberation do. Like all specific democratic struggles and demands, we place them within our overall strategy of advancing the class struggle as a whole. We evaluate each *concrete* case, in all its ramifications and in its specific context. We assess it from the angle of what best furthers the development of class consciousness and self confidence of the working class: what the workers can gain or lose from it, how it can strengthen or weaken them, how it can unite or divide them. This is important, because any democratic demand, including the demand for self-determination, can, at certain times and under certain conditions, serve as a cover behind which the capitalists advance *against* the working class, to divert, blunt, or weaken the struggle. In that case, the formal content of the demand can turn into its opposite.

This is especially true during big revolutionary upheavals, when the capitalists' immediate and vital interests are threatened. To maintain their dominance and to halt and turn back the revolutionary process, they will use any tool that is available, even one that fits uncomfortably in their hand and that they intend to discard as soon as it has performed its function. Formalist methods of thought, hazardous for a revolutionary under any circumstances, are even more likely to be fatal the closer you get to a living revolution. You can wind up facing the wrong direction, and being shot down by your own troops.

Let us cite one historical example. The Russian empire under the tsar, like Ethiopia under Haile Selassie, was a prisonhouse of oppressed nationalities. Recognition of the right to self-determination of these oppressed peoples was a central plank in the program of the Bolsheviks. However, as Trotsky pointed out in 1922, ". . . our party did not for a minute turn the democratic principle of self-determination into a dominating factor over all other historic requirements and tasks" (Trotsky, *Between Red & White* [London: Communist Party of Great Britain, 1922], p. 83). In 1918, following the seizure of state power by the Russian working class, the Menshevik government of Georgia, an oppressed nation within the old Russian empire, declared Georgia's independence from the new Soviet state. On a formal level, the Georgian government had exercised its right to self-determination. But in the specific context of the class struggle as it was unfolding in the midst of revolution, civil war, and imperialist intervention, the imperialists and other reactionary forces turned "independent" Georgia into a dagger aimed at the very heart of the Russian revolution. The Bolsheviks realized that under those circumstances defense of the revolution took primacy over other questions, and acted accordingly. In February 1921, the Red Army marched into Georgia, and, in conjunction with a revolutionary upheaval, helped overthrow the counterrevolutionary Menshevik regime.

A more contemporary, though admittedly hypothetical, example further illustrates this point. In Iran, the liberation of the oppressed nationalities is no less a central axis of the developing revolution there than it was during the Russian revolution or than it is in Ethiopia today. But if the capitalist Turkish regime today sent its army into Azerbaijan under the guise of "liberating" the oppressed Azerbaijani Turks, or if the Iraqi regime today sent its troops into Arab-inhabited Khuzestan for similar stated reasons, could we determine our stand on such an invasion by considering only the national question involved, abstracted from the class struggle inside Iran, and in isolation from the struggle between the Iranian revolution and world imperialism?

Exclusive focus on the question of national liberation per se can lead to serious oversights of the broader class conflicts involved in such revolutionary upheavals.

'Armed struggle of the Somali people' or capitalist invasion?

Flint and Levine also have a wildly inflated assessment of the "revolutionary" capabilities of the neocolonial bourgeoisie. Although they apparently would deny that they consider the Somalian ruling class capable of leading progressive struggles, this assumption is implicit throughout their article and underlies much of their analysis of the Ethiopia-Somalia war.

What else can one conclude from the following statement?

> In sum, all the evidence at hand indicates that the attack by the Somalian army constituted an armed struggle of the Somali people in support of their national liberation and reunification. The main instrument of that struggle was the Somalian army, which is in simple fact the most powerful military force at the disposal of the Somali nation (p. 135).

Do Flint and Levine really think that the Somalian army—the army of a capitalist state and an instrument of class rule—is "at the disposal" of all Somali classes, "the Somali nation"? Can military action by the army of Somalia constitute "an armed struggle of the Somali people"? Do they think that this capitalist army can carry out a struggle for Somali "national liberation and reunification"?

We can only conclude that Flint and Levine would answer these questions affirmatively. They describe the Somalian army as the "progressive forces" (p. 138), the "insurgent forces" (p. 138), or, more simply, the "Somali forces" (p. 130). The invasion by this army becomes a "continuation of the Somali struggle for national liberation and unification" (p. 131), a struggle by the "oppressed and exploited" (p. 135).

These characterizations indicate that Flint and Levine reject the Trotskyist assessment of the role of the colonial and neocolonial bourgeoisies in this era of imperialist domination and permanent revolution.

One of the basic premises of Trotsky's theory of the permanent revolution, a premise that has been borne out by subsequent historical experience, is that the bourgeoisie is no longer capable of leading or carrying through struggles for basic democratic rights, such as political democracy, agrarian reform, or national liberation. In an age when the proletarian revolution is already on the agenda, the capitalists realize that such democratic conquests will inevitably serve as weapons in the hands of the working class for the seizure of power. They fear the mobilization and independent action of the masses.

In the neocolonial countries of Africa, Asia, and Latin America, the domination of those countries by imperialism is an additional—indeed overwhelming—factor standing in the way of the completion of the democratic tasks of the bourgeois revolution. The bourgeoisies in those countries stand in a dependent and subservient partnership with the imperialists. As much as they might chafe at the tight grip of the imperialist powers, the local capitalists' fear of the power of the workers and peasants is so deep that they are unwilling to challenge any basic imperialist interests. They do not put their army "at the disposal" of the workers and peasants. Ever.

From time to time, the neocolonial bourgeoisies can be forced to take some measures against imperialism as a result of mass pressure, or to improve their conditions within the framework of their subservient relationship. But those cases do not change their overall position as a dependent class. Indeed, the limited nature of the measures they undertake further testifies to it.

It is, of course, possible to argue that *under intense mass pressure* the bourgeois government of Somalia was forced to take action to advance the fight for national liberation of the Somali people even though the Siad Barre regime is in no way progressive. However, neither Flint, Kramer, Levine, Keil, nor Wohlforth demonstrate that to be the case. They make no effort to do so because it cannot be done. There is absolutely no evidence of any upsurge of the Somali masses—in the Ogaden or in Somalia—that could have forced Siad to act, in order to protect his own rule, by placing himself at the head of the Somali national liberation struggle. We will return to this later.

Historical analogies

Flint and Levine invoke some examples from history in an effort to reinforce their argument. Their examples are notable for what they *don't* prove. Never has the Marxist movement decided to support one side in a war because that side cloaked its war aims in the mantle of national liberation of an oppressed people.

The comrades invoke the nineteenth century precedent of Bismarck's efforts to unify Germany, efforts that were supported by Marx and Engels as progressive despite the reactionary manner in which they were carried out. But what does that prove? The one-hundred plus years between Bismarck and Siad Barre span two rather distinct periods. Bismarck was in power when the bourgeoisie was still capable of playing some progressive role. But this period is finished, and has been for some time. The bourgeoisie in the age of capitalism's decline, the age of imperialism, is different. This is a rather basic lesson: no more Bismarcks.

Next, Comrades Flint and Levine invoke the example of the Fourth International's military support to Chiang Kai-shek against the Japanese imperialists. The example itself is well-known and indisputable, but what does it tell us about the Ethiopia-Somalia war? We sided with Chiang Kai-shek in the war against Japan, because the Chinese workers and peasants would be in a stronger position to overturn capitalism, and Chiang Kai-shek, if they could win liberation from Japanese imperialism. *If* we were to agree with Flint and Levine's premise that the Somalian invasion of Ethiopia aided the struggle against imperialism and national oppression, then the example of the Sino-Japanese war would tell us that it would be permissible to side with Siad Barre's army in the war, despite his "unsavory" character. But we *don't* agree with their premise. That's what we are debating. So the example doesn't help at all.

Flint and Levine then recall the case of the struggle of the Kurds against the government of Iraq. In that specific struggle, in which the Kurds were fighting for autonomy, we insisted that the fact that the Kurds received aid from the shah of Iran and from the CIA did not change the character of their struggle as one that deserved our support. The Stalinists tried to smear the Kurds as "proimperialist" because they took arms and money from wherever they could get it.

This proves . . . what? What does it tell us about the Ethiopia-Somalia war? Suppose the specific and concrete situation in Iraq were different. Suppose Iraq were in the midst of a deepgoing social revolution, one that imperialism was desperately trying to weaken. Suppose Syria, with imperialist backing, sent troops to fight alongside the Kurds in the name of Kurdish self-determination? Suppose . . . But why go on? Each case is *concrete*. The fact that we supported the Kurds against Iraq does nothing to tell us which side we should have supported in the Ethiopia-Somalia war. Not a thing.

Next we turn to what Flint and Levine present as the "classic case"—Ireland. "What would we do," they ask, "if the Republic of Ireland sent an 'invading' army northward to force the issue of reunification? Wouldn't we consider this progressive?" (p. 133) We respond by asking, Has it? They themselves are forced to admit that it has not.

But this, perhaps they will say, is a hypothetical example. However, the *actual* case speaks more forcefully than its hypothetical opposite. It is a compelling illustration of why it is wrong to hope that the army of a bourgeois regime can be placed "at the disposal" of an oppressed nationality. End of "classic case."

Flint and Levine continue: "Other examples of the same general [!] phenomenon can easily be produced: the liberation and unification of Germany and Italy in the nineteenth century, of Vietnam in the twentieth, and so on" (p. 134). We have already explored the example of Germany; Italy falls into the same category.

But Vietnam? Since Vietnam is a workers state, we doubt that very many comrades will be convinced that it is an appropriate example.

The very fact that national reunification in Vietnam was achieved in the course of the socialist revolution is itself another confirmation of the basic difference between the nineteenth and twentieth centuries. Where did the Vietnamese capitalist class stand on the questions of reunification and national liberation? The Stalinists of the Vietnamese Communist Party, though they tried mightily, were unable to find a "progressive" Vietnamese capitalist class.

The logic of 'state capitalism'

The use Comrades Flint and Levine make of their example of Vietnam is revealing in another respect. It shows that their errors on the Ethiopia-Somalia war flow to a great extent from their mistaken view of the overall world political situation. They flow from their theory of state capitalism.

In Flint, Kramer, and Levine's conception of the world, there are no workers states. They do not think Vietnam is a workers state, that China is a workers state, that the Soviet Union is a workers state, or that Cuba is a workers state. In their view, they are all examples of "state capitalism."

Their view of the world and of the international relationship of class forces is fundamentally false. They cannot, therefore, distinguish clearly between forces of revolution and forces of counterrevolution.

Because they consider the Soviet Union to be capitalist, they are opposed to defending the Soviet workers state against imperialism. Rather, they see "Soviet imperialism," like American imperialism, seeking to carve out "spheres of influence," sending troops from "capitalist" Cuba to do its bidding.

That is one of the reasons why they so brusquely dismiss Soviet and American involvement in the Horn of Africa as simply a game of power politics in which two equivalent imperialist powers are competing for influence and control.

The state-capitalist line leaves one with no way to orient politically toward the international class struggle. It denies that an important form of the world class struggle is the basic, overall, and irrepressible conflict between imperialism on the one hand and the workers states and the developing colonial revolution on the other. Without such a framework, the international class struggle dissolves into a series of isolated or scarcely connected wars, conflicts, and regional upheavals, in which local actors head the bill and in which imperialism is relegated to a subordinate role.

Flint, Kramer, and Levine's serious misperception of the existing workers states inevitably clouds their vision regarding capitalism itself, especially, as we have seen, concerning the character of the neocolonial bourgeoisies.

If the social gains of the Vietnamese and Cuban revolutions are possible under capitalism, then how can we say that the bourgeoisie, at least in the semicolonial world, is no longer progressive? How can we say the national bourgeoisies are incapable of standing up resolutely to imperialism, of waging successful national liberation struggles, of carrying through sweeping land reforms? If "capitalist" Vietnam can fight off American imperialism and achieve national reunification, then why can't the capitalist Somalian regime? If "bourgeois" Vietnam can overthrow Pol Pot and improve the conditions for advancing the class struggle in Kampuchea, why can't bourgeois Somalia overthrow Mengistu and do the same? Perhaps the Somalian bourgeoisie is progressive after all. That is the clear direction in which Flint, Kramer, and Levine's logic is pointed, and they have not hesitated to follow it.

We ask Flint, Kramer, and Levine: Was Trotsky wrong when he maintained that the national bourgeoisie, in the epoch of imperialist domination, was unable to carry through the unfinished tasks of the bourgeois-democratic revolution? Was he wrong when he argued that only the working class could lead the struggle for the completion of those tasks, and would have to do so against the bourgeoisie?

In response to the view that Cuba is state capitalist, we asked, in "In Defense of the Cuban Revolution: National Committee Majority Report" (p. 39):

> If we say that Cuba is capitalist, then we have to say that something new has appeared in the world. A new kind of progressive capitalist class has developed. A variety of capitalism has emerged that is superior, at least from the standpoint of the Cuban workers and peasants, to any capitalism they have ever known. . . .
>
> But if Cuban *capitalism* can carry through a radical land reform, can achieve national independence from American imperialism, can advance the level of human dignity—if Cuban *capitalism* can do all that, then what happens to the theory of the permanent revolution?

We have seen exactly what happens to the theory of the permanent revolution in Flint and Levine's discussion article. It gets left behind. Of what use is there for it when the invasion launched by the capitalist regime of Somalia "constituted an armed struggle of the Somali people" and when the regime's army was "at the disposal of the Somali nation"?

Mogadishu and the Ogaden

Flint and Levine accuse the party majority of making a "false dichotomy" by pointing to the differences between the Somalian regime and the struggles of the Somalis in the Ogaden.

They state that one of the purposes of the party's position is "to impose a rigid demarcation between the Somali national struggle in the Ogaden and the invasion of the Ogaden territory by the army of the Somalian state. Apparently, the only legitimate form of national struggle in the Ogaden would be one conducted solely by residents of the Ogaden. Presumably the same yardstick applies to national struggles by the Somalis imprisoned in Kenya and Djibouti. Only indigenously Kenyan-Somali or Djibouti-Somali movements can be considered legitimate national struggles worthy of our support" (p. 132–33).

Two things are lumped together in this passage. We do, as we have already pointed out, recognize the dichotomy between the Somalian *regime* and the national struggles of the oppressed Somali masses. It is a class dichotomy. No, we do not think "the only legitimate form of national struggle in the Ogaden would be one conducted solely by residents of the Ogaden." We have no fixation about borders, nor do we accept, as Flint and Levine claim, "the borders imposed on the oppressed as the proper basis for judging whether their struggle is legitimate or illegitimate." In the context of a real struggle for Somali liberation Somalis on both sides of the border would of course try to coordinate their struggles and aid each other against their oppressors.

Nevertheless, we cannot ignore the existence of different states. Whatever their artificiality, borders do affect the tempos and direction of national struggles. They determine, first of all, *who* the particular struggles are directed against. The immediate oppressor of the Somalis in the Ogaden is the Ethiopian state. That of the Somalis in Kenya is the Kenyan state. That of the Somalis in Djibouti is the Djibouti state. *And that of the Somalis in Somalia is the Somalian bourgeois state.* Flint, Levine, Kramer, Wohlforth, and Keil seem to forget that the citizens of Somalia are themselves nationally oppressed—by imperialism via the intermediary of the neocolonial Somalian state, which helps to perpetuate that oppression. Imperialism is, in fact, the main national oppressor of *all* the peoples in the Horn of Africa, as in the rest of the colonial and semicolonial world. That means that in whatever state they find themselves, the Somalis, in order to truly and consistently fight against national oppression, must confront not only their immediate oppressors, but imperialism as well.

That the Somalian regime has decidedly not done. Quite the opposite.

Since its foundation in 1960, the Somalian capitalist regime has been a relatively loyal dependent of the imperialist powers. Though it claims to follow "scientific socialism" and has in the past had trade and other ties with the Soviet Union, the Somalian state has always remained under imperialist domination. To preserve capitalist rule from any working class threat, it has not hesitated to imprison Marxists. It has left one of the two biggest sectors of the Somalian economy, the cultivation of bananas, under the ownership of Italian capital (southern Somalia used to be a direct Italian colony). The other main sector, livestock husbandry, is still controlled by private merchants, who sell the cattle on the world capitalist market. Despite repeated pleas by the regime in Mogadishu for closer ties with the United States, Washington was largely uninterested for a number of years, that is, as long as its more valuable ally, Selassie, was still in power next door. Since the Ethiopian revolution, American imperialism's interest in using the Somalian regime as a more direct instrument against the struggles of the oppressed masses in the region has risen considerably.

Has the Somalian regime's record on behalf of Somalis elsewhere been any better than its record within Somalia? Since Flint and Levine maintain that the Somalian regime sent its army into Ethiopia to "liberate" the Somalis there, let us look at its past role in that regard.

Since the present Somalian state was formed in 1960 through the merger of the former British- and Italian-ruled Somalilands, it has demagogically claimed to favor the establishment of a "Greater Somalia," incorporating the Somali-inhabited areas of Ethiopia, Kenya, and Djibouti. Yet like its more recent claims that its policies are "scientific socialist," this was largely rhetoric, designed to win some popularity. But it has consistently shown its deep fear of a real struggle *by the masses* of Somalis themselves to attain that objective. The reason is not hard to fathom, since such a struggle would inevitably challenge the survival of the Somalian capitalist state.

In the early 1960s, there was a rise in Somali nationalist activity in Ethiopia, with the Somali guerrillas receiving modest amounts of assistance from the Somalian regime. In 1963, Emperor Haile Selassie sent troops and planes against the rebels, and initiated a brief war against Somalia. The rebellion was crushed, and the border war convinced the Somalian authorities that the stability of their regime could be best preserved by improving ties with Selassie and avoiding similar clashes in the future. It moved in a more concerted fashion than before to bring the leadership of the Somali struggle in the Ogaden under its firm control.

Under the circumstances in which they found themselves, the Somalis in the Ogaden had little choice but to accept aid from wherever it was offered, and they were justified in doing so. But the Somalian regime took advantage of that dependency by attaching political strings to its assistance. It also moved to co-opt the petty-bourgeois leaders of the Somali movement, partly by incorporating some of them directly into its army, making them subject to the orders of the Somalian military command.

This increased control over the movement in the Ogaden was used by the Somalian regime to dampen the struggle there. In 1967, the Somalian regime of Prime Minister Mohammad Ibrahim Egal reached a diplomatic understanding with both the Ethiopian and Kenyan regimes that effectively ended the guerrilla actions of the Somalis in those countries.

The Somalian regime at the same time sought to use its control over the guerrillas in the Ogaden as a diplomatic bargaining chip in its dealings with Selassie and as a ploy to elicit greater assistance from the imperialists. In July 1968, for instance, Somalian President Abdirashid Shermarke told U.S. Ambassador Raymond L. Thurston that keeping the Somali guerrillas quiet required money. He said that "it costs from 200 to 800 shillings a month to pay off the liberation fighters. Sultans cost from 1500 to 2000 shillings a month" (*Horn of Africa*, April–June 1978, p. 14. A shilling was worth about US$0.14 at that time).

In October 1969, the Egal regime was ousted by the Somalian army under Gen. Mohammed Siad Barre. For purposes of public consumption, Siad slightly escalated the rhetoric about Somali national liberation and unification. But this was a complete smokescreen. According to I. M. Lewis, "Contrary to what might have been expected of a military government, the new regime not only continued to follow Egal's conciliatory path in seeking to build stronger and more effective links with both Ethiopia and Kenya, but has displayed little evidence of adopting a more militant stance on the issue of Somali unification. . . . Indeed, it seems most significant that of the many accusations made against Korshell [a vice-president arrested by Siad in 1970], one of the most damning was that he was allegedly intriguing to create trouble with the Ethiopians—open evidence of General Siad's private nightmare. . . ." (I. M. Lewis, "The Nation, State, and Politics in Somalia," in David R. Smock and Kwamena Bentsi-Enchill [eds], *The Search for National Integration in Africa* [New York: The Free Press, 1975], pp. 301–02.)

Until Selassie's overthrow in 1974, the Somalian regime's relations with the emperor remained cordial and the struggle in the Ogaden was kept on ice. Not surprisingly, however, the powerful revolution that toppled the monarchy, destroyed the Ethiopian feudal landholding class and set Ethiopia's workers, peasants, and oppressed nationalities into motion shocked the Somalian authorities. They worried about the impact of that revolution within Somalia itself. Their relations with the Ethiopians turned markedly hostile. The issue of the Ogaden Somalis was only the most convenient public excuse. The regime's fear of the Ethiopian revolution was shown by Siad's visit to Washington in October 1974, just after Selassie's overthrow. In a bid to solidify ties with American imperialism, he offered refueling and supply facilities for American naval vessels, an offer that was repeated in July 1975 (*New York Times*, July 8, 1975).

Washington turned down Siad's offers. As we have already seen, the U.S. was more interested at that time in trying to transform the Dergue into a stable, pro-American entity that could put the reins on the Ethiopian revolution. It was only after the failure of that attempt had become clear that the American imperialists turned more seriously toward the Somalian regime as an instrument for its counterrevolutionary policies.

As the Somalian regime's hostility to the Ethiopian revolution escalated, it began preparations to reactivate the guerrilla forces in the Ogaden. Precisely when the original Western Somali liberation Front (WSLF) was formed is unclear, since different officials have given different years, although it appears to have been sometime in the 1960s. In any case, it was extensively reorganized during a conference in January 1976, with the full backing of the Somalian regime.

For the first time, the WSLF extended its territorial claims to cover all of the four Ethiopian provinces of Hararge, Bale, Arussi, and Sidamo, an area with a total population of 7.4 million people, of whom only about 1.4 million are Somalis (the bulk are Oromos and Sidamos).

A second guerrilla wing, the Somali Abo Liberation Front (SALF), was formed at this conference as a political cover for the expanded territorial claims of the WSLF and the Somalian regime. In what must have come as something of a surprise to most Oromos, the participants in the conference proclaimed that they were not Oromos after all, but—Somalis! Magically, overnight, the Somali population in Ethiopia was expanded severalfold, and now lived in a vast territory extending to within fifty miles of the Ethiopian capital of Addis Ababa. These newly christened "Somalis" were assured that the SALF would help "liberate" them. From all the available evidence, however, the SALF never amounted to much more than a paper organization, a transparent cover for the Somalian regime's counterrevolutionary attacks on the Ethiopian revolution.

As for the WSLF itself, the Somalian regime has admitted that a portion of its cadres are actually regular Somalian troops. That indicates that the WSLF, to a great extent, had been transformed into a direct auxiliary force of the Somalian army. At the same time, however, we can assume that it at least partially continued to reflect the aspirations of the Somalis in the Ogaden for an end to their national oppression.

The Ogaden and beyond

Comrades Flint and Levine affirm that the Somalian invasion "received the wholehearted support of the Somali workers and peasants within Somalia proper as well as in the Ogaden" (p. 137). They also claim that we implied that the invasion had "no support from the Ogaden's Somali population" (p. 134).

The last point is false. Simply because we raise questions about the reports in the capitalist press about the supposed *unanimity* of Somali support for the invasion, they think we are trying to prove the opposite extreme.

First, let us concede, for the sake of argument, that *all* the news reports of Somali support for the invasion were true. Would that change our position on the war? No, it would not. We did not assess the character of the war on the basis of the particular level of consciousness of the Somali population at the moment. Just because many of the Somali nomads might have believed they were being "liberated" wouldn't necessarily make it so.

Most Blacks in the United States have many illusions in capitalist politicians, especially Black Democrats, and even back some of them with much enthusiasm. That does not change our attitude toward these politicians one iota. It simply means we have to patiently work to expose them and to explain to workers, Black and white, why they should not give any Democrat support.

In Ethiopia and Somalia, revolutionists would do the same thing: while continuing to support any actions the Somali masses may take against their national oppression or class exploitation, explain to them why the Somalian invasion was not in their class *or national* interests, since a defeat of the Ethiopian revolution and a victory for imperialism would have been a major setback for all peoples struggling for their emancipation.

That being said, let us throw in a note of caution concerning the "wholehearted support the Somali workers and peasants" were said to give to the invasion.

The reports in the capitalist press of mass support among the Ogaden Somalis should be evaluated critically, not swallowed whole. To begin with, there were only a handful of direct eyewitness reports from the Ogaden, since the Somalian authorities generally barred reporters from visiting the war zones (for obvious reasons, since they were trying to hide the direct and massive involvement of regular Somalian troops). The reporters were taken around by officials of the WSLF, and were presumably shown what the WSLF wanted them to see. The enthusiastic tone of the reports also makes one somewhat suspicious, since the capitalist press rarely tries to portray national liberation struggles with favor.

There are also indications of Somali non-support for the invasion. Somali workers in Diredawa (the only significant proletarianized section of the Somali population in Ethiopia) fled *from* the Somalian invasion. Flint and Levine try to dispute that by saying that those Somalis were simply getting out of the way of Somalian artillery shells. That may be, but the fact remains that they fled *in the direction* of the Ethiopian forces, not toward the Somali-held regions, as did other Somali refugees. A further aspect of the situation in Diredawa was that the Ethiopian People's Revolutionary Party (EPRP) had a strong base among the Oromo and Somali workers of the city. The EPRP, which called for the overthrow of the Dergue and also supported the right to self-determination of the oppressed nationalities (including their secession if they so choose), *opposed* the Somalian invasion as a reactionary attack against the revolution. It is quite likely that the EPRP's position was supported by at least some of the Somali workers, who were among the most radicalized of all Somalis in Ethiopia.

The situation in the Ogaden following the war also provides some evidence of a political differentiation among Somalis. After discussions with WSLF leaders, correspondent Jean-Claude Pomonti reported from Mogadishu in October 1978 that "the WSLF itself is divided. Some of its military leaders have gone over to the enemy." He went on to quote a WSLF representative: "We have carried out a campaign among our people to explain to them that President Barre could not remain in the Ogaden to fight at our side. Of course, the Ethiopians are profiting from this. They are playing on tribal ties. They are saying to the Somali population: 'The Somalians abandoned you. Come with us. It's your land. You can govern yourselves.' But the people do not believe them. Not more than half are collaborating with the Ethiopians." (*Le Monde*, October 22–23, 1978.)

"Not more than half"! A far cry from the picture painted at the time of the war. And this representative of the WSLF does not ascribe their "collaboration" to physical intimidation (though we might assume there was at least a little), but to political persuasion.

Flint and Levine's belief in the progressive character of the Somalian invasion also leads them into the unenviable position of trying to justify the Somalian army's attacks beyond the Ogaden against the non-Somali peoples of Ethiopia, in particular the Oromo and Sidamo peasants of Bale, Arussi, and Sidamo provinces.

Those attacks indicate the fraudulent nature of the claims by the Somalian regime and the WSLF that their purpose was to "liberate" the oppressed Somalis. It is further evidence of the invasion's true goal, especially since these non-Somali areas were among the strongest bastions of the Ethiopian revolution.

If the aim of the Somali forces was really national liberation, why did they drive deep into the Oromo and Sidamo areas, forcing peasants to flee the land they had just seized from the old landlords a few years before? Flint and Levine attempt to brush this aside by referring to the needs of military strategy. But this simply ignores the fact that *it was the publicly stated aim of the WSLF that those Oromo and Sidamo areas be annexed to Somalia*, not just temporarily occupied. As we have seen, the Oromos were redefined as Somalis for this purpose.

Flint and Levine go further, however. They cite the WSLF's supposed alliance with three other "national liberation" groups, the Afar Liberation Front, the Oromo Liberation Front, and the Somali Abo Liberation Front, then go on to proclaim, "In view of this multinational alliance, one would *assume* that the insurgent forces would set out to liberate not merely Somali territory but the territory of their allies as well" (p. 138, emphasis in original). So now the progressive Somalian army is "at the disposal" not only of the Somali masses but other oppressed peoples in Ethiopia as well. What a truly amazing capitalist regime Siad Barre is head of!

The Afar Liberation Front is a *rightist* group led by dispossessed landlords. The Somali Abo Liberation Front was created at the January 1976 conference of the WSLF, and seems to be little more than a propaganda cover for the WSLF's claims to Bale, Sidamo, and Arussi provinces. The Oromo Liberation Front is a rather obscure outfit. Perhaps it really exists, perhaps it doesn't. But judging from the extent of information on it, it certainly hasn't done much to draw anybody's attention. The WSLF claimed at the time of the war that it was in alliance with it, although at the January 1976 conference a WSLF leader emphatically denied any connection with the Oromo National Liberation Front, which may or may not be the same group.

In any case, it would be rather risky to "assume" anything from such alliances, let alone that the Somalian army and the WSLF "would set out to liberate not merely Somali territory but the territory of their allies as well."

Why Siad Barre went to war

As Comrades Flint and Levine portray it, the war that broke out in mid-1977 was a direct continuation of the Ethiopian revolution and of the struggles of the Somalis for their national liberation and unification.

But as in most of their discussion article, their arguments on this point are quite schematic. They make little attempt, in the concrete, to try to show *how* the war reflected the ongoing mass struggles. If the Somalian invasion was, indeed, preceded by a mass upsurge of the Somali people, why don't they try to show how that upsurge built up to it? The fact is that there was very little that actually happened before 1977, either in the Ogaden or in Somalia, that they could point to, certainly nothing massive enough to compel Siad Barre to go to war against his militarily superior neighbor.

So Flint and Levine are reduced to deducing—from their original premise—that an upsurge in the Somali national struggle in the Ogaden *must* have taken place. As "documentation," they cite an article in *Intercontinental Press/Inprecor* quoting a leader of the WSLF claiming that they had been "inspired" by the downfall of Selassie. But the quotation is not a solid foundation for their case. What else would a leader of the WSLF, or an official of the Somalian regime, say? Would they dare tell the truth, that the real objects of their attack were the social gains of the Ethiopian revolution? For instance, the rightist guerrilla forces now fighting in Afghanistan against the revolution in that country claim as their inspiration . . . the Iranian revolution! Would Flint and Levine believe them for a minute? Maybe, but no one else would.

All the available evidence indicates that it was a conscious, coldblooded decision by the Somalian regime to start the war. Flint and Levine might agree with that. What is at dispute, however, is why, and to what purpose. If, as we have demonstrated, the Somalian regime did not initiate the war to advance the Somali national liberation struggle, the question is posed: Why did it start the war? Let us now turn to the answer the facts provide.

By offering Washington military facilities in Somalia in 1974 and again in 1975, the Somalian regime had already signalled its growing concern over the deepening of the Ethiopian revolution and its willingness to serve imperialism's counterrevolutionary aims. The failure of other maneuvers against Ethiopia convinced Washington by early 1977 to play the Somalian card—weak as it was—since any open American military move was out of the question due to antiwar sentiment at home.

As early as February 14, 1977, Andrew Young publicly stated that the White House should foster closer ties with the Siad regime.

Just one week later, some 1,500 Somalian troops, supported by tanks, made an initial thrust into Ethiopia.

In early April, Carter ordered his close aides to "get Somalia to be our friend" (Fred Halliday, "US Policy in the Horn," in *Review of African Political Economy*, September-December 1977, p. 20).

By May, some 3,000 to 6,000 well-organized and well-armed Somali troops, ostensibly under the flag of the WSLF, began major operations against the Ethiopian forces. The WSLF commander claimed May 25 that they were active in all of the four provinces claimed by the WSLF and Somalian regime. In June, both the Ethiopian regime and WSLF representatives were reporting major clashes. The American overtures to the Siad regime directly preceded the escalation of the Somalian drive into Ethiopia. Is it conceivable they had nothing to do with each other?

The clearest proof of American backing of the Somalian invasion came in mid-June. According to a report by Arnaud de Borchgrave in the September 26, 1977, *Newsweek*, Kevin Cahill, an American doctor with State Department connections, played a major role as intermediary:

> Cahill, who is no stranger to the world of secret diplomacy, flew to Mogadishu in mid-June [1977] after conferring with Matthew Nimetz, the top trouble-shooter for Secretary of State Cyrus Vance and one of his former law partners. Cahill told Siad Barre that he had a message from "the very top" of the U.S. Government. Washington was "not averse to further guerrilla pressure in the Ogaden," he said, and was now prepared to "consider sympathetically Somalia's legitimate defense needs." In return, the United States wanted Somalia to drop its territorial claims to parts of northern Kenya and to the former French colony of Djibouti [but note, not to Ethiopian territory, including its large non-Somali majority].
>
> Siad Barre immediately cabled his son-in-law, Dr. Abdullahi Addou, the Somali ambassador in Washington. Addou conferred with Carter twice and assured Siad Barre that the Cahill message was legitimate. A few days later, Vance went on record with the offer of arms aid, and President Carter himself declared that he wanted to "aggressively challenge, in a peaceful way, of course, the Soviet Union and others for influence" in "crucial" areas like Somalia.
>
> At the same time, Siad Barre also made a secret visit to Saudi Arabia where officials advised him they had been in contact with Washington and were ready to ship French and British weaponry to Somalia immediately. Six other nations also weighed in with offers of arms. By mid-July, Siad Barre felt absolutely confident he could supply his armies without Soviet help, and he kicked off the Ogaden offensive.

Is this not enough to indicate what real American policy toward the war was?

After Cahill's message to Siad was exposed by de Borchgrave, the White House lamely tried to cover up by claiming that Siad had "misinterpreted" what was meant. Anyone gullible enough to believe that is welcome to.

Cahill himself later explained that Siad was enthusiastic about the prospect of more American involvement, stating that the general had a "sincere desire for a greater American presence." Do Flint and Levine think it is possible not only for a neocolonial regime to lead a national liberation struggle, but that it can do so at the same time that it is forging a closer alliance with American imperialism?

Following the secret contacts between Carter and Siad, Secretary of State Vance for the first time openly indicated, in a July 4 speech, that American aid to Siad would be made available. Siad correctly took this as further confirmation of American backing for his military operations in the Ogaden.

By mid-July, 1977, the regular Somalian army pushed into Ethiopia in force, including the deployment of tanks, armored cars, MIG jet fighters, and thousands of troops.

On July 26, it was reported that "Carter has discussed Somalia, Ethiopia and the international maneuverings around them with Egyptian President Anwar Sadat, Saudi Arabian Crown Prince Fahd, and European leaders at the London summit" (*Washington Post*, July 26, 1977). That same day, the State Department made its official offer to supply arms to the Somalian regime.

This sequence of events from February through July tells us several things about how the war started:

(1) The American imperialists knew about the Somalian thrusts into the Ogaden weeks, and perhaps several months, *before* their public arms offer.

(2) The White House approved of the incursions, and encouraged the Somalian forces to drive deeper into Ethiopia by telling Siad that it was "not averse to further guerrilla pressure in the Ogaden."

(3) The Somalian regime launched its full-scale invasion, which appears to have begun around mid-July, under the prodding of the imperialists and with the full expectation that it would receive imperialist assistance for the invasion. According to de Borchgrave, "The Somalis claim that they began their all-out invasion of Ethiopia's Ogaden

region last July because of the prospect of U.S. arms aid—and because they had received a secret U.S. message which they interpreted as a go-ahead to conquer the area" (*Newsweek*, September 26, 1977).

Since we know that American imperialism is not in favor of the Somali people winning real national liberation, and since we know that it is opposed to the Ethiopian revolution and has attacked it in the past, the only rational conclusion we can draw from the facts is that the imperialists encouraged the Somalian invasion as a way to attack the Ethiopian revolution.

Our characterization of the war is not based on the purely "subjective" views of Carter, Siad Barre, or the WSLF leaders, as Flint and Levine claim. It is based on the *objective* reality of the class forces in motion. The subjective intentions of the main participants are merely an indication of that.

Still, against all the evidence, Flint and Levine proclaim that "at no time did the U.S. encourage or anticipate the kind of full-scale invasion of the Ogaden which Siad Barre actually launched" (p. 145). The invasion, they insist, "flew directly in the face of the key principles of U.S. policy in the Horn and, indeed, in Africa as a whole." (We will come back later to these "key principles.") They also state that "there is nothing here [in the Ethiopia pamphlet] to prove that the actual escalation of the fighting in the Ogaden occurred on the orders or under the control of U.S. imperialism" (p. 142).

They support this conclusion only by neglecting to mention almost everything that happened before July. They simply leave out entirely one of the key indicators of Washington's position on the war, Cahill's message to Siad from Carter, cited in the pamphlet on page 30.

Flint and Levine do note rather vaguely that "in early 1977, the U.S. government offered economic and military assistance to Mogadishu, hoping to bring the latter within its orbit." But is that all it was after? Then why did Carter, through Cahill, ask Siad to escalate his involvement in the Ogaden?

Flint and Levine's blind spot on the Cahill affair is even more interesting since in their apparently thorough perusal of past articles on the war they overlooked the details of the U.S. encouragement, which we reported in the October 3, 1977, *IP/I*. Despite our own initially incorrect position on the war, we did not close our eyes to such facts. The article itself was prophetically entitled, "Carter Stoking Fires in Horn of Africa?"

Before moving on, let us take up Flint and Levine's criteria that it is necessary for us to prove that the Somalian invasion was "under the control of U.S. imperialism" or that "U.S. or U.S.-allied troops or military advisers" had to be directly involved for us to oppose the invasion.

It is precisely because of the weakening of the ability of the U.S. to intervene openly against the colonial revolution, especially the heightened sensitivity of the American working class to foreign military actions, that American imperialism tries to accomplish its objectives in a less open way. Peking's invasion of Vietnam is a recent example. The fact that Washington doesn't exercise direct or open control over a military operation, or that it takes a public stance of "neutrality" or even "opposition" doesn't change anything. It is necessary to look behind the public lies to determine the real forces at work. We will see in a few minutes how dangerous it is to take Carter's "plausible denials" of U.S. involvement in the Ethiopia-Somalia war for good coin.

'Facts' and facts

In Flint and Levine's attempts to outline American policy toward the Ethiopia-Somali war, they list sixteen points, which they label "facts" (see pp. 143–45). The general impression that is given by them is that Washington opposed the Somalian invasion of Ethiopia and exerted pressure on the Somalians to withdraw.

These sixteen "facts" consist largely of formal statements by American officials, reports from the capitalist press trying to interpret official policy, and newspaper editorial statements. We'll examine each of them.

The first four "facts" can be taken together.

"Fact" #1: A news report that the State Department, in August 1977, had told a Somalian military aid mission that no U.S. arms could be supplied while the war continued.

"Fact" #2: A public announcement by the State Department on September 1, 1977, withdrawing the earlier offer to openly sell arms to the Somalian

regime. "We have decided that providing arms at this time would add fuel to a fire we are more interested in putting out," a U.S. government official said.

"Fact" #3: A report that Washington had forbidden its allies to transfer U.S. arms to Somalia.

"Fact" #4: A long quote from an article in the October 2, 1977, *New York Times* claiming that the public arms offer had been withdrawn *after* Washington "suspected" that Somalian troops had invaded the Ogaden.

Flint and Levine interpret Washington's withdrawal, in September 1977, of its public offer to provide arms to the Somali regime as a shift in policy, made once the fact that Somalia had invaded the Ogaden became known to Washington. But as we have already seen, Washington did not just "suspect" that Somalian troops were in Ethiopia at the time the offer was made. It *knew*. Cahill had told Siad back in June that Carter favored *further* activity in the Ogaden.

Then why was the offer publicly withdrawn? Simple. For the same reason Washington could not intervene openly itself. The antiwar sentiment in the U.S. would not allow it. So for political reasons Washington could not afford to be seen to be aiding the aggressors in the war. It backed off *publicly* and officially took its distance from the invasion, while at the same time *continuing to encourage it from behind the scenes*. We will see how it did so shortly.

The reason the State Department official gave for withdrawing the arms offer is pure rhetoric. If there is one lesson we have learned about how the U.S. ruling class conducts its foreign policy, it is that it lies through its teeth. If we were to believe everything the rulers said about their aims, our ability to analyze conflicts involving American imperialism would be seriously impaired, to say the least.

Do Comrades Flint and Levine forget that Washington publicly stated it had nothing to do with the South African and Zaïrian invasion of Angola? Haven't the American imperialists claimed to be "neutral" in the fighting in Indochina? Don't they pretend to be "benevolent mediators" in Zimbabwe?

The fact is that Washington often has little choice but to lie, to cover up its true aims. The widespread antiwar sentiment in the United States forces it to cloak its attempts at foreign aggression under the most incredible verbiage. More than ever, it has been compelled to carry out its interventions in as indirect a manner as possible, covertly through the CIA and other channels, or through third parties and "proxies." That sometimes makes U.S. intervention less apparent and less effective than the direct dispatch of American troops, but it makes the interventions no less real.

We also have to look carefully at how the capitalist press reports things, especially concerning the government's policy aims. It, too, lies. It is crucial to have a clear political framework that we can use to judge what is true and what is not.

In trying to assess the American role in any given conflict, we cannot confine ourselves to what Washington or the bourgeois press says on the matter. We must look at what Washington *does* in practice. That's how we have approached the U.S. intervention in the Horn of Africa.

Comrades Flint and Levine, for all their emphasis on official policy statements, also make an error as to what the White House's diplomatic stance actually was. They claim that following the withdrawal of the open arms offer, Washington "demanded that the invasion be terminated" (p. 143). Where did they get that idea? It is not true. The thrust of its diplomatic position was to call for negotiations. That is, while the Somalian army was in occupation of much of eastern Ethiopia, most of which was non-Somali, Washington did not press for a Somalian withdrawal, but asked "both sides" to negotiate to "resolve" the dispute. In whose favor? Later, when the Ethiopians began to receive increased Cuban assistance, Carter added the stipulation that Moscow and Havana should stop "interfering" in Ethiopia. The White House maintained this stance as late as January 12, 1978, when Carter said at a press conference, "Our hope is that the Somalis might call publicly for negotiations to begin immediately to resolve the Ogaden dispute." It was only a month later—*when the Somalians were already being defeated on the battlefield*—that the White House, in an obvious move to cover its tracks, finally called for the Somali army to withdraw—before the Cubans wiped them out.

The hand behind the invasion

How do Marxists interpret the kind of "facts" that Flint and Levine have cited? By looking at what the imperialists actually did during the course of the war.

Was the Somalian regime as isolated internationally as Flint and Levine would have us believe? Did it get only "offers" and "promises" of backing for its war? Did the U.S. really try to block its allies from shipping arms to Mogadishu?

While it is possible that the Somalian regime got more assistance than has to date been revealed, enough has already been reported to paint a convincing picture of the direct and indirect imperialist backing to the Somalian invasion *while it was in progress.*

In July 1977, at the same time that Carter was publicly offering arms to the Somalian regime,

> France, which has historic colonial interests in the area and has just given independence to its port enclave of Djibouti, is reported to have agreed to provide military equipment to Somalia. Britain, which once was the colonial ruler of much of Somalia, has agreed in principle to supply equipment, informed sources said.
>
> An Islamic country with a potentially strategic location on the Indian Ocean and the Gulf of Aden, Somalia is of special interest to Saudi Arabia. The Saudi leadership, which met Somali President Siad Barre most recently July 13, is reported ready to finance Somali arms purchases from European countries. *Some new arms from Arab sources are already being received.* [*Washington Post*, July 26, 1977. Emphasis added.]

Reporting from Mogadishu, the capital of Somalia, correspondent David Lamb revealed in mid-October, at the height of the Somalian invasion of Ethiopia:

> Every day a Boeing 707 jet freighter lands here on a mystery flight from the Middle East, its cargo hold laden with supplies for Somalia's war against Ethiopia.
>
> The plane bears no markings to identify it by owner or country of origin. A seal on the tail has been covered with yellow paint. The plane stays only long enough to unload its cargo and within hours is thundering off for home, wherever that may be.
>
> There is much speculation in Mogadishu about the plane. Some say it is U.S. and carried arms paid for by the CIA. Others say it is from Syria or Saudi Arabia. The best bet, according to Western intelligence sources, is that it comes from Iraq. [*Los Angeles Times*, October 17, 1977.]

"Fact" #5: An editorial in the November 18, 1977, *New York Times* urging "an American diplomatic approach to persuade Somalia to pull back from its dangerous adventure...."

If it is risky to accept, uncritically, news stories in the *New York Times* as fact, it is doubly dangerous to present editorials as fact.

Sometimes editorials in the *New York Times* can provide a clue to the thinking of a section of the ruling class. Sometimes they are examples of obfuscation. In any case, we cannot assume they reflect actual government policy. Again, we have to look at them in the context of American imperialism's real aims. In this case, the *Times* editors did not even pretend to be stating government policy. They were expressing a certain unease among ruling circles over the risks involved in continuing the Somalian invasion, especially in light of the possibility of an increasing role by Cuba's revolutionary army.

"Fact" #6: "As the Somalian invasion deepened, the Carter administration not only barred assistance to it but also maintained economic support to Ethiopia and made overtures for a resumption of closer U.S.-Ethiopian ties." We have already seen why the first part of the sentence is inaccurate. The second part, while true, doesn't show what the authors intend at all. The fact that, while Ethiopia was under attack, the U.S. made overtures to the Dergue does not indicate the U.S. was opposed to the Somalian invasion. During the height of the American-backed invasion by South African troops into Angola in 1975, for instance, the American imperialists made similar overtures to the MPLA as a probe to see if it was ready yet to make any concessions. And significant economic ties were maintained between the MPLA and Gulf Oil for a number of months during the war.

"Fact" #7: Public denunciations by Somalian officials of the U.S. withdrawal of the open arms offer.

The Siad regime was no doubt disappointed that Washington chose not to follow through on its promises to openly ally with it. The South African regime, it should be recalled, also condemned Washington for "betraying" it by not coming across with greater *public* assistance.

The Somalians, for political reasons, hoped for a more *open* American commitment to the invasion. But they were mollified to an extent by the continued covert assistance they were receiving.

By late November 1977, the pro-U.S. regime in Saudi Arabia had already provided Siad with about $300 million (*Economist*, December 3, 1977). That was the most substantial contribution to the Somalian invasion from a single source up to that time. Were the Saudis acting on their own? Or did they get U.S. approval? Was that one of the things discussed when Carter met with Prince Fahd earlier in the year?

Toward the end of 1977, at least $7 million worth of weapons was flown into Somalia *directly* by Washington in a covert CIA operation (Halliday, "U.S. Policy in the Horn," p. 21).

Although the official U.S. posture was that Washington's allies had not been given an official okay to transfer arms to Somalia (an approach known as "deniability"), the American imperialists knew about such shipments.

> U.S. officials acknowledge privately that Iran and Saudi Arabia are financing or otherwise helping to supply non-American arms to Somalia, purchased on the world market or obtained from other Middle Eastern nations.
>
> "I am afraid I am going to have to dodge that question," State Department spokesman John Trattner said yesterday, when asked at a formal briefing if Saudi or Iranian weapons are going to Somalia.
>
> Trattner said he could not go into details of the talks that President Carter had about the Ethiopia-Somali conflict in his recent stops in Iran and Saudi Arabia.
>
> "It's no secret," said the spokesman, "that the Iranians and Saudis are very concerned about the extent of Soviet involvement in Ethiopia, as we are." [*Washington Post*, January 14, 1978.]

Trattner failed to note that the arms aid to the Somalian regime began well before the big increase in Soviet assistance to the Ethiopian regime, or the initial arrivals of Cuban troops, in mid-to-late December 1977.

"Fact" #8; In January 1978, the State Department again turned down a Somalian request for open arms aid, and again gave as its reason: "We will not contribute to a conflict by pouring gasoline on it."

The gasoline, as we have seen, had already been poured.

"Fact" #9: A public statement in January 1978 by the American, British, French, West German, and Italian governments pledging to support an Organization of African Unity effort to negotiate an end to the war.

The statement by these five imperialist governments did not call for a Somalian withdrawal. It was a continuation of Washington's smokescreen of calling for negotiations. Meanwhile, the arms continued to flow.

In January, the German government publicly admitted that it had extended credits to the Somalian regime worth about $12 million (*Der Spiegel*, February 13, 1978).

In early February, Sadat of Egypt revealed that he had already provided $30 million worth of arms to the Somalian regime (*Christian Science Monitor*, February 8, 1978).

Around the same time, it was reported:

> In a further escalation of the arms buildup in the war-torn Horn of Africa, Somalia has begun receiving French-built tanks from a third country, believed to be Saudi Arabia, according to western diplomatic sources. . . .
>
> Western sources reported that about 60 AMX tanks recently arrived in Somalia but did not say from which country the French-built equipment had come. [*Washington Post*, February 8, 1978.]

Also in early February, Washington dispatched two warships to the Red Sea as a direct warning to the Ethiopians and the Cuban troops who were helping them.

The arms shipments to Somalia continued:

> Despite the government's denials, Somalia is secretly getting major arms shipments from the Middle East, including West German tanks and Soviet and U.S. missiles, diplomatic sources in Mogadishu said yesterday [February 16].
>
> Unlike previous shipments, the arms are highly sophisticated and are giving the Somalis confidence that they can contain Ethiopia's offensive in the Ogaden desert.
>
> The sources said the arms include at least 60 West German tanks, hundreds of Soviet-made RPG7 anti-tank missiles, and American, British and West German surface-to-air missiles.
>
> One source said at least 2,000 air defense missiles have reached the Somalis, whose own air force has been grounded since October by the superiority of the Ethiopians—a major factor in Ethiopia's recent successes.
>
> The sources said the shipments began two weeks ago on major scale, with some 30 cargo ships unloading at Somali ports. . . .
>
> In an effort to keep the supply operation secret, the Somalis directed most of the cargo ships to Mecra, 80 miles south of Mogadishu. The arms have so overwhelmed the port of Mecra that Somali authorities were forced to send 14 arms ships to the deep water port at Mogadishu, where longshoremen labor though the night to remove the cargo in secrecy. [New York *Trib*, February 17, 1978, based on wire dispatches.]

Arnaud de Borchgrave provided further details of the international network that had been set up to supply the Somalian army:

> Somalia, I have learned, has enlisted a European consortium to supply it with arms and pilots. Siad Barre ordered his ambassador in Paris to seek help from France, and secret meetings were held in London, Paris, Rome and Madrid. Soon, 43 Cobra helicopter gunships were ordered from a Bell Augusta plant in Italy for shipment to Somalia via Madrid. The deal, financed by Saudi Arabia, also covered millions of rounds of ammunition, 300 cannon turrets and anti-aircraft missiles. Shipments were arranged by a Madrid firm, F. Internacional, which performs topographical work for the Spanish Government but also acts as an arms-sales agent. Two weeks ago, two Spanish military officers were sent to Somalia as expediters. [*Newsweek*, February 20, 1978.]

Comrades Flint and Levine emphatically state, "At no time during the course of the war did the Somalians receive any military assistance from the United States. . . .

> Once it became clear that the Somalis had definitely *lost* the struggle—primarily because of Russian and Cuban intervention on the side of the Dergue *then* the U.S. promised and its allies gave modest amounts of military assistance to the Somalis (p. 145, emphasis in original).

As we have seen, the arms and financial assistance began well before the Somalian defeat, hundreds of millions of dollars worth of it, primarily through third parties such as the Saudi and Iranian regimes. It was obviously not enough, since the Somalians were defeated—thanks largely to the internationalist assistance of the Cuban fighters and the antiwar sentiment in the United States that limited Washington's options. But we don't decide to oppose an imperialist-supported intervention only if it seems like it has a good chance of succeeding.

"Fact" #10: The *New York Times* reported on February 11, 1978, that Secretary of State Cyrus Vance "in effect demanded that Somalia withdraw its forces from the Ogaden region. . . ." (Let's examine this one in connection with #12 and return to #11 in a moment.)

"Fact" #12: The Somalian regime agreed to withdraw in early March, and the *New York Times* reported that Carter had sent a letter to Siad urging such a withdrawal.

What Flint and Levine fail to point out is that the Somalian troops were by that time already being *defeated in battle*. It was not the White House that got them to withdraw. *It was thousands of Cuban troops*.

Once the Somalian troops were beginning to

be driven out, and Washington saw no feasible way of heading off the setback, then it calculated that it had everything to gain by piously calling for a withdrawal that was, in any case, unavoidable. It also saw the need to cover its tracks and attempt to maintain its self-assumed image as a "peacemaker."

Imperialism and the 'sanctity' of borders

"Fact" #11: Flint and Levine stress a statement made by Carter at a March 9, 1978, news conference, in which he claimed that the White House favored a solution to the conflict between Ethiopia and Somalia, that would *"ensure the territorial integrity of all countries in the region and the honoring of international borders"* (italics added by Flint and Levine). This is presented as a clear statement of "the principles" of U.S. policy in Africa. A little later, Comrades Flint and Levine declare that one of the reasons Washington did not "strongly encourage and materially support Siad Barre's invasion" was because it "was a clear and open violation of one of the key principles of the neocolonialist OAU—that is, that the state boundaries imposed upon Africa by colonial rule must not be tampered with, especially through armed force" (p. 146). Keil also refers to "the imperialists' fears of instability implied in changing boundaries in Africa." (*SWP Discussion Bulletin*, Vol. 36, No. 2, April 1979, p.30.)

Must we again remind the comrades that the only sure way of determining imperialism's policy is not to listen to what it says, but to look at what it does?

Washington's own past record on this question shows that the imperialists are not reluctant to "dishonor" existing borders. They favor their retention *only when it suits their interests*, only when it helps maintain capitalist stability. They are equally ready to violate or change them in pursuit of their counterrevolutionary aims.

To give a few examples in Africa, where Washington claims it respects the "sanctity" of the borders left by the departing colonial powers:

• In 1960–61, American imperialist interests favored the reactionary Moïse Tshombe's secessionist movement in the Katanga province of the Congo (now Zaïre) as a way of weakening the central government of Patrice Lumumba, whom the CIA feared could become "another Castro." Later, when Lumumba had been done away with, Washington shifted against the Katanga secession, because then it became a question of building up a stable, procapitalist central government.

• In 1963, a brief war broke out between Morocco and Algeria. Algeria had just won its independence from France, the capitalists had been swept out of the government, mass mobilizations were growing, and a workers and peasants government under Ben Bella had been established. The mass pressures for carrying through more and more thorough-going anticapitalist measures were great. The Moroccan regime, with American approval, attacked Algeria, using as a pretext a long-standing claim to some territory that it was trying to annex. But the border dispute itself was not the real reason for the war. What was actually involved was an armed attack against the Algerian revolution. The Fourth International supported the Algerian side in the war on that basis. (Incidentally, the Cubans sent some military instructors to aid the Algerians during the war.)

• To a much lesser extent, Washington, while adopting a formally "neutral" position, leaned toward the Biafran secessionist movement in Nigeria during the civil war of 1967–70. Other imperialist powers, most notably France, Portugal, and, it has recently been learned, South Africa, gave more assistance to the Biafran movement. In this case, the Biafran secessionist movement did not represent an attack on a revolutionary upheaval, but was simply being backed to an extent by some imperialist powers in an effort to weaken the Nigerian state and make some inroads into a country that was largely dominated by an imperialist competitor, Britain. Although there is very little evidence to indicate that these imperialist powers actually controlled the Biafran movement (it was largely a result of very real nationality conflicts within Nigeria), their attitude does indicate that the imperialists do not necessarily oppose a change of borders and the creation of new states.

• The most recent example before the Somalian attack on Ethiopia is the conflict in the Western Sahara. In 1975, Spain, which had ruled the territory for decades, agreed to the Western Sahara's partition between Morocco and Mauritania, without consulting the Saharan people themselves. The Moroccan monarchy of King Hassan II, backed by Paris, Washington, and other imperialist powers, claimed the annexation as a victory for Moroccan "reunification," since the territory had been ruled by Morocco's Alawi dynasty in the days before the colonial conquests. Hassan was even successful in whipping up considerable popular support within Morocco for his "national liberation" of the Sahara. The Saharans, however, have resisted these annexations as violations of their right to national self-determination. Under the leadership of the Polisario Front, they are fighting for the restoration of the Western Sahara's borders, as originally drawn up by the Spanish colonialists. The Fourth International has supported this struggle, because of the revolutionary content of the Saharan people's democratic fight for self-determination.

These examples show that general formulas, such as the supposed desirability of scrapping all the colonial-imposed borders, or imperialism's opposition to any change in them, are less than helpful. What is important to revolutionists is not whether the borders are changed, but *who* is fighting to change them, and *for what purpose*. Each particular national conflict needs to be examined on the basis of its own dynamics.

Post-war ties

Flint and Levine's remaining four "facts" all deal with the period after the war.

"Fact" #13: In June 1978, Washington renewed its offer to openly provide arms to the Somalian regime, but this was, according to Flint and Levine, "a relative pittance" compared to what the Ethiopians got from Moscow. Moreover, Flint and Levine continue, "this U.S. offer was made dependent upon assurances from Siad Barre that the weapons would not be used outside of Somalia's boundaries."

Flint and Levine apparently think that it is possible to gauge the degree of American backing to the Somalian regime by looking only at the amount of aid that is openly offered. They tend to ignore everything else, including Washington's *political* role.

Washington's unwillingness to rush in, publicly, with massive amounts of aid indicates two things:

1. The continued political difficulties of openly allying with the Somalian regime, which only yesterday was the open aggressor in the Ethiopia-Somalia war.

2. An apparent decision, once the Somalians had been defeated, to shelve the idea of another invasion (at least for the moment). But that does not rule out using the Somalian regime to apply continued pressure against the Ethiopians, at a less intense level, through guerrilla-type actions in the Ogaden (both by forces of the WSLF and by Somalian troops).

As for the "assurances" that U.S. weapons would not be used outside Somalia's borders, Comrades Flint and Levine should remember that Washington demands similar "assurances" from many of the regimes that it provides arms to. They are meaningless, as shown by the Israeli regime's open use of American weapons in Lebanon. Such "assurances" are simply a convenient way for Washington to try to beg off direct responsibility for the military actions of its allies, even when those have received American approval.

"Fact" #14: Flint and Levine write: "During the same month [June 1978], an American military mission to Kenya recommended to the White House that U.S. military aid to that country be boosted to offset any possible threat of renewed Somalian attempts to seize Somali-inhabited territories outside Somalia's borders."

Flint and Levine cite an article in the June 7, 1978, *New York Times* as their source, but in their summary of the information in the article, they distort it slightly. The relevant portion of the article reads: "The American military mission, which was headed by Gen. John Hill, is recommending increased arms sales to Kenya, which recently acquired a squadron of F-5 fighters. The sales would be designed *in part* to compensate for any *United States military supplies to Somalia*, which has turned to the West and to the Arabs for arms since it cut off its military ties with the Soviet Union" (emphasis added).

It is true that the Kenyan regime expressed some concern about the repercussions of the Ethiopia-Somalia war on its own Somali population and might fear that the Somalian regime, at some future date, could renew assistance to Somali dissidents within Kenya. Washington has been trying to allay those fears, and when Cahill encouraged Siad Barre to move deeper into the Ogaden, he at the same time urged him to renounce any claims to Kenyan territory. In any case, as the

New York Times article implied, Washington had other reasons for stepping up military aid to the Kenyan regime. Not least among them was its desire to bolster one of its staunchest allies in Africa against the prospects of growing instability in the region—instability that the Ethiopian revolution has greatly contributed to.

The fact that the Somalian invasion of Ethiopia may have disturbed the Kenyan regime does not prove anything regarding the American backing for that invasion.

"Fact" #15: The failure of Siad Barre, "despite a personal trip to Europe" in July 1978, to obtain any open and acknowledged arms assistance from the French, British, Italian, West German, and Dutch governments.

"Fact" #16: Carter's unwillingness as of February 1979 (and we might add, through the time of this writing) to fulfill his June 1978 offer of arms.

In answer to these two "facts," we simply refer the reader back to the response to "fact" #13. The same reasons for the imperialists' general hesitancy to publicly supply military equipment still apply.

However, that does not mean that arms have not been arriving in Somalia in indirect and covert ways. The Somalian regime is reported to have obtained via Saudi Arabia French anti-tank missiles and via other sources, British Rapier anti-aircraft batteries (*Le Monde*, October 22–23, 1978). There may be more that has not come to light.

Comrades Flint and Levine also ignore the fact that despite the imperialists' caution on the question of arms, they have nevertheless moved to consolidate their alliance with Siad Barre in other ways. Washington has provided millions of dollars in financial assistance ($13 million in 1978, $15 million in 1979, and a scheduled $20 million in 1980). With its eyes toward the future, the White House has also posted an American military attaché to Mogadishu. The Saudi Arabian regime has continued to pour in money, as have the West German imperialists, who provided some $45 million in 1977 and 1978 alone. (*Le Monde*, October 22–23, 1978).

The Somalian regime has continued its counterrevolutionary activities within Ethiopia, seeking to keep up pressure against the Ethiopian forces. Following the Somalian defeat, Western diplomats reported that the Somalian forces reverted to hit-and-run tactics. "After the withdrawal, some of the soldiers shed their uniforms and put on desert robes and switched tactics," one diplomat was quoted in the June 7, 1978, *New York Times*. "We believe they are getting full support of the Mogadishu regime while purporting to be the Western Somali Liberation Front." Toward the end of 1978, such "guerrilla" actions were stepped up considerably, and there have been reports as recently as this April of continuing casualties from the conflict.

This completes our disposition of the sixteen "facts." Before leaving the subject, however, it is worthwhile to look at one more source of information that confirms in virtually every detail what we have seen to be the actual course of events. On March 15, 1978, Fidel Castro gave a speech in which he detailed the role of Cuba's internationalist fighters in the Ethiopia-Somali war and the attitude of the Cuban government toward that war. (Excerpts from the speech were printed in *Intercontinental Press/Inprecor* on April 17, 1978.)

"First of all," said Castro, "we would like to say that we deeply regret the conflict between Somalia and Ethiopia; we did all we could to avoid it. Roughly a year ago, around this time—perhaps it was later than March 20, I don't remember exactly—we organized a meeting in Aden between the leaders of Ethiopia, Yemen and Somalia and ourselves in an effort to solve the problems between Somalia and Ethiopia, precisely to avoid a war. . . .

> Today we realize that when we met with Somalia's leaders in March of last year in Aden they had already worked out the plan—which they later put into practice—to invade Ethiopia, because they felt that the historical opportunity had arrived since Yankee imperialism and the NATO nations would welcome news of the invasion of Ethiopia with open arms.
>
> You know that there are many revolutionary Arab countries but that there is also a group of reactionary Arab countries. These reactionary Arab countries were also delighted with the attack on Ethiopia to destroy the Revolution. One of those countries, Saudi Arabia, which is ruled by an archaic monarchy, was one of the most interested in the destruction of the Ethi-

opian Revolution because when you see your neighbor's house on fire you take precautions. Since an Emperor had been overthrown, the Emperor or King of Saudi Arabia or whatever they call him was very worried about the downfall of the Ethiopian Emperor.

The same thing happened in Iran, a reactionary ally of Yankee imperialism with a criminal repressive government, a country also ruled by a Shah—Shah means Emperor, King, or well, I'm not exactly sure what it means. (LAUGHTER) It is another feudal monarchy, an absolute monarchy that was also bent on destroying the Ethiopian Revolution and encouraging Somalia to attack.

In view of these favorable circumstances for them, the reactionary faction [in Somalia], who hoped to get a flood of petrodollars from Saudi Arabia and Iran and economic aid from NATO and the United States, took advantage of the fact that there was a revolution in Ethiopia and foisted on this country their policy of war and aggression. This is the Somalian leadership's great crime: invading Ethiopia to destroy a revolution on behalf of the reactionary nations of the area, NATO and imperialism. . . .

Castro then went on to rip to shreds the lies and denials from Washington that the U.S. was in any way involved in promoting the Somalian invasion. "The imperialists have assumed a very hypocritical position during the conflict, because they knew that Somalia was invading Ethiopia right from the start, in July. The United States and the NATO countries knew about it and remained silent; they didn't say a word and they were delighted. They provided weapons for the aggressors—weapons from the United States and from NATO member states—by way of Saudi Arabia, Iran and other countries, and as the Somalians advanced they didn't say a word. When Somalia had occupied nearly all of Ogaden, the imperialists were optimistic; but when the Ethiopians began receiving internationalist aid, when they started to get weapons from the socialist camp and internationalist Cuban fighters began to arrive, the imperialists raised a real hue and cry. Then they insisted that there had to be a meeting of the OAU, the UN, etc., etc., and they talked about the need for a cease-fire. When, though, did they start talking about a cease-fire? When the aggressors started to lose the war.

As long as Somalia's forces advanced, the imperialists didn't say a word. When things started to change after the Ethiopians' first successful battles, when they realized that the situation could change quickly, then they raised the hue and cry and unleashed a propaganda drive all over the world, talking about the Cuban internationalist fighters—the Cuban troops as they call them—in Ethiopia. When the tables began to turn, they started to talk about a cease-fire, something which they hadn't done for all those months when the reactionary aggressors advanced. Of course the Ethiopian Government quite correctly said that there could be no cease-fire as long as part of its territory was occupied. That's also our revolutionary philosophy: there can be no cease-fire as long as there is occupied territory. (APPLAUSE)

The first counterattacks and the offensive followed, and the enemy troops were roundly defeated. They had to pull out in great haste, leaving behind tanks, cannon, artillery, all kinds of weapons, to escape being surrounded and captured because they had been defeated, completely defeated. We must point out that there was nothing voluntary about the withdrawal of Somalia's troops. If they had stayed four more days, just four more days, virtually all their troops in Ogaden would have been surrounded. Due to the way the revolutionary forces advanced and captured the main communication centers, if the enemy hadn't undertaken a speedy withdrawal, the remains of Somalia's army would have been surrounded in Ogaden. Thus, the aggressors have been forced to leave. They can't fool anybody at all by saying that the Somalian Government made the gesture of withdrawing its troops, because had the Somalians not done so they would have lost what little they had left. That's the situation: they left as a result of the military operations in which they were defeated. . . .

The war, the Dergue, and Eritrea

Based on the evolution of the imperialist offensive against the Ethiopian revolution and on the facts of the war itself, we have concluded that the overwhelmingly dominant element of the war was an imperialist-initiated and imperialist-backed invasion aimed at weakening and driving back the social gains of that revolution. The other factors in the war—the reactionary character of the Dergue, the nationalist aspirations of the Somalis in the Ogaden, and even the specific intentions of the WSLF or Somalian leaders—were all secondary and did not in any appreciable way alter the basic counterrevolutionary dynamic of the Somalian invasion.

Under the circumstances, it was the duty of revolutionists to defend that revolution from attack and support an Ethiopian and Cuban victory against the Somalian invaders.

Such a position does not mean that we extend political support to the reactionary Dergue, nor that we bear any responsibility for how the Dergue might seek to take advantage of the Somalian defeat for its own counterrevolutionary policies.

Flint and Levine claim, "It was the defeat of the Somalis in the Ogaden—and the leading role played in that defeat by Cuban troops—which rescued the Dergue's army and freed its troops for use against the people of Eritrea" (p. 152).

Along similar lines, Wohlforth states, "The Cuban-led victory in the Ogaden has made it possible for the Dergue to concentrate its forces on the Eritrean front" (SWP *Discussion Bulletin*, Vol. 36, No. 2, April 1979, p. 11). Comrade Keil follows a variation of this theme: "In the events of 1977–78, the Somalian military action helped the Eritrean liberation fighters and weakened the Ethiopian Dergue in face of the revolutionary masses" (Ibid., p. 30).

Their logic runs like this: The Eritrean struggle, which we support, suffered a serious setback at the hands of the Dergue *because* the Ethiopian side was victorious in the war. *Therefore*, we should have supported the Somalian invasion, which would have aided the Eritrean struggle.

The comrades are here trapped in their own formal logic.

If we applied their method to a situation like that in Angola, for example, we would have to say that a victory by the MPLA and Cuban forces against the South African and Zaïrian invasion of 1975–76 enabled the MPLA to crack down against the Angolan left (including the Angolan Trotskyists). Would they argue that we should therefore have supported those invasions, because they would have weakened the MPLA "in face of the revolutionary masses"? Of course not. Even they recognized that a victory of the South African and Zaïrian forces would have been a severe defeat for the Angolan masses in general.

If we adopted the comrades' way of thinking we would not have been able to support Chiang Kai-shek against the Japanese imperialists, because we knew that he would seek to take advantage of any defeat of the Japanese to then turn around and go after the Chinese masses themselves. We would not be permitted to fight alongside Allende in Chile in the heat of the rightist military coup of 1973. The Bolsheviks would not have been allowed to bloc with Kerensky to fight off Kornilov's reactionary attack against the Russian revolution in August 1917.

Are the comrades arguing that we should abandon our defense of regimes in the neocolonial world that are under imperialist attack—on the very grounds that they are capitalist? If we did that we would be taking a big step in the direction of sectarian ultraleftism.

Revolutionists, of course, make a clear distinction between defending such regimes from imperialist attack and giving them political support. We give them no political confidence, because we know that they are unable to really fight off imperialism and that they will continue to repress their own workers and peasants the first opportunity they get, even during the war itself.

The Dergue's actions in Eritrea, as well as its other reactionary policies, underscore why it is important for us to continue to oppose it politically, to fight to maintain the independence of the working class, while at the same time backing any progressive measures that the regime might undertake as a result of mass pressure, such as promulgating the land reform, kicking out the American military advisers, or fighting off the Somalian invasion.

Revolutionists are for the overthrow of the Dergue, yes. But we are not indifferent to *what forces* do the overthrowing, *how* it is done, or *for what purpose*.

If the Dergue is swept away by a mass upsurge of the Ethiopian working class and its allies, that would help to advance the revolution, and greatly improve the prospects for establishing a government of the workers and other toiling masses. If the Dergue is toppled by the imperialists, however, or a neocolonial capitalist regime in alliance with imperialism the new government established will be in an even stronger position to move against the concrete social conquests of the revolution itself.

And let us add, a defeat for the Ethiopian revolution would have been a severe setback for the Eritrean struggle as well. Do not think for one minute, comrades, that if the most reactionary forces opposed to the Ethiopian revolution were successful in toppling the Dergue and establishing a more directly proimperialist regime that they would rush to grant the Eritreans' right to self-determination. With the defeat of the Ethiopian revolution, they would be in an even stronger position than the Dergue is today to move against the Eritreans.

In the final analysis, what the Dergue is able to get away with depends on the relationship of class forces within Ethiopia. If a revolutionary working class party had existed and was sufficiently strong, it would have been able to utilize the defeat of the imperialist-inspired attack to push the revolution forward even further, and thus better defend the Eritreans. The brutal truth remains that there was no such party. If there was anything that enabled the Dergue to move against the Eritreans as it did in late 1978 and early 1979, it was that.

To sum up: The first task of revolutionists, in the context of the Ethiopian revolution, is to defend the gains of the revolution from all attacks, whether they come from the imperialists or from the Dergue. Only on that basis can we hope to advance it.

We seek to advance and defend the independent struggles and organizations of the working class and its allies. We fight in the most principled manner for recognition of the right of the oppressed nationalities to self-determination; that is the only real way to forge the broadest unity among the peoples in the region and undercut imperialism's efforts to use the national conflicts for its own purposes.

Above all, revolutionists work to build a proletarian combat party capable of leading the working class and its allies among the oppressed nationalities to take power and begin to institute policies in their interests.

That is the only way to safeguard the gains that have already been won and to advance the revolution further.

Cuba, Eritrea, and the African revolution

Despite the differing estimates of the class character of the Cuban state by the five comrades (Flint, Kramer and Levine think it is state capitalist, Wohlforth and Keil that it is a deformed workers state), they all condemn the Cuban role in Ethiopia, employing similar arguments.

We have already shown why we think the Cuban participation in the war against the Somalian invasion was a revolutionary act. Let's turn now to their arguments about Cuba and Eritrea.

Comrades Flint and Levine confine themselves to apportioning guilt by association. That is, the Cubans, by aiding the Ethiopians against the Somalian invasion, were assisting the Dergue to crack down harder on the Eritreans. We have just seen why that is not the case.

Comrades Wohlforth and Keil use similar arguments, but in addition they denounce the Cubans for direct involvement in the Dergue's military campaign against the Eritreans.

"There have been some reports," Wohlforth writes, "of Cuban troops stationed as an occupying army in Asmara and other Eritrean cities. There have even been reports of Cuban pilots as well as Soviet ones flying in the military action. It is not possible to judge the accuracy of these reports because the Dergue has closed the region to reporters" (Ibid., p. 12). Comrade Keil goes so far as to accuse the SWP of not defending "the Eritreans very well *in practice* because the *Militant* has in effect covered up Cuba's sizable intervention against them and protests by Eritrean forces against this intervention" (Ibid., p. 29).

While Wohlforth at least concedes that the reports in the bourgeois press are unverifiable, Keil does not let an element of doubt enter his argument. He is fully convinced that the Cuban government has carried out a "sizable intervention" against the Eritreans.

Keil's "proof"? He cites an article in the July 27,

1978, *New York Times* claiming that "the several thousand Cubans inside Eritrea—along with many thousands more in Tigre province to the south—are reported to have taken a back-up role, providing help in logistics, communications, and strategic [*sic*]." The source of this information? The *Times* reporter cites "Western diplomats." Keil also relies on a few quotes by various figures from the Eritrean People's Liberation Front (EPLF) claiming that Cubans were aiding the Ethiopian forces militarily.

The first thing that should be noted is that none of the "evidence" against the Cubans is concrete. There is no evidence, anywhere in all this, that the Cubans were involved in a "sizable intervention" against the Eritreans. In fact, there is no reliable evidence that the Cubans were directly involved *at all* in the Ethiopian war against the Eritrean independence struggle.

Keil maintains that we had no "reason to disbelieve the Eritrean charges of Cuban intervention." What he really means is that *he* had no reason to disbelieve the charges from one of the two Eritrean groups against the Cubans, while he had every reason to reject Cuban statements that they were *not* involved in the fighting. Since he is already convinced that Cuban foreign policy is counterrevolutionary, even unsubstantiated charges against Cuba serve as ammunition for his position.

But let's see if there is any "reason to disbelieve" the accusations against the Cubans. Reason one: the Cubans themselves have repeatedly denied any military involvement in Eritrea. Their general policy has been to openly take credit for their military involvement—in Angola, in the Ogaden, and elsewhere. Therefore there is no reason to doubt the truthfulness of their statements on Eritrea. If they were involved they would say so.

Reason two: even the U.S. Department of State had to admit on November 30, 1978—after the massive military offensive by Ethiopian forces began—that it had no evidence that Cubans were intervening in the fighting in Eritrea.

Reason three: other statements from Eritrean sources have contradicted the charges levelled against Cuba by the EPLF representatives. The Eritrean Liberation Front, the other main group in Eritrea, has frequently *denied* that Cubans were involved in the fighting against them. Even the charges from the EPLF have not been consistent. Keil cites a report in the November 22, 1978, *Guardian* that quoted EPLF leader Issayas Afewerki as saying, "The Cubans and Russians are distributed on all fronts. Whenever there is any offensive from the Ethiopian side, it is sure that there are Russians and Cubans participating." That was before the Dergue launched its massive offensive against the Eritreans. But just three weeks later, *after the offensive had begun,* the *Guardian* published a statement by the EPLF on the offensive, in which there is *not one word* about Cuba or any Cuban involvement (*Guardian*, December 13, 1978).

The fact is that, lacking any substantial evidence that the Cubans are lying, we have no reason to support the accusations against them. It is more likely that the charges are false. Did the EPLF representatives who made the charges perhaps think that by contributing to the anti-Cuba propaganda barrage they could elicit some assistance from Washington or some other imperialist capital? It cannot be ruled out.

We don't accept every anti-Cuban remark or report as true. We have recently come across some evidence confirming the wisdom of that approach.

In late 1977, the White House approved the launching of a covert CIA program to discredit the Cubans on the question of Eritrea. It had the direct blessing of Carter and of his Special Coordinating Committee, a cabinet-level body headed by National Security Adviser Zbigniew Brzezinski that oversees clandestine operations.

Citing "well-placed sources," *New York Times* correspondent Seymour Hersh revealed three of these programs in a report in the June 1, 1978, edition. Two of the operations involved sending clandestine radio and other communications gear to the Egyptian and Sudanese governments.

"In addition," Hersh continued, "the C.I.A. organized an *anti-Cuban propaganda operation* during intensified fighting between Ethiopia and insurgents in Eritrea. . . ." (emphasis added.)

Could that be one of the sources of the strangely persistent reports in the bourgeois press of Cuban military involvement against the Eritreans? Everything points in that direction.

We should also note the Cubans' *differing* political attitude toward the Eritrean struggle from that of either Moscow or the Dergue. In contrast to the

Cubans' role in fighting off the Somalian invasion, they have studiously avoided falling in behind the Dergue's reactionary drive in Eritrea, insisting repeatedly that they believe a political solution to the conflict is in order, not a military one. Cuban Vice-president Carlos Rafael Rodríguez summarized this stand in late 1978 when he said, "We helped the Eritreans in their fight for self-determination from the time of Haile Selassie onward. We feel there has to be some political solution to the Eritrean problem and there have to be talks between Eritreans and the central government."

While *Pravda* effusively hailed the Dergue's military advances in Eritrea, *Granma*, the newspaper of the Cuban Communist Party, said not a word about them.

This differentiation in stance by the Cubans comes despite considerable pressure from both Moscow and the Dergue to come out against the Eritreans.

Nevertheless, the Cuban government has opposed the Eritrean right to self-determination, that is, their right to establish an independent state. We think they are wrong, and have stated so. The Cuban position on this score weakens not only the Eritrean revolution but also the Cuban revolution.

Comrades Wohlforth, Keil, Flint, Kramer, and Levine bolster their rather weak arguments by openly denying or trying to play down the anti-imperialist role of Cuba in Africa. They do so by dismissing the danger of imperialist intervention—an especially risky course if we ourselves are to be ready to respond to foreign aggression by Washington.

We have already seen how the comrades minimize the threat from imperialism in the Horn of Africa. Comrades Wohlforth and Keil go further, however. They follow their logic backwards in time to rewrite the history of the imperialist aggression against Angola.

This is not the place to go into a detailed account of the Angolan war. Comrades who are interested can go back and look at our press coverage at the time, or read the book, *Angola: The Hidden History of Washington's War,* by Ernest Harsch and Tony Thomas (New York: Pathfinder Press, 1976).

But it is instructive to note at least what Wohlforth and Keil say about one of the key aspects of that war: why Cuba intervened and why the imperialists intervened.

"Let us remember," Wohlforth states, "Cuban troops did not enter Africa to fight off a South African invasion—that happened later" (Ibid., p. 11). Wohlforth's memory must be faulty. The first South African military thrusts into Angola came in August 1975. The first Cuban military instructors did not arrive until October, and thousands of Cuban troops did not arrive until after the South Africans had begun their large-scale invasion that same month. Thus Wohlforth's trick memory makes it possible for him to dismiss the real reason for the Cuban intervention in Angola: to beat back an imperialist attack.

Comrade Keil approaches this question with even more abandon. Repeating Wohlforth's charge that Cuban forces came to the assistance of the MPLA before the South Africa intervention, he goes on to state, "This military policy had helped open up Angola to the South African imperialists in the first place, with the U.S. behind them" (Ibid., p. 33).

Keil's logic leaves one stunned. Was Cuba responsible for the South African invasion?

We would suggest that Keil and Wohlforth reexamine their assessment of the Cuban revolution and the character of the Castro leadership, for it seems to be taking them further and further from the real world.

Revolution versus counterrevolution

The fact that the Cuban armed forces came to the defense of the Ethiopian revolution against the imperialist-backed Somalian invasion tells us something about the anti-imperialist character of Cuba's foreign policy. It also helps us to understand the significance, from the standpoint of the international class struggle, of the revolution in Ethiopia.

Unfortunately, Comrades Kramer, Levine, Flint, Keil, and Wohlforth are on the wrong side not only on Ethiopia but also on Cuba. They think that Cuba's anti-imperialist intervention in the war against Somalia was counterrevolutionary. They think that Somalia's counterrevolutionary invasion of Ethiopia was revolutionary.

All five comrades make the fundamental mistake of justifying their wrong line on the Ethiopia-Somalia war by viewing the national question in an abstract and schematic way, isolating it from and elevating it above the concrete clash of class forces in the Horn of Africa.

Comrades Kramer, Flint, and Levine, who hold the state capitalist point of view, see no qualitative difference between the Cuban workers state and states that are capitalist. They think the working class should put an equals sign between the Soviet workers state and American imperialism. Comrades Keil and Wohlforth can't see any difference at all between Cuba's revolutionary leadership and the Kremlin's counterrevolutionary leadership.

If the party adopted these five comrades' approach, method, or line, we would be unable to distinguish between revolution and counterrevolution. That would be a disaster.

TWO INTERPRETATIONS OF THE CUBAN REVOLUTION
By Joseph Hansen

Although I do not agree with his conclusions, I think Comrade David Keil has done a service to the party by raising the question of our position on Cuba. No doubt this will help lead to a fruitful discussion, particularly by inducing comrades to check what has been said in previous debates over the meaning of the Cuban revolution.,

The position of Comrade Keil—and of Comrade Scott Cooper, who agrees with him—is indicated in the title they gave to a joint article in the Discussion Bulletin (Vol. 35, No. 4): "For a Political Revolution in Cuba: Against the Stalinist Cuban Communist Party: Draft Theses."

Neither the Socialist Workers Party nor the Fourth International has called for a political revolution in Cuba. If the bureaucratic deformations of the Cuban workers state were to grow to such an extent as to place in power a hardened bureaucratic caste, then undoubtedly the course of the Cuban revolution, particularly our form of defending it, would have to be reassessed. Up to now neither the SWP nor the Fourth International has declared that such a qualitative change has occurred. They have held that the outcome of the Cuban revolution in this respect still remains to be seen.

Comrade Steven Beren has defended this position in an article, "What Framework for the Discussion on Cuba: Trotsky's Method or Keil's Schematism?" (Discussion Bulletin, Vol. 34, No. 10.) His arguments are compelling, it appears to me.

Against this view, Comrades Keil and Cooper hold that the original analysis of the course of the Cuban revolution was wrong—it should have been seen at the time that the Cuban workers state was born deformed, that a Stalinist caste was present from the beginning, and that it quickly became hardened. Consequently, they argue, we should have been fighting for a political revolution in Cuba since about 1961. They call for adoption of this view.

It should be noted, however, that they place greater weight on the new political course they propose than on the grounds they advance in its behalf:

"The evidence presented above and in the article by David Keil," they say, "proves that Cuba is a deformed workers state headed by a party which has been Stalinized since 1961. We are proposing that this position be formally adopted.

> Of course, if agreement exists among revolutionary socialists on the political tasks ahead, but not on historical questions, different views on these historical questions should not be counterposed to each other in voting. Votes are taken on political tasks, not on historical assessments.
>
> If someone puts forward a motion to call for political revolution in Cuba and replacement of the Stalinist Cuban CP by a Marxist party, we are ready to consider withdrawing our proposal. But we believe our draft theses present the most consistent position and hence are the most convincing.

It is in general correct to indicate priorities in this way. In the struggle to advance revolutionary Marxism, political tasks take precedence. For the sake of agreement on a correct political course, differences over historical interpretations and even the assessment of past political differences can be placed on a secondary level and deferred for later discussion or even left to the historians to decide. However, Comrades Keil and Cooper do not indicate why the importance of the historical question can be discounted *in this instance.*

The fact is that the considerations they advance for changing the party's position on Cuba require giving priority to the historical question. They contend that a wrong analysis was made. If their view on this stands up, everything else follows. On the other hand, if the original analysis was correct, they have lost their case.

Of course, there may be other comrades who might agree that the original analysis was correct but who would contend that changes have occurred since then so deepgoing as to compel us to say that the Cuban revolution, for whatever causes, has degenerated beyond any possibility of reform, thus invalidating our present political position.

However, this is not the stand taken by Comrades Keil and Cooper. While they would agree with the political conclusion, as they indicate, they would not agree with the reasoning behind it. They would consider it a case of correct political positions being reached through faulty thinking.

It appears to me that this view would necessitate shifting the discussion to a different level. In processes of such depth and complexity as the Cuban revolution, how can invalid reasoning lead to valid political conclusions? Wouldn't Comrades Keil and Cooper be duty bound to raise the question of the status of dialectics in our movement? And even if the differences over tasks and slogans were overcome, wouldn't those who disagreed with their premises still face the job of explaining why Comrades Keil and Cooper were wrong?

Origin—an item of key importance

Comrades Keil and Cooper agree that the Castro leadership was non-Stalinist in origin. However, they do not consider this fact to deserve much attention. In none of his articles urging that the SWP and the Fourth International adopt a new political line in relation to Cuba does Comrade Keil take up this question. It is dismissed in a phrase such as "The Castroist leadership, non-Stalinist in origin, capitulated to the Stalinist Popular Socialist Party and fused with it in 1961 to form the Integrated Revolutionary Organizations."

I will take up the question of Castro's alleged capitulation further on. Here I merely want to emphasize that the non-Stalinist origin of the Castroist leadership was one of the most striking features of the Cuban revolution. It proved that forces other than the Stalinists can come to power in a revolutionary upheaval. It proved that such forces are capable of bypassing a Stalinist party standing in the way of the revolution. It provided strong evidence against the thesis that a leadership trained in the school of Stalinism is more likely to move in a revolutionary direction than one free of such training.

The victory of the Cuban revolution inspired a generation of rebel youth on a worldwide scale. In the working-class movement internationally, the victory constituted a new devastating blow to the revolutionary pretensions of the Soviet ruling caste, thereby accelerating the erosion of Stalinism.

The most remarkable fact about the Castroist leadership is that it began with radical democratic positions, found itself heading the first socialist revolution in the Americas, and after the victory announced its conversion to revolutionary Marxism. It is worth recalling some of the milestones in the development of this grouping, particularly those bound up with the career of its main figure.

If we leave aside his campus experiences, Castro began his political career as a congressional candidate of the radical bourgeois Ortodoxo Party (Partido del Pueblo Cubano) in the elections scheduled for June 1, 1952. The electoral campaign was cut short by Batista's coup on March 10, 1952.

By March 24, Castro had resorted to the courts, filing one brief demanding that Batista's seizure of power be declared unconstitutional and another demanding that the appropriate penalties for the crimes committed, amounting to 100 years in prison, be imposed on the usurper.

The courts rejected the first lawsuit and ignored the second. The attitude of the Stalinists paralleled that of the judges. Class-collaborationist to the marrow, the Stalinist leaders were looking ahead to serving as labor lieutenants for the dictator.

The outcome in the courts was not unexpected to Castro. While the legal basis of his move was unassailable, he had a political objective in mind; namely, to demonstrate that the Cuban people could not hope to redress their grievances by relying on appeals to a judiciary that was subservient to a dictator. Stronger means were required to oust Batista and obtain justice.

Castro had in mind an appeal to arms. On that question, the Stalinists stood to the right of the so-called liberal bourgeoisie in Cuba.

The attack on the Moncada Barracks on July 26, 1953, was of course an adventure. It was only by the greatest good luck that Castro did not lose his life as did others in his small band. Nonetheless the commitment of these rebels to a just cause could only arouse a most sympathetic response among revolutionists everywhere, however severe their judgment might be of the suicidal nature of such tactics.

It must be recognized that the consequences of this particular adventure were not *absolutely* negative. Because of the sensational nature of the action, Castro managed to utilize the subsequent trial to gain wide publicity for his program, which included a scathing denunciation of the crimes of Batista. Along with this he and his comrades gained recognition as dedicated revolutionists, a type completely opposite to the bootlicking Stalinists who had supported Batista in the past.

In the program advanced by Castro at that time, the stress was on democratic demands: majority rule, equality before the law, punishment of those who had usurped power. A deepgoing agrarian reform was undoubtedly the single most significant demand. Besides this the program called for the sharing of profits with the workers; the confiscation of the property of malfeasants in office, including those in all previous governments who had handed down their ill-gotten gains via inheritances; nationalization of the electric trust and the telephone trust; and rebates for unlawful excesses charged in their rates.

"The problem of the land," Castro said in his speech to the court, "of industrialization, the problem of housing, the problem of education, the problem of unemployment and the problem of the health of the people—here are the six problems whose solution our efforts would have resolutely begun, together with public liberties and political democracy."

In October 1953, Castro began serving a fifteen-year sentence. Popular pressure for his release became so intense, however, that he and his comrades were granted amnesty by congress, a measure signed by Batista on May 13, 1955. The experience in prison, part of it in solitary confinement, did not dampen Castro's independent attitude. By July he was in Mexico planning a guerrilla training camp.

The training period ended with the famous *Granma* expedition and its landing on the western coast of Oriente Province on December 2, 1956. The operation was not a notable military success; in fact, it was something of a disaster.

What was notable, however, was Castro's skill at wringing favorable publicity from the action. For the sake of his political objectives, Castro even accepted higher odds against a military success by publicly notifying the world (and Batista) in advance of the projected landing.

In this same period, Castro continued to move leftward. In July 1955 he came under the influence of Che Guevara, forming a fast friendship with the Argentine revolutionist, who was anything but a Stalinist. On March 19, 1956, Castro broke from the Ortodoxo Party. Building the July 26 Movement became his central concern. While the July 26 Movement concentrated on advancing guerrilla war, it was more than a mere guerrilla current; it also constituted a political party, a fact that can be overlooked or incorrectly downgraded in importance if you hold that the advance of the Cuban revolution is to be explained primarily by the military struggle initiated and kept up by a few hundred rebels.

Batista made the mistake of disregarding Castro's politics and of thinking that the challenge could be reduced to the military level where the relationship of forces was such that not much more than a brutal police crackdown was needed to liquidate the upstarts. The dictator left out of account the meaning of the rising restlessness among the peasants, the workers, and sectors of the middle class.

The political task facing Castro was to strengthen and broaden the linkup he had already established to a certain degree with the masses and prove to them that the July 26 Movement offered not only an attractive but a realistic alternative to Batista's dictatorship. Castro succeeded in this task within two years. It was the mobilization of the masses throughout Cuba that assured the victory over Batista on December 31, 1958.

The Stalinists had nothing whatsoever to do

with this revolutionary struggle save to stand in its way.

The victory over the Batista government was not registered by the July 26 Movement immediately assuming power. Instead a coalition government was set up.

On December 14, 1957, in maneuvering with some other political currents, Castro had proposed that Manuel Urrutia, a judge who had helped the rebels during the Moncada period, be named provisional president in a "caretaker government" to be set up when Batista was overthrown. He repeated the proposal after Batista fled from the island, and Urrutia was sworn in on January 4, 1959. José Miró Cardona, another liberal bourgeois figure, was named premier.

Castro himself did not take any posts at first. In speeches that ran hour after hour on nationwide television, he concentrated on explaining the revolution to the masses. It was part of an intensive effort to mobilize them on a revolutionary basis.

The sector of the bourgeoisie that had favored the struggle against Batista resisted Castro's course, and the State Department did what it could to bolster the wing in the coalition government representing these forces.

Rifts soon began to appear in the coalition. Under pressure from the left wing, Miró Cardona resigned on February 13, 1959, and Castro took his place as premier. The coalition began to come apart at the seams.

The next outstanding battle was over Urrutia's anti-Communist orientation. On July 17, 1959, Castro resigned as premier, and went on television to explain the situation. Urrutia resigned during Castro's speech. Castro soon resumed his governmental post, and Dr. Osvaldo Dorticós Torrado was designated provisional president.

The disintegration of the coalition government reflected the sharpening of the class struggle, particularly over putting into effect the agrarian reform, which had been enacted on May 17. The process reached a qualitative turning point within a few months. On November 26, Felipe Pazos, who had been appointed president of the National Bank of Cuba, was replaced by Che Guevara. Governmental power had now been assumed directly by the central leadership of the July 26 Movement. The new government was characterized by the SWP and the Fourth International as a "workers and peasants government."

The July 26 Movement itself was deeply affected by the rapidly changing political situation. The right wing, whose commitment had been only to topple Batista's dictatorial rule and establish democratic bourgeois rule, drew back from the measures that had to be undertaken to carry out the promised thoroughgoing agrarian reform. The movement was, in fact, being torn asunder.

The response of the Castro team to this situation again showed its independent character and its commitment to advancing the revolutionary process no matter what the consequences. In face of the popular support won by Castro, the right wing of the July 26 Movement collapsed.

Washington displayed a more and more belligerent attitude toward the new government in Havana as it proceeded along the path of "intervening" (expropriating) property held by American interests. For each move by the Eisenhower administration, the Castro regime replied with further "interventions." By October 1960, the economic basis for a workers state had been firmly established in Cuba. It was an auspicious opening for the socialist revolution in the Western Hemisphere.

Particularly notable was the speed with which the process, from the defeat of Batista to the expropriation of the capitalists, was carried out. This was a consequence of the firm adherence displayed by the Castro leadership in practice to the class struggle. They avoided a crushing defeat of the kind that occurred in China in the twenties and in Indochina in the post-World War II period because of the policy of class collaborationism practiced by the Stalinist leaderships in those instances.

The Castro team, with the exception of Che Guevara, was a native Cuban formation. It led a revolution that arose out of the social, economic, and political situation in Cuba under American domination, and it did so in opposition to the Cuban Stalinists, who followed a class-collaborationist policy. In the process, the Castro team transcended its major petty-bourgeois limitations.

To carry out measures of a democratic bourgeois nature such as a deepgoing agrarian reform, it found itself compelled to follow a course of action going beyond bourgeois democracy—and it did so. It expropriated the capitalists both foreign and domestic and imposed a monopoly on foreign trade, thus establishing a workers state, including the introduction of a planned economy. This course of action confirmed in an unconscious way one of the main tenets of Trotsky's theory of permanent revolution: that the capitalist system in its dying stage is incapable of solving the tasks of the democratic revolution, therefore they become tasks of the socialist revolution. In the end, these leaders recognized that the Cuban revolution was socialist in character.

I think that the above analysis of the nature of the Castro leadership and its course remains correct. The non-Stalinist origin of the Castro team remains a prime fact. It is crucial to keep it in mind, in my opinion, if we are to reach a correct appreciation of the principal moves made by this leadership in the subsequent years.

What the events of 1961 showed

On July 26, 1961, Castro announced the merger of the July 26 Movement, the Revolutionary Directorate, and the Popular Socialist Party (the Stalinists). The fused organization was named the Integrated Revolutionary Organizations. On March 8, 1962, the composition of the national leadership was made public. It consisted of twenty-five persons, including thirteen from the former July 26 Movement, ten from the former PSP, and two from the former Revolutionary Directorate.

In 1963 the name was changed to United Party of the Socialist Revolution, and in October 1965 it was further changed to the "Communist Party of Cuba."

The highest body in the CPC is a Political Bureau consisting of eight persons. The eight include both Raul and Fidel Castro and Dorticós. Fidel Castro heads the party with the post of secretary general.

Comrade Keil holds that Castro's July 26, 1961, speech announcing the formation of the Integrated Revolutionary Organizations was proof positive that he had capitulated to Stalinism. Thus he says in his article "Cuba: Trotsky's Method Versus Maitan's Liquidationism," which was published in the SWP Discussion Bulletin Vol. 34, No. 6 (July 1976):

> Parallel to the Stalinization of the Castro leadership's foreign policy was its organizational Stalinization. The decisive step was the creation of the Integrated Revolutionary Organizations (ORI), in my opinion. The ORI's formation was announced by Castro at a rally held July 26, 1961. (P. 18.)

Comrade Keil says further:

> The fusion with the Stalinists was prepared organizationally as well. At the Eighth Congress of the PSP in August 1960, Blas Roca called for all revolutionary forces to enter 'fusion' and become 'a single movement.' This Stalinist-initiated fusion was formally begun at the end of October, 1960, when the Stalinist youth organization merged with the youth group of the July 26 Movement to form the Jóvenes Rebeldes. It was thus not surprising for the Castroists to merge with the PSP itself. It was more in the nature of the final, well-prepared collapse of Castroism as an independent current. (P. 20.)

The evidence, however, calls for a different interpretation of the fusion, in my opinion. Above all, we must consider the context in which it took place; that is, the efforts of the Eisenhower and Kennedy administrations to crush the Cuban revolution by economic and military means.

Following intense diplomatic pressure against the Cuban revolution in 1959, Eisenhower asked Congress in January 1960 for authorization to modify the quota for importation of sugar from Cuba. On April 8 he accused Fidel Castro of having "betrayed" the ideals of the Cuban revolution. On July 5 he cut off Cuba's sugar quota. On October 19, he went to the length of declaring an embargo on trade with Cuba.

The year 1961 opened ominously for the Cubans. On January 3, in one of his last acts in office, Eisenhower broke off diplomatic relations with Cuba. Secretly, he had already ordered a military invasion designed to touch off a counterrevolution and drown the Cuban workers state in blood.

John F. Kennedy, who was sworn in on January 20, took over command of this secret war waged by the most formidable imperialist power on earth against a small population on a small island located in a most vulnerable geographical position.

The military invasion began on April 15 with raids by camouflaged planes on the airports at Santiago and Havana. The next day at the services for those killed, Castro responded to the raids politically by declaring that the Cuban revolution was socialist in character.

On April 17, the expeditionary forces equipped by the CIA and the Pentagon landed at Playa Girón in the Bay of Pigs. The Cuban populace mobilized throughout the island; and in view of the evident miscalculation as to the popularity of the Castro government, Kennedy left the invaders to their fate.

In what way did Castro utilize these events to advance the "final, well-prepared collapse of Castroism as an independent current"? By taking charge of the military defense at Playa Girón, personally participating in the engagements, defeating the invasion within forty-eight hours and capturing 1,200 prisoners?

Kennedy found himself in the embarrassing position of having to negotiate with Castro over releasing the prisoners of war. Stalinist class collaborationism did not now suddenly flower. Castro asked for 500 bulldozers by way of exchange. The negotiations dragged on. Finally Castro agreed to accept $53,000,000 worth of food and medicine. The money was raised "privately" in the United States, and Kennedy relaxed the embargo to permit purchase and shipment of the goods.

Did Kennedy decide to turn over a new leaf and forswear war with Cuba? Hardly. On February 3, 1962, he made the embargo on trade with Cuba complete. In a speech to the released Cuban prisoners of war, who presented him with their brigade flag in Miami on December 29, 1962, Kennedy said: "I can assure you that this flag will be returned to this Brigade in a free Havana."

It is now known, of course, that Kennedy continued the secret CIA war against the Cuban revolution. Besides burning crops, blowing up planes, infecting Cuban livestock with contagious diseases, and so on, a key objective was the assassination of Castro. The recent revelations about the CIA's use of murder in overthrowing governments show that the spy agency made a number of attempts on Castro's life. Washington's experts in these matters clearly believe that it is more practical to kill Castro than to lure him into the trap of collaborating with American imperialism.

But what about the fusion projected by Castro on July 26, 1961? Doesn't that prove his willingness to capitulate to the Stalinists, who are certainly class collaborationists?

First of all, let us note that it was the Cuban Stalinist leaders—not Castro—who capitulated to Washington's puppet, Batista. From this fact we are entitled to suspect that if Castro had been just another Batista, as the Healyites aver, the Cuban Stalinists could have been counted on to capitulate to the new Batista with equal readiness, if given the opportunity. It would at least be logical to suspect it.

Of course, Castro was not another Batista. He was a revolutionary leader who succeeded in bypassing the Stalinists and mobilizing the masses into a powerful striking force which he led to victory against Batista's rule, ending the domination of American imperialism, and ending capitalism in Cuba. Castro followed this up in 1961 by leading a successful defense against an armed invasion. Consider his position now: the most popular figure in Cuba, the most influential member of the team running the July 26 Movement, the government, the armed forces, and the economy.

Yet, according to the scenario proposed by Comrade Keil, this powerful political figure was only preparing for the crowning act—capitulation to the Stalinists, who coolly displayed their leadership capacities by taking over and running things from then on in Cuba.

To construct this implausible interpretation, Comrade Keil has to leave out of account a fact essential to correctly understanding the play of political forces—*the effect of the rise of the July 26 Movement on the ranks of the Stalinists.*

As in other Communist parties, many of the rank and file were revolutionary minded. However much the leadership sought to disparage Castro, the ranks of the PSP were impressed by the revolutionary example he and his team set in practice.

K.S. Karol notes in his book *Guerrillas in Power* that "the Communists could not help feeling anxious about the growing popularity of the July 26th Movement, particularly during 1953–56." (P. 140.)

This uneasiness may have helped keep the PSP

in the opposition—if only in a catatonic way—following Batista's 1952 coup.

The PSP's decline in membership provides another instructive indication of its growing isolation. In 1942 the party claimed to have 87,000 members. In 1952 the figure was down to 20,000; and by the time of the victory of the July 26 Movement, it had fallen to 7,000.

Although the details have not yet been revealed, we do know that the leadership began to dispute among themselves on what to do about the July 26 Movement, which was becoming more and more formidable in its challenge for leadership of the masses. The outcome was the designation of Carlos Rafael Rodríguez to go to the Sierra Maestra to talk with Castro.

Aníbal Escalante, the organizational strong man of the PSP, gave Rodríguez a memorandum on what to lay down in the conversations. Escalante's line was to keep Castro from getting radicalized and doing something that might break friendly relations with the United States.

Rodríguez paid no attention to the memorandum. He was the under the pressure of PSP members who were becoming Fidelistas.

This pressure mounted greatly after the victory as Castro initiated measure after measure advancing the *socialist* revolution in Cuba. In view of its disintegrating base, the PSP faced a bleak perspective. It could collapse or it could possibly join the July 26 Movement. To succeed in the latter move it had to prove its reliability and loyalty to the July 26 Movement.

On August 21, 1960, Blas Roca, the general secretary of the PSP, made a collective self-criticism of the party's past errors, particularly the error of not having recognized the historic merits of Fidel Castro. The ranks of the party had already demonstrated their views by the way they pitched in to carry out the immense tasks facing the country. And during the Bay of Pigs invasion the following April they showed their capacity to carry out the directives issued by the government.

From this it ought to be clear to everyone that in moving toward a fusion of the July 26 Movement, the Revolutionary Directorate, and the PSP, Castro was engaging in a simple political operation. He was responding positively to overtures from political forces that had previously fought the July 26 Movement and had committed grave errors. He did this in a generous way, making it easier for his former opponents to complete their turn. He did not even insist that the name of his own organization be kept. He assured posts for the leaders of the former groups in the top bodies of the new formation. All his moves were calculated to bring the greatest possible unity among these disparate currents in facing American imperialism.

At the same time there could be no doubt that one of the conditions of the fusion was recognition of the Castro team as the central leadership. Lee Lockwood noted the following fact when the United Revolutionary Socialist Party of Cuba became the Communist Party of Cuba on October 3, 1965: "More than 80% of the PCC's new 100-man central committee were former members of Castro's 26th of July or other non-Communist revolutionary organizations."

Obviously what Castro foresaw was not a peaceful development of the Cuban revolution, but continuation of the American blockade, of American military intervention, of fierce diplomatic pressure against Cuba on a worldwide scale. As a small fortress besieged by the mightiest imperialist power on earth, Castro understood the need for maximum unity and maximum reinforcement of his leadership within that fortress.

This interpretation of the fusion appears to me to be the most reasonable and the most in accordance with the facts. If this is true, then Comrade Keil's interpretation, and his political position along with it, have to be rejected.

Soviet aid and the first round with Escalante

The worst problem facing the Castro team was defense of the Cuban revolution, in view of its extreme vulnerability to economic blockade and military intervention. On the material side, the Cuban revolution required not only economic aid but arms sufficient to discourage attack by the aggressive power standing at the head of the world capitalist system and ready in behalf of that system to use the most fiendish weapons, including nuclear bombs. On the political side, the defense of the Cuban revolution called for policies such as those employed by the Soviet Union in the days of Lenin and Trotsky.

In the entire world there was only one possible

source of material aid on the scale needed. This was the Soviet Union. In return for material aid, however, the Stalinist regime demanded political payment; that is, for the arms and other commodities required to defend the Cuban revolution, the Kremlin demanded propaganda painting up the rule of the bureaucracy in the USSR and its policy of "peaceful coexistence" (class collaboration) with capitalism.

Castro accepted these conditions, although with some reservations. It can be argued that this was an incorrect decision, and that it would have been preferable to reject the onerous terms. However, there is little to be gained speculating over what the course of history might have been if the Cubans had flatly told Khrushchev, "No." They would have shortly faced the murderous fire of the Pentagon. As they fell, with virtually no weapons to defend themselves, perhaps they could have comforted themselves with the thought that their example of intransigence against Moscow would long be remembered. On the other hand, their martyrdom would have signified a defeat for the Cuban revolution bearing very grave consequences for the world revolution as a whole.

Rather than accept the swift crushing of their revolution, the Cubans chose to take the material aid even if the price amounted to a holdup.

The agreement negotiated with Deputy Prime Minister Mikoyan in February 1960 included purchases of sugar by the Soviet Union and a credit of $100,000,000 at 2.5 percent interest to buy Soviet industrial plants and machinery, and to pay for the cost of technical aid. A secret agreement was also reached concerning supplies of arms. This was a little more than a year before the Bay of Pigs invasion.

In my opinion, if blame is to be assigned in this situation, it should be placed squarely on the Soviet bureaucrats for attaching political strings to the material aid needed to defend a small country under attack from American imperialism, particularly one carrying out a socialist revolution.

It must be recognized that the price demanded by Moscow for granting material aid weakened the political defense of the Cuban revolution and served to foster the growth of bureaucratism in Cuba. Nonetheless, it seems to me to be unwarranted to conclude from these negative developments taken in isolation that a hardened bureaucratic caste has appeared in Cuba.

Comrade Keil's view—if I understand him correctly—is somewhat different. He believes that a bureaucracy existed in Cuba from the very beginning; that is, even before Soviet aid became available. He draws the further conclusion that "the bureaucracy had hardened into a caste by the time of the 1960 social transformations." ("For a Change in Our Position on Cuba," p. 29.) This clearly implies that the very process that established a workers state in Cuba simultaneously established a parasitic ruling caste, with the first shipments of Soviet aid serving to help the caste emerge.

There seems to be no theoretical linkage between this position and Comrade Keil's agreement that the leadership of the Cuban revolution was non-Stalinist in origin.

Up to now, we have held that the non-Stalinist origin explained not only the outstanding features of the first developments—such as the swift victory over Batista and the rapid appearance of a workers state—but also some outstanding features of subsequent events.

The non-Stalinist origin of the Cuban revolutionary leadership is evinced in actions or positions independent from and sometimes in contradiction to Moscow's course. Unfortunately, Comrade Keil pays no attention to the persistence of this feature; his schema rules out its importance and even its existence. Yet if it is left out of account it is very difficult, if not impossible, to draw correct conclusions about Cuba's political role in the international class struggle.

Some examples of this aspect of Cuban politics are well worth considering, in my opinion.

We can begin with the mistake made by some of the old Stalinist hacks who concluded that Castro had capitulated when he projected the fusion of the July 26 Movement, the Revolutionary Directorate, and the PSP. Perhaps these dyed-in-the-wool Stalinists thought that Castro wanted to be only the nominal head of the united organization and that he might not object to their assuming some of the tedious organizational responsibilities. Or they may have thought that Castro was really naive in party politicking and would not notice what they were up to.

In any case, under the guidance of Aníbal Escalante, who had been general secretary of the party in the days when it supported Batista, these case-hardened Stalinists went ahead with the kind of factional operation in which they were past masters, putting their cronies in advantageous positions in the new party formation, and bypassing, undercutting, or straight-arming those with a background in the July 26 Movement. Thus the outlines of a bureaucratic machine began to appear, helping to nourish the growth of bureaucratism in general.

Castro began his preparations. He had granted an interview to the editors of *Izvestia* and *Pravda*. This was published in Moscow on January 26, 1962, but in such a way that Castro's views appeared to be the same as those of Khrushchev on such issues as "peaceful coexistence." Four days later in Havana, *Revolución* published the correct text. Entire passages proclaiming the necessity for revolutionary struggle had been deleted from the text published in Moscow. One of the sentences that had been scissored out was the following: "No coexistence is possible between the exploited masses of Latin America and the Yankee monopolies."

On February 4, Castro followed up by proclaiming the *Second Declaration of Havana*. The central theme of this revolutionary statement was: "The duty of every revolutionary is to make the revolution." It explicitly rejected the possibility of the national bourgeoisie playing a progressive role in Latin America.

Then on March 26, 1962, eight months after his announcement of the fusion, Castro gave a television speech in which he leveled a blistering attack on Escalante and the growth of bureaucratism in Cuba. The speech made an international sensation. It was recognized everywhere as an attack on Stalinism, a judgment concurred in by the Trotskyist movement.

Comrade Keil takes a different view of the meaning of the action:

> Castro's denunciation of Anibal Escalante, a Stalinist leader, on March 26, 1962, was considered by the Fourth International to be the beginning of a revolutionary campaign against bureaucratism. It was nothing but a bureaucratic purge, however. Escalante was made the sole culprit and was not allowed to defend himself. Castro proposed no concrete measures to combat bureaucratism—except Escalante's bureaucratic ouster. . . . It is not surprising that the Kremlin and the majority of Cuban Stalinists supported Castro against Escalante. If Castro's speech had been a telling blow against bureaucratism, these Stalinists would not have applauded, as they did. ("For a Change in Our Position on Cuba," p. 30.)

The analysis is defective; it does not advance our understanding of the issues involved in the confrontation. The *assertion* is made that it was "nothing but a bureaucratic purge." If that was actually the case, what were the reasons for the "bureaucratic purge"? Why did it occur at this particular time? Did it have no relation with other important events in the headlines at the time? We are not told. Yet "bureaucratic purges" cannot be dismissed as meaning nothing—not if we follow the dialectical method.

On the other hand, if we look for the elements in Castro's course that are in line with the non-Stalinist origin of his political current, then we have no trouble in discovering the politics involved in the confrontation.

1. The struggle led by Castro against bureaucratism was genuine and not an elaborate show designed to cover up a frame-up of Escalante.

2. Escalante's ouster was one of the consequences of a sharp factional fight involving his continuation of bureaucratic practices in the new organization that were completely consistent with his entire previous life as a Stalinist bureaucrat.

3. Among other things, the development of Escalante's secret faction represented a challenge to the leadership of Castro. In meeting the challenge, Castro reasserted his leadership.

4. Castro's action served warning on the Kremlin, which might have been intervening and giving encouragement to Escalante and his cronies, that this would not be permitted even if it meant splitting the fused organization and driving out all of Escalante's followers.

Comrade Keil is quite accurate in noting that Castro's action met with applause from the Kremlin and the "majority of Cuban Stalinists" (whatever that means). This was not because they regarded Castro's political response to Escalante's Stalinist hatchet work and the rising threat of bureaucratism as meaning nothing, but because they saw no alternative.

The missile crisis

On October 22, 1962, seven months after the ouster of Escalante, President Kennedy made a nationwide broadcast in which he revealed that Moscow was sending nuclear-tipped missiles that Castro could use to defend Cuba. He issued an ultimatum, demanding among other things immediate recall of the missiles. Kennedy made it clear that if Khrushchev did not concede, he was prepared to launch a nuclear war. Kennedy mobilized the U.S. army and prepared to invade Cuba on an overwhelming scale, with the missile sites targeted for immediate obliteration. On October 28, after six days in which humanity agonized over Kennedy's brinkmanship, Khrushchev submitted to the ultimatum. A nuclear war between the United States and the Soviet Union was averted for the time being.

Khrushchev claimed that in his negotiations with Kennedy he gained a pledge that the U.S. would not engage in any military invasion of Cuba. Kennedy, however, was equivocal on this, hedging with provisos. As is now known, he ordered the CIA to conduct a secret war against Cuba with Castro marked for assassination. Kennedy's presidential successors kept up the secret war. Obviously the White House has no difficulty distinguishing between a Castro and a Khrushchev.

Who took the initiative in seeking to boost Cuba's military defense by emplacing short-range defensive missiles? Contradictory versions have been offered on this and the facts still remain obscure. Arthur Schlesinger sums up what was known in 1965 at the time he wrote his book *A Thousand Days*:

> The Soviet Union had never before placed nuclear missiles in any other country.... Why should it now send nuclear missiles to a country thousands of miles away, lying within the zone of vital interest to their main adversary, a land, moreover, headed by a willful leader of, from the Russian viewpoint, somewhat less than total reliability? Castro, with characteristic loquacity, later produced a confusion of explanations. He told a Cuban audience in January 1963 that sending the missiles was a Soviet idea; he repeated this to Claude Julien of *Le Monde* in March 1963; in May he described it to Lisa Howard of the American Broadcasting Company as 'simultaneous action on the part of both governments'; then in October he told Herbert Matthews of the *New York Times* that it was a Cuban idea, only to tell Jean Daniel of *L'Express* in November that it was a Soviet idea; in January 1964, when Matthews called him about the Daniel story, Castro claimed again that it was a Cuban idea; and, when Cyrus Sulzberger of the *New York Times* asked him in October 1964, Castro, pleading that the question raised security problems, said cagily, 'Both Russia and Cuba participated.'

As for the Russians, Khrushchev told the Supreme Soviet in December 1962, 'We carried weapons there at the request of the Cuban government.' (As quoted by Herbert L. Matthews in *Fidel Castro*, pp. 224–25.)

In his memoirs, published in 1970 as *Khrushchev Remembers*, Khrushchev changed what he had said previously:

> It was during my visit to Bulgaria that I had the idea of installing missiles with nuclear warheads in Cuba without letting the United States find out they were there until it was too late to do anything about them. I knew that first we'd have to talk to Castro and explain our strategy to him in order to get the agreement of the Cuban government.... In addition to protecting Cuba, our missiles would have equalized what the West likes to call 'the balance of power.' ... The Caribbean crisis was a triumph of Soviet foreign policy and a personal triumph in my own career as a statesman and as a member of the collective leadership. (As quoted by Maurice Halperin in *The Rise and Decline of Fidel Castro*, p. 174.)

Whatever the truth may be as to precisely who deserves credit for the initial conception, it is plain that the Cubans were in on the planning from the very beginning. The idea could well have emanated from Castro within the context of discussions in which Khrushchev came to see—all on his own—that it might well advance Moscow's interests to a high degree and certainly could do them no harm. It is difficult to imagine Castro not fostering any additional positive feelings Khrushchev might have displayed such as a tendency to think of himself as the seminal source of the scheme.

The Cubans were not acting as tools of Moscow. They viewed the installation of nuclear missiles as a qualitative upgrading of the military defense of the Cuban revolution that also signified an improvement of the defense of the Soviet Union and the defense of the socialist revolution as a whole.

The independent aspect of their involvement in the installation of missiles was shown in the most striking way in the aftermath of the crisis. The Cuban government objected with particular sharpness to the way Khrushchev and Kennedy settled the crisis without so much as consulting the Cubans.

Khrushchev had acceded to Kennedy's demand that a United Nations delegation be permitted to enter Cuba to inspect the missile sites. Castro refused point-blank to agree to this. Posters displaying a photograph of Lumumba and the slogan "Cuba is not the Congo!" went up all over Cuba as a pointed reminder of how the leader of the Congolese revolution was assassinated and his government destroyed during the intervention of United Nations forces there.

For months the Cuban government displayed its displeasure with the Kremlin because of not having been consulted in the dealings with Kennedy.

In an interview in 1965, Lee Lockwood asked Castro: "Do you think that Khrushchev acted in a personal and highhanded manner in the Missile Crisis?"

Castro replied: "With regard to us, yes. Khrushchev had made great gestures of friendship toward our country. He had done things earlier that were extraordinarily helpful to us. But the way in which he conducted himself during the October Crisis was to us a serious affront."

Further on in the interview, Castro, while saying good things about Khrushchev, told Lockwood that at the time Khrushchev was replaced (October 1964), "our relations with him had reached their lowest point." The lowest point, "With him personally and consequently with his government." After he was deposed, the "situation improved considerably."

Exploring this point, Lockwood elicited more from Castro, including the following:

LOCKWOOD: You thought he should have taken a tougher line with the United States?
CASTRO: Just that, essentially.
LOCKWOOD: But there was nothing else which he did that contributed to the weakening of relations?
CASTRO: I have mentioned the October Crisis and the subsequent climate of distrust, which could never be completely overcome.
LOCKWOOD: Distrust by Cuba of the Soviet Union?
CASTRO: I would say distrust between Khrushchev and ourselves." (*Castro's Cuba, Cuba's Fidel*, pp. 225–26.)

These facts are difficult to explain on the basis of the theory that the Castro team is operated by remote control from the Kremlin. The difficulty vanishes if you keep in mind the non-Stalinist origin of this team and the persistence with which it has affected their relations with all other currents.

To bring things up to date, the following bit of information should be mentioned. During a trip to Cuba in May 1975, Senator George McGovern interviewed Castro. McGovern said later that among other things Castro told him: "I was furious when [Khrushchev] compromised [with Kennedy]. But Khrushchev was older and wiser. I realize in retrospect that he reached the proper settlement. . . . If my position had prevailed, there might have been a terrible war. I was wrong."

In passing it is worth mentioning that James P. Cannon was of the opinion at the time that in face of Kennedy's threat to plunge the world into a nuclear war there was no choice but to withdraw the missiles. (See Appendix.)

Guevara's criticisms

Another example testifying to the influence of the non-Stalinist origin of the Castro team was the speech given in Algiers by Che Guevara February 25, 1965, at the Economic Seminar of Afro-Asian Solidarity.

Although Che spoke rather diplomatically, his

sharpest points were directed at the Kremlin, as everyone understood.

"The practice of proletarian internationalism," he said, "is not only a duty of the peoples who are struggling to assure themselves a better future, it is, besides, an ineluctable necessity . . . for the socialist countries.

"The development of the countries which have today taken the road to freedom, must be underwritten by the socialist countries; this is my profound conviction."

He scored the practice of selling goods at world market prices to countries struggling to break out of the imperialist grip. "It is the duty of socialist countries to end their tacit complicity with the exploiting countries of the West."

On the need for solidarity with peoples struggling for their freedom, Guevara said: "Arms must not constitute a merchandise in our world; one must deliver them without any payment and in the quantities required by the peoples who need them."

Guevara took up other points—the aims of imperialism and the need to struggle against them, the effect of imperialist investments on dependent countries, the necessity to go beyond capitalism to socialism, practical steps to be taken in forging anti-imperialist alliances, and so on.

What stood out, however, was the impression he gave of the Castro team's disagreement with the Kremlin's antirevolutionary practices.

Other expressions of this attitude could be cited. Suffice it to call attention to Guevara's famous message of April 16, 1967, calling for "two, three, many Vietnams . . ."

Consider the following paragraphs:

> When we analyze the isolation of the Vietnamese we feel anguished over the logic of its meaning for humanity.
>
> North American imperialism is guilty of aggression. Its crimes are immense, extending over the whole world. We already know this, gentlemen!
>
> But they are likewise guilty who at the decisive moment vacillated in making Vietnam an inviolable part of socialist territory—yes, at risk of a war of global scale, but also compelling the North American imperialists to make a decision.
>
> And they are guilty who keep up a war of insults and tripping each other, begun some time ago by the representatives of the two biggest powers in the socialist camp. (*Che Guevara Speaks* [New York: Pathfinder Press, 1967, 2000], p. 182 [2013 printing].)

Words spoken by a stooge of Moscow? Of Peking? Or as a representative of a bureaucratic ruling caste in Cuba? No, Guevara was one of the top leaders of the Castro team, a new political current marked by its non-Stalinist political origin and its leadership of a successful socialist revolution.

The second Escalante case

Comrade Keil does not take up the second case involving Aníbal Escalante. Perhaps he views it as not differing essentially from the first case, which he dismisses as amounting to a Stalinist purge. Yet the second case really offers more material than the first for his interpretation of the evolution of the Cuban revolution. It is in any case worth noting.

In 1962 Escalante had been sent into exile in Prague. Permitted to return to Cuba in 1964, he was given a post as administrator of a state farm. He seemed to have passed into obscurity. However, he was not without influence among his old cronies of PSP days, who formed a social circle that gossiped about party affairs. This, of course, was their democratic right.

On January 28, 1968, Radio Havana announced that after a three-day session, the Central Committee of the Communist Party of Cuba had decided to expel Escalante. He and eight other former members of the PSP were to be turned over to the courts. Later, twenty-seven "accomplices," who were not members of the CPC, were also put on trial. All of them were given long prison terms, Escalante, for instance, receiving fifteen years.

The rights of the defendants were not safeguarded—they were violated—a fact that led to sharp criticisms from various partisans of the Cuban revolution.

First of all, the main charge leveled at the defendants was engagement in factional activities, which was not a crime under Cuban law. Secondly,

Escalante's "microfaction," as it was dubbed, was so small and its leader so discredited that it seemed to represent no serious danger. Why all the excitement? Finally, the procedure was bureaucratic and utterly out of line with the practices of a party built on the Leninist model.

These criticisms were justified. The procedure *was* antidemocratic. Nonetheless it would be a mistake to overlook the underlying clash of forces; otherwise our independent analysis of the political meaning of the removal of Escalante from the scene would prove to be defective.

1. The elimination of Escalante was a warning to the Kremlin in language it understood to stop throwing its weight in the internal affairs of the Communist Party of Cuba. This was a real issue; in 1967 a second secretary of the Soviet embassy had become involved in the "microfaction" and had been sent back to Moscow.

2. The strain of the blockade, coupled with economic errors made by the Cuban government, had begun to have an effect on the populace. Escalante's followers responded sensitively to the grumbling and helped to circulate it. The Castro team undoubtedly feared that in the context of siege conditions, the "microfaction" could rapidly become a "macrofaction," particularly if it was fostered by the Kremlin. The crackdown was a preventive measure against that possibility. (I am leaving aside the important question of how this situation might have been met in a better way.)

3. In the Communist Party of Cuba, the attack on Escalante also constituted a fresh blow to the old PSP elements and reinforcement of the younger layers with a background in the July 26 Movement or experience in the first years following the revolutionary victory.

4. Also involved was the dispute over "armed struggle" versus the "peaceful road" to socialism, which had reached high intensity at the OLAS Conference held in Havana August 4–11, 1967. The discussion was still going on, with the Cubans pitted against the Latin American Communist parties, which were backed by Moscow. Escalante epitomized the old Stalinist hacks who opposed the line of "armed struggle" from the standpoint of parliamentary politicking.

Thus at bottom the struggle was between a Stalinist "peaceful coexistence" current favored by the Kremlin and a revolutionary current of non-Stalinist origin hampered by Cuba's need for material aid from the Soviet Union.

The attacks on Trotskyism

As part of his thesis that Castro and Guevara "came under the thumb of a discredited Stalinist party" ("Cuba: Trotsky's Method Versus Maitan's Liquidationism," SWP Discussion Bulletin Vol. 34, No. 6, July 1976, p. 17) during the two-year period of 1959–61 in which they overturned capitalism in Cuba, and definitively sold out to Stalinism by July 26, 1961, Comrade Keil bears down heavily on the suppression of *Voz Proletaria* and the destruction of the type set for Trotsky's *Permanent Revolution* in 1961, as well as Castro's denunciation of Trotskyism in 1966.

These attacks were well answered by our movement at the time and it would seem unnecessary to go into them again. However, Comrade Keil's presentation leaves out some facts that not all comrades may know about.

For example, he describes *Voz Proletaria* as being Trotskyist. It was, however, one of the newspapers of the Posadas grouping. While Posadas claimed to be a Trotskyist and was at one time a member of the Fourth International, it would be difficult to imagine anyone worse qualified to represent Trotskyism in Cuba.

The source of his positions was an inner voice to which he gave free expression, recording the results in rambling dissertations that filled *Voz Proletaria* and other publications under his control. It ought to be sufficient to recall that one of his nostrums for speeding up the advance to socialism was a preemptive nuclear strike by the Soviet Union against the United States, for capitalism could not survive an atomic war while socialism could be built on the smoking ruins.

Quotations from *Voz Proletaria* were deftly used by the Stalinists to smear the Fourth International.

Why Comrade Keil calls the Posadist group "Trotskyist" is not clear. Perhaps it is overzealousness in trying to substantiate his thesis. It contrasts particularly with his saying that Comrade Maitan "is not a Trotskyist and has no idea what Stalinism is. . . ." (Ibid., p. 11.) Yet Posadas is a Trotskyist and knows what Stalinism is? Comrade Keil makes other assertions of similar kind that do not help clarify the issues; for instance: "Such people as Maitan have a way of deserting the revolutionary movement." (Ibid., p. 27.) And the "Trotskyist" Posadas?

We Trotskyists, of course, uphold the democratic right of every tendency in the workers movement to express its opinion through its press and through public assembly. At the same time, it must be flatly stated that the Posadas tendency—because of misrepresenting itself as "Trotskyist"—did the Trotskyist movement no good. In fact it facilitated, however unwittingly, the dirty work of Stalinists of the Escalante stripe.

Castro's attack on Trotskyism occurred on January 15, 1966. It was occasioned by a split in Yon Sosa's MR-13 guerrilla movement in Guatemala. The splitters, led by Luis Turcios, alleged that members of "the Fourth International" were playing a disruptive role in the organization. These "Fourth Internationalist" participants in the Guatemalan guerrilla movement were all members of the Posadas tendency.

Castro's denunciation created a storm of protest in the left internationally, and he backed off. It was soon evident that his reference to the "Fourth International" was actually to the Posadas tendency. The material on which he based his reference had been compiled by the Stalinists. It consisted of an amalgam of quotations from utterances by Posadas and attacks featured in the Healyite press in London. (For an account, see my article "Stalinism or Trotskyism in the Cuban Revolution?" in the *International Socialist Review*, summer 1966, p. 96.)

To finish with the Posadist "Trotskyists"—they were put on trial a few months later (April 29–30, 1966) by the MR-13. The charges were taking funds from the movement without authorization. The trial was completely fair, full rights being given to those on trial to defend themselves.

They did not deny the charges. Instead, they sought to justify their actions by claiming that the money was used for a worthy cause, having been sent to Posadas to finance his publications. As a result three of them were expelled from the MR-13. (For documentation on the trial, see *World Outlook*, July 15, 1966, pp. 28–36.)

The scandal was another serious blow to our movement because of the identification of Posadas with "Trotskyism." Let us hope that in his next contribution, Comrade Keil will join us in pointing out the false credentials used by Posadas.

Genuine Trotskyists existed in Cuba. In Havana a small group gave support to the July 26 Movement beginning about the time the guerrilla training camp was set up in Mexico. One of them, whom we saw from time to time, did work in the Cuban community in New York collecting funds.

With the victory in 1959, these Trotskyists were among the most active in facing the mountainous practical tasks that fell on the small revolutionary forces suddenly thrust into governmental power. Eventually they were absorbed by the July 26 Movement.

Following the victory, other Trotskyist cadres developed within the July 26 Movement. Under the ban on factions and tendencies it was not easy for them to spread their views, and some became discouraged. It is difficult to ascertain the present status of these loyal defenders of the Cuban revolution.

Besides this, other aspects must be taken into account in considering the possible influence of Trotskyism in Cuba. In the beginning, the mood was propitious to the growth of Trotskyist ideas. I.F. Stone summed up what he saw by coining the term "unconscious Trotskyists." Comrade Keil ridicules the term as illogical and as playing into the hands of the Healyites, who with their customary ill will and antipathy to the Cuban revolution attacked the formulation. However, it was Stone's honest impression, and all the more valuable because he was neither a Trotskyist nor unconscious.

Stone, and I think C. Wright Mills, concluded that an atmosphere favorable to Trotskyism existed because of what they heard from cadres who were both revolutionary and anti-Stalinist.

Some of these cadres had been members of the PSP in the fifties. Shaken up by the invasion of Hungary and Khrushchev's report on the crimes of Stalin, they quit the PSP. In other words, the PSP experienced a crisis like many other Stalinist parties at the time, and lost members, particularly intellectuals, who moved in various directions, the best ones toward the July 26 Movement. Some cadres who had lived abroad were aware of the main positions of Trotskyism and could talk intelligently about them, further impressing figures like Stone and Mills.

The fact that Guevara carried a book by Trotsky in his knapsack in Bolivia was not an anomaly but an indication of the attractiveness of Trotsky's analyses and outlook to at least some members of the Castro team. Guevara, of course, was especially friendly to some of the figures of the Fourth International (the real Fourth International).

It should be added that Trotskyists had no problem visiting Cuba and even giving lectures at the university, a situation that lasted up to and including the OLAS Conference in 1967.

The guerrilla orientation

Comrade Keil is mistaken, in my opinion, in his interpretation of the guerrilla orientation projected by the Castro leadership, following the establishment of a workers state in Cuba. He argues as follows:

> The 1973 LTF resolution acknowledges, 'The guerrillaism of the Cubans was quite logically coupled with depreciation of the validity and importance of revolutionary political principles.' (p. 15) This was because the principles followed by the Cuban CP were counterrevolutionary Stalinist principles. The Castroist leadership sought to frighten the U.S. and Latin American capitalists by promoting guerrilla struggle in Bolivia and other countries. This represented no break with Stalinism; at the same time that the Cuban leadership was developing the guerrilla warfare strategy, its Stalinist line became more and more hardened. The guerrilla strategy was nothing more than a peasant strategy constructed along Stalinist lines. There was no contradiction between the 'armed struggle' line and the policies of class collaboration. ("For a Political Revolution in Cuba: Against the Stalinist Cuban Communist Party: Draft Theses." SWP Discussion Bulletin, Vol. 35, No. 4, June 1977, p. 9.)

This position flows logically from Comrade Keil's thesis that the Cuban leadership "came under the thumb of a discredited Stalinist party" and that Castro and Guevara capitulated definitively to Stalinism in 1961. With a discredited Stalinist party in power in Cuba, anything it did in any field would naturally be Stalinist. In the guerrilla arena, its orientation would be "counterrevolutionary," designed only to "frighten the U.S. and Latin American capitalists." It stands to reason, doesn't it?

But it appears to me that a contradiction in Comrade Keil's position becomes visible at this point. He agrees that the Castro team had a non-Stalinist origin. Its origin, as we well know, was a guerrilla movement inside Cuba. Consequently *that* guerrilla movement was not Stalinist.

If we accept Comrade Keil's thesis, we are faced with the problem of explaining the transition from a non-Stalinist guerrilla orientation to a Stalinist one. To begin on firm ground, Comrade Keil is duty bound to explain, first of all, why the guerrilla movement organized, developed, and led by the Castro team was non-Stalinist in character.

He has already fulfilled the second requisite, describing what he considers to be the fraudulent nature of the succeeding *Stalinist* guerrilla orientation.

That leaves us with the third step—at what point did the original non-Stalinist guerrilla orientation change qualitatively into its opposite? What are the proofs?

There are important associated questions that likewise call for answers. For example, if Guevara succumbed to the outlook of a narrow bureaucratic caste in Cuba—becoming one of its leaders, according to Comrade Keil's thesis—why did he consider it necessary to risk his life leading a guerrilla movement in Bolivia? And why did Castro open up such a harsh struggle with the Latin American Stalinists over "armed struggle"?

I think that the interpretation of the Cuban guerrilla orientation given by our movement as a whole up to now matches the facts better than Comrade Keil's interpretation.

We based ourselves on the simple proposition that Castro and his comrades sought to project on an international level the same non-Stalinist guerrilla orientation that had brought them to power in Cuba. They well understood that the fate of the Cuban revolution hinged on international aid, the best and most solid form being the immediate extension of the Cuban revolution into Latin America.

They based themselves on their own experiences in struggling for power, on the immense international popularity of their achievements, and the effect of their success on the radicalization of the youth on a worldwide scale. Guerrilla movements based on following the Cuban example sprang up repeatedly all over Latin America.

All of this was real. For the Trotskyist movement—with its small forces—it meant linking up with the youth who had been inspired by the Cuban revolution, even if this required keeping in association with them while they went through the guerrilla experience. Our aim, of course, was to bring them to Trotskyism and to show them the advantages of building a Leninist-type party.

While demonstrating our solidarity with the Cuban revolution, we opposed the Castroist guerrilla orientation in Latin America. This was not because we considered it to be "Stalinist." The source of our opposition was the political calculation that the success won in Cuba could not be repeated in Latin America under the given relationship of class forces. Something more powerful was required; namely, a Leninist-type party. And we advocated—as we still advocate—that the Cubans should turn in this direction.

Later, in 1969, the majority of the Fourth International changed its opinion on the guerrilla orientation. A minority stuck to the original position. These different views constituted the principal grounds for the subsequent division of the Fourth International into contending factions.

The persistence of the Cubans in fostering guerrilla war and urging others to follow the example they had set in Cuba explains the rabid nature of the hostility displayed by the White House and the State Department—their blockade of Cuba, their vindictive campaign on the diplomatic level, their reprisals on ships that made deliveries to Cuba, their military forays and sabotage, their decision to murder Castro, as well as their broader policies such as expenditures on counterguerrilla operations, support of ultrareactionary governments and assistance in putting them in power through operations of the CIA. It is impossible to make all this vanish with a few phrases about "counterrevolutionary" guerrilla actions designed solely to "frighten the U.S. and Latin American capitalists," the better to gain Castro's real goal of class collaboration with these same enemy forces.

The persistence of the Cubans in pursuing a non-Stalinist guerrilla orientation also explains the factional in-fighting with the Latin American CPs who hypocritically praised the line but secretly resisted it and sabotaged it. This fight, as already mentioned, reached its high point at the 1967 OLAS Conference with Castro's condemnation of the Venezuelan CP. For those who attended that conference the sincerity of the Cubans was beyond question.

In reality, of course, the guerrilla orientation was in trouble. Instead of gaining successes, it was accumulating setbacks. One of the reasons was the sabotage of the Latin American CPs. Another was the inability of the Cubans to offer aid to guerrilla movements on a large scale; they were in a difficult situation themselves.

Yet the need for a breakthrough was obvious and compelling. In addition, the Cubans felt great solidarity toward the Vietnamese, engaged in a frightful conflict with the same imperialist enemy. It may well have been that in considering the declining chances of the Latin American guerrillas, Castro and Guevara concluded that one of the main defects was inadequate leadership. If this could be made up, a single breakthrough would alter the whole situation. Out of such calculations and perhaps others, Guevara decided to make a try in Bolivia.

Guevara's death on October 8, 1967, signified more than the end of a dedicated revolutionist, it marked the end of the guerrilla orientation as a major policy. It was evident that trying to repeat the Cuban example, even under the direct leadership of a Guevara, was not sufficient to win. The task of maintaining a beleaguered fortress under terrible strains was to last much longer than had been expected.

However, Guevara's death became a fresh factor in the international radicalization of the youth. During the May–June 1968 days in Paris, his photograph was the most prominent at the Sorbonne. He became enshrined among broad sectors of the revolutionary-minded youth.

Thus, ironically enough, Guevara's death and his inspiring example of dedication to the revolutionary cause also became one of the factors that influenced the majority of the Fourth International to adopt a guerrilla orientation in 1969, precisely as the guerrilla movement as a whole ebbed away in Latin America.

Eventually the failure of the guerrilla orientation enabled the Latin American Stalinists to make a come-back with their line of a "peaceful road to socialism." One of the tragic consequences was the disaster in Chile, which further isolated the Cuban workers state.

In the Fourth International, where the guerrilla orientation led to painful defeats in Bolivia and Argentina, the majority faction finally drew up a self-critical balance sheet of the experience.

The invasion of Czechoslovakia

Just ten months after the death of Che Guevara and seven months after the second crackdown on Escalante, the Cubans were confronted with a new crisis of major dimensions. On August 21, 1968, Moscow sent 350,000 troops into Czechoslovakia to crush the incipient political revolution against Stalinist rule.

Although the Cubans had nothing to do with this action, they were forced to take a stand. In a speech August 23, in which he took as his basic premise that the danger of a counterrevolution in Czechoslovakia was real, Castro reluctantly supported the invasion.

Moscow's action, of course, violated the democratic right of the Czechs and Slovaks to determine their own fate, a right fully supported by the Bolsheviks in the time of Lenin and Trotsky. To support the action, as Castro did, was in violation of the basic program of revolutionary socialism. It was obvious to political experts why he felt compelled to make this concession. Not to have done so would have endangered the sole source of material support to the Cuban revolution at a time of increasing economic difficulties under the American blockade. Because of the nature of the case, Castro only hinted at this. ("Some of the things that we are going to state here . . . will constitute serious risks for our country.") Castro's reticence on this aspect of the situation made it easier to picture him as a Stalinist puppet.

Comrade Keil uses Castro's support of the invasion as part of his evidence that the program of the Communist Party of Cuba is "counterrevolutionary"; and he goes so far as to say, among other things, that "there is no evidence of any critical comments from within the Cuban leadership" on the invasion of Czechoslovakia. ("Additional Material Relating to Cuba," SWP Discussion Bulletin, Vol. 33, No. 14, p. 44.)

This is inaccurate. It fails to mention the critical comments made by Castro in the very speech in which he sided with Moscow's action. A few quotations from the text of the speech as published in three successive issues of *Intercontinental Press* (September 2, September 9, and September 16, 1968; pp. 694, 720, and 759) will show how sharply Castro spoke:

> . . . it is not enough to simply accept the fact and nothing more—that Czechoslovakia was headed toward a counterrevolutionary situation and that it was necessary to prevent it. . . .
>
> What are the factors that created the necessity for a step which unquestionably entailed a violation of legal principles and international norms that, having often served as a shield for the peoples against injustice, are highly esteemed by the world?
>
> Because what cannot be denied here is that the sovereignty of the Czechoslovak state was violated. To say that it was not would be a fiction, an untruth. And the violation was, in fact, of a flagrant nature.

Quite logically this experience and this action constitute a bitter and tragic situation for the people of Czechoslovakia. . . . We must analyze the causes, the factors and the circumstances that made possible a situation in which, after twenty years of communism in Czechoslovakia, a group of personalities—whose names, incidentally, do not appear anywhere—found it necessary to appeal to other countries of the socialist camp to send their armies to prevent the triumph of the counterrevolution in Czechoslovakia and the triumph of the intrigues and conspiracies of the imperialist countries interested in tearing Czechoslovakia away from the community of socialist nations.

Gentlemen, is it conceivable that a situation

could occur, under any circumstances, after twenty years of communism in our country, of communist revolution, of socialist revolution, in which a group of honest revolutionaries, in this country, horrified by the prospect of an advance—or rather a retrogression—to counterrevolutionary positions and toward imperialism, could find themselves obliged to request the aid of friendly armies to prevent such a retrogression from occurring? What would have happened to the communist consciousness of this people? What would have happened to the revolutionary consciousness of this people? To the dignity of this people? To the revolutionary morale of this people? If such a situation could arise some day, what would be left of all these things which, for us constitute in essence the revolution?

What kind of communists would we be and what kind of communist revolution would this be, if, at the end of twenty years, we were to find ourselves forced to do such a thing in order to save it?

and, we repeat, how were these circumstances possible? An analysis of the factors involved must be undertaken. . . .

Obviously, this is not the time to make or pretend to make that profound analysis. But we can cite some facts and ideas. Bureaucratic methods in the leadership of the country, lack of contact with the masses—a decisive question for every true revolutionary movement—neglect of communist ideals. And what do we mean by neglect of communist ideals? We mean forgetting that men in a class society, the enslaved, struggle for a whole series of ideals, and when they speak of socialism and communism they are not only speaking of a society where exploitation does actually disappear and the poverty resulting from that exploitation disappears, but they are speaking also of all those beautiful aspirations that constitute the communist ideal of a classless society, a society free from selfishness, a society in which man is no longer a miserable slave to money, in which society no longer works for personal gain, and all of society begins to work for the satisfaction of all needs and for the establishment among men of the rule of justice, fraternity, equality and all those ideals of human society and of the peoples who have always aspired to achieving these objectives. And these objectives are possible, as we have explained on other occasions, as we explained amply last July 26.

We can say—and today it is necessary to speak clearly and frankly—that we have seen to what extent these ideals and international sentiments, that state of alertness and awareness of the world's problems, have disappeared or are very weakly expressed in certain socialist countries of Europe.

We would not say in all these countries, but in more than one socialist country of Europe. Those who have visited these countries, including Cuban students on scholarships, have often come back completely dissatisfied and displeased and have said to us: 'Over there the youth are not being educated in the ideals of communism and in the principles of internationalism: the youth there are highly influenced by all the ideas and tastes prevalent in the countries of Western Europe. In many places the main topic of conversation is money and incentives of this or that type, material incentives of all kinds, material gains and salaries.' As a matter of fact, an internationalist and communist conscience is not being developed in those places.

Added to all this is the preaching of peace. In the socialist countries peace has been incessantly and widely preached. And we ask ourselves, what are all these campaigns leading up to? Do we say this because we are in favor of war? Do we say this because we are the enemies of peace? We are not the enemies of peace; we are not in favor of wars; we do not advocate universal holocausts. I feel obliged to say this because when we analyze these questions, right away it always brings up the cliché, the schemata, the accusations of warmongering, of promoting war, of being irresponsible, and so on and so forth. . . .

The real promoters of war, the real adventurers, are the imperialists. Now, then, these dangers are real; they are a reality. And this reality cannot be changed by simply preaching, in one's own house, an excessive desire for peace. In any case, the preaching should be done in the enemy's camp and not in one's own camp, because this would only contribute to stifling militancy, to weakening the people's readiness to face the risks, sacrifices, not only the possible ultimate sacrifice of one's life, but also material sacrifices.

And when the peoples know that the realities of the world, the independence of the country, and internationalist duties demand investment and sacrifices in the strengthening of the defense of the country, the masses are much better prepared to work with enthusiasm to achieve this, to make sacrifices, understanding this need, being conscious of the dangers that arise when the people have been stirred up and softened by a constant, foolish and inexplicable campaign in favor of peace. It is a very strange way of defending peace. That is why we who at the beginning did so many foolish things out of ignorance or naïveté, for a long time now have not painted any signs around here saying, 'Long Live Peace,' 'Long Live This,' 'Long Live That.'

Because at the beginning, out of mimicry, by imitation, we repeated things as they arrived here, until we reached a point, well, what is the meaning of 'Long Live Peace'? Let's put up that sign in New York: 'Long Live Peace' in New York, 'Long Live Peace' in Washington.

A series of standards, a series of ideas, a series of practices incomprehensible to us, which have really contributed to slackening and softening the revolutionary spirit of the socialist countries; ignorance of the problems of the underdeveloped world, ignorance of the shocking misery which exists; tendencies toward maintaining trading practices with the underdeveloped world which are the same as those carried on by the developed bourgeois capitalist world. I'm not talking about all the socialist countries, but some of them.

. . . when we give some technical aid, we do not think of sending a bill to anyone, because we think that the least a developed country, a socialist country, a revolutionary country, can do to help the underdeveloped world is to send technicians.

We cannot imagine sending a bill to anyone for arms which we give him or sending a bill to anyone for technical aid, or even reminding him of it. Because if we are going to give aid and if we are going to bring up the fact every day, what we will be doing is constantly humiliating those whom we are aiding. I don't think there is any need to go around preaching about it too much.

All of us know that the leadership which Czechoslovakia had, generally, for twenty years was a leadership plagued with many vices: dogmatism, bureaucracy, and, in short, many things which cannot be presented as examples of truly revolutionary leadership.

When we speak here, when we present our thesis about the 'liberaloid' nature of this group, so warmly greeted by imperialism, it does not mean in any way that we are expressing our solidarity with the former leadership. We must bear in mind that that leadership, with which we had relations from the very beginning, even sold this country, at a high price, many weapons which were spoils of war seized from the Nazis, weapons for which we have been paying, and are still paying for today, which belonged to Hitler's troops that occupied Czechoslovakia. . . .

On many occasions they sold us very outdated factories. We have seen the results of many of the economic concepts on which they base their business transactions, on which they base their eagerness to sell any old junk, and it must be stated that these practices led to their selling old, outdated junk to a country which is making a revolution and has to develop.

There is a series of questions that disturb us. It disturbs us that, so far, there has been no direct charge against Yankee imperialism in any of the statements made by the countries that sent their divisions to Czechoslovakia, or in the explanation of the events.

We have been informed exhaustively concerning all the preceding events, all the facts, all the deviations, all about this or that liberal group; we have been informed of their activities. The activities of the imperialists and in the intrigues of the imperialists are well known, and we are disturbed to see that neither the Communist party nor the government of the Soviet Union, nor the governments of the other countries that sent their troops to Czechoslovakia, have made any direct accusation against Yankee imperialism for its responsibility in the events in Czechoslovakia.

It is understandable that the countries of the Warsaw Pact sent their armies to destroy the imperialist conspiracy and the progress of counterrevolution in Czechoslovakia. However, we have disagreed with, been displeased at, and protested against the fact that these same countries have been drawing closer economically, culturally and politically to the oligarchic governments of Latin America, which are not merely reactionary governments and exploiters of their peoples, but also shameless accomplices in the imperialist aggressions against Cuba and shameless accomplices in the economic blockade of Cuba. And these countries have been encouraged and emboldened by the fact that our friends, our natural allies, have ignored the vile and treacherous role enacted by those governments against a socialist country, the policy of blockade practiced by those countries against a socialist country.

. . . we ask ourselves if that policy of economic, political and cultural rapprochement toward those oligarchic governments that are accomplices in the imperialist blockade against Cuba will come to an end.

One of them, Argentina, even shelled a Soviet fishing vessel—shelled it! I believe they even wounded one of the members of the vessel's crew. Afterwards they were like beasts over there, lying in wait for another boat. They commit flagrant, indecent actions against everybody, yet that soft line has been followed in regard to them—a line which, in our opinion, only encourages their position as accomplices in the aggressions against Cuba.

Something similar is happening to the Communist parties of Europe, today trapped in their own indecision. And we wonder whether possibly in the future the relations with Communist parties will be based on principled positions or whether they will continue to be guided by their degree of willingness to maintain a spineless attitude, to be satellites, lackeys—a situation in which only those that maintain a spineless attitude, say 'Yes' to everything and never assume an independent position on anything, would be considered friendly.

So there you have those who criticized us on innumerable occasions, today overwhelmed by the worst kind of confusion.

Our party did not hesitate to help the Venezuelan guerrillas when a rightist and treacherous leadership, betraying the revolutionary line, abandoned the guerrillas and entered into shameless collusion with the regime. At that time we presented our analysis as to which side was right—that scheming, politicking group that betrayed the combatants, that betrayed those who had given their lives, or those who kept the flag of rebellion flying. . . .

I ask myself, in the light of the facts and in the light of the bitter reality that persuaded the nations of the Warsaw Pact to send their forces to crush the counterrevolution in Czechoslovakia, and—according to their statement—to back a minority in the face of a majority with rightist positions, if they will also cease to support these rightist, reformist, sold-out, submissive leaderships in Latin America that are enemies of the armed revolutionary struggle, that oppose the peoples' liberation struggle.

And, with the example of this bitter experience before them, I wonder whether or not the parties of those countries, in line with the decision made in Czechoslovakia, will cease to support those rightist groups that betray the revolutionary movement in Latin America.

We do not and cannot believe in the possibility of an improvement in relations between the socialist camp and the U.S. imperialist government as long as that country performs the role of international gendarme, aggressor against the peoples and enemy and systematic opponent of revolutions everywhere in the world. Much less can we believe in any such improvement in the midst of an aggression as criminal and cowardly as that being waged against Vietnam.

Our position on this is very clear: one is consistent with world realities and is truly internationalist and genuinely and decidedly supports the revolutionary movement throughout the world, in which case relations with the imperialist government of the United States cannot be improved, or relations with the imperialist U.S. government will improve, but only at the cost of withholding consistent support from the worldwide revolutionary movement.

Additional pertinent passages could be quoted from this speech, including a cutting attack on Titoism that Castro associated with the anti-revolutionary attitude of the Warsaw Pact governments. However, these extracts should be sufficient to show that Castro did not click his heels and salute when the Soviet armies invaded Czechoslovakia.

We said at the time that "it is dubious that Castro's speech will be published in the Soviet Union or any of the East European countries." To this day it has been kept in the closet in those countries.

Castro's "critical comments" remain inexplicable if you hold to the thesis that he sold out to Stalinism in 1961. They are easily explained if you keep in mind the non-Stalinist origin of the Castro leadership.

The Cuban role in Angola

In his polemic against Comrade Maitan, Comrade Keil argues as follows:

> At least we are in favor of Castro supporting Puerto Rican independence, but we cannot be in favor of what Castro did in Angola. Cuban troops were sent, not to support a revolution or a national liberation struggle against imperialism, but to support one nationalist movement with a pro-capitalist leadership against two other similar movements. Cuban policy was to support the MPLA in a fratricidal war. . . . If Castro's policy on Angola was 'internationalist,' so was Brezhnev's identical policy, to which Cuban policy was subordinated. (P. 13.)

It is doubtful that Castro's policy in sending troops to Angola was either identical to Brezhnev's policy or subordinated to it. True, such a conclusion follows directly from Comrade Keil's thesis that Castro sold out to Stalinism in 1961. However, if that thesis is mistaken, we must examine the Cuban role in Angola carefully to see if any trace can be found of the non-Stalinist origin of the Castro leadership.

Before proceeding, let us pause to consider the view that the policies of Castro and Brezhnev in Angola are "identical." If this is true we are compelled to ask: "Has Brezhnev initiated a new Soviet foreign policy qualitatively different from that of the past? Does the Kremlin now project intervening in Africa—and elsewhere—with armed force? Was the dispatch of Cuban troops the opener in this new policy?"

If these questions are answered affirmatively, then it is imperative to analyze the reasons for the shift and determine what our political attitude should be towards it.

I do not think that the Kremlin has begun an aggressive foreign policy, but it is implied if you equate the foreign policies of Havana and Moscow and hold that the real command is exercised by Brezhnev.

The alternative interpretation, which in my opinion comes closer to the reality, is that Castro should be credited with originating the idea. It is reminiscent of all his bold plays, going back to the Moncada incident and including the episode of the nuclear missiles in 1962.

By checking the sequence of events, we can see this perhaps more clearly.

Cuban aid first became substantial in the spring of 1975 when the coalition government formed by the three Angolan liberation movements collapsed and the People's Movement for the Liberation of Angola (MPLA) asked the Cuban government to send advisers. The Cubans responded by sending 230 military technicians. This was *before* Soviet advisers had appeared in the Angolan capital of Luanda.

On October 23, 1975, when the South Africans suddenly sent armed forces into Angola, it was alleged that 1,500 Cuban troops were present in the country.

On November 10, the Portuguese government announced that it was transferring sovereignty in its former colony to "the Angolan people"; and the next day many governments, including Havana, recognized the MPLA as the government in power.

The Cubans continued to step up their aid. The Associated Press reported November 19 that 1,000 more Cuban soldiers had arrived. The Ford administration said December 11 that the number of Cuban troops present in Angola had risen to 5,000. The December 26 issue of *Granma* reported that the number present had "doubled" to 7,500. By January 21, 1976, when Havana halted the airlift, Kissinger's estimate of the number of Cuban troops present in Angola was 11,000.

It is thus clear that the transport of troops did not occur in a single dramatic operation, but was stretched out over a period of possibly seven months. Moreover, the Cubans had to rely on their own very limited means of transport. When the accumulation of Cuban troops became noticeable in Angola, Washington resorted to heavy diplomatic pressure to bar Cuban planes from refueling stops in places like Guyana, Canada, and the Azores.

The relative roles of Moscow and Havana in sending Cuban troops to Angola was, of course, of keen interest to State Department officials. We know a little about their calculations from a report that appeared in the February 5, 1976, issue of the *New York Times*.

Kissinger, the *Times* said, had concluded that Cuba had resumed "exporting revolution" on its own initiative. As head of the State Department he had decided not to express himself publicly, preferring instead to press the Soviet Union to end its intervention in Angola. Kissinger reasoned that he had no diplomatic leverage with Cuba, while he did have leverage with the Soviet government because of the détente.

Kissinger rejected the theory that Havana had been forced by Moscow to send troops to Angola: "I believe the Cubans went in there with flags flying."

Two unidentified Soviet officials were likewise quoted by the *Times* as echoing Kissinger. One of them said: "We did not twist their arms. We didn't even have to twist their arms. The Cubans wanted to go in."

Did Kissinger make a gross error in brushing aside the theory, widely voiced in the communications media at the time, that Castro was acting on Brezhnev's orders? It is hardly likely. Kissinger had very good sources of information; and he utilized them in determining a line of action that would best meet the realities from the imperialist point of view. We should carefully note that he did not equate Brezhnev and Castro; he viewed Castro as the initiator of the move of sending Cuban troops to Angola.

The reaction of the masses in Africa should also be noted. While no poll has been taken of their opinion, a good gauge is offered by the contrast in applause given to Castro and Podgorny on their joint tour of African countries in March of this year. The ovations went to Castro; lukewarm applause acknowledged the presence of the old Stalinist bureaucrat.

Let us now consider Comrade Keil's assertion that Cuban troops were sent "not to support a revolution or a national liberation struggle against imperialism, but to support one nationalist movement with a pro-capitalist leadership against two other similar movements." On this, Comrade Keil appears to have modified his position somewhat. Together with Comrade Cooper, he uses the following phrasing in the document "For a Political Revolution in Cuba":

> 12. Cuban intervention in Angola in 1975 and 1976 had two sides. On the one hand, the Cuban presence stayed the hand of imperialism, South African imperialism in particular. On the other hand, the Cuban military policy was not to offer aid to all three Angolan nationalist groups against imperialist intervention. Rather it was to side with one nationalist group, the MPLA, in a fratricidal civil war. When the MPLA won, this led to Cuba training and advising the police and military forces of the neocolonial regime which the MPLA established. This part of Cuban policy in Angola was a criminal betrayal of the Angolan masses and a service to imperialism. (P. 11.)

It is good that Comrades Keil and Cooper have recognized that the action taken by the Cubans in sending troops to Angola was directed against imperialism, although it was not only the imperialism of South Africa but, more importantly, the imperialism located ninety miles from Cuba. The action of the Cubans effectively countered the CIA undercover operations organized by Kissinger in collusion with the Vorster regime. In this way, the Cubans acted as our allies in the struggle against imperialism. They helped us to block Ford and Kissinger from escalating the U.S. intervention in Angola up to the level of another Vietnam. That was certainly a service to humanity and to the cause of socialism.

Verification of the accuracy and effectiveness of the Cuban blow came from Washington itself. Part of the evidence was the high-pitched screaming in the White House and the State Department. Who can ever forget how President Ford, between bumping his head on door frames and tumbling down airplane landing steps, cursed Castro as an "international outlaw"?

In Miami February 28, 1976, in a voice that ought to have carried across the Straits of Florida to Havana, Ford bellowed: "My Administration will have nothing to do with the Cuba of Fidel Castro. It is a regime of aggression. And I solemnly warn Fidel Castro against any temptation to armed intervention in the Western Hemisphere. Let his regime, or any like-minded government [Brezhnev's?], be assured the United States would take the appropriate measures."

There you have it—the pitiful giant slapping at a Cuban wasp.

Washington's alarm over the presence of Cuban troops in Angola was genuine. The reason was the increase in instability this introduced into Africa. The explosive end of the Portuguese empire in southern Africa might still set off a new chain reaction. The Cuban troops, although actually small in numbers, might provide an element assuring such a development.

How about the other side of the Cuban move: (1) the failure "to offer aid to all three Angolan nationalist groups against imperialist intervention"; and (2) the support given to the MPLA?

If the three contending factions had proved capable of forming and maintaining a joint government, it would have certainly made it easier to secure aid from other countries, including Cuba. But they could not work together. Despite holding programmatic positions that had much in common, their internecine struggle degenerated into a power fight in which all three resorted to force of arms to settle the issue. Each of them sought material aid from whatever sources were available.

The MPLA won out in this civil strife, which the imperialists had sought to turn to their own advantage. The result was thus the installment of an MPLA government, and this fact—whether for good or bad—became a new element in the situation. The imperialists took as their immediate task the toppling of this government. However, they soon saw that this was a futile course in view of the balance of forces, and they shifted to the longer range objective of subverting the MPLA.

The Leninist Trotskyist Faction and the Socialist Workers Party certainly never opposed the anti-imperialist aspects of the liberation struggle of the Angolans. We were, in fact, in the forefront of the struggle against Portuguese, South African, and American imperialism. We urged the three factions in Angola to unite against Portuguese colonialism. We put the interests of that battle against Lisbon in first place at every significant turn. We sought, for instance, at an appropriate point to turn the demand for the withdrawal of Portuguese troops into a main slogan. This would have facilitated the international campaign in favor of the Angolan liberation movement.

But we never identified politically with any of the three Angolan factions. We pointed out that this was excluded because of the nature of their programs. We called attention to the fact that none of them, including the MPLA, had a socialist program. We went to some lengths to analyze the social and political nature of the three factions in Angola because of the apprehension aroused in us by the fact that some comrades in the Fourth International tended to take a soft attitude politically toward the MPLA and to engage in wishful thinking that the MPLA, under the pressure of events, might take a socialist course. That could easily lead to placing political confidence in the MPLA; in other words, beginning to feel that the MPLA would certainly act in accordance with Trotskyist wishes.

On this question we have a sharp difference with the Cubans. It does sow illusions to present the MPLA as committed to socialism. It does hamper the struggle for socialism to fail to point out the bourgeois nature of their program.

At the same time, we are committed to the Leninist tactic of drawing a distinction between the imperialist powers and the bourgeoisie or incipient bourgeoisie of a colonial or semicolonial country. Revolutionary Marxists are not only permitted but enjoined to make alliances when possible with such forces against imperialism even if the alliances prove to be but temporary because of the vacillations and undependability of the leaders of these antisocialist class forces. Moreover, so long as an alliance with them remains in effect, a friendly attitude should be maintained, including in educational material and polemics explaining why the revolutionary Marxists insist on proceeding under their own banner.

To exclude an anti-imperialist alliance with a colonial, semicolonial, or neocolonial government or liberation movement is completely sectarian—at least according to the norms of Leninist politics.

In foreign policy, the Castro leadership has sought anti-imperialist alliances from the beginning, particularly in Latin America. The gauge has been the attitude of the bourgeois governments toward the Cuban revolution. Concretely this has meant their stand on diplomatic relations with Havana and especially their attitude toward the blockade. If a Latin American government refuses to recognize the blockade and maintains friendly diplomatic relations, this is taken by the Cubans as sufficient evidence of an anti-imperialist stand.

In each instance, the Cubans have failed to indicate the antisocialist nature of these governments, which may have been required by governmental diplomatic necessities but which stood in violation of the principles of Leninism. The violation has been compounded by the inordinate public praise lavished on the governments that refused to bow to State Department pressures on these questions. In other words, Castro gave them political support, including the attribution of virtues that none of them possessed, in return for helping to break the blockade, an objective that was ultimately gained.

The political price paid by Havana was a high one. The failure to draw programmatic distinctions fostered class collaborationism in these countries, hampered the building of revolutionary-Marxist parties, and helped the Stalinists make a comeback.

One of the consequences was the debacle in Chile. (We should not, however, overlook the responsibility of the Trotskyist movement for the paucity of revolutionary-Marxist cadres when the opportunities opened up on a giant scale.) Castro, who visited Chile from November 10 to December 4, 1971, may not have been as optimistic as he made out at the time. Besides calling for sacrifices by the workers in support of Allende, he dwelt on the "fascist" danger in the country and the need to mobilize against it. His parting personal gift to Allende was, significantly, a submachine gun.

In the case of Agostinho Neto, whom Castro evidently views in much the same light as he viewed Allende, not only were guns supplied but troops to use them and to show the Angolans how to stand up firmly against imperialism. The biggest defect was the failure to indicate the political limitations of the MPLA.

Dangerous developments in Cuba

In defending the Cuban revolution, the Castro leadership has been compelled to rely on Soviet material aid. At the same time the principal requirement in expanding the revolution is opposition to the political strictures placed on that aid. This is the most glaring contradiction facing the Cubans in foreign policy. The constant threat emanating from American imperialism has forced them to remain within Moscow's orbit.

When they realized that the relationship of class forces in Latin America made a duplication of the pattern of the Cuban victory quite unlikely, the Castro leadership gave up the policy of offering substantial support to the declining guerrilla movements. But the correct lesson was not drawn. A shift was not made to the strategy of building Leninist-type parties. Instead, with the collapse of their guerrilla perspective, the Cubans retreated. They turned to securing the indispensable safety line of material aid from the USSR. As part of this effort, they sought to integrate the country's economy as much as possible into the economic framework of the Soviet Union and the East European countries.

Concomitantly, they sought to remove whatever political obstacles might exist to achieving this elementary goal. Undoubtedly they felt too weak and vulnerable to do otherwise in view of the collapse of the guerrilla strategy and the danger of being crushed by American imperialism. The result was increasing adaptation to the pressures emanating from Moscow.

Our movement has reported the successive steps, criticizing them sharply and pointing to the increased chances of degeneration of the revolution if this course were pursued to its logical end.

The democratic rights that constituted the main program of the July 26 Movement were the first to suffer damage, beginning about 1961. The blows included restrictions on freedom of speech and assembly, on the right to organize political groupings whose support of the revolution was unquestionable but who had criticisms of the leadership to offer.

An extension was the banning of tendencies and factions within the Communist Party of Cuba. The absence of a Leninist-type party governed by the rules of democratic centralism closed off the possibility of easy rectification of mistaken courses; for instance, the effort to obtain a harvest of ten million tons of sugar in 1970, which was well above the capacities of the country.

Internationally, too, the absence of a Leninist-type party has been costly. Such a party could analyze the political programs of movements or governments independently of governmental diplomatic needs. With but a single authoritative voice, that of Fidel Castro, the contradiction between the need to speak independently and the need to maintain favorable diplomatic relations is difficult to resolve.

Freedom of the arts has also suffered. In the early years, Cuba offered a refreshing contrast to the insufferable bureaucratic controls imposed in the other workers states. The arrest of Heberto Padilla, one of Cuba's major poets, on March 20, 1971, marked a turning point in this area. After about five weeks in jail and after having written a long statement repudiating his own works and "confessing," that he was guilty of "moral and cultural turpitude," Padilla was released. Included in his public "self-criticism" was a denunciation of K.S. Karol and René Dumont as CIA agents "beyond any doubt."

Since both Karol and Dumont were outstanding sympathizers of the Cuban revolution, the charges leveled against them as well as the handling to which Padilla had been subjected led to a storm of protest from leftist intellectuals everywhere. Castro brushed all this aside, and a deep rift appeared between the Cubans and these supporters of the Cuban revolution.

Instead of moving toward the establishment of a soviet form of government on the model that existed in the Soviet Union under Lenin and Trotsky, the Castro leadership moved toward electoral forms resembling those set up by Stalin.

The actual power of decision is exercised by a tiny group—in the final analysis by Fidel Castro himself. This is one of the features of the present governmental forms that is most dangerous to the Cuban revolution.

According to the theory of the Trotskyist movement, a personal dictatorship is not excluded in extremely exceptional circumstances; however, it is considered to be a great danger and a sure sign of the weakness of the revolution.

In Cuba it puts in question the consolidation of the revolution on the basis of proletarian democracy. While big advances have been made, the narrow basis of power has also increased the incidence of serious mistakes, and it leaves perpetually unsettled the question of succession.

The growth of bureaucratism has been registered by the introduction of ranks in the armed forces and the granting of some privileges in governmental layers. Nonetheless this incipient bureaucratic stratification must be weighed against such achievements as the elimination of racism, the liquidation of illiteracy, and the great emphasis on developing housing, educational opportunities, and medical and other social services for the populace as a whole despite the general poverty. The first concern of the Castro leadership has truly been the well-being of the poor and not the development of a parasitic bureaucracy.

It has been observed quite correctly that the Cubans have made no contributions to Marxist theory. We can add that in the first years they even tended to ridicule theory, giving *action* almost mystical powers. But this is not a telling argument against them. It is better to admit that they had a certain justification for their depreciation of theory—they had led a socialist revolution to victory without being theoretical experts. Consequently they felt that their experience could be repeated; *action* was what counted. "The duty of every revolutionary is to make the revolution."

In making a revolution, Marxist theory counts nonetheless. It enabled us to forecast that the guerrilla orientation had become outmoded in Latin America. But the same theory also enabled us to recognize that the Castro leadership represented something new. We recalled Trotsky's words in "An Open Letter to Comrade Burnham": "In the next epoch we can expect great revolutionists of action but hardly a new Marx." (*In Defense of Marxism* [New York: Pathfinder Press, 1942, 1995], p. 155 [2012 printing].) Castro, Guevara, and their comrades marked the appearance on the world political scene of revolutionists of action. As more of this type appear, we can be sure they will increasingly feel the need for a good guide to action. And they will find this in revolutionary-Marxist theory as maintained and developed by the Trotskyist movement.

Despite the encroachments of bureaucratism in Cuba, I am of the opinion that the trend has not reached the point of qualitative change; that is, the appearance of a hardened bureaucratic ruling caste. Consequently, as I see it, to call for a political revolution is premature to say the least; and the proposal of Comrades Keil and Cooper to take that stand should be rejected.

The main course of the SWP in defense of the Cuban revolution should continue to be political action against American imperialism paralleling the anti-imperialist defense efforts of the Castro leadership. That is what is most important politically for us who are located within the imperialist monster. We should register our criticisms but subordinate them to this prime need.

Appendix

Los Angeles, California
October 31, 1962

New York, New York

Dear Farrell:

Now that the crest of the Cuban crisis seems to have passed, everyone is assessing its outcome. This is the trend of our thinking in informal discussions here.

We must keep our eyes on the main issues and not get sidetracked by subsidiary considerations. What was the situation?

1. The U.S. naval blockade was set for a clash with Soviet ships which could escalate into nuclear war. Kennedy gave clear notice that the U.S. would not stop at the use of the most forceful measures.

2. The Pentagon was ready to bomb and invade Cuba and crush its revolution. Newspaper accounts report that this was one of the alternative moves considered even for the start, and it was to be put into effect if Moscow did not yield on the missile bases.

In the face of these direct and immediate threats to world peace and the Cuban revolution, Khrushchev drew back, agreed to pull out the missiles, and dismantle the bases under U.N. supervision. He received in return a suspension of the blockade and public assurances that Cuba would not be invaded.

What else could he have done under the given circumstances? It would have been foolhardy to risk setting off a thermonuclear war and daring the U.S. to come and wipe out the Cuban bases in view of Washington's evident determination to go the limit if necessary.

In our opinion Khrushchev sensibly backed away from such a showdown, thus saving the world from war and the Cuban revolution from attack by overwhelming forces for a *time*. But this *time* is of decisive importance!

The retreat was unavoidable and the concessions, as we know about them, did not give up anything essential. Those who judge otherwise should tell us what alternative course the Kremlin should have followed on the military and diplomatic fronts at that excruciating point of decision. Should Khrushchev have defied the embargo or refused outright to withdraw the missile bases?

The crisis over Cuba is of immense importance. But we should not forget it is only one sector in a world-wide conflict between imperialism and the workers states which has witnessed in the past, and will see again, advances and retreats by one side or the other. As revolutionary realists, we have not criticized or condemned heads of workers states or union leaders for retreating and making concessions when the balance of forces was unfavorable. Lenin traded space for time at Brest-Litovsk. As we know from our Minneapolis experiences, even the most militant leadership which is up against the gun may have to give ground before the insuperable power of the employer in order to save the existence of the union and fight another day.

The grim fact was that both the Soviet Union and Cuba not only had guns, but even more fearsome weapons, poised over their heads and ready to be used.

For this reason we do not believe that Khrushchev's course was incorrect on the level of military affairs and state relations. To condemn it and cry "betrayal" would only help the Stalinists get off the hook where they are really vulnerable. That is their policy of supporting Kennedy, Stevenson and other "peace-loving" Democratic capitalist politicians. This attitude, flowing from the Kremlin's doctrine of peaceful co-existence, has again been exposed as criminal.

Although we should carefully watch their development, we should be cautious and not jump to conclusions about the relations between Castro and Khrushchev. The latter's unilateral decisions and divergent aims may have created friction between them but it would be unwise to substitute speculations for solid facts. Khrushchev's declarations have not indicated any abandonment of Cuba, and it would be difficult for him to do so with the eyes of China, the colonial peoples and the Soviet militants upon him. On the other hand, Castro deeply needs Soviet aid.

The principal point—and you make it in the editorial—is that the world, the socialist movement and the Cuban revolution have gained time. The bombs are still there. But they were not dropped anywhere. And we are heartily in favor of that!

Despite gleeful claims by the American press that Kennedy's strong stand has given a stern lesson and severe setback to "Soviet aggression," people unaffected by imperialist propaganda have, I believe, breathed relief over the settlement and thank Khrushchev for his sanity. Bertrand Russell and Nehru expressed themselves along that line.

We must remember that nuclear war would mean the greatest defeat for humanity and socialism. We must avert that terrible eventuality, not, to be sure, by stopping the class struggle against imperialism, but by utilizing every means that will give the workers time enough to wake up & organise themselves for that purpose.

Jim Cannon

THE CUBAN REVOLUTION AND WORLD POLITICS

October 1962
The 'Missile' Crisis as Seen from Cuba
TOMÁS DIEZ ACOSTA

In October 1962 Washington pushed the world to the edge of nuclear war. Here the full story of that historic moment is told from the perspective of the Cuban people, whose determination to defend their sovereignty and their socialist revolution blocked US plans for a devastating military assault. $17

Red Zone
Cuba and the Battle against Ebola in West Africa
ENRIQUE UBIETA GÓMEZ

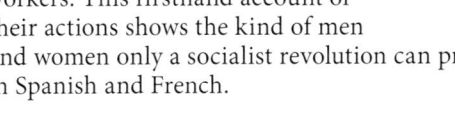

When three African countries were hit in 2014–15 by the Ebola epidemic, Cuba's revolutionary government sent what no other country even pretended to provide: more than 250 volunteer doctors, nurses, and other medical workers. This firsthand account of their actions shows the kind of men and women only a socialist revolution can produce. $17. Also in Spanish and French.

The First and Second Declarations of Havana

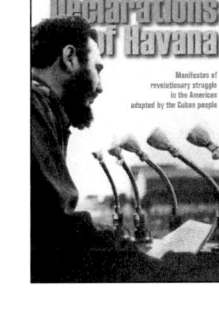

Nowhere are the questions of revolutionary strategy that today confront men and women on the front lines of struggles in the Americas addressed with greater truthfulness and clarity than in these uncompromising indictments of imperialist plunder and "the exploitation of man by man." Adopted by million-strong assemblies of the Cuban people in 1960 and 1962. $10. Also in Spanish, French, Farsi, Arabic, and Greek.

The Inevitable Battle
From the Bay of Pigs to Playa Girón
JUAN CARLOS RODRÍGUEZ

The rout of US-organized and -financed forces at Girón Beach on Cuba's Bay of Pigs in April 1961 was Washington's greatest military defeat in the Americas. It has marked the course of history for the last sixty years. $20. Also in Spanish.

Our History Is Still Being Written
The Story of Three Chinese Cuban Generals in the Cuban Revolution
ARMANDO CHOY, GUSTAVO CHUI
MOISÉS SÍO WONG
MARY-ALICE WATERS

"What was the key measure to uproot discrimination against Chinese and blacks in Cuba? It was the socialist revolution itself." New edition sheds light on Chinese Cubans' involvement in Cuba's internationalist course, including in Africa and Latin America. $15. Also in Spanish, French, Farsi, Greek, and Chinese.

Cuba and Angola: The War for Freedom
HARRY VILLEGAS ("POMBO")

The story of Cuba's unparalleled contribution to the fight to free Africa from the scourge of apartheid. And how, in the doing, Cuba's socialist revolution was strengthened. $10. Also in Spanish, Farsi, and Greek.

Cuba and the Coming American Revolution
JACK BARNES

This is a book about the struggles of working people in the imperialist heartland, the youth attracted to them, and the example set by the Cuban people that revolution is not only necessary—it can be made. It is about the class struggle in the US, where the revolutionary capacities of workers and farmers are today as utterly discounted by the ruling powers as were those of the Cuban toilers. And just as wrongly. $10. Also in Spanish, French, and Farsi.

Che Guevara Talks to Young People

Guevara challenges the youth of Cuba and the world to work. To become disciplined. To join the vanguard on the front lines of struggles, small and large. To become a different kind of human being as they fight together with working people of all lands to transform the world. $12. Also in Spanish and Greek.

WWW.PATHFINDERPRESS.COM

Also from Pathfinder

The Communist Manifesto
Karl Marx and Frederick Engels

Communism, say the founding leaders of the revolutionary workers movement, is not a set of ideas or preconceived "principles" but workers' line of march to power, springing from a "movement going on under our very eyes." $5. Also in Spanish, French, Farsi, and Arabic.

Socialism: Utopian and Scientific
Frederick Engels

"To make men the masters of their own form of social organization—to make them free—is the mission of the modern proletariat," writes Engels. A classic guide to the operations of capitalism and struggles of the working class. $10. Also in Farsi.

The Teamster Series
Farrell Dobbs

Four books on the strikes, organizing drives, and political campaigns that transformed the Teamsters across the Midwest in the 1930s into a militant industrial union movement. Written by Farrell Dobbs, the general organizer of these Teamster battles and leader of the Socialist Workers Party.

A tool for workers seeking to use union power in every workplace and advance the fight for an independent labor party. $16 each, series $50. Also in Spanish. *Teamster Rebellion* is also available in French, Farsi, and Greek.

The Jewish Question
A MARXIST INTERPRETATION
Abram Leon

Why is Jew-hatred still raising its ugly head? What are its class roots—from antiquity through feudalism, to capitalism's rise and current crises? Why is there no solution under capitalism? The author, Abram Leon, was killed in the Nazi gas chambers. Revised translation, new introduction, and 40 pages of illustrations and maps. $17. Also in Spanish and French.

New International
A MAGAZINE OF MARXIST POLITICS AND THEORY

CAPITALISM'S LONG HOT WINTER HAS BEGUN
JACK BARNES

Today's global capitalist crisis is but the opening stage of decades of economic, financial, and social convulsions and class battles. Class-conscious workers confront this historic turning point for imperialism with confidence, Jack Barnes writes, drawing satisfaction from being "in their face" as we chart a revolutionary course to take power. In *New International* no. 12. $14. Also in Spanish, French, Farsi, Arabic, and Greek.

OUR POLITICS START WITH THE WORLD
JACK BARNES

The huge economic and cultural inequalities between imperialist and semicolonial countries, and among classes within them, are accentuated by the workings of capitalism. To build parties able to lead a successful revolutionary struggle for power in our own countries, vanguard workers must be guided by a strategy to close this gap. In *New International* no. 13. $14. Also in Spanish, French, Farsi, and Greek.

U.S. IMPERIALISM HAS LOST THE COLD WAR
JACK BARNES

The collapse of regimes across Eastern Europe and the USSR claiming to be communist did not mean workers and farmers there had been crushed. In today's sharpening capitalist conflicts and wars, these toilers are joining working people the world over in the class struggle against exploitation. In *New International* no. 11. $14. Also in Spanish, French, Farsi, and Greek.

The Low Point of Labor Resistance Is Behind Us
THE SOCIALIST WORKERS PARTY LOOKS FORWARD
Jack Barnes, Mary-Alice Waters Steve Clark

The global order imposed by victors of the inter-imperialist slaughter of World War II is shattering, with explosive ramifications for workers and farmers worldwide. A long retreat by the working class and unions has come to an end. More and more workers of all ages, skin colors, and both sexes are saying, "Enough is enough!" This book highlights opportunities ahead for class-conscious workers to forge a labor party built on the unions. And a mass proletarian vanguard able to lead the struggle to end capitalist rule, opening a future for humanity. $10. Also in Spanish and French.

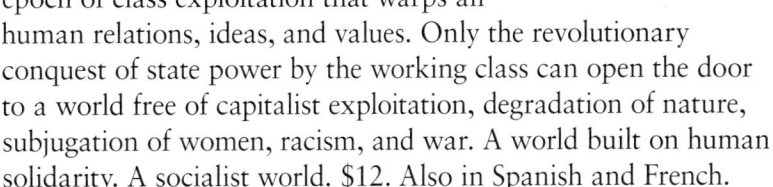

Labor, Nature, and the Evolution of Humanity
THE LONG VIEW OF HISTORY
Frederick Engels, Karl Marx George Novack, Mary-Alice Waters

Without understanding that social labor, transforming nature, has driven humanity's evolution for millions of years, working people are unable to see beyond the capitalist epoch of class exploitation that warps all human relations, ideas, and values. Only the revolutionary conquest of state power by the working class can open the door to a world free of capitalist exploitation, degradation of nature, subjugation of women, racism, and war. A world built on human solidarity. A socialist world. $12. Also in Spanish and French.

America's Revolutionary Heritage
MARXIST ESSAYS
George Novack

A materialist explanation of the American Revolution, Civil War and Radical Reconstruction, genocide against the Indians, rise of American imperialism, first wave of the fight for women's rights, and more. $23

WWW.PATHFINDERPRESS.COM

EXPAND YOUR REVOLUTIONARY LIBRARY

Are They Rich Because They're Smart?
Class, Privilege, and Learning under Capitalism
JACK BARNES

Exposes growing class inequalities in the US and the self-serving rationalizations of well-paid professionals who think their "brilliance" equips them to "regulate" working people, who don't know what's in our own best interest. $10. Also in Spanish, French, Farsi, and Arabic.

Socialism on Trial
Testimony at Minneapolis Sedition Trial
JAMES P. CANNON

The revolutionary program of the working class, presented in response to frame-up charges of "seditious conspiracy" in 1941, on the eve of US entry into World War II. The defendants were leaders of the Minneapolis labor movement and the Socialist Workers Party. $15. Also in Spanish, French, and Farsi.

Democracy and Revolution
GEORGE NOVACK

The limitations and advances of various forms of democracy in class society, from its roots in ancient Greece through its rise and decline under capitalism. Discusses the emergence of Bonapartism, military dictatorship, and fascism, and how democracy will be advanced under a workers and farmers regime. $17

Puerto Rico: Independence Is a Necessity
RAFAEL CANCEL MIRANDA

One of the five Puerto Rican Nationalists imprisoned by Washington for more than 25 years and released in 1979 speaks out on the brutal reality of US colonial domination, the example of Cuba's socialist revolution, and the ongoing struggle for independence. $5. Also in Spanish and Farsi.

Women's Liberation and the African Freedom Struggle
THOMAS SANKARA

"There is no true social revolution without the liberation of women," explains the leader of the 1983–87 revolution in the West African country of Burkina Faso. $5. Also in Spanish, French, and Farsi.

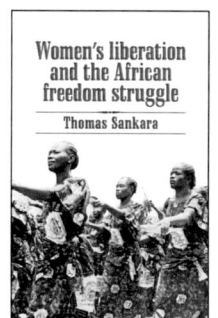

Cosmetics, Fashions, and the Exploitation of Women
JOSEPH HANSEN, EVELYN REED
MARY-ALICE WATERS

How big business reinforces women's second-class status and uses it to rake in profits. Where does women's oppression come from? How has the entry of millions of women into the workforce strengthened the battle for emancipation, still to be won? $12. Also in Spanish, Farsi, and Greek.

50 Years of Covert Operations in the US
Washington's Political Police and the American Working Class
LARRY SEIGLE, FARRELL DOBBS
STEVE CLARK

How class-conscious workers have fought against the drive to build the "national security" state essential to maintaining capitalist rule. $10. Also in Spanish and Farsi.

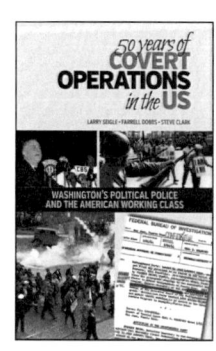

Feminism and the Marxist Movement
MARY-ALICE WATERS

From the earliest days of the modern revolutionary workers movement, Marxists have championed the struggle for women's rights and explained the economic roots in class society of women's oppression. $5. Also in Farsi.

The Struggle against Fascism in Germany
LEON TROTSKY

Writing in the heat of struggle against the rising Nazi movement, a central leader of the Bolshevik Revolution in Russia draws lessons from that first victorious proletarian revolution, examines the petty bourgeois class roots of fascism, and presents a revolutionary political course to defeat it. $25

Imperialism's March toward Fascism and War
JACK BARNES

"There will be new Hitlers, new Mussolinis. That is inevitable. What is not inevitable is that they will triumph. The working-class vanguard will organize our class to fight back against the devastating toll we are made to pay for the capitalist crisis. The future of humanity will be decided in the contest between these contending class forces." In *New International* no. 10. $14. Also in Spanish, French, Farsi, and Greek.

Capitalism's World Disorder
Working-Class Politics at the Millennium
JACK BARNES

The social devastation and financial crises, the coarsening of politics, the cop brutality and acts of imperialist aggression accelerating around us— all are products not of something gone wrong with capitalism but of its lawful workings. Yet the future can be changed by the united struggle and selfless action of working people conscious of their power to transform the world. $20. Also in Spanish and French.

Revolution in the Congo
DICK ROBERTS

Describes the 1960 victory of Congolese peasants and workers, led by Patrice Lumumba, against Belgian colonial rule. And the role, under United Nations cover, of US and Belgian imperialism in the overthrow and assassination of Lumumba. $5. Also in Farsi.

The Transitional Program for Socialist Revolution
LEON TROTSKY

The Socialist Workers Party program, drafted by Trotsky in 1938, still guides the SWP and communists the world over. The party "uncompromisingly gives battle to all political groupings tied to the apron strings of the bourgeoisie. Its task—the abolition of capitalism's domination. Its aim— socialism. Its method—the proletarian revolution." $17. Also in Farsi.

Colombia: Fidel Castro on the Debate around Revolutionary Strategy and Lessons of the Cuban Revolution
FROM THE PAGES OF THE *MILITANT*

Excerpts from Fidel Castro's *Peace in Colombia* and articles from the *Militant*. In describing the Cuban leadership's efforts to end decades of war between the FARC guerrilla movement and Colombia's brutal regime, Castro in his prologue, afterword, and other statements explains why Cuban revolutionaries, unlike FARC leaders, rejected taking hostages and organized working people to win state power, not pursue a "prolonged people's war." $5. Also in Spanish.

Pathfinder Press accessible ebooks for the blind, those with low vision, or other challenges reading print books

For a list of current accessible titles, go to: pathfinderpress.com/collections/books-for-the-blind.

Visit Bookshare.org for information on how to sign up.

WWW.PATHFINDERPRESS.COM

Malcolm X Talks to Young People

"The young generation of whites, Blacks, browns, whatever else—you're living at a time of revolution," said Malcolm in 1964. "And I for one will join with anyone, I don't care what color you are, as long as you want to change this miserable condition that exists on this earth." Four talks and an interview in the last months of Malcolm's life. $12. Also in Spanish, French, Farsi, and Greek.

The History of the Russian Revolution
LEON TROTSKY

How, under Lenin's leadership, the Bolshevik Party led millions of workers and farmers to overthrow the state power of the landlords and capitalists in 1917 and bring to power a government that advanced their class interests at home and worldwide. Unabridged, 3 vols. in one. Written by one of the central leaders of that socialist revolution. $30. Also in French and Russian.

Maurice Bishop Speaks
The Grenada Revolution and Its Overthrow, 1979–83

The triumph of the 1979 revolution in the Caribbean island of Grenada under the leadership of Maurice Bishop gave hope to millions throughout the Americas. Invaluable lessons from the workers and farmers government destroyed by a Stalinist-led counterrevolution in 1983. $20

Voices from Prison
THE CUBAN FIVE

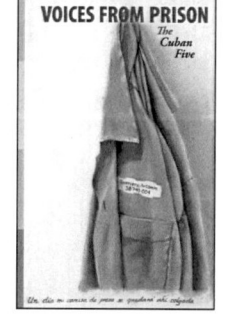

Cuban internationalists Gerardo Hernández, Ramón Labañino, Antonio Guerrero, Fernando González, and René González, known to millions worldwide as the Cuban Five, were framed up and imprisoned by Washington for up to 16 years. In the voices heard here from fellow prisoners, freedom fighters, and family members their revolutionary integrity, humanity—and humor—emerge ever more clearly. $7. Also in Spanish, French, Farsi, and Arabic.

The Clintons' Anti-Working-Class Record
Why Washington Fears Working People
JACK BARNES

What working people need to know about the profit-driven course of Democrats and Republicans alike over the last three decades. And the political awakening of workers seeking to understand and resist the capitalist rulers' assaults. $10. Also in Spanish, French, Farsi, and Greek.

The Revolution Betrayed
What Is the Soviet Union and Where Is It Going?
LEON TROTSKY

In 1917 workers and peasants of Russia were the motor force for one of the deepest revolutions in history. Yet within ten years a political counterrevolution by a privileged social layer, whose chief spokesperson was Joseph Stalin, was being consolidated. The classic study of the Soviet workers state and its degeneration. $17. Also in Spanish, Farsi, and Greek.

Women in Cuba: The Making of a Revolution within the Revolution
VILMA ESPÍN
ASELA DE LOS SANTOS
YOLANDA FERRER

The integration of women in the ranks and leadership of the Cuban Revolution was intertwined with the proletarian course of the leadership of the revolution from the start. This is the story of that revolution and how it transformed the women and men who made it. $17. Also in Spanish, Farsi, and Greek.

How Far We Slaves Have Come!
South Africa and Cuba in Today's World
NELSON MANDELA, FIDEL CASTRO

Speaking together in Cuba in 1991, Mandela and Castro discuss the role of Cuba in the history of Africa and Angola's victory over the invading US-backed South African army. That victory accelerated the fight to bring down the racist apartheid system. $7. Also in Spanish and Farsi.